GEORGE MASON

FORGOTTEN FOUNDER

GEORGE MASON

Forgotten Founder

Jeff Broadwater

The University of North Carolina Press | Chapel Hill

© 2006 The University of North Carolina Press
All rights reserved
Manufactured in the United States of America

Designed by April Leidig-Higgins
Set in Sabon by Copperline Book Services, Inc.

This book was published with the assistance of
the Fred W. Morrison Fund for Southern Studies
of the University of North Carolina Press.

The paper in this book meets the guidelines for permanence
and durability of the Committee
on Production Guidelines for Book Longevity
of the Council on Library Resources.

Library of Congress Cataloging-in-Publication Data
Broadwater, Jeff. George Mason, forgotten founder /
Jeff Broadwater.
p. cm.   Includes bibliographical references and index.
ISBN-13: 978-0-8078-3053-6 (cloth: alk. paper)
ISBN-10: 0-8078-3053-4 (cloth: alk. paper)
1. Mason, George, 1725–1792.   2. Statesmen—
United States—Biography.   3. Politicians—
Virginia—Biography.   4. United States—History
—Colonial period, ca. 1600–1775.   5. United States
—History—Revolution, 1775–1783.   6. United States—
History—Confederation, 1783–1789.   7. Virginia—
History—Colonial period, ca. 1600–1775.   8. Virginia
—History—1775–1865.   9. United States. Constitution.
1st–10th Amendments.   10. Constitutional history—
United States.   I. Title.
E302.6.M45B76 2006
973.3092–dc22   [B]   2006010729

10 09 08 07 06   5 4 3 2 1

Contents

A section of illustrations follows page 132.

Preface

WHO WAS GEORGE MASON? He has been called "an almost forgotten man in the pantheon of revolutionary heroes." Almost forgotten, but not quite. A large state university bears his name; a postage stamp once bore his likeness. The Colonial Dames of America maintain his home, and Gunston Hall is open every day for inspection by schoolchildren and curious tourists seeking a glimpse of something presumably important—something virtually sacred—in America's past. Mason's statue has long stood on the statehouse grounds in Richmond. In the Capitol Building in Washington, D.C., his likeness hangs alongside those of history's other great lawgivers, among them Hammurabi, Moses, and Blackstone. In the spring of 2002 Mason attracted a flurry of attention when the Wendy Ross statue of a seated, accessible, avuncular Mason, with book in hand, was unveiled near the National Mall.[1]

Biographical sketches appear occasionally in the popular media, and in 2001 a small press reprinted Helen Hill Miller's *George Mason: Constitutionalist*, which had first appeared in 1938.[2] Mason usually merits a passing reference in the standard textbooks. They may mention his influence on Thomas Jefferson, who adopted the second paragraph of the Declaration of Independence from the Declaration of Rights that Mason had written as a preamble to the Virginia Constitution of 1776. Mason's insistence at the Philadelphia Convention of 1787 that a bill of rights be appended to the federal Constitution is routinely credited with initiating the movement that culminated in the first ten amendments. If he typically receives a respectful hearing, his Anti-Federalist views have drawn scorn. One venerable text, first published in 1930 when few writers questioned the wisdom of the Framers, attributed Mason's refusal to sign the Constitution to "wounded vanity" because some of his "pet projects were not adopted."[3]

But what do we really know about him? Probably not much, and some of what we think we know is probably wrong. A National Park Service website explains that Mason refused to sign the Constitution because it failed to abolish the foreign slave trade or to adequately protect individual liberty. The Park Service is about half right. Although Mason was a careful student of what today would be called constitutional law, he was not a lawyer. Although he opposed slavery in principle, he was not an abolitionist. Although he has a legitimate claim to be called the "Father of the Bill of Rights," he did not oppose ratification of the United States Constitution solely, or even primarily, because it lacked a bill of rights. While he is frequently praised as a man of principle and integrity, which he was, he was also human; he did on more than one occasion use his political influence to advance his personal interests. And few of his contemporaries would have described him as avuncular.

The small community of Mason scholars has occasionally attempted to explain its subject's relative obscurity. His age has been identified as one culprit. Mason died in 1792, too soon to play a major role in the politics of the new federal government. But Patrick Henry, Benjamin Franklin, and Paul Revere rested claims to immortality on service to the nation that predated the political struggles of the 1790s. More persuasive is the notion that Mason, because of his opposition to the Constitution, has often been dismissed as a disgruntled loser, a type that does not fare well in the public memory. Above all else, Anti-Federalism came to be seen—I think wrongly—as almost entirely a move to restrict the expansion of federal power. That notion, for purposes of Mason's reputation, proved to be a two-edged sword. Kate Mason Rowland's sympathetic biography, which appeared in 1892, could laud Mason as the intellectual godfather of a generation of unreconstructed Confederates. It was a fleeting sort of fame. As states' rights became increasingly identified as a synonym for segregation, and as attitudes toward segregation began to change, Mason's alleged defense of state sovereignty made him unlikely to appeal to a broad audience.

Attempts to blame the neglect of Mason on the historian's preference for more triumphal figures no longer seem convincing. Contemporary historians are drawn to characters who lived outside the mainstream. Anti-Federalism, in particular, has enjoyed a surge of respectability in recent years. Conservatives can appreciate the Anti-Federalists' suspicion of government. Libertarians can appreciate their demand for a bill of rights. Partisans on the left can sympathize with their opposition to a Constitution that seemed to launch an age in which the economic opportunities offered by liberal capitalism produced increasing social and political inequality.[4]

We come closer to the truth when Mason's relative obscurity is explained by his own reluctance to seek the historical spotlight. Mason never sought national office. He never wrote his memoirs. He made no concerted effort, as best as we can tell, to preserve his papers. Even more important is the elusive nature of Mason's accomplishments. Before the American Revolution, Mason was a mentor to George Washington. Mason played a critical role in the movement to use economic coercion to force a change in British imperial policies in the decade before the Revolution. He took the lead in drafting Virginia's first state constitution and its famous Declaration of Rights, which influenced not only Thomas Jefferson and the Declaration of Independence but constitution writers ever since. Mason must rank among the most effective delegates to the federal Constitutional Convention, and ironically, during the ratification debate, he became the Constitution's most intellectually formidable opponent. It is an impressive résumé, but Mason remained one step away from the dramatic event or the single line—he never said anything like "Give me liberty, or give me death"—that could ensure certain immortality.[5]

Yet if, as John Adams once said, the real American Revolution took place in the minds of the American people, George Mason deserves attention for what he thought. The political scientist Clinton Rossiter once suggested, "John Adams and George Mason might well ask their critics whether the Massachusetts Constitution and the Virginia Declaration of Rights were not among the world's most memorable triumphs in applied political theory."[6] The linkage to Adams is telling. Adams and Mason shared a similar eighteenth-century republican faith. Despite their commitment to representative democracy and civil liberties, they took a jaundiced view of unchecked individualism, transient popular majorities, and the inherent virtue of the marketplace. They feared government because they feared corruption in the political process, and they worried about political corruption in large part because they feared the people themselves could become corrupt. With the triumph of classical liberalism in the 1800s, and its emphasis on individual initiative unregulated by government action, American politicians could echo republican strictures against the whims and excesses of arbitrary government, but few politicians would suggest that the marketplace, or even the people themselves, could present a threat to democracy. As Joseph Ellis has written in explaining our tendency to undervalue Adams, "In the search for a usable past, too much in Adams was simply not usable." Adams, Ellis explained, "represents a cluster of political principles that do not fit comfortably within the framework of our national political mythology."[7] Mason can create a comparable discomfort. Adams at least realized he might not get all the historical credit he thought he deserved. "The history of the Revolution," he once said, "will be one continued Lye from one end to the other."[8]

If John Adams can help illuminate Mason's political philosophy by comparison, Carter Braxton, Mason's fellow Virginian, can serve the same purpose by contrast. In 1776, as the newly independent American states were preparing to draft new constitutions, Adams published his "Thoughts on Government." In response, Braxton wrote a pamphlet entitled "An Address to the Convention of the Colony and Ancient Dominion of Virginia; on the Subject of Government in General, and Recommending a Particular Form to Their Consideration." Braxton feared an excess of democracy, and if he was a poorer political philosopher than Adams or Mason, he may have been a better prophet. Republican government, they all agreed, depended on the virtue of the people, or more specifically, Braxton wrote, on their public virtue, which he defined as "a disinterested attachment to the public good, exclusive and independent of all private and selfish interests." Unfortunately, he argued, public virtue "though sometimes possessed by a few individuals, never characterized the mass of people in any state." Widespread virtue might be theoretically possible in an egalitarian society where the economic interests of the great majority of the citizens—and of the state—were the same. "Hence," Braxton wrote, "in some ancient republics, flowed those numberless sumptuary laws, which restrained men to plainness and similarity of dress and diet."[9]

Braxton did not believe public virtue could long endure in America. Sumptuary laws "may be practicable in countries so steril by nature as to afford a scanty supply of the necessaries and none of the conveniences of life: But they can never meet with a favourable reception from people who inhabit a country in which providence has been more bountiful."[10] Wealth would come too easily in the new nation, class divisions would develop, and competing economic interests would destroy the equality of condition that could fuse self-interest and the public interest. Braxton's solution was to accept the inevitable and design a new political order accordingly: the democratic element in the new American governments should be minimized because Americans would lack the virtue to support a more vigorous democracy. The state, Braxton argued, should abandon sumptuary legislation and other attempts to promote an individual identification with the public interest, and citizens should be left free to exploit the opportunities America offered them. Braxton's pamphlet laid bare a paradox: more freedom meant less democracy.[11]

Braxton's argument received a chilly reception, and Virginia's 1776 convention essentially ignored his advice. He is important for our purposes as the anti-Mason. Nothing could have appalled George Mason more than the suggestion that Virginia's political elite ought to abandon both the quest for civic virtue in an egalitarian society and the ideal of a truly representative government. Thirteen years later, Mason wrote of Braxton, "I know him well, and I think there are few men in the United States less deserving Trust or Confidence, with Respect either to his Circumstances, Principles, or Character; tho' he is a very plausible Man."[12] Braxton had seen the future, but Mason was more in step with his times, and, as we shall see, elements of Mason's brand of republicanism eventually formed a major strand in American political life.

Braxton presumably agreed with Mason—John Adams certainly did—on the importance of political ideas. Mason called them "first principles," and he enthusiastically embraced the republican first principles of the American Revolution. He soon came, however, to doubt the virtue of his fellow citizens and to see the republican state governments created by the Revolution as a threat to liberty. Even Mason's own state of Virginia was not immune to corruption. So Mason went to Philadelphia in 1787 prepared to support a reinvigorated central government that could serve as a check on the state legislatures. Practical considerations influenced Mason's first principles. As the summer of 1787 wore on, Mason grew more fearful that the emerging Constitution failed to protect the interests of minorities, especially the southern states. The South's commitment to slavery helped set it apart from the rest of the new nation, and slavery proved to be the insoluble dilemma for Mason. He could not in good conscience endorse the expansion of slavery, which would have served the South's political interests. At the same time, he could not envision the end of slavery in the near future, even though abolition, and with it the reform of southern agriculture, would have eliminated the single greatest distinction between the South and the rapidly developing West.

As a result, Mason opposed ratification of the Constitution, and he lost. Yet if defeat tarnished his reputation, too many of his fellow citizens shared his first principles for those ideas to disappear completely from American history. The concern for public virtue, which Mason's generation saw as fundamental, would virtually vanish in the dynamic nineteenth century, but Mason's fear of the abuse of government power would remain one of the central themes of American political debate.

THIS BOOK WOULD NOT have been possible without the assistance of numerous individuals and institutions. My colleagues William J. MacLean and Charles Bolton made useful, and encouraging, comments on my initial drafts. Jon Kukla and Rosemarie Zagarri read the entire manuscript on behalf of the University of North Carolina Press. Paula Wald, Brian MacDonald, Katy O'Brien, Amanda McMillan, and Charles Grench at the University of North Carolina Press were as helpful and responsive as editors can be. Kevin Shupe, Gunston Hall's librarian, assisted in many ways during my repeated trips to northern Virginia. I think those who produce the manuscript do the hardest work. Sharon Piazza and Bev Gryczan helped put it in a readable form, and Katie Bennett, Steve Ferriter, and Courtney Ferriter helped me through innumerable computer problems. Sue Randolph in Hackney Library's Inter-Library Loan Office responded to my many requests promptly and efficiently. Mrs. Billie Rees West provided hospitality and moral support on my research trips to Richmond. Authors make constant demands on spouses and family. In my case, Cyndi indulged my work, learned to appreciate George Mason, and presented me with my own copy of Robert Rutland's long-out-of-print edition of *The Papers of George Mason*.

The Center for Professional Development at Barton College provided much appreciated financial support. Thanks are also due to the Davis Library at the University of North Carolina at Chapel Hill, the Library of Virginia, and the Virginia Historical Society, where much of the research for this book was done. The staffs of the Library of Congress and the Virginia Museum of Fine Arts helped me locate illustrations.

One of the great pleasures of writing about American history in the revolutionary and founding periods is the excuse it offers to enjoy the work of other historians. No era in American history has produced a richer literature or attracted the attention of a more impressive group of scholars. We all owe a special debt of thanks to the editors and publishers of the modern letterpress editions of the papers of the Founders and of the other documentary collections from the period.

Of course, what I made of the help I received is for the reader to judge.

GEORGE MASON

FORGOTTEN FOUNDER

Chapter One

A Retreat of Heroes

E WAS THE FOURTH George Mason in America with, by eighteenth-century standards, deep roots in his native Virginia. According to family tradition, the first George Mason to reach the Old Dominion was a Royalist who fled England after the defeat of pro-Stuart forces at the battle of Worcester in 1651.[1] In March 1655 George Mason I patented in northern Virginia 900 acres based on eighteen headright claims.[2] He quickly entered the ranks of the local gentry. His first wife, Mary French, gave birth to George Mason II, apparently an only child, around 1660. As an adult, the second George Mason bought hundreds of additional acres in northern Virginia. Among his new holdings was Dogue's Neck, a stubby peninsula that juts out between Pohick and Occoquan creeks into the Potomac River. Mason settled there, and it eventually came to be known as Mason's Neck. When he and his third wife died during an epidemic in 1716, he owned more than 8,000 acres and two dozen slaves.[3]

Again according to family tradition, George Mason III was born in 1690 on Dogue's Neck. He may have approached even more closely the ideal of the Virginian aristocrat than had his father or grandfather. According to one contemporary observer, Virginia "improved in wealth and polite living" more in the early 1700s than it had in all its previous history.[4] Mason rose with the rising tide, and he made a fortuitous marriage. Ann Thomson was the daughter of Stevens Thomson, a prominent lawyer who had been educated at Cambridge and the Middle Temple. Thomson later served as Virginia's attorney general. Ann was the only Thomson child who survived to adulthood and was the sole heir to a substantial estate. Ann gave birth to the couple's first child, George Mason IV, on 11 December 1725, at Dogue's Neck.[5]

George Mason III expanded the family's holdings in northern Virginia and into Charles County, Maryland, generally preferring to lease land to white tenants than to work it with his own slaves. London merchants considered the local Orinoco tobacco inferior to the sweet-scented tobacco grown farther south. But a market existed for Orinoco tobacco on the continent, and Mason established a close and lucrative relationship with Glasgow merchants willing to trade in what the English considered to be trash tobacco. Mason moved his family to a new plantation, on Chicka-muxon Creek in Charles County, Maryland, in 1730, but he retained business interests in Virginia: thousands of acres of land, three ferries, and a fishing monopoly on Simpson's Bay at the mouth of Occoquan Creek.[6] They all undoubtedly required frequent trips across the Potomac, which were often dangerous. Hugh Jones, a professor of mathematics at the College of William and Mary, complained that the worst part of travel in colonial Virginia was crossing the area's many rivers and creeks. Jones had lost a brother in an accident on the Chickahominy ferry. The traveler, Jones wrote, was often in "much danger from sudden storms, bad boats, or unskillful or willful ferrymen."[7] On a trip from Maryland to Virginia on 5 March 1735, Mason's boat capsized and he drowned.

Mason's death at forty-five left Ann alone with ten-year old George and two younger children, Mary, who was four, and Thomson, who was only two. Returning to Virginia, she settled on Thomson family property on Chopawamsic Creek, which was just a short distance north of where the first George Mason had built his first plantation. Ann never remarried, which was unusual for a wealthy, young widow in a society in which serial marriage, because of high rates of mortality, was common. It was even more unusual in that, by all accounts, Ann was an attractive and intelligent woman. But she had little practical need for a husband. A careful businesswoman, she kept meticulous records and made some shrewd investments. We know from her records, for example, that she bought George a beaver hat, a wig, a razor, and some school books in 1742. Because his father died intestate, the family's landholdings, under the law of primogeniture, would go to George. Worried about leaving the younger children impoverished, Ann bought 10,000 acres in Loudoun County for Mary and Thomson. The family later joked that, as adults, Mary and Thomson were wealthier than George.[8] When Ann died in November 1762, the *Maryland Gazette* eulogized her: "She discharged her duty, in her several characters of a Wife, Parent, a Mistress, a Friend, a Neighbor and a Christian with that distinguished Lustre, which everyone would wish to imitate, but few have ever equaled."[9]

Little more can be said about George Mason's early life other than what can be reasonably inferred from circumstantial evidence. He may have taken from his mother an eye for detail and a prudence with money, traits he would show in later life. Mason likely spent much time outdoors, fishing and hunting. "There is no Custom more generally to be observed among the Young Virginians," one English official wrote, "than they all Learn to keep and use a gun with Marvelous dexterity as soon as ever they have strength to lift it to their heads."[10] George probably traveled little other than short trips to neighboring plantations, the parish church, or across the Potomac to Maryland. As the eldest son of a wealthy planter in a hierarchical society, he likely would have acquired early in life an air of command, an understanding that he belonged to a class that was expected to dominate Virginia society.

We do know that in 1736, shortly after she returned to Virginia, Ann hired a Master Williams to tutor George in a schoolhouse on the Chopawamsic plantation. It must have been a one-room, neighborhood school. Mason recalled in later years at least one classmate from Williams's school, Richard Hewitt, the son of a local Anglican minister. From 1737 to 1740, George is believed to have attended a school in which Williams taught in Maryland. In 1740 George returned home and completed his formal education—probably in grammar, Latin, and mathematics—under a Dr. Bridges. Colonial tutors were almost invariably itinerant Scottish divines whose breeding and abilities were often questioned by native-born Anglicans. George's uncle, John Mercer of Marlborough, had a low opinion of tutors in general, and of George's in particular. "They are almost to a man bred Presbyterians and tho none of them scruple to become Episcopalians for a parish, their religion is to be much questioned, I mean whether they have any or no, for I have known some without either religion or morals, & I attribute it to George Mason's tutor that I have long doubted with a good deal of concern that he had very little improved in either."[11]

Mercer, who became George's co-guardian, along with Ann, after the death of Mason's father, may have had more influence on the boy than any of his tutors. There were, to be sure, other influences. Alexander Scott, the rector of Overton Parish who had received a master's degree from the University of Glasgow, ordered books for Mason from England. But Mercer, who had married Ann's sister, must have been one of the more strong-willed characters in Mason's early life. A scholarly but combative lawyer, Mercer's irrepressible temper led to his disbarment—on more than one occasion. During one of his involuntary absences from the bar, Mercer prepared an impressive digest of all the laws of colonial Virginia. The library on Mercer's Marlborough plantation boasted several hundred volumes, making it one of the largest in the colony. Perhaps half the collection consisted of legal treatises, including an extensive collection of the writings of the great English jurist Sir Edward Coke, but Mercer's tastes were eclectic, running from classical works such as the *Iliad*, the *Odyssey*, and Plato to more pedestrian handbooks on farming, gardening, and medicine.[12]

Given Mason's intelligence, his meager formal education, and the erudition he demonstrated later in life, it seems reasonable to assume Mason spent long hours with Mercer's books. Mason was often—and sometimes still is—mistaken for a lawyer; he had a legalistic caste of mind that may have originated under Mercer's tutelage and in his library. Mason's younger brother Thomson was admitted to the bar and became one of the colony's leading barristers, but George Mason never considered, as far as we know, a legal career. The irascible Mercer's battles with the local courts may have discouraged Mason, and lawyers, in Mason's boyhood, did not enjoy the status they would later acquire. As the planter Langsdon Carter observed in his diary, "Attorneys were always looked upon as so many copyers and their knowledge only lay in knowing from whom to copy properly."[13] Mason, by contrast, would be content to live the life of a great planter.

GEORGE MASON RETURNED to Dogue's Neck sometime after his twenty-first birthday in 1746. Dogue's Neck lay in Fairfax County, which had been carved out of Prince William County in 1742, which itself had been split from Stafford County in 1731. Fairfax County took its name from Lord Fairfax, who held most of Virginia's Northern Neck as a proprietary grant originally made by Charles II. The arrangement allowed the Fairfax family to collect quitrents from local landholders. Despite the vestiges of feudalism, the Northern Neck was, according to one contemporary observer, "a most delightful Country." Undemocratic and hierarchal, the Northern Neck, nevertheless, in the words of two recent historians, had "a strong tradition of service, right conduct, and the rule of law."[14] Nowhere else in Virginia were the great planters more numerous or more influential.

On 4 April 1750 Mason married sixteen-year-old Ann Eilbeck, the only child of Colonel William Eilbeck, a wealthy planter and merchant whose Mattawoman plantation lay near the Masons' Maryland estate. Small, delicate, with dark eyes and hair and a light complexion, Ann had, according to family legend, attracted the unrequited attention of a fourteen-year old George Washington. "In the Beauty of her Person, & the Sweetness of her Disposition, she was equaled by few, & excelled by none," Mason later wrote. Their first child, George Mason V, was born in April 1753, and by spring the following year, she would be pregnant again. Nine children survived to adulthood.[15] No writings from Ann have survived, but based on records left by Mason and by John, the couple's fourth son, the marriage appears to have been a happy one.

In 1754 Mason began work on a new house for his growing family. William Buckland had come to America as an indentured servant to Mason's younger brother Thomson. Impressed by Buckland's skill and character, Mason put Buckland in charge of what would become known as Gunston Hall, which was named for the ancestral seat of Mason's maternal grandfather, Gerald Fowkes. Begun by a local builder, the floor plan and exterior lines of the house came from the standard pattern books of the day. But Buckland took charge of the interior design. Another Englishman, William Bernard Sears, did much of the actual carving, and Gunston Hall's intricate woodwork shows the hand of a master craftsman. Buckland went on to become one of the most distinguished architects in early America. If Gunston Hall was dwarfed by Sabine Hall or Montpelier, it was nevertheless grand by the standards of the times, when most Virginians, white and black, lived in one or two room cabins.[16]

Gunston Hall faced northwest, setting between the King's Highway to the west and the Potomac River to the east: Mason had a dock where Pohick Creek entered the river. His house was one of the first brick structures in northern Virginia. Wood construction predominated, not only for private homes but even for churches and courthouses, until at least the 1740s. Sandstone quoins from a quarry on Aquia Creek further distinguished Gunston Hall. George Washington would later order Aquia Creek quoins for the White House; Gunston Hall's floor plan resembled Mount Vernon's before it was expanded. The exterior seemed perfectly symmetrical; there were double chimneys on each end, and on the landward side of the first story, there were two windows on either side of a small porch. The second story featured five dormer windows, the middle one centered above the porch. The rear of the house, oriented toward the river, was similar, except for a more elaborate entrance. There a five-sided porch, its entryway a high, rounded arch flanked by a lower, peaked entablature, overlooked a large formal garden.

Inside, a wide central hall connected the landward and garden entrances. As a guest entered from the landward side, a staircase to the left led to the second floor. The baseboard, chair rail, and cornice typified the intricate woodworking that made Gunston Hall architecturally significant, but a pair of elliptical arches that framed the stairway and the rear half of the hall dominated the foyer. Supported by pilasters, they were joined by a pine-apple pendant. To the right, or southwest, was a formal drawing room in the Palladian style. Caryatids, or draped female figures, supported a marble mantel. Arched and recessed cabinets stood on either side of the fireplace. Pilasters around them ended in broken pediments. Pilasters also enclosed the windows, where hinged blinds folded flush against the embrasure. The drawing room opened directly into a formal, Chippendale dining room; its less elaborate woodwork was considered in its day more modern. Gunston Hall exemplified Buckland's ability to combine a variety of styles—Chippendale, Palladian, rococo, and baroque—in an elegant and innovative synthesis.[17]

If the Palladian and Chippendale rooms reflected Mason's wealth and taste, the rest of the house demonstrated his more practical side and the demands of a large family. To the left of the landward entrance stood a modest master bedroom that was distinguished mainly by two closets on either side of a fireplace. Ann Mason kept her clothes and "the Green Doctor"—a riding crop used to spank the children—in one. The other served as a pantry for sweets and other delicacies. Across a narrow hall running perpendicular to the foyer was a small room that apparently doubled as Mason's office and as a family dining room. He cluttered the windowsill and bookcase with papers. Upstairs, a central hallway divided the front and rear of the house, with five separate rooms on each side, enough for the children, a few guests, and perhaps a servant or two.[18]

Mason's estate occupied more than 5,000 acres on Dogue's Neck and was, except for a few luxury goods, relatively self-sufficient. Mason farmed four separate tracts, each under its own overseer, of 400 to 500 acres apiece. The principal crops were tobacco and corn, but wheat became more important as time went by, and Mason also kept cattle and hogs. Deer abounded on the two-thirds of the estate that was kept in timber; a fence across the landward side of the peninsula restrained the deer.[19]

The big house itself stood among a network of smaller buildings—a smoke-house, a school, a spinning and weaving house, a laundry, a blacksmith's shop, a stable, barns, and, at some distance, the slave quarters. Gunston Hall had its own orchard; its own distillery to make, among other things, persimmon brandy; and its own barrel-making operation to provide storage for its produce. Most of the work was done by some ninety slaves. John Mason recalled later that his father "had among his slaves carpenters, coopers, sawyers, blacksmiths, tanners, curriers, shoemakers, spinners, weavers, and knitters." Even the distiller was a slave, as was the operator of Mason's Occoquan ferry. There were a few exceptions. During the Revolutionary War, when cloth was in short supply, Mason hired white artisans to supervise the slave spinners and weavers.

Although Mason's sons may have studied briefly at local academies, Mason employed, as was the custom, a series of Scottish tutors for the boys. A Mrs. Newman taught the girls needlework, cooking, etiquette, dance, and music. From time to time, Gunston Hall served as a home for members of Mason's extended family, and when it did, Mason assumed responsibility for their problems. Mason tried, without success, to get a military commission for his young cousin French Mason as, he told George Washington, "the only means of getting him clear of a very Foolish Affair he is likely to fall into with a Girl in this neighborhood."[20]

What Edmund Randolph called "that baleful weed tobacco" was "the only commodity which could command money for the planter on short notice." Randolph listed tobacco's shortcomings in his history of colonial Virginia: it sustained the "pollutions and cruelties of slavery"; it exhausted the soil; and by swallowing up "in its large plantations vast territories," it discouraged the immigration of white settlers. Planters generally did not use fertilizer or rotate crops, and because tobacco plants were kept free of weeds or grass, erosion was a problem. Three successive years of tobacco production would exhaust a field for a generation, although it might be used for a short time for corn or wheat.[21] Planters like Mason developed an almost obsessive, but understandable, preoccupation with acquiring land. According to one of the standard agricultural textbooks of the day, "there is no plant in the world that requires richer land, or more manure than tobacco. . . . This makes the tobacco planters more solicitous for new land than any other people in America." Considering the land required for corn, pasture, and timber, the planter was estimated to need fifty acres per worker.[22]

Yet tobacco by 1750 accounted for 85 percent of the value of Virginia's exports to Great Britain and, as Randolph suggested, was one of the colony's few sources of foreign exchange. Tobacco cultivation could be profitable, even if it did not consistently generate profits sufficient to support the lavish life-styles of the great planters. Despite depressions in the late 1740s and early 1760s, tobacco prices generally rose from Mason's boyhood until the eve of the Revolution. Mason's generation saw the value of its land and slaves appreciate substantially. More fortunate and more astute than most, Mason, eager to protect himself from the gyrations of the tobacco market, shifted acreage from tobacco to wheat in the 1760s, and by 1768 he was experimenting with sheep production.[23]

Mason must have been a busy man, one with an eye for detail and definite opinions. Ten years after building Gunston Hall, he remembered the exact combinations of lime and sand he had used to make mortar, one formula for outside work and another for inside. And when his neighbor, Alexander Henderson, began his own cellar, Mason freely shared his views, down to his advice on the best sand to use—"good pit sand, out of your cellars or well."[24] Despite plantation society's reputation for gaiety, one contemporary foreign visitor observed that "he now seems best esteemed and most applauded who attends to his own business, whatever it might be, with the greatest diligence."[25] Unlike many large planters, Mason kept his own books and personally managed a sprawling enterprise that may have ultimately included 75,000 acres in northern Virginia, in Maryland, and on the western frontier. Such personal staff as he had usually consisted of one or two slaves, especially a trusted mulatto named James who stayed at Mason's side for years, and, as they grew older, Mason's sons.[26]

The noted artist John Hesselius painted Mason's portrait shortly after his marriage to Ann Eilbeck. The Hesselius portrait has since been lost, but a later copy depicts a bland and pudgy Mason. It is, perhaps, Mason's best-known likeness, but nothing in the picture suggests the strong will, the stubborn independence, or the acerbic tongue for which Mason would become known. Mason wore a club wig; the hair hung straight but curled up in back and was tied with a black ribbon in what was called a "club." Mason owned several. James would keep one dressed and powdered at all times. Mason shaved his head twice a week and washed his head in cold water every morning until shortly before he died. Wigs were not worn constantly. John Mason recalled his father wearing a white linen cap at home in the summer, and when he went out of doors in cold weather, he wore a green velvet cap under his hat. Others remembered a vigorous Mason, a tall, muscular, dark-eyed man, his skin brown from long hours outdoors, some of them spent at the racetrack.[27]

In the room Mason used as his study, two windows overlooked the garden. The study had its own entrance, and in good weather, Mason would take several walks a day in the garden. John Mason later recalled his father walking out of doors "wrapped in meditation," wholly oblivious to anyone around him. The children knew not to interrupt Mason when he was in his study or in the garden. Mason, in turn, would eat with the family, but between his preoccupation with business and politics and the challenge of keeping up with nine children, one of them could be gone for several days before Mason would notice.[28]

We can only speculate as to Mason's politics before the events leading up to the American Revolution thrust him into public life; we know more about what he may have been reading. As was typical for a Virginia planter, Mason's library included the Book of Common Prayer, a handbook for justices of the peace, and a form book for real-estate conveyances. Almost equally predictable were the classics and ancient history, and Mason almost surely owned volumes of Cicero and Lucretius. He also owned a copy of John Locke's *Two Treatises of Government* and probably copies of legal treatises by Coke and Pufendorf. Mason's reading seems to have been weighted toward the writings of the Whig opposition: Algernon Sidney's *Discourses Concerning Government*, *Cato's Letters* by John Trenchard and Thomas Gordon, and Edward Wortley Montagu's *Reflections on the Rise and Fall of Antient Republics.*[29]

We know more about his health. By the time he was thirty, Mason suffered from health problems that would plague him for the rest of his life. In August 1755 he wrote his neighbor, George Washington, "I fully intended to have waited on you this evening at Belvoir," the Fairfax plantation halfway between Dogue's Neck and Mount Vernon, "but find myself so very unwell after my Ride from Court, that I am not able to stir abroad." Mason's letter to Washington, the oldest surviving document in a series of chronic complaints of ill health, identified no specific ailment, but by 1762 Mason had been afflicted by erysipelas, a painful skin condition.[30]

More troubling would be persistent gout. Here Mason was in good company. His fellow sufferers included Horace Walpole, Samuel Johnson, Benjamin Franklin, and Edward Gibbon. Indeed, the eighteenth-century experienced something of a "gout wave." Gout was caused by high levels of uric acid in the blood. Deposits of sodium urate could collect in the joints and form painful crystals. Commonly associated with the upper classes, the prevalence of gout in Mason's day may have reflected the growth of protein-rich diets and the popularity of strong wines like Port and Madeira. One modern theory blames the spread of the disease on lead-lined wine casks and the use of lead-based additives in the wines themselves. Gout came in different forms. Irregular gout did not involve the joints. Atonic gout caused stomach pains. Other symptoms included headaches, fainting, and kidney stones. Mason's gout affected his stomach, hands, and feet. Attacks typically began about two o'clock in the morning. The pain would usually start to subside within twenty-four hours, but soreness could persist for weeks.[31]

No evidence exists that Mason sought professional help and, given the state of eighteenth-century medicine, it was probably just as well. Doctors tended to agree that inactivity, gluttony, drunkenness, and stress of almost any kind—from overwork to sexual excess—could weaken a patient's resistance to the disease. Richard Blackmore, a London doctor, blamed gout on what he called "fright," or the stresses of life in the hectic eighteenth century. According to one authority, gout attacked those "who follow their studies too closely, especially in the night, with an intense application of mind."[32] The description fit Mason. He also liked to enjoy a toddy and two or three glasses of wine at dinner every night, which for his system was probably too much. The medical authorities disagreed on whether the disease was hereditary, on whether it was curable, and on treatment options. The most sensible prescriptions were matters of common sense: rest, exercise, and moderation in food and drink. The experts debated the value of more extreme remedies, which included sexual abstinence, drugs of varying degrees of effectiveness, purges, bleedings, and blisterings. The more heroic measures surely did more harm than good. Mason used homemade medicines. Painful as it was, gout was neither completely debilitating nor necessarily fatal. Victims often enjoyed perfectly good health between episodes; his contemporaries frequently commented on a healthy Mason's robust constitution. Some doctors even believed gout served a useful purpose. It was, they speculated, the body's way of forcing dangerous elements away from vital organs and into the extremities.[33]

FINISHING SECOND among the twelve successful candidates, George Mason was elected to the vestry of Truro Parish in 1749, the year the parish boundaries were reorganized and a new Cameron Parish was spun off from the old Truro. As would Gunston Hall, Truro Parish became one of the constants of Mason's life. He remained on the vestry until 1785, and he served four separate terms as a church warden.[34]

As a member of the Truro vestry in the established church, Mason's duties were primarily administrative, as was common for vestries throughout the colony. He served, for example, on the committee overseeing the construction of a new glebe house, or parsonage, which brought predictable headaches, including a complaint to the builder that "none of the bricks . . . are fit to put into the walls" and that the work already done should "be pulled down & done with good bricks." In addition to their responsibility for the construction and maintenance of church buildings, the vestrymen also supervised the preparation of financial reports, the collection of the parish levy, and the relief of the poor. Despite the episcopal nature of the church, the vestry hired and fired ministers. An entry in the vestry minutes for 12 November 1759 is typical: 400 pounds of tobacco were allotted to Elizabeth Palmer "towards the support of her child, a Lame Idiot." Indeed, in part because of its responsibility for the aid of the destitute and disabled, Truro Parish had a larger budget than Fairfax County. Parish levies throughout Virginia typically exceeded the county tax. The county court rarely served as a check on the vestry because the membership of both groups, drawn as it was from the large planters, tended to overlap. The vestry was essentially self-perpetuating; after an election by parishioners, future vacancies were filled by a vote of the remaining vestrymen. Anglican Virginia, however, was not Puritan New England. The vestries acquired a reputation, perhaps undeserved, for laxity in pursuing moral offenses—fornication, bastardy, and missing church services—and neglecting their legal duty to register all marriages in the parish record book.[35]

Bishop Meade, the nineteenth-century Virginia historian, traced the Virginia Framers' commitment to civil liberty, and especially freedom of religion, to the experience of the church vestries, which had long insisted on local autonomy from the Anglican hierarchy. "They had been slowly fighting the battles of the Revolution for a hundred and fifty years. *Taxation and representation* were the only other words for *support and election of ministers*. The principle was the same." More recently, Jack Rakove has suggested that the concern of eighteenth-century Americans for freedom of conscience laid the foundation for a subsequent commitment to other individual and minority rights.[36]

Ironically, Virginia's Anglican gentry had not initially supported religious freedom. It came to America in part as a result of British action. Royal authorities insisted that the English Toleration Act, which allowed licensed dissenters to worship publicly, be enforced in the colonies. Only gradually did the ideal of religious tolerance—even of Protestant dissenters—take root. As Virginia society became more diverse, the notion of an established church became increasingly unpopular and unworkable. By 1775 less than a third of white families in the Chesapeake region may have participated in Anglican communion, and some 40 percent may have been wholly un-churched. Indeed, the Framers' commitment to the separation of church and state may have stemmed in part from a certain skepticism about the claims of the church. As Gordon Wood has written, "at best most of the revolutionary gentry only passively believed in organized Christianity and, at worst, privately scorned and ridiculed it."[37] Whatever his motives, Mason defended religious freedom as steadfastly as did any patriot of his era.[38]

In attempting to reconstruct his religious views, we have for Mason nothing as revealing as Thomas Jefferson's letter to Peter Carr, advising his nephew to "Read the bible . . . as you would read Livy or Tacitus" and candidly admitting a critical reading could lead to atheism. Nor did Mason produce the equivalent of a Jefferson Bible, a harmonized version of the Gospels exorcised of the miraculous and the supernatural.[39] Jefferson, of course, endured fierce attacks from his enemies for his alleged infidelity, but even though Mason generally shared Jefferson's views on church-state relations, Mason's faith was never questioned. Mason may have been philosophically closer to James Madison, whose beliefs did come under suspicion because of his association with Jefferson. Bishop Meade, who interviewed Madison concerning his religious views, concluded that Madison was generally orthodox, if "his creed was not strictly regulated by the Bible."[40]

One recent study of the faith of several prominent Founders has described Mason as a man of "conventional piety." Mason made orthodox, and presumably sincere, professions of faith on appropriate occasions; he was not the type to hide his opinions behind clichés. When the present-day Pohick Church was completed in 1774, Mason dutifully bought two pews—numbers three and four on the south aisle. Mason's will, which he wrote in middle age and never revised, began with an expression of religious sentiment that was at once orthodox and disarmingly optimistic. He resigned his soul to an "Almighty Creator . . . who hateth nothing that he hath made," and "willingly and cheerfully" trusted the "unbounded mercy and benevolence . . . of my blessed Savior, (for) a remission of my sins."[41]

Mason was not a fundamentalist or an evangelical in the modern sense, but he could easily have been "conventionally" pious by eighteenth-century standards. Faith was by no means irreconcilable with a Whig view of history. Edward Wortley Montagu, one of the most popular of the Whig historians, argued that Epicurus had helped bring about the collapse of the Roman Republic by undermining the belief that "all things here below are directed, and governed by divine providence." Montagu condemned "the principles of modern deism" as "in reality the same with those of Epicurus." As a vestryman, Mason presumably took the oath "to be conformable to the Doctrine and Discipline of ye Church of England." That doctrine should not have placed inordinate demands on Mason's credulity. Mason's church respected the scientific advances of the Enlightenment. The Anglican orthodoxy of Mason's day mediated the literal Scripture with human reason. Minimizing miracles and theological disputation, it emphasized ethical behavior, order, and tolerance. Putting the evidence Mason left behind into the context of the middle and late 1700s suggests a few basic conclusions about his thoughts on church and state: he saw religion as a prod to the virtue he believed essential to republican government, but he came quickly to the belief that while the state ought to encourage virtue, it should neither impose on its citizens a religious orthodoxy nor support an ecclesiastical establishment.[42]

MASON'S DEVOTION to Gunston Hall rivaled his distaste for ordinary politics in its intensity. Yet Mason could not escape the demands of public service, and no one did much more to transform the political life of Virginia, however unimpressive his initial forays into politics may have been. What then of political Virginia when Mason came of age?

Under a 1736 statute, any free white male who was over twenty-one and who owned a farmhouse and 25 acres, a city lot and a house, or 100 unoccupied acres could vote in colonial Virginia. Besides Indians, women, and the landless poor, Jews and practicing Catholics were also disenfranchised. Slaves, of course, could not vote, but neither could free blacks or mulattoes. Because colonial records are spotty, historians have long debated how many potential voters were disenfranchised by the property requirements. They were, it is clear, less stringent than they may seem at first glance because long-term leases were treated as the equivalent, for suffrage purposes, of a fee simple title. Thomas Jefferson believed less than half of adult white males could vote; one modern study, by contrast, pegged the figure at slightly more than 85 percent.[43] More plausible, especially in Mason's Fairfax County, would be about two-thirds. Two points should be kept in mind. First, eligibility rates were not static. As population increased and land became harder to obtain, eligibility rates declined, falling in Fairfax County from 66 percent in the 1740s to 35 percent in the 1770s. Second, eligibility did not equal participation. Voter turnout fluctuated from county to county and from year to year: the available evidence suggests between 40 and 65 percent of eligible voters would vote in any given election.[44]

How democratic the system was in practice is another question. Forty or so wealthy families dominated Virginia politics, largely monopolizing positions in the House of Burgesses and, at the local level, on the county courts and the parish vestries. As the historian A. G. Roeber has written, positions such as justices of the peace were passed down "from father to son, from uncle to nephew."[45] As the legislature grew in power after the English revolution in 1688, small planters, whose votes could determine elections to the House of Burgesses, increased in their political respectability. If Virginia was not an egalitarian society, and it was not, planters large and small had common interests: the maintenance of high tobacco prices and of white supremacy. Mason worried about the effect of slavery on the white character, but slavery may have made white Virginians value freedom and free citizens all the more. Undoubtedly, the emerging republican ideology, to use a much contested term, exalted the small farmer as the ideal citizen. Jackson Main's study of the 100 wealthiest Virginians in the 1780s suggests a critical point: wealth may have been a virtual prerequisite to political office in eighteenth-century Virginia, but it did not always guarantee a planter a position of political prominence. Mason ranked forty-second on Main's list. Many of those ahead of Mason were much wealthier than he was, and of that group, many played no important role in the politics of the day and have been forgotten to history.[46]

Until his campaign for a seat in the Virginia ratifying convention of 1788, the only electorate George Mason ever faced was the voters of Fairfax County. Although the county grew rapidly during his lifetime, it remained small. Politics was personal. In 1749, the year Mason became a vestryman, Fairfax County had fewer than 5,000 adult white males and fewer than 2,000 slaves. At least half the population comprised tenants, but slavery, which was already widespread, was increasing and becoming more concentrated. Slaves represented 28 percent of the county's population in 1749, but more than 40 percent by the 1780s. Mason weathered the economic trends well. With 22 slaves, he was one of the largest slave owners in the county in 1749, but several of his neighbors owned many more. By 1782 Mason owned 128 slaves, second then only to George Washington, who held 188. And politics in the Northern Neck tended to be more deferential than elsewhere, giving large planters like Mason and Washington obvious advantages.[47]

The county court was probably the single most important unit of government in colonial Virginia. The court appointed the county clerk and made recommendations to the governor for sheriff and other local officials, including new members of the court. The governor normally accepted the court's recommendations. A single justice of the peace could decide a case involving less than twenty shillings or 200 pounds of tobacco. Two justices could probate a will or close an ordinary for violating the Sabbath. As a body, the court set rates for ordinaries and fixed the county levy. The justices shared responsibility with the parish vestry for aiding orphans, the aged, the disabled, and the mentally incompetent. Serious crimes were referred to the General Court in Williamsburg, but the county court tried minor offenses, especially breaches of the moral order such as swearing, drunkenness, or having a child out of wedlock. Punishment could be severe. In 1749 Rebeckah Davis, an indentured servant, was sentenced to fifty lashes or a fine of 500 pounds of tobacco for giving birth out of wedlock. As an indentured servant, she presumably accepted the lashes.[48]

Nevertheless, many critics believed that the courts did a poor job of maintaining morality, and as communities grew and became more diverse, the courts seemed anachronistic. The justices were not lawyers. They were usually planters who had taught themselves what law they knew. As one Scottish visitor observed of the Virginians, "They diligently search the Scriptures, but the Scriptures which they search are the Laws of Virginia: for though you may find innumerable families in which there is no Bible, yet you will not find one without a Law-book."[49] Over time the colony's dependence on a part-time, volunteer court became burdensome on the planter-justices and unsatisfactory to litigants. In the 1740s the courts typically met two days a month, but by the 1760s week-long sessions were common. Yet the courts struggled to stay current with their caseloads. Conventional wisdom holds that the experience in self-government Virginians gained through the county courts helped prepare them for the state and nation building required by the American Revolution.[50] Despite the claims of earlier biographers, Mason's experience supports another view.

Mason was named a justice of the peace for Fairfax County on 22 April 1747, but he rarely attended the court's monthly meetings. The other justices, including Mason's friend Daniel McCarty, attended faithfully. Mason compiled the worst attendance record of any of the justices. In the three years prior to 20 April 1752, when Mason was dropped from the court, the justices met on fifty-seven days. Mason attended court for three full days and part of a fourth. He did not show up at all in 1750. He lost his seat, apparently, as part of a broader purge by Williamsburg authorities against inactive justices whose frequent absences caused troublesome delays by depriving the courts of needed quorums. Mason was reappointed to the court in November 1764, but his attendance never improved. Senior justices, moreover, rotated in the office of sheriff, but Mason, even though he ranked second in seniority by 1770, never took his turn. Mason's service on the county court, it seems safe to conclude, did not instill in him a particular affinity for local government, lend him any great insights into the needs of his fellow citizens, or contribute to the development of his political ideas.[51]

Mason's indifferent performance on the county court did not prevent him from seeking a seat in the House of Burgesses in June 1748 at the age of twenty-three. He finished fourth in a five-candidate race for two seats. Lawrence Washington, one of the incumbent burgesses, and Richard Osborne, a longtime vestryman and former justice, won easily, but Mason's entry into politics was not necessarily premature. The other incumbent, John Colville, finished third, just a few votes ahead of Mason. Incumbent burgesses rarely lost; Colville may have been unpopular and Mason may have seen an opportunity to exploit Colville's weakness. Mason's youth was not an insurmountable obstacle. James Monroe won election to the House of Burgesses at twenty-four, James Madison and Thomas Jefferson at twenty-five, and George Washington and Richard Henry Lee at twenty-six. Yet Mason's record as justice of the peace may have suggested a lack of maturity, even though his performance on the court did not improve with age. Mason conceded as much at the Constitutional Convention in 1787 when he persuaded a majority of his fellow delegates to fix the minimum age for service in Congress at twenty-five. As he told the convention, "every man carried with him in his own experience a scale for measuring the deficiency of young politicians; since he would if interrogated be obliged to declare that his political opinions at the age of 21 were too crude and erroneous to merit an influence on public measures."[52]

Ten years later a more established Mason sought a seat in the House of Burgesses under more auspicious circumstances. Neither of the incumbents, John West nor George William Fairfax, sought reelection, and Mason faced only two opponents, George Johnston, a large planter and successful lawyer, and Charles Broadwater, a vestryman, justice of the peace, militia officer, and former sheriff. Virtually no details of the race have survived, but Mason and Johnston prevailed. At least one contemporary account of the election exists, from an eyewitness who seemed unimpressed. Reporting the results to George Washington the day after the voting, John Kirkpatrick, an Alexandria merchant, observed wearily, "An Election causes a Hubub for a Week or so—& then we are dead for a While."[53]

The colonial legislature to which Mason was elected did not meet in fixed sessions or serve for prescribed terms. The governor would call new elections after the death of the king; to attempt to resolve a political crisis; or upon the appointment of a new governor or, more accurately, a new lieutenant governor because it was normally the lieutenant governor who actually lived in Virginia, discharged the gubernatorial responsibilities, and assumed the title. Indeed, Francis Fauquier's appointment as lieutenant governor necessitated the elections of 1758. A small executive council advised the governor.

Although the council represented the largest planters in the colony and although the governor and council set together as the General Court, Virginia's highest judicial body, it was the House of Burgesses that had, by 1758, become the dominant political institution in Williamsburg. The House boasted an impressive cadre of leaders, including Richard Bland, Edmund Pendleton, and George Wythe, and a host of rising stars. Mason's freshman class included his younger brother, Thomson, elected as a delegate from Stafford County, and Richard Henry Lee from Westmoreland. The assembly's power derived in part from the wealth and influence of its members and, perhaps, from a relative unity of interests and opinions. Virtually every burgess was a planter, and most held local offices, usually as a vestryman and justice of the peace. A few were merchants, an occupation to which, despite possible stereotypes, no stigma was attached. Lawyers labored under a stigma that never wholly disappeared, but as the Revolution approached, the planter-lawyer emerged as the most significant force in the assembly, both in terms of numbers and influence. More than a third of the legislators were land speculators. No political parties or formal divisions existed in the House, but there were a few personal rivalries, which centered around two groups of rival claimants for western land: a Northern Neck faction led by the Lees, with which, as we shall see, Mason allied himself, and a James and York rivers faction headed by the venerable Speaker of the House, John Robinson, and by Attorney General Peyton Randolph, who succeeded Robinson as Speaker in 1766. By the 1760s a geographic divide had also emerged between the aristocratic Tidewater counties and the newer, more western, and presumably more democratic, counties on the frontier.[54]

The French and Indian War, which had erupted in 1754, still raged when Mason took his seat in the House of Burgesses in September 1758. Although the war would drag on for five more years, the immediate threat to Virginia had passed. The French fortress at Louisburg had fallen in July, and the French would abandon Fort Duquesne before the end of November. As the danger eased, Governor Fauquier struggled, with mixed results, to persuade the lawmakers to keep Virginia's troops in the field, supporting British regulars as they carried the war into Canada. Mason, accordingly, was appointed to a series of ad hoc committees to prepare military measures.[55]

He was also appointed to the Committee of Privileges and Elections, and his legislative duties kept him in Williamsburg until early November.

Mason was apparently absent when the burgesses reconvened in February 1759, but on 6 March he was reappointed to the Committee of Privileges and Elections, and on 8 March he was added to the Committee of Propositions and Grievance, which welded jurisdiction over local matters ranging from the authorization of new ferries to licensing fees for peddlers. A fairly typical freshman, Mason left few footprints at the capitol, but as a member of the committee, he helped pass a controversial bill creating Fauquier County out of Prince William County.[56]

Besides the war with France, the great issue of the late 1750s was the fate of the Two Penny Act, a temporary measure that provided for the payment of the Anglican clerics at a rate of two cents for every pound of tobacco they would normally have received as salary. Intended to prevent a windfall to the clergy during a period of rising tobacco prices, the Two Penny Act provoked bitter opposition from many of the ministers. The privy council disallowed the measure in August 1759, although by then the act had expired. The disgruntled ministers sought back salaries in Virginia's courts; Patrick Henry's successful defense of the principle behind the Two Penny Act in the famous Parson's Cause helped make his reputation. Mason, as far as we know, followed the spectacle from his study at Gunston Hall. In fact, Mason made little more impact on the House of Burgesses in his first term than he had made on the Fairfax County Court. Judging from his committee assignments, his colleagues valued his judgment, or saw his potential, but he did not return for subsequent sessions in 1759, 1760, or 1761. When new elections were called in 1761, Mason did not seek a second term.

Mason's support of the Fauquier County bill put him at odds with Lord Fairfax, and some Mason scholars have speculated that the controversy underlay Mason's decision not to seek reelection. But two years intervened between that legislative fight and the next election, during which time Mason showed no interest in the affairs of the burgesses. It seems more likely that Mason was motivated by a lack of interest in ordinary politics that bordered on contempt. Mason had reason to dislike public service. It took five days to travel from Gunston Hall to Williamsburg; the trip was an ordeal for a man with Mason's physical ailments. In all likelihood, Mason sometimes exaggerated his illnesses—they never seemed to prevent him from discharging an obligation that caught his fancy—but gout plagued him all his life. Nor should the seamy side of even eighteenth-century politics be overlooked. During the November 1758 session, for example, one delegate, William Ball from Lancaster County, was expelled from the House for "uttering forged and counterfeit Treasury Notes, knowing them to be so." The

House, moreover, was frequently called upon to resolve disputed elections, an often contentious and tedious task.[57]

For the period in which George Mason was an important public figure, the 1770s and 1780s, the surviving records of his life are more plentiful than they are for the early years, and a distinct personality emerges from the documents. Mason possessed an incisive intellect and a commanding personality, but he was not inclined to suffer fools gladly or to compromise his own opinions. Given his nature, the mystery may not be why Mason initially showed little interest in the day-to-day business of government, but why he sought public office at all. The will Mason wrote in 1772 is as revealing as any document he ever produced. In it he recommended to his sons "from my own Experience in life, to prefer the happiness of independence & a private station to the troubles and vexations of Public Business."[58] Eighteenth-century Virginians often feigned indifference to political office, but in Mason's case the sentiments were undoubtedly sincere.

BESIDES HIS LOVE of Gunston Hall, his loyalty to Truro Parish, and his impatience with politics, the other constant in Mason's life was his preoccupation with the Ohio Company. In the Treaty of Lancaster of 1744, the Six Nations of the Iroquois League sold their claims in the western reaches of Virginia to the English for £400. Three years later, Thomas Lee, who had been a member of the Virginia delegation at the Lancaster conference, organized the Ohio Company to exploit the Indians' concession. Lee wanted to establish a trading monopoly with the Indians along the Ohio River, until white tenants, probably German Protestants from Pennsylvania or the Rhineland, could be settled in the area. Lee could argue that the Ohio Company's plan would solidify English relations with the Indians and check French expansion, but one modern historian has called it "a great feudal leap backward in English America."[59] Ultimately, the company would help stop the French, but only by provoking a war with both France and the Indians.

Lee and eleven partners submitted a petition for a land grant to Lieutenant Governor William Gooch and the council of state in October 1747, but even though Lee was soon to become president of the council, Gooch balked at the company's request. He may have realized that a large land grant in the Ohio Valley would antagonize the French, and at the same time he undoubtedly felt pressure from other influential speculators with competing projects of their own. John Robinson would soon organize the rival

Greenbriar Company, and a Robinson ally, Edmund Pendleton, helped to organize yet another group, the Loyal Company. Gooch stalled by referring the Ohio Company's petition to the Board of Trade in London. After an exchange of reports between the board and the privy council, the council, on 16 March 1749, issued instructions to Gooch, on the terms Lee proposed: the company would receive title to 200,000 acres north, west, and south of the forks of the Ohio River provided that, within seven years, the company would build a fort and settle 100 families in the region, after which the company would receive an additional 300,000 acres. Gooch finally issued the grant on 13 July 1749. The almost two-year delay between the company's initial petition and Gooch's action was one of several setbacks that would, collectively, prove fatal to the venture.[60]

The company, to be sure, began operations on a limited scale even before it received its grant. By late 1747 two well-known frontiersmen, Thomas Cresap and Hugh Parker, had been hired, presumably to solicit business with the Indians. Soon the company began raising money to buy trade goods through John Hansbury, a prominent London merchant who had been brought into the company to lobby British officials after Gooch sent the company's petition to London. On 21 June 1749, according to the minutes of a company meeting at Stafford County Courthouse, the members "agreed to receive Mr. George Mason then present as a partner upon paying his share." In late September, Mason replaced Nathaniel Chapman as the corporate treasurer, a position Mason would hold, doggedly executing the attendant duties, for the rest of his life. His entry into the company almost surely reflected its need for capital, although he never invested more than he could afford to lose.[61]

Meanwhile, Hugh Parker built a two-story log trading post on the Virginia side of the Potomac opposite the mouth of Wills Creek, near present day Cumberland, Maryland. Mason worried that the company's delay in beginning full-scale operations had given its Pennsylvania competitors an opportunity to prejudice the Indians against it, but the company attracted the patronage of white settlers. In May 1750 Zacheus Ruth opened an account to buy two hoes, and James Ross bought, on credit, a half barrel of gunpowder and 100 pounds of lead. By the middle of September, Mason had filed, on behalf of the company, the first of dozens of lawsuits he would bring against nonpaying customers. The Wills Creek facility was soon expanded, and another storehouse was built at Rock Creek, near what is today Georgetown. Strategically located at a divide connecting the Potomac with a branch of the Monongahela, the Wills Creek post became the center of the company's operations. In 1751–52, the Ohio Company built a road from Wills Creek to the mouth of Red Stone Creek on the Monongahela near modern Brownsville, Pennsylvania, and then built a storehouse there and another one further up the Monongahela. The company authorized Mason to purchase three male slaves and two women for work at Wills Creek who were to be, enigmatically, "used to the country business." The company's executive committee, on which Mason served, approved a plan by Christopher Gist, a noted explorer, to settle at least 150 families "on the branches of the Mississippi to the westward of the great mountains." Gist was also dispatched on a series of expeditions to explore land north and south of the Ohio River.[62]

Gist reported back that hopes for white settlement were premature. The Lancaster treaty notwithstanding, the Indians were hostile, and, in any event, the company's grant apparently included land not subject to the treaty. The company's prospects were more tenuous than a brief survey of its activities might suggest. The company's grant had not conveyed title to any particular piece of property; the company in essence enjoyed a right to try to find and develop what land it could in western Virginia. Virginia's own territorial claims ran north and west of the western border of Pennsylvania, but Pennsylvania and Virginia could not agree on how far that border extended. Pennsylvania ultimately had its way; if the Ohio Company had prevailed, Pittsburgh would today be part of West Virginia. According to one historian of the company, uncertainty over the border between Pennsylvania and Virginia discouraged investment and delayed organized white settlement. It also engendered an animosity toward the company among Pennsylvania traders and public officials, who saw the Virginians as both economic rivals and as a political threat. One official's description of company agent Thomas Cresap as "that vile fellow Cresap" typified feelings in Pennsylvania.[63]

Worse yet, the company lost much of its leadership before it could establish permanent settlements and a real foothold west of the Alleghenies. Thomas Lee died of tuberculosis in November 1750. Lawrence Washington, George Washington's much respected half brother, replaced Lee as president, but Lawrence lived only until July 1752. Hugh Parker died in 1751. Two prominent shareholders, William Fairfax and Thomas Nelson, a York County burgess, withdrew from the company and, to make matters worse, joined the Loyal and Greenbriar companies. Unlike a modern corporation, the Ohio Company had no paid professional management. Much of the day-to-day business of the company fell to Mason. In 1751 John

Mercer, Mason's uncle, was retained to draft a formal agreement among the partners. Mercer became a shareholder and the corporate secretary, and he and Mason functioned, for all practical purposes, as the company's principal executive officers.[64]

A new lieutenant governor, Robert Dinwiddie, arrived in Williamsburg on 20 November 1751 and almost immediately became a member of the Ohio Company. Dinwiddie assured Thomas Cresap that he had "the Success and Prosperity of the Ohio Company much at heart." It was, obviously "a time when there was no such thing as the modern notion of conflict of interest."[65] In fairness to Dinwiddie, if the Ohio Company expected favors from the new lieutenant governor, he disappointed them. Dinwiddie promptly made grants to other speculators in Ohio Valley land that the Ohio Company claimed, and he may have been more interested in using the company as an instrument to promote British expansion than as a source of personal profit.[66]

Dinwiddie did, however, move to address one problem that plagued Mason and his associates, the continuing hostility of the Iroquois to further English settlement. In the summer of 1752 Dinwiddie convened a conference with the Indians at Logstown, an Indian village about eighteen miles south of present-day Pittsburgh. Christopher Gist was to represent the Ohio Company, and Mason drafted written instructions for Gist that were both humane and naive. The Indians, Mason wrote, were to be made to understand that the company would "supply them with goods at a more easier rate than they have hitherto bought them." Settlement, Mason believed, would facilitate the very trade the Indians wanted. He offered to make "some further satisfactions" to the Delawares, Iroquois allies who hunted along the Ohio but did not consider themselves bound by the Treaty of Lancaster. Because Mason believed the Iroquois had relinquished their claims to the land in the Lancaster treaty, there was nothing disingenuous in his offer to make land available to individual Indians. In order "to convince our brethren the Indians how desirous we are of living in strict friendship and becoming one people with them," Gist was to tell them that Ohio Company land would be made available to them "upon the same terms and conditions as the white people have." The Indians, Mason wrote, should "enjoy the same privileges . . . as far as is in the company's power to grant."[67]

The company's efforts at Logstown met with only partial success. The conference produced a treaty in which the Indian representatives reaffirmed the Lancaster land grant of 1744 and agreed to the construction of a fort at the forks of the Ohio. But their agreement was contingent upon the approval of the Onondaga council, a caveat the Virginians blithely ignored. The agreement also ignored the claims of the Delaware and other tribes who hunted in the Ohio Valley. Worse yet, Gist may have misrepresented the intentions of the Ohio Company, minimizing its interest in large-scale settlement. And, of course, the Logstown treaty did nothing to pacify the French. Within a week of the end of the Logstown conference, the French incited a bloody raid by their Chippewa and Ottawa allies on the pro-English Twightwee at Pickawillany on the Upper Great Miami River.[68] Dinwiddie organized another conference, at Winchester, in the fall of 1753, but it failed to unite the Indians under English hegemony.

The company's goal continued to be the colonization of the backcountry with German Protestants. German and Swiss Protestants enjoyed an enviable reputation for piety and industry, and efforts to recruit them were common. When the Ohio Company received an inquiry from John Pagan, a merchant who was considering helping a group of Germans immigrate, Mason, Mercer, and fellow stockholder James Scott responded with a glowing invitation. German Protestants, Pagan was told, would enjoy religious freedom, could become citizens, and would be allowed to vote. They would enjoy the protection of "the English Laws of Liberty and Property," which were "universally allowed to be, the best in the World for securing the people's lives and fortunes against Arbitrary power." Virginia's "moderate" taxes "don't amount to above the value of eight shillings per poll," and food and clothing went untaxed. In fact, the legislature had recently exempted foreign Protestants settling west of the mountains from all taxes for ten years. Neither did they have anything to fear from a professional army or an overbearing church. "Our Militia renders soldiers useless and we have no Ecclesiastical courts."[69] But a global war made it impossible for the Ohio Company to make good on its invitation.

The Ohio Company became the catalyst for the almost inevitable French and Indian War, the last in a series of wars between France and Great Britain for control of North America. The company's aggressive construction program alienated the Indians and prodded the French to assert their claims in the Ohio Valley. Emboldened by the Logstown treaty, the Ohio Company made plans to build a fort on Shurtees, or Chartier, Creek about two miles below the fork of the Allegheny and Monongahela rivers. Mason, in July 1753, ordered twenty swivel guns for the fort from John Hansbury in London. Captain William Trent was sent to take charge of construction. Trent and a small party met Gist and Cresap at the site in the early spring of 1754, but apparently informed that a large French force was on the move,

Trent left to seek reinforcements. A young ensign Edward Ward was left in command. The French arrived on 17 April, before Trent could return and before the fort was completed. Ward had little choice but to surrender the post, which the French quickly finished and renamed Fort Duquesne. Sent to check the French advance, George Washington hastily built a crude stockade, aptly named Fort Necessity, at Great Meadows, but in July 1754 a superior French force compelled Washington to abandon the fort.[70]

The outbreak of hostilities ended the Ohio Company's efforts at colonization and brought ruin on its trading posts. Ward and his men had retreated to the Red Stone fort, but the French caught up with them and destroyed the company's storehouse and goods. By the middle of July 1754, the company had fallen back to Wills Creek, which became the key to British defenses. The military commanders seized the company's property and, in Mason's view, never fully compensated the company. In reality, the distinction between the company's interests and those of the empire, which had never been sharp, virtually disappeared in the fog of war. The catastrophic defeat of General Edward Braddock at the Battle of the Wilderness, outside Fort Duquesne, in July 1755, ended all hope of further English settlement in the West within the foreseeable future.[71]

Mason enlisted in the war effort, apparently functioning from Gunston Hall as a quartermaster for Virginia troops. Mason procured powder and lead for Washington's men, and complained to Washington about colonial officials who refused to make full and timely payments for the supplies they bought, a practice that had been "highly detrimental to the public, as well as greatly injurious to many private people." In September 1756 Mason was commissioned a colonel in the militia, whence he was known ever after as Colonel Mason.[72] One contemporary English commentator observed wherever a visitor traveled in the South, "your Ears are constantly astonished at the Number of Colonels, Majors, and Captains that you hear mentioned. In short, the whole country seems at first to you a Retreat of Heroes."[73]

Late in November 1758, a British-American force led by General John Forbes recaptured Fort Duquesne. The victory at what became known as Fort Pitt, however, did not revive the Ohio Company's fading prospects. The Treaty of Easton, negotiated by Pennsylvania with the Shawnee and the Delaware in October, foreshadowed a change in British policy, one with ominous consequences for Mason and his partners. The treaty prohibited white settlement in Pennsylvania territory west of the Allegheny Mountains without the consent of the Indians. Amid the bloodshed of the French and Indian War, royal authorities wanted to avoid further provoking the tribes.

Francis Fauquier replaced Robert Dinwiddie the same year the treaty was signed. Although the new governor wanted to pursue Virginia's western land claims, Fauquier was under pressure from British officials, especially Colonel Henry Bouquet, the commander at Fort Pitt, to adhere to the principle endorsed at Easton: no white settlement west of the mountains without the unequivocal agreement of the Indians.[74]

As the French were beaten back and the political tides, ironically, turned against the Ohio Company, Mason took the offensive. In September 1761 the company, through an executive committee on which Mason served, submitted a petition to George III asking the king to confirm earlier royal instructions to the governor to issue the company a land grant. The deadline to complete the first phase of settlement had passed, but the war constituted an extenuating circumstance. Until fighting had begun, the company had done everything asked of it. The war reduced its frontier trade to shambles; its "debtors in those parts, were for the most part either killed, dispersed, or ruined." Above all, "your petitioners . . . have been from time to time put off, by divers pretences, particularly, that the Indians would not suffer the said lands to be settled."[75]

The company retained Charlton Palmer, a London solicitor, to press its case before the king, and Mason tried to use Robert Dinwiddie as a lobbyist. "As we may expect a peace next winter," Mason wrote the ex-governor in September 1761, "his Majesty's subjects" will soon be at liberty "to settle the lands on the Ohio." Mason seemed willing to accept any relief that would revive the company, but he hoped for a positive reaffirmation of the company's grant from the king, "rather than to be remitted to the Government here, who from jealousy or some other cause have ever envisioned to disappoint us in every design we could form to settle and improve the lands."[76] Dinwiddie, however, had never been a particularly effective advocate— his pledge as governor to make tens of thousands of acres available to Virginia's war veterans had thrown one more complication into the company's plans—and Mason failed to recognize the extent to which the Ohio Company had lost Whitehall's support.[77]

In July 1760 Thomas Cresap had offered Henry Bouquet 25,000 acres and an interest in the company if he would help it settle Swiss and German immigrants on the frontier. In a letter to his superior, General Jeffrey Amherst, Bouquet treated Cresap's letter as bribe, and it is hard to find a better word for it, unsuccessful though it was. On 30 October 1760 Bouquet issued an order prohibiting further settlement west of the Alleghenies without the permission of the colonial governor. The Ohio Company nevertheless made another equally unsuccessful effort to influence the British commander in late December. George Mercer, John Mercer's son and Mason's cousin, offered to sell Bouquet an interest in the company. No direct evidence links Mason to either overture, but it seems unlikely that two company representatives would undertake similar initiatives without the knowledge of the executive committee. As the historian Francis Jennings has observed, "the writer who refuses to recognize corruption among his own people will miss a lot of history."[78]

Bouquet had correctly anticipated the course of imperial policy. In April 1762 the Board of Trade ruled that the Lancaster and Logstown treaties were "vague and void of precision." "A few Indians," the board concluded, could not convey land on behalf of all the tribes. In a decision that was upheld by the privy council, the board ordered that no further land grants be made in Indian territory. King George's more famous Proclamation of 1763 formalized a territorial policy that had been in the works since the Treaty of Easton in 1758: there would be no English settlement west of the Appalachian Mountains in the immediate future; settlers already in the area were to leave; no more western land could be purchased from the Indians; and the Indian territory would be ruled by a military commander.[79]

John Mercer wrote Charlton Palmer after the king's decree that Mason had concluded "that the proclamation was an express destruction of our grant." Mason believed that the company should change its strategy and seek compensation "for the great trouble and expense we had been at."[80] Although Mason never entirely abandoned his dream of a real-estate empire in the Ohio River Valley, he soon began to hedge his bets by collecting headrights in his own name. He would not rest all his dreams on the Ohio Company grant.

The Ohio Company had been an ill-fated venture from the beginning. Some of the obstacles it faced—competition from rival land companies, opposition from the French, the Pennsylvania-Virginia border dispute—were beyond its control. Mason believed the Six Nations had conveyed title to the land he coveted, but the Logstown and Lancaster treaties were of dubious legality. The company showed no qualms about influence peddling; at one time or another twenty-five stockholders served in the House of Burgesses. Yet the company never wielded its political clout with much effect. It enjoyed little support among the burgesses as a group or among the general public, in part because fertile land was available to the south, along Virginia's lateral valleys, with less risk of provoking an Indian war.

A demand existed for western land, but enterprising colonists could extend the frontier without the assistance of the Ohio Company. Orderly settlement collapsed after the frontier crossed the Appalachians. As Francis Fauquier complained to Lord Shelburne, "people will run all risques whether from Governments or from Indians" to settle between the mountains and the Ohio "without the least plea of right."[81] The virtual monopoly the Ohio Company wanted might have done more to retard westward expansion than to encourage it. Mason, of course, saw matters differently. The Ohio Company's agents had helped map the Ohio Valley, which opened up the area to white settlement, and they had exposed "French Incroachments then . . . altogether unknown or unattended to." Mason argued that "there cannot be a stronger proof of the public principles upon which the Company have acted that that they have expended a much larger sum in searching and discovering the inland parts of this Continent" than it would have cost to acquire land in "the inhabited parts of the Colony."[82]

Could the making of a revolutionary be seen in Mason's failure to persuade imperial authorities to make good on the terms of the Ohio Company's 1749 grant? Mason, in such an interpretation, should have been radicalized by the Proclamation of 1763. If it did not stop squatters, it did frustrate the land companies. Their business required clear titles.[83] Mason felt even more frustration, however, with local authorities who had, he thought, opposed the company at every step. His experience with the Ohio Company may have gnawed at Mason's allegiance to Britain, but he would have other reasons to embrace a revolution.

Chapter Two

Our All Is At Stake

A S BRITISH POLICY CHANGED in the 1760s, imposing new imperial duties on the American colonies, Mason gravitated from the periphery to the center of the colonial resistance. His role in the controversy over the 1765 Stamp Act was noteworthy mainly for his inclusion of a critique of slavery into his personal protest against the act. By 1769, however, Mason had become a leader in Virginia's efforts to organize a boycott of British goods and thereby force Parliament to repeal the Townshend Duties. If Mason took his time in assuming a position of leadership, he recognized immediately the explosive character of the imperial crisis, and understood that, if mishandled, it could lead to war.[1]

Apart from an occasional levy on personal property, Virginians paid three direct taxes, each essentially a poll tax. A public levy, imposed by the House of Burgesses, financed the colonial government. The county courts levied a county tax to support local government, and the parish vestries collected a separate assessment. All free white males sixteen years of age and older were considered tithables, and slave owners paid taxes on each adult slave they owned, male or female. Slave women were taxed because, unlike white women, they were expected to work in the fields and were, therefore, a source of income. Direct taxes had fallen dramatically since the 1660s. In 1753 George Mason calculated that annual taxes were no more than eight shillings per person, and Mason noted, in his letter to the German Protestants, that "no Tax or Imposition is laid on anything necessary for food or raiment or the Subsistence of Life." The decline in direct taxes had been made possible by increasing revenues, as tobacco production increased, from an export duty on tobacco and by newer tariffs on liquor, slaves, and servants, but the duties were not overly burdensome.[2]

Great Britain itself may have collected less than £2,000 a year from all the American colonies before 1763. The Molasses Act of 1733 had imposed a tax of six pence a gallon on molasses and rum imported into the colonies from the Caribbean. The act exempted staples from the British West Indies.

Designed to protect British planters from foreign competition, not to raise revenue, the act was routinely ignored by American smugglers. By the 1750s British customs officials had given up trying to collect more than a penny and a half a gallon.[3]

The Proclamation of 1763, however, heralded a fundamental change in British policy. The end of the French and Indian War left Britain with a vast new domain to administer, a large standing army, and a large and growing national debt. Britain's national debt had increased from about £70 million in 1755 to more than £122 million by 1763. Despite the mounting indebtedness, British taxpayers believed their taxes were already high. Worse yet, the British economy was mired in a postwar recession.[4]

In the spring of 1764, the new chancellor of the exchequer George Grenville pushed through the House of Commons, over scant opposition, a legislative package intended to put the empire on a sound financial footing. The American Revenue Act, better known as the Sugar Act, imposed a series of new or increased export duties. To encourage compliance with the Molasses Act, the duty on foreign molasses was reduced to three pennies a gallon. Other provisions, also designed to crack down on smuggling and to enforce the Navigation Acts regulating American trade, were more ominous. A new vice-admiralty court, with jurisdiction over all the American colonies, was established in Halifax, Nova Scotia. Americans feared the new court where a crown-appointed judge, not a jury of one's peers, decided guilt or innocence, and where the burden of proof rested on the defendant. A separate measure, the Currency Act, struck directly at Virginia. Parliament had, since 1751, prohibited the issuance of legal tender paper money by the New England colonies. The Currency Act extended the ban southward. The House of Burgesses had issued paper money to finance Virginia's participation in the French and Indian War, but Parliament did not want Virginia planters to repay their debts to British merchants in depreciated colonial dollars. A clumsy attempt to address the eighteenth century's chronic monetary chaos, the Currency Act imperiled Virginia's already limited ability to deal with shortages of cash and contractions of credit.[5]

Americans protested the new regime, and the change in British policy led them to explore the limits of Parliament's authority. A virtual consensus quickly emerged in the colonies that, although Parliament could make law for Americans, it could not, because Americans were not represented in Commons, impose a tax on them. According to English constitutional theory, taxes were a gift made by the people to the sovereign, and according to the American argument, because Parliament did not represent the colonists, it could make no such gift on their behalf. Many members of Parliament did not understand the American position, and it was not always communicated clearly. Confusion arose from the Americans' seeming willingness to accept customs duties imposed for purposes of regulating imperial trade. Some British leaders seemed willing to concede that Parliament could not impose an internal tax on the colonies to raise revenue, but they insisted on Parliament's right to impose external taxes on American imports and exports. Colonial agents in London occasionally appeared to accept the more politic distinction. But at home, American lawyers like James Otis of Massachusetts and Daniel Dulany of Maryland, in popular and widely read pamphlets, flatly rejected the internal-external dichotomy.[6]

Grenville and his allies responded with the doctrine of "virtual representation." Members of Parliament, so the theory went, were not elected to represent any particular constituency, but as an institution Parliament represented all the king's subjects, including the Americans. Given Great Britain's limited suffrage and grossly malapportioned electoral districts, virtual representation was an almost plausible explanation of how the House of Commons functioned in the British Isles. But it made no sense to Americans, whose formative experiences had been with colonial legislatures in which they were actually, not virtually, represented. However self-serving the American logic may have been, it was not without foundation. William Pitt, who had served brilliantly as head of the government during the French and Indian War, recognized the distinction between legislation, which did not require popular consent, and taxation, which did. And Pitt, surely the most distinguished English politician of his day, ridiculed the notion of virtual representation, calling it in a speech to the House of Commons in January 1766, "the most contemptible idea that ever entered into the head of man."[7]

Although the Sugar Act was intended to raise revenue, it could be rationalized as a trade regulation and, hence, as a legitimate exercise of Parliament's legislative power. A more egregious threat to colonial rights soon overshadowed the Sugar Act. Passed in March 1765, the Stamp Act imposed a direct, internal tax by requiring Americans to buy stamps for printed material ranging from legal pleadings to playing cards. Grenville had decided, as a "friendly gesture," to appoint Americans to administer the act, and loyal patriots applied for the positions. Benjamin Franklin recommended a political ally, John Hughes, for the post of Pennsylvania stamp agent, and Richard Henry Lee expressed interest in the Virginia position. The appointment went instead to Mason's cousin, George Mercer, who had been in England to press the claims of the Ohio Company when the Stamp Act was passed.[8]

Opposition to the act, legal, illegal, and extralegal, coalesced before Mercer could return to Virginia. In Massachusetts, a mob ransacked the home of Lieutenant Governor Thomas Hutchinson. Boston, New York, and Philadelphia merchants organized boycotts of British goods. The Virginia House of Burgesses, urged on by Patrick Henry, passed a set of resolves opposing taxation without representation, and a Stamp Act Congress, meeting in New York and representing nine other colonies, condemned the Stamp Act and called for its repeal. When Mercer arrived in Williamsburg on 30 October, two days before the Stamp Act was to take effect, a mob demanding his resignation met him as he stepped off the ship. Francis Fauquier intercepted a dazed Mercer on the front porch of the Coffee House, later the site of Christiana Campbell's Tavern, and escorted him to the Governor's Mansion. Despite the royal governor's intervention, Mercer resigned his commission the next day. Fauquier reported to the Board of Trade that Mercer's father, John—Mason's former guardian—and Mercer's two brothers were "frightened out of their senses for him."[9]

The act presented a dilemma for justices of the peace, lawyers, and litigants because the county courts could not legally function without stamped paper. It was, Fauquier told the board, "a most melancholy prospect at First View, for what Ideas can we well form of a more miserable Condition, than a State of general Outlawry." The more radical course was to hold court in open defiance of the act; the more prudent approach was to find a way to operate without the courts. Only Rhode Island blatantly ignored the act. In Virginia, practice varied from county to county. In December, Edmund Pendleton expressed the view the courts should meet to do "as many things . . . as can be done without stamps." By February 1766 Pendleton had become convinced that the temporary, partial shutdown had served a useful purpose. British merchants deprived of the ability to bring debt actions in Virginia's courts were pressuring Parliament to repeal the stamp tax. But, Pendleton warned, litigation could not be delayed indefinitely; Virginians would eventually have to accept the stamps or proceed without them, and "not one in 1000" would agree to use the stamps.[10]

George Washington and George William Fairfax, then Fairfax County's delegates to the House of Burgesses, may have asked Mason for help. In any event, he provided them with a scheme to address one of the principal issues raised by the suspension of litigation, the problem of collecting delinquent rent. Under the common law, a landlord could restrain, or seize, a debtor's property for nonpayment of rent. The debtor, in turn, could replevin, or recover, the seized property by posting a bond. But under the Stamp Act, the tenant could not post a legal bond without purchasing a stamp, and if he did, as long as the courts were closed, the landlord could not sue to collect on the bond. Mason's proposal was to allow the tenant to submit a "confession of judgment" for back rent to a single justice of the peace, who could enforce the judgment without convening the other justices if the tenant failed to satisfy the debt within a reasonable period.[11]

Mason's "Scheme for Replevying Goods & Distresses For Rent" demonstrated an impressive knowledge of English land law, and it showed Mason's willingness to help sabotage the Stamp Act, but among all the Stamp Act protests, it stands out for another reason. Mason's replevin scheme began with an antislavery preamble that is his oldest extant attack on the institution: "The Policy of Encouraging the Importation of free People and discouraging that of Slaves has never been duly considered in this Colony, or we should not at this Day see one Half of our best Lands in Most Parts of this Country remain unsettled, and the other cultivated with Slaves." Slavery not only discouraged settlement, but it undermined the character of whites. Pointing to the decline of the Roman Republic, Mason went on to describe "the ill Effect such a Practice has on the Morals & Manners of our People: one of the first Signs of the Decay, & perhaps the Primary Cause of the Destruction of the most flourishing Government that ever existed was the Introduction of great Numbers of Slaves—an Evil very pathetically described by the Roman Historians—but 'tis not the Present Intention to expose our Weakness by examining this Subject too freely."[12]

Mason told Washington and Fairfax that the replevin proposal was "much longer than it might have been," but he asked them to excuse it "as a natural Effect of the very idle Life I am forced to lead," an apparent reference to his poor health. Mason presumably feared they would think his comments on slavery had unnecessarily extended the draft. The relevance of his remarks was strained. Mason justified the replevin scheme as a way to encourage white tenancy, which was preferable to the ostensible alternative, African slavery. Because Mason never freed his own slaves, the depth of his hostility to slavery is suspect, but the tenuous relevance of the preamble to the replevin scheme suggests that slavery did deeply trouble him. He could have easily avoided the subject. If Mason's actions conflicted with his rhetoric, his rhetoric was consistent. As he explained to Washington and Fairfax, the antislavery preamble to the replevin scheme "inculcates a Doctrine I was always fond of promoting, & which I cou'd wish to see more generally adopted than it is like to be."[13] Over the next quarter of a century he would return repeatedly to the arguments he first raised in the replevin scheme.

MASON'S CONDEMNATION OF slavery echoed the criticisms of other established planters in the Northern Neck and Tidewater. As early as 1759, Richard Henry Lee had supported heavier duties on imported slaves as a way to discourage the slave trade. In a speech to the House of Burgesses, Lee attacked slavery as both a moral blight and as an impediment to Virginia's economic progress. Impressed by Pennsylvania's prosperous German farmers, Lee feared Virginia was falling behind its neighbors because of the colony's dependence on slave labor. More than even slavery itself, the slave trade became a frequent target of contempt, partly for economic reasons. Virginia's slave population tripled between 1740 and 1770, largely due to natural increase, and large planters had little need for imported slaves. Northern Neck planters, as they shifted from tobacco production to wheat, which was less labor intensive, needed fewer slaves of any kind. In 1772 the House of Burgesses petitioned the crown for authority to stop the traffic in slaves. British officials ignored the plea. After independence was declared, the Virginia legislature, in 1778, passed its own bill prohibiting the practice.[14]

The views of Patrick Henry mirrored those of Mason and Lee. Henry, moreover, raised the question that has long perplexed historians: how could the generation that produced the Declaration of Independence, declaring as it did the equality of all men, have done so little about the problem of slavery? Writing in 1773 to the Virginia Quaker Robert Pleasants, who had freed his own slaves, Henry asked, "Is it not amazing that at a time, when the rights of humanity are defined and understood with precision, in a country, above all others, fond of liberty, that in such an age and in such a country we find men . . . adopting a principle as repugnant to humanity, as it is inconsistent with the bible, and destructive to liberty?"[15]

As the author, in the Virginia Declaration of Rights, of the assertion that "all men are created equally free and independent," Mason would have been as well suited as anyone to answer Henry's question. Unfortunately, the surviving records yield little direct evidence of how Mason reconciled, in his own mind, his commitment to freedom and democracy, his antipathy toward slavery, and his ownership of dozens of black slaves. Yet a myriad of ideas and assumptions about work, race, and government permeated

Mason's world and served to limit his capacity to deal effectively with the problem of slavery. If they do not fully explain the tragic juxtaposition of American slavery and American freedom, they do offer some clues to the origins of Mason's ambiguous legacy.

To begin with, while Mason cast a critical eye on slavery, it was an eighteenth-century eye. Mason had firsthand experience with the cruelty involved in keeping people in bondage. In 1754 one of Mason's slaves, a man named Dick, had his ear cut off for running away and for stealing, probably a hog. Dick died during a second escape attempt. In 1767 two of Mason's slaves were executed for attempting to poison their overseers, and according to a newspaper report, the slaves' "Heads were cut off, and fixed on the chimnies of the Court-House." Minor offenses could result in brutal, corporal punishment, and slave owners were generally constrained only by their own consciences and economic self-interest.[16] But given the criminal codes and working-class living standards of the day, more affluent whites could see the slaves' routine as little worse than that of indentured servants or English peasants. In the words of one contemporary observer, "the Negroes, though they work moderately, yet live plentifully, have no families to provide for, no danger of beggary, no care for the morrow."[17]

Although Mason later condemned slavery as a violation of the human rights of American blacks and Africans, his first public attack on the institution focused on its effect on Virginia's development and on white morality. In the debate over slavery, the interests of blacks never, during Mason's lifetime, became paramount. Black rights were always weighed against, and diluted by, concerns about the interests of white society. Prejudice against blacks ran too deep for it to be otherwise. Benjamin Franklin and Thomas Jefferson, perhaps the two finest minds in eighteenth-century America, both expressed views on race that today would be condemned as blatantly racist. Franklin, in his "Observations Concerning the Increase of Mankind," admitted his partiality to "the Complexion of my Country." Why, Franklin asked, "increase the Sons of Africa, by planting them in America, where we have so fair an opportunity, by excluding all Blacks and Tawneys, of increasing the lovely White and Red?" Jefferson, although he labeled slavery a "great political and moral evil" and prepared a plan for gradual emancipation, expressed the "suspicion," in his *Notes on the State of Virginia*, that "the blacks, whether originally a distinct race, or made distinct by time and circumstances, are inferior to the whites in terms of the endowments both of body and mind."[18]

Hostility toward slavery, in reality, stemmed in part from a hostility toward blacks, which in turn crippled the antislavery cause. Racial prejudice worked to perpetuate American slavery, even if it was not essential to sustain the institution. Slavery, serfdom, and peonage had existed elsewhere without racial connotations. Indeed, bondage had been so historically ubiquitous one might well ask why, by the 1760s, it had come to trouble so many white Americans so much. The answer lies in part—and this part helps explain why people like Mason did not act more aggressively on their concerns —in the reservations many whites felt about living alongside members of a supposedly inferior race, whether slave or free. The problem was inherent in American slavery, and emancipation, by undermining white control, would only make it worse.[19]

Prejudice toward blacks had several sources. Most white Virginians routinely encountered blacks only in the degraded conditions of slavery, and as Winthrop Jordan has observed, "once the Negro became fully the slave, it is not hard to see why white men looked down upon him."[20] The Africans' perceived heathenism further depressed their status. Englishmen had made Christianity, and in fact Protestant Christianity, a virtual prerequisite for participation in civil society. A society that marginalized Jews and Catholics could not be expected to embrace pagans, and as late as the American Revolution, only a minority of slaves had converted to Christianity. But more fundamentally, blacks were simply dismissed as intellectually inferior; the only real debate was whether that inferiority was innate or the product of environmental forces. Most educated whites blamed the environment.[21]

However white Virginians explained what they saw as black inferiority, their perceptions about blacks led them to conclude that they could not live with large numbers of freed slaves, and 40 percent of America's black population lived in Virginia. Mason shared widespread concerns about the capacity of slaves to adjust to freedom. According to one account, he dissuaded Jefferson from proposing the immediate abolition of slavery. Mason reportedly told Jefferson, probably in the 1770s, that before emancipation could be considered, the state should establish county grammar schools for young, male slaves. "Each of us knows, that the Negro considers work as punishment," Mason said. "If they were not educated before being freed, the first use they would make of their liberty would be loafing, and hence they would become slaves out of necessity." Mason did support a ban on the foreign slave trade and the legalization of private manumissions.[22] Before the Revolution, only the governor and council could emancipate a slave, and only then for meritorious service to the colony. Until the law was changed in 1782, private manumissions were prohibited.[23]

Concerns about living with a large free black population led many of Mason's contemporaries to give serious consideration to linking general emancipation to colonization. As Jefferson explained: "Why not retain and incorporate the blacks into the State, and thus save the expense of supplying, by importation of white settlers, the vacancies they will leave? Deep rooted prejudices entertained by the whites; ten thousand recollections, by the blacks, of the injuries they have sustained; new provocations; the real distinctions which nature has made; and many other circumstances, will divide us into parties, and produce convulsions which will probably never end but in the extermination of the one or the other race."[24]

Yet colonization was wholly unrealistic. Even apart from the moral question raised by a forcible relocation, where would the former slaves go, and who would replace them? Large-scale colonization would have required massive governmental intervention completely foreign to the limited American governments of the eighteenth century. At best, it suggests an African American version of the Cherokees' Trail of Tears: a bloody, forced march to some desolate wilderness. As early as 1766 Patrick Henry reluctantly expressed a more realistic white view. "The disadvantages from the great number of slaves may perhaps wear off, when the present stock and their descendants are scattered through the immense deserts in the west. To re-export them now is impracticable, and I am sorry for it."[25]

Only a clear and coherent ideology of universal equality might have overcome prejudices so engrained that they could lead a person of Jefferson's intelligence to consider a scheme so desperate as colonization, and on the question of slavery, the ideology of the Revolution was neither clear nor coherent. As Mason would argue time after time, in their confrontation with Great Britain, the colonists were insisting on their rights as Englishmen, a legal claim which failed to include Africans. John Hancock's response to the Stamp Act illustrated the distinction. "I will not be a Slave, I have a right to the Libertys & privileges of the English Constitution, and as an Englishman will enjoy them."[26] The idea that all people enjoyed certain inalienable rights as a matter of natural law, best exemplified in the writings of John Locke, offered a more expansive concept of "Libertys & privileges." Locke's belief that every individual was entitled to enjoy the fruits of his or her own labor seems to be an express repudiation of slavery, but Locke was personally complacent about the institution. Locke, moreover, believed that the purpose of government was to protect private property, a view Mason did not question, and Locke defined property liberally enough to include slaves.[27] To Mason's generation, property rights enjoyed a privileged position because they involved more than considerations of personal comfort or convenience. The ownership of property meant personal independence, and independence conferred on a citizen the ability to participate actively in the political life of the community, free from the pressures and temptations that might lead to the compromise of the public good for personal gain.[28] Ironically, as property slaves helped support the republican order; but if emancipated, they could not, without property of their own, be readily admitted into civil society.

The existence of African slavery in an age of political enlightenment may not, in retrospect, be so "amazing" after all, and Mason's failure to act more forcibly on his antislavery sentiments should be no mystery. Indeed, Edmund Morgan and others have argued that slavery allowed Virginia's planters to embrace democracy to an extent that would not otherwise have been expected of a landed gentry. Political theorists had long wrestled with the problem of accommodating democracy to the existence of the poor, whom no one trusted to participate responsibly in government. Slavery allowed the planters to minimize their society's need for a large class of the working poor and to exclude their African substitutes from civil society. A desire to maintain white rule, moreover, helped to unify white Virginians regardless of their economic status.[29] History usually appears inevitable in hindsight, and in the case of slavery and the American Revolution, it may have been. The revolution ought not to be seen as a missed opportunity to put slavery on a road to an early death. The attacks of Mason and others helped to undermine the legitimacy of the institution, and the eventual prohibition of the slave trade may have helped confine slavery to the South,[30] but racial fears and animosities pervaded white society too deeply during Mason's lifetime for much more to be done.

THE STAMP ACT proved to be unenforceable. Faced with an angry mob, George Mercer, for example, claimed there were no stamps for the Williamsburg customhouse, when in fact he had brought stamped paper with him from England. Mercer's deception gave ship captains an excuse for their noncompliance. The American boycott hurt the British economy, and in January 1766 a group of London merchants petitioned the House of Commons to repeal the Stamp Act. Lord Rockingham replaced Grenville, and in March, with Pitt leading the opposition to the Stamp Act, it was repealed.[31] Mason's replevin scheme never took effect.

Parliament had only yielded to political reality and economic necessity; it still refused to take the American constitutional arguments seriously. In

May 1766 the *Virginia Gazette* published a letter to America from a committee of London merchants warning the Americans not to gloat in the
repeal of the Stamp Act. The colonies' violent protests had been counterproductive, the merchants claimed, and further resistance could return
Grenville to power.[32] The letter provoked one of the earliest and longest
of Mason's political writings. In a response finished in June 1766, Mason
ridiculed the merchants' condescending attitude, which he likened to "the
authoritative Style of a Master to a School-Boy." Mason caricatured the
merchants' position: "We have, with infinite Difficulty & Fatigue got you
excused this one Time; pray be a good boy for the future; do what your
Papa and Mamma bid, & hasten to return to them your most grateful
Acknowledgements for condescending to let you keep what is your own."
Mason would have none of it. "Is this not a little ridiculous, when applyed
to three millions of us loyal & useful Subjects as any in the British Dominions, who have only been contending for their Birth-right."[33]

When it repealed the Stamp Act, Parliament also passed the Declaratory
Act, asserting Parliament's right to legislate for the colonies "in all cases
whatsoever," without specifically mentioning Parliament's power to tax
them. Mason knew that Pitt and others sympathetic to America recognized
the difference between legislation and taxation. If Mason had been privy
to Parliament's debate on the act, he would have known the intent of the
legislation was to reassert Parliament's authority to tax the colonies, but the
proceedings in Parliament had been kept secret. Mason suspected the truth.
If the Declaratory Act set forth any "unconstitutional Principles," Mason
declared, "to become 'waste paper' would be the most innocent use that
could be made of it." Parliament should have expressly rejected the claim
of a right to tax the colonies. "Nothing (except hanging the Author of the
Stamp Act) would have contributed more to restore that Confidence which
a weak or corrupt ministry had so greatly impaired."[34]

Parliament could, Mason conceded, legislate for the colonies, but it could
not exercise its legislative power in a way that discriminated against them.
He went on to castigate the procedures of the vice-admiralty courts and
to question the wisdom of the Navigation Acts. Relaxing restrictions on
American commerce would not cause colonial entrepreneurs to compete
with British industry. "Our Land is cheap and fresh . . ., while we can live
in Ease & Plenty upon our Farms, Tillage & not Arts, will engage our Attention." Americans, Mason believed, wanted British goods. If Americans
were free to seek the best price for their staples abroad, "all our superfluous
Gain will sink into Your Pockets, in Return for British Manufactures."[35]

Mason also made some astute predictions. "Such another Experiment as the Stamp-Act wou'd produce a general Revolt in America," a revolt that would invite foreign intervention in support of the Americans. "There is a Passion natural to the Mind of Man, especially a free Man, which renders him impatient of Restraint." At the same time, he professed his loyalty to "his Majesty's sacred Person & Government," and rested his case squarely on "the Liberty & Privileges of Englishmen." Americans, Mason believed, were legally equal to the English, and morally superior. "Let our fellow-subjects in Great Britain reflect that we are descended from the same Stock as themselves, nurtured in the same Principles of Freedom; . . . that in crossing the Atlantic Ocean, we have only changed our Climate, not our Minds, our Natures & Dispositions remain unaltered; that we are still the same People with them, in every Respect; only not yet debauched by Wealth, Luxury, Venality, & Corruption."[36] Their greater virtue made Americans more apt to defend their rights, and by force if necessary. Mason's letter was apparently never published in England, but it placed Mason firmly in the camp of the more advanced advocates of American rights.

Despite the Declaratory Act, Anglo-American relations entered a period of relative calm after the repeal of the Stamp Act. Parliament revised the Sugar Act, and although the duty was now imposed on all imported sugar products, it was lowered to a penny a gallon. And yet the Stamp Act crisis left permanent scars. Mason may have considered himself an Englishman, but he knew the English government considered him to be a rude provincial. Edmund Randolph later wrote that "until the era of the Stamp Act almost every political sentiment, every fashion in Virginia appeared to be imperfect unless it bore a resemblance to some precedent in England." Virginians had chafed under British rule before, but they saw the Stamp Act as a turning point in the relationship.[37]

BESIDES DAMPENING the colonists' ardor for things British, the Stamp Act crisis also helped to unify Americans around a common set of ideas about how governments should function, or what writers of the period called "first principles." The notion of political first principles reflected an eighteenth-century preoccupation with the idea of balance and circularity in the physical universe. Good health, for example, depended on maintaining a proper balance of the humors of blood, phlegm, and bile. Aging and decline were part of the normal cycle of life, but disease and death could at least be temporarily arrested by restoring the humors to their original balance. Governments likewise tended to decline into despotism, unless citizens could intervene and restore a proper balance of political power within the state.[38]

Mason derived his first principles from a variety of sources—John Locke, the writings of the English Whig opposition, the common law, the European *philosophes*, the Scottish Enlightenment, and Virginia's own political and legal history. Long considered the philosophical godfather of the American Revolution, Locke, the great champion of natural rights liberalism, has fallen into some disfavor over the past quarter century or so. He has, to an extent, been displaced by a handful of radical Whig writers who propounded a republican ideology that could be traced through Machiavelli and Renaissance Italy to the Roman Republic and the ancient Greek city-states. Assigning primacy to one tradition over another can be treacherous business. Clear lines do not divide them, the Founders did not always bother to divulge their sources, and the relative influence of different writers fluctuated with the needs of the moment. Locke seemed tailor-made to justify armed resistance to George III, but when it came time to establish a central government for the new nation, he had to step aside in favor of Montesquieu.[39]

Locke's *Two Treatises of Government*, often seen as providing the intellectual justification for the Glorious Revolution of 1688, propounded a rational liberalism based on reason and experience. In Locke's view, government had been established to act as a trustee of the people's interests—largely the preservation of their property—and possessed no legitimate interests of its own. Locke's view of the state's role was essentially negative, leaving citizens alone to pursue their own self-interest. Some powers were strictly denied the government. A ruler could not discriminate among his citizens or tax them without their consent. Locke did not repudiate the monarchy as an institution, but a ruler who violated Lockean principles effectively made himself an enemy of the people, and they were justified in resisting him. Mason agreed completely.[40]

Yet despite a few dissents, Locke has lost ground among historians in recent years to writers like Algernon Sidney, Thomas Gordon, and John Trenchard. Critical of the English state, the Tories, and even the Whig establishment, republican writers took a dim view of human nature in general and of political leaders in particular. "It is the nature of power," Trenchard and Gordon warned, "to be ever encroaching."[41] Only constant vigilance, and an active participation in the political life, could check it. Corruption, virtue, and luxury were the key concepts in republican thought. Corruption meant not so much private debauchery as the pursuit of one's private interests at the public's expense. Radical Whigs could applaud personal probity, but they equated virtue with patriotism or love of country. The road from virtue to corruption was paved with luxury. Wicked rulers promoted luxury to distract the people's attention from signs of approaching tyranny; "they cannot be persuaded to see distant dangers, of which they feel no part."[42]

The actual influence of republicanism on Mason and his contemporaries may be a subject of debate, and the difference between Lockean liberalism and the radical Whigs' republicanism on the great issues of the Revolution ought not to be drawn too starkly. Undoubtedly, however, the language of virtue and corruption appealed to the Puritan strain in the American psyche, and a desire to avoid contamination by the spreading corruption of the British state contributed to the eventual decision for independence. It is, moreover, difficult to read Trenchard and Gordon and Mason's writings and speeches without appreciating the extent to which Mason adopted the rhetorical style of the radical Whigs. The bitter sarcasm of his letter to the London merchants is but one example.[43]

That style was not subtle. One historian of the Revolution has suggested that the "most potent weapon colonial leaders held was their assertive language and their public style."[44] Despite his reputation as a serious thinker, Mason's reading tastes sometimes ran to partisan polemics. Writing his friend George Brent to thank him for sending him a copy of *Junius's Letters*, Mason praised them profusely. "Junius's Letters are certainly superior to anything of the kind that ever appeared in our Language." Junius, in fact, was an anonymous propagandist whose writings ridiculing the British government and its ministers appeared in London's *Public Advertiser* between 1767 and 1772. The essays, sometimes attributed to Sir Philip Francis, were too topical, too personal, and too scurrilous to have lasting significance. The Duke of Grafton was a favorite target, and the attacks on Grafton typified Junius's approach. After criticizing Grafton for consorting with a mistress, Junius then lambasted Grafton for a lack of chivalry when he abandoned her. Along the way, Junius only feigned to spare the woman's feelings, remarking sarcastically that he would not "insult the memory of [her] departed beauty."[45]

Junius may have helped undermine Mason's faith in the British government, but Junius could not have been the source of many substantive political ideas. *Cato's Letters*, by Trenchard and Gordon, would have given Mason a more systematic introduction to radical thought and rhetoric, and if Mason had not already discovered Algernon Sidney on his own, which seems unlikely, they would have directed him toward the work of the lead-ing seventeenth-century republican theorist.[46] Besides a love of virtue, a hatred of corruption, and a fear of luxury, Mason took from the radical Whigs an acute sensitivity to prospective tyranny. Because it was in the na-ture of government to abuse the rights of the people, even a trivial violation of those rights could be the precursor to full-scale despotism. "So danger-ous a thing is an ill precedent," Trenchard and Gordon wrote, "which is often an inlet to an endless train of mischiefs; and so depraved is the nature of man, that we justify ourselves in our wickedness by examples that can-not be justified." Republicanism may also help explain Mason's aversion to politics. While it was a postulate that the citizen should be engaged in the public debate, republicans also understood it was difficult for a politi-cian to maintain his virtue. "A good man will choose to live in an innocent obscurity, and enjoy the internal satisfaction resulting from a just sense of his own merit, and virtue, rather than aim at greatness by a long series of unworthy acts and ignoble actions."[47]

Eighteenth-century republicanism should not be confused with modern libertarianism. Mason believed in a fairly broad-based suffrage and in in-dividual rights; few did more to enshrine notions like freedom of religion or the right to due process of law in the American political creed. Yet those ideas have evolved since Mason's day. Mason, and the political theorists on whom he drew, saw the right to representation as the paramount political freedom. The people's rights were more collective than individual, more dependent for their protection on the legislature than the courts. Mason candidly admitted that the economic boycotts American patriots used to protest British tax policy could violate the rights of individuals, but Mason believed the interests of the community justified those violations. "Every Member of Society is in Duty bound to contribute to the Safety & Good of the Whole; and when the Subject is of such Importance as the Liberty & Happiness of a Country, every inferior Consideration, as well as the Incon-venience to a few Individuals, must give place to it; nor is this any Hardship upon them; as themselves & their Posterity are to partake of the Benefits resulting from it."[48]

Likewise, the republican commitment to equality must be defined in eigh-teenth-century terms. Republicans feared extremes of wealth and poverty. "As great riches in private men is dangerous to all States, so great and sud-den poverty produces equal mischiefs."[49] Ordinary citizens possessed the competence to decide whether or not their state was well governed. "Every cobbler can judge, as well as a statesman, whether . . . the market where he buys his victuals, be well provided."[50] But republican notions of equality did not translate into an egalitarian commitment to bring all citizens into the political life of the state. Gordon explained that, by "the people," he meant "not the idle and indigent rabble under which name the people are often understood and traduced, but all who have property without the privileges of nobility."[51]

Few topics illustrate the difference between the eighteenth-century world and modern sensibilities better than do the republicans' support for sumptuary laws. Intended to regulate vices like drinking, gambling, lewd entertainment, and idleness, sumptuary laws also sought to discourage luxury and conspicuous consumption. Difficult to reconcile with modern notions of personal freedom, or with the demands of a free market, sumptuary laws were not intended simply to promote social equality. They were also intended to protect the virtue on which the republican state rested, and they had an appeal beyond the fringes of radical Whiggery. At different times, Benjamin Franklin, John Adams, and Montesquieu endorsed them. The various nonimportation agreements the colonists adopted before the Revolution were of a kindred spirit. Americans believed that boycotts of English fineries would not only help alter British policy, but they would help preserve an austere, self-reliant, and hardy American character. As late as 1787, Mason argued that a sumptuary provision ought to be incorporated into the Constitution.[52]

Although it is convenient to think of republicanism as an intellectual tradition distinct from Locke's supposedly more modern liberalism, Mason made no such distinction. Contemporaries like Franklin, Jefferson, Landon Carter, and James Otis drew equally on both Sidney and Locke. It is telling that the editors of the modern versions of *Cato's Letters* and of Sidney's *Discourses on Government* seem to believe that their subjects agreed with Locke more often than not, and leading contemporary studies of both Locke and Sidney reach similar conclusions. Locke put relatively more emphasis on individual rights and the equality of all citizens before the law. But republicans and liberals alike believed that citizens enjoyed certain natural rights as a matter of natural law. Both Locke and Sidney believed in limited, representative government, in the sanctity of private property, in the need for some division of political power within a society, and in the right to revolt against an oppressive government.[53] What is sometimes seen as the tension between republican virtue and liberal rights was, more likely, in Mason's mind a delicate balance in which the safety of economic, religious, and political freedom rested in large measure on the virtue of the citizenry. Rights and virtue need not have been in conflict when, as in Mason's day, debates over rights usually involved not conflicts between the public good and individual rights but those between majority rights and an undemocratic government.[54]

Categorizing the political philosophy of Mason and his contemporaries is difficult because they not only synthesized traditions that were never entirely distinct but also filtered those traditions through their own unique experiences. The Virginians had a native ability to turn political molehills into constitutional mountains.[55] To a very large extent, many of the revolutionary theories of Mason, Jefferson, Henry, and Lee were indigenous, planted originally by the now almost forgotten Richard Bland. A lawyer and graduate of the College of William and Mary, Bland represented Prince George County in the House of Burgesses from 1742 until 1775. Bland died in 1776, but not before serving with Mason on the committee of the Virginia Convention that drafted the Virginia Declaration of Rights and Virginia's first state constitution. Once described as looking "something like the old parchments which he handled and studied so much," Bland was a legislative workhorse and, during his lifetime, the burgesses' leading constitutional theorist. In 1753, when Lieutenant Governor Robert Dinwiddie proposed to collect a pistole, a Spanish dollar, for every land patent issued, Bland emerged as a leading advocate of the legislative prerogative over such fees.[56]

Bland authored the Two Penny Act of 1758 and defended it in a 1764 pamphlet, "The Colonel Dismounted," which anticipated arguments Mason and others would use to oppose the Stamp Act.[57] Because Virginians were not a conquered people, Bland argued, they enjoyed the same rights as Englishmen. "Under an English government all men are born free, are only subject to laws made with their own consent, and cannot be deprived of the benefit of those laws without a transgression of them."[58] Because Parliament ceased to represent the colonists when they came to America, Bland concluded that Virginia should be self-governing in its internal affairs, subject only to the common law and statutes of Parliament "in force at the time of our Separation."[59]

Bland entered the Stamp Act debate with "An Inquiry into the Rights of the British Colonies," which was published in Williamsburg and in London, and which may well have been the first published statement of the American position on Parliament's right to tax the colonies.[60] Assuming an English citizen could not be taxed without his consent, Bland breezily dismissed the theory of virtual representation: "That nine Tenths of the People of Britain are deprived of the high Privilege of being Electors . . . shows a great

Defect in the present Constitution."[61] In leaving England, the colonists had removed themselves from England's civil society and had returned to a state of nature, which necessitated a new "compact with the Sovereign." Virginia's colonial charters embodied that contract, and because the charters were issued by the king, not by Parliament, Bland could find no legal justification for Parliament's exercise of jurisdiction over Virginia.[62] Mason would eventually reach the same conclusion.

Mason, moreover, broke completely with English liberal and republican principles on the question of religious liberty, and even moved ahead of many of his fellow Virginians. English reformers associated Catholicism with Stuart absolutism, censorship, and the Inquisition. Locke feared the power of Rome, and the title of a 1722 essay by Trenchard and Gordon illustrated their attitude: "The necessary Decay of Popish States shown from the Nature of Popish Religion." But the English experience with the Stuarts had little relevance to Mason. The Board of Trade in London had endorsed some measure of religious freedom in the colonies as a way of attracting settlers, and Mason and his political allies appreciated the economic value of religious toleration. Mason had seen colonial Virginia's relatively permissive religious climate as a magnet for potential immigrants as early as 1753, when the Ohio Company formulated its plan to settle German Protestants west of the Appalachian Mountains. "A general toleration of Religion," Patrick Henry wrote in 1766, "appears to me the best means of peopling our country."[63]

Yet a willingness to tolerate Catholics, and to withdraw state aid from religion in general, was not inevitable. Catholics enjoyed little popular support in eighteenth-century Virginia. When the Quebec Act recognized the rights of Canadian Catholics, Richard Henry Lee exploded that the adherents of "this bloody and intolerant religion" were poised "to carry slaughter and destruction into the free protestant colonies."[64] Mason never engaged in such rhetoric. In addition to seeing the economic utility of tolerance, Mason had a philosophical predisposition toward freedom of opinion. "Persecution in Matters of Religion," he wrote, "serves not to extinguish, but to confirm the Heresy." Mason's opinions on church-state relations put him in the forefront of Virginia reformers, leading him to disagree even with Lee and Henry over the propriety of state aid to organized religion.[65]

Mason's views on the proper relationship between organized religion and civil government illustrate a more fundamental point. If the American Revolution was a conservative revolution in the sense that it was not attempting to remake American society,[66] Mason and his compatriots, including Lee and Henry, had a vision of a republican state that went beyond the mainstream of Whig thought. Their assault on Parliament's authority ran contrary to the fundamental Whig premise that Parliament constituted the primary bulwark of the people's liberties against monarchial abuse. Mason's claim, which was commonplace in the colonies, that the Americans wanted only to enjoy their rights as Englishmen stretched the truth. As Gordon Wood has pointed out, the American demand for actual, as opposed to virtual, representation, expanded freedoms of speech and religion, and other reforms exceeded what English law afforded even the inhabitants of the British Isles.[67] Mason owed philosophical debts to many sources, but he and his fellow revolutionaries developed their own unique political ideology.

IN THE SUMMER OF 1766, George III dismissed Rockingham and asked William Pitt to organize a new government. Pitt hoped to form a "Ministry of all the talents," a broad coalition government that would be assembled to squelch as much partisan bickering as possible. Plagued by gout and failing mentally, Pitt declined to serve as the first lord of the treasury, the de facto prime minister, and instead accepted a largely symbolic post as lord privy seal, as well as a peerage, which removed him from the House of Commons. Loyalty and competence were not prerequisites for service in the new government. A reluctant and dissolute Duke of Grafton became prime minister, but he lacked both the inclination and the experience to lead the ministry. Pitt, now Lord Chatham, seemed strangely disengaged from his own government, and the new chancellor of the exchequer, Charles Townshend, stepped forward to fill the void.

To reduce the burden on the British treasury, Townshend wanted to move the army from the American frontier to the Atlantic seaboard, where the troops could be supplied more easily, and he wanted to shift more of their expenses to the Americans. In a January 1767 debate in Parliament, the government revealed that the annual budget of the army might be as much as £400,000. Townshend promised to bring forth new revenue measures. In February, Parliament passed legislation reducing British property taxes by £500,000, which only exacerbated Townshend's financial woes.

Townshend responded by proposing new duties on imported tea, paint, lead, glass, and other items. Townshend defended the new levies as external taxes, which, in 1767, a British minister could have believed in good faith might have been acceptable to a majority of Americans. But the Townshend

Duties, as they came to be known, were expected to produce only about £40,000 a year, hardly enough to make a dent in the army's expenses, and Townshend wanted to earmark at least some of the revenue for royal officials in the colonies, thus making them financially independent of the colonial legislatures. Other components of Townshend's program seemed equally intented to break the back of colonial resistance. He proposed the New York legislature be suspended until it complied with the Quartering Act, requiring it to supply British troops in New York. He advocated the creation of an American Board of Custom Commissioners, located in Boston, to supervise personally the enforcement of British trade regulations. Parliament passed the Townshend Act, to take effect on 20 November 1767, in June. Other provisions included new vice-admiralty courts in Charleston, Philadelphia, and Boston, and increased use of writs of assistance, broad search warrants that could be used against American smugglers. Having worked his will on Parliament, Townshend took a fever and died early in September 1767.[68]

John Dickinson's "Letters from a Farmer in Pennsylvania," which began appearing in December 1767, should have disabused British officials of any lingering illusions they may have had about the Americans' willingness to accept even an external tax. Beginning in Boston in the fall of 1767, patriots in the larger American cities organized associations to protest the Townshend Duties by refusing to import British goods. By March 1769 merchants and legislatures in most of the northern and middle colonies had joined in the nonimportation movement.

Virginia faced several disadvantages in attempting to respond to the Townshend Duties. The House of Burgesses had not been in session since April 1767, and Governor Fauquier feared the consequences of calling them back to Williamsburg. But when Fauquier died on 1 March 1768, John Blair, president of the council and acting governor, convened the delegates, who responded with a strong protest against the new duties. At the same time, however, Virginia seemed ill-suited to enforce a meaningful nonimportation agreement. With little manufacturing, the Chesapeake and southern colonies relied more heavily on British imports than did New Yorkers or New Englanders. Virginia planters tended to buy directly from factors representing British merchant houses. Unlike Boston, New York, or Philadelphia, trade with Britain could not, in Virginia, be strangled by putting pressure on a relatively small number of centrally located American merchants to stop dealing in English goods.[69]

In early April 1769 George Washington sent Mason copies of correspondence between Annapolis and Philadelphia merchants and a copy of a nonimportation agreement signed by the Philadelphia merchants on 10 March. Dr. David Ross of Bladenburg, Maryland, had sent the documents to Washington, and apparently unknown to Washington, Ross had also sent copies to Mason. The Philadelphia agreement lamented America's considerable indebtedness to Great Britain and the many obstacles Americans faced in paying off those debts, "in particular . . . the last unconstitutional Acts imposing Duties on Tea, Paper, Glass & c for the Sole purpose of raising a Revenue." The merchants expressed the twin hopes that "their Example will Stimulate the Good People of this Province to be frugal in the Use & Consumption of British Manufacture," and that British merchants and manufacturers would help the Americans "to obtain Redress of those Grievances under which the Trade and Inhabitants of America at present labor." Except for certain specified items, mainly necessities not readily available in the colonies, the Philadelphia merchants agreed to import or buy no English goods as long as the Townshend Duties remained in effect.

"Our lordly Masters in Great Britain," Washington wrote from Mount Vernon, "will be satisfied with nothing less than the deprivation of American freedom." Washington believed an economic boycott might be an effective middle way between further "Addresses to the Throne, and remonstrances to Parliament," which had been unavailing, and an appeal to arms, which Washington saw as "the last resource." He had doubts about the practicability of nonimportation "in the Tobacco colonies where the Trade is so diffused, and in a manner wholly conducted by Factors." Washington also worried about whether work toward a boycott could begin before the House of Burgesses met in May. But Washington believed a nonimportation agreement could serve a useful purpose even if it did not alter British policy: it might at least curb the spending of Virginia's notoriously profligate planters. "I am somewhat in doubt," Washington told Mason, "& should be glad to know your opinion."[70]

Probably because he had already received his copy of the packet from Ross, Mason answered Washington's letter immediately. Mason agreed that no formal action could be taken until the General Court or the general assembly met. Mason had, however, begun a draft for "our Gazettes" to prepare Virginians for economic warfare. He had been "unluckily stop'd by a Disorder which affects my Head & Eyes in such a Manner, that I am totally incapable of Business," but Mason promised, "so soon as I am able, I shall resume it." Although Mason believed the established trade of American raw materials for British manufactured goods served the best interests of both countries, he also believed the Anglo-American relationship had reached a critical point, one that justified commercial sanctions. "Our All is at Stake, & the little Conveniencys & Comforts of Life, when set in Competition with our Liberty, ought to be rejected not with Reluctance but with Pleasure." A nonimportation scheme, Mason realized, would have to be adapted to economic reality in Virginia, which he thought would permit a boycott of "all manner of Superfluitys" and "Finery of all Denominations." Mason even raised the prospect Virginians might "refrain from making Tobacco."[71] Mason may have thought then that an actual tobacco strike might hurt Virginia as much as it would hurt Britain, but the threat, by contrast, likely as it was to raise prices, could only benefit the colony.

We do not know exactly what happened next. The Truro Parish vestry met the following week and Washington and Mason may have discussed the nonimportation plan at that meeting. According to Washington's diary, Mason spent 21 April at Mount Vernon and signed a contract to sell Washington 100 acres on Little Hunting Creek. On 23 April, Mason, back at Gunston Hall, sent Washington a copy of a nonimportation agreement for Virginia, with a few suggested changes. The authorship of the draft Mason revised is a matter of debate. Historians from Jared Sparks to Julian Boyd attributed the resolves to Mason, largely because the oldest surviving copy of them, which was in Washington's papers, was believed to be in Mason's handwriting. In fact, Washington's copy was in an unknown hand, which led Robert Rutland to conclude that Mason could not have been the author.[72] The handwriting evidence, of course, is not conclusive. Mason could have copied someone else's work, or another writer could have copied his, before the original manuscript disappeared. The real author might have dictated to an amanuensis.

Rutland buttressed his conclusion by pointing to Mason's statement in his letter of 5 April that he was too ill to write, but Mason might easily have recovered in a few days. If he was able to travel to Mount Vernon on 21 April, it seems logical to assume he was well enough to write a few days earlier. Mason promised Washington on 5 April that he intended to complete a draft essay defending nonimportation as soon as he could; preparation of the agreement itself would have gone hand in hand with such an article. Perhaps the best reason why Mason's illness does not point toward another author may be inferred from the relevant documents themselves. The actual nonimportation agreement is not much longer than the letter Mason wrote on 5 April, when he said he was too sick to write: despite his claim of disability, Mason's illness, at least by the fifth, would not have prevented him from acting as the drafter.

No evidence points directly toward another author, and he, or she, would have had little time to do the work. Because of the similarities among the Philadelphia agreement, Mason's letter of 5 April, and the Virginia agreement, Rutland concedes that the author of the Virginia agreement must have had access to both the Philadelphia document and Mason's letter. In order to have written the Virginia agreement in time for Mason to have sent a revised draft to Washington by 23 April, another author would also have needed to have received a copy of Mason's letter, from either Mason or Washington, within a few days of its writing, no insignificant consideration given eighteenth-century modes of transportation. Presumably, there would have been some further consultation with Mason, and perhaps with Washington. Yet if Mason or Washington communicated with someone else, those communications produced no surviving documents, which is possible if not entirely probable. Mason may have worked at Gunston Hall with a coauthor, or Mason may have used an assistant—someone had to make the copy Mason revised—but the evidence does not support the existence of another writer working independently of Mason, and there is no obvious candidate for the role.[73]

In any event, the Mason draft, if we may call it that, was not radically different from the Philadelphia agreement. Mason expanded the preamble slightly, adding a complaint that the people of Virginia had been beset by "Grievances and Distresses" that threatened to reduce "them from a free and happy people to a Wretched & miserable State of Slavery." The agreement committed subscribers to refrain from buying goods subject to the Townshend Duties, and rather than listing goods that could be imported, as the Philadelphia patriots had done, Mason specified the other items that were to be proscribed—mainly liquor, foodstuffs, furniture, and luxury goods. More significantly, Mason went on to prohibit the importation of slaves and to threaten an embargo of naval stores and tobacco.[74]

Washington took Mason's draft with him to Williamsburg. On 16 May the House of Burgesses passed a series of resolutions that, among other things, asserted its exclusive right to tax Virginians, causing the new governor, Norborne Berkeley, Baron de Botetourt, to dissolve the assembly. Undeterred, the burgesses reassembled in the Apollo Room at the Raleigh Tavern, and eighty-eight of them signed a nonimportation agreement. Save for the threat to stop tobacco production, which was deleted, the final agreement generally tracked Mason's proposal.[75]

Washington's concerns about the ability of a planter elite to enforce nonimportation in an economy as decentralized as Virginia's proved prophetic. In the year after the burgesses endorsed the nonimportation agreement, tea imports declined, but overall imports actually increased. Higher prices for tobacco, wheat, and lumber meant more money for ordinary planters, and they spent it on British goods. But the boycotts in the northern and middle colonies told a different story. The Townshend Duties produced less than half the revenue Charles Townshend had originally expected, and losses to British merchants approached a staggering £700,000.[76] With Townshend's plan in shambles, the British cabinet voted to repeal the duties, except, at George III's request, for the tax on tea. The king insisted "that there must always be one tax to keep up the right, and as such I approve of the tea duty."[77] On 5 March 1770, the day of the Boston Massacre, Lord North, who had replaced Grafton as prime minister, introduced legislation in Parliament to repeal all the Townshend Duties, save for the one on tea.

Mason knew, as he told Richard Henry Lee in June 1770, that "the Custom-House Books shew'd that the Exports to Virginia in particular were very little, if at all, lessened" by the agreement of the previous year. Yet Mason was not willing to submit to a tax on tea, and he was not ready to give up on nonimportation. "We must avoid even the appearance of violence," but local committees, composed of "the most respectable men," needed to be organized to enforce the economic sanctions against Great Britain. Those who traded with the British should be publicly shunned: "If Shame was banished out of the World, she wou'd carry away with her what little Virtue is left in it." Mason was not present when the House of Burgesses reconvened in Williamsburg later in the month, but Lee, as a delegate from Westmoreland County, was and the burgesses adopted a revised nonimportation association incorporating the local committee structure Mason had recommended to him.[78]

Despite the new enforcement mechanism, and Mason's personal efforts to promote nonimportation in Fairfax County—where perhaps as many as a third of the voters signed the nonimportation pledge—the 1770 agreement proved no more effective than the earlier association. A tax on tea alone imposed too light a burden on most Virginians to justify a general boycott of British goods. Mason reported to George Brent in December 1770 that the nonimportation efforts "are at present in a very lanquid State," and he conceded the colonies ought to have adopted a boycott "in the Nature of a Sumptuary Law, restraining only Articles of Luxury & Ostentation" and goods subject to a tax. By the middle of 1771 Mason had concluded that the boycott should be limited to tea and any other items the British might tax. Mason, meanwhile, denied British claims that the patriots' real goal was independence. As he wrote Brent, "there are not five Men of Sense in America who wou'd accept of Independence if it was offered." Yet, Mason warned, "shou'd the oppressive system of taxing us without our consent be continued, the Flame, however smothered now, will break out with redoubled Ardour."[79]

Chapter Three

The Fundamental Principle

MASON REACHED middle age with few noteworthy public accomplishments. He had regained his seat on the Fairfax County Court, but he never seemed to take seriously his duties as a justice of the peace. His service in the French and Indian War consisted of the mundane work of procuring supplies far from the front lines. After spending a few uneventful weeks in the House of Burgesses, he sought neither reelection nor higher office. Gunston Hall had produced no widely read state papers, and if Mason had poured great effort into the Ohio Company, he had barely been able to keep the enterprise afloat. His description of himself in his letter to the London merchants seemed fitting; he was, he wrote, "a Man, who spends most of his Time in Retirement, and has seldom medled in public Affairs."[1]

Yet Mason had been a driving force behind the nonimportation movement, and he would continue almost single-handedly to press the Ohio Company's claims. Between the summer of 1774 and the spring of 1776, a troubled Mason would draft a revolutionary manifesto, the Fairfax Resolves; serve reluctantly in a provisional government; and help organize first a militia and then an army to wage war against the British Empire. Indeed, by 1776 Mason would become one of the two or three dominant figures in Virginia politics. Mason lacked Washington's physical presence, Jefferson's intellectual versatility, or Madison's commitment to public service. Mason could not command the popular following that Patrick Henry enjoyed, and he could not match Richard Henry Lee's long experience in public office. Both exceeded him as an orator. But Mason's colleagues recognized him as an indispensable ally, and during Mason's lifetime, only Washington ranked higher in public esteem.[2] Years later Jefferson recalled Mason as a one of Virginia's "really great men, and of the first order of greatness." Henry Lee ranked Mason ahead of Jefferson as a legislator. Madison, with whom Mason would spar repeatedly at the Constitutional Convention, pronounced him simply "the ablest man in debate he had ever seen." Mason "saw to the bottom of every proposition," Edmund Randolph wrote. "His elocution was manly sometimes, but not wantonly sarcastic."[3]

The Stamp Act crisis and a political scandal had created an opportunity for a new generation of more radical leaders to challenge the Tidewater aristocrats who had long dominated the House of Burgesses. Two of the newcomers, Richard Henry Lee and Patrick Henry, would be among Mason's closest allies. After the Speaker of the House John Robinson died in 1766, it gradually became apparent that Robinson, who was also the colonial treasurer, had secretly loaned his friends and political allies money he had collected in taxes that was supposed to be retired as an anti-inflationary measure.[4] As a delegate from Westmoreland County, Lee demanded a thorough investigation, which earned him a reputation as a champion of political virtue and made him a hero in the Northern Neck. The third son of a large family with nine children of his own, Lee, unlike Mason, needed the income he received from a series of government posts, and Lee embraced the republican virtues of self-sacrifice and self-denial almost from necessity.[5] Mason would spend many days at the Chantilly estate Lee rented from his older brother Thomas Ludwell.[6]

Lee brought to the patriot cause an early and unwavering commitment to American independence and a sense of drama that Mason lacked. "His face was on the Roman model," an early biographer wrote, "the whole contour, noble and fine." Lee had lost four fingers on his left hand in a hunting accident. He kept the crippled hand wrapped in a black silk bandage, and when he spoke, he flashed the bandaged hand with such polished grace it was said he must have practiced the gesture in a mirror.[7]

With a "deep and melodious voice," Lee, according to contemporaries, played Cicero to Patrick Henry's Demosthenes.[8] In May 1774 Mason heard Henry debate the burgesses' response to the Boston Port Bill, which closed the port to most commercial traffic. "He is in my opinion the first man upon the continent," Mason wrote his neighbor Martin Cockburn, "and had he lived in Rome about the time of the first Punic war, when the Roman people had arrived at their Meridian glory, and their virtue not tarnished, Mr. Henry's talents must have put him at the head of that glorious Commonwealth." Edmund Randolph later credited Henry as being the first politician in Virginia to challenge successfully the political monopoly of the planter aristocracy, but many of Mason's fellow revolutionaries saw glaring flaws in the rough-hewn, homespun orator. Henry's greatest flaw, to use William Wirt's term, was "indolence," which manifested itself in a chronic inattention to legislative detail. As Wirt described it, Henry possessed an "unconquerable aversion to every species of systematic labor." Mason over-looked Henry's foibles.[9]

Mason seemed to have more in common with George Washington—independent means, steady judgment, a distaste for politics, and a commitment to the American cause that involved more principle than passion—but the relationship between Mount Vernon and Gunston Hall was ambiguous. Until the Revolutionary War took Washington north, Mason and Washington saw each other regularly and communicated frequently. Over the years, Mason sent Washington dozens of pear, cherry, and apple grafts; Washington dutifully recorded each arrival in his diary.[10] Washington hunted deer with Mason on Dogue's Neck; Mason would sometimes stop at Mount Vernon on his way home from court in Alexandria.[11] Mason advised Washington on the selection of a tutor for Washington's stepson Jackie Custis, and Washington, on a trip to Williamsburg, bought two pairs of snap earrings for Mason's daughters. In the spring of 1770, Mount Vernon and Gunston Hall alternated as the site of Francis Christian's dancing school for the young people in the neighborhood.[12] On at least two occasions, Washington and Mason served together as arbitrators in legal disputes between their neighbors,[13] and they collaborated on what was for both of them a pet project, legislation to create a company to make the Potomac navigable as far west as Fort Cumberland.[14]

But the relationship may have been proper and polite, rather than close and personal, at least on Washington's part. Washington rarely spent the night at Gunston Hall, and he wrote Mason far less often than Mason wrote him. Washington tended to keep acquaintances at arm's length. Older, more affluent, and more cerebral, Mason, one historian has suggested, may have slightly intimidated Washington. Washington, who left Mount Vernon time after time in the service of his country, may have thought Mason was overly preoccupied with his health, his children, and his personal affairs. Washington could have resented Mason's effort to collect on a note Washington had cosigned for his spendthrift friend John Posey.[15] Mason and Washington clashed, perhaps good naturedly, perhaps not, when Truro Parish decided to rebuild Pohick Church. Mason wanted to rebuild on the old site, which was only about three miles from Gunston Hall. Washington preferred a location closer to Mount Vernon; Washington carried the day when he appeared at a vestry meeting with a survey showing the site he preferred was more centrally located. They also exchanged words over the validity of the title Mason conveyed to Washington when Mason sold him 300 acres on Hunting Creek.[16] A more serious crisis arose in early 1775.

Washington and Mason, on the eve of war, advanced the money to create an independent militia company for Fairfax County. Afterward, Washington accused Mason of trying to keep all the money collected to repay the debt. Washington's accusation provoked an anguished denial from Mason. It was not the kind of exchange that might be expected between two men who liked and trusted one another.[17]

Yet Washington undoubtedly relied on Mason for political advice and instruction. Washington later explained how, in 1769, he became involved in the nonimportation movement: "Much abler heads than my own," Washington said, convinced him that the Townshend Act was "not only repugnant to natural right, but subversive of the laws and constitution of Great Britain itself." Given Mason's views on the subject and the frequent communication between the two men, the reference is undoubtedly to Mason.[18]

Poor health and family responsibilities did often preoccupy Mason. Gout and other complaints continued to plague him.[19] He would also face tragedy at Gunston Hall. Between 1753 and 1770, Ann Mason gave birth to ten children, nine of whom survived to adulthood. In December 1772 she gave birth prematurely to twin boys. Neither child lived. Ann had fallen ill during her pregnancy and never recovered. Dr. James Craik, George Washington's close friend and personal physician, attended her, but she died in March 1773, Mason wrote, "of a slow fever . . . after a painful tedious Illness." Ann's death devastated Mason. John Mason later recalled that his "father for some days paced the rooms, or from house to the grave (it was not far) alone." Mason started on his own will, which ran to fifteen pages, and he wrote a moving eulogy to Ann in the family Bible, which ended: "Her . . . irreparable Loss I do, & ever shall deplore; and tho' Time I hope will soften my sad impressions, & restore me greater Serenity of mind than I have lately enjoyed, I shall ever retain the most tender and melancholy Remembrance of One so justly dear."[20] Six years later, Mason wrote George Brent that after Ann's death he was overcome by a "settled melancholy . . . from which I never expect, or desire to recover."

Mason also told Brent that he had "determined to spend the Remainder of [my] Days in privacy & Retirement with my children,"[21] but that was a commitment, try as he might, that Mason could not keep. By the eve of the Revolution, Mason's influence among the leaders of the revolutionary movement in Virginia had spread too far for him to remain in permanent seclusion at Gunston Hall. Even casual observers recognized the quality of Mason's mind and the force of his personality. Philip Mazzei, an Italian doctor and writer who came to Virginia in December 1773 to help develop

a local wine industry, met Mason in Williamsburg within days of arriving in America. Mazzei was immediately overwhelmed. "In my opinion,"
Mazzei wrote, "he is not well enough known. He is one of those brave, rare
—talented men who cause nature a great effort to produce." The Italian
ranked Mason alongside Dante, Machiavelli, Galileo, and Newton as one
of the intellectual giants of Western civilization. Mazzei exaggerated, but
Mason won wide respect for his intelligence, independence, and utterly
transparent lack of personal political ambition.[22]

If Mason, as late as 1774, had few public accomplishments to his credit
apart from his role in the nonimportation movement, he had demonstrated
considerable business acumen. His ability to manage successfully a large
plantation displayed a skill many of Virginia's chronically indebted planters never mastered, and he had risen to a position of dominance within
the Ohio Company. Politically, Mason's philosophical inclination toward
advanced but not extreme positions served a practical purpose. Holding
the revolutionary movement together meant keeping radicals like Henry,
Lee, and Jefferson marching in concert with cautious men like Richard
Bland. "The Sanguine are for rash Measures without consideration," Edmund Pendleton explained, "the Flegmatic to avoid that extreme are afraid
to move at all, while a third Class take the middle way and endeavor by
tempering the first and bringing the later into action to draw all together
to a Steddy, tho' Active Point of defense."[23] Mason, a solid patrician whose
views on American rights usually did not run too far ahead of those of his
fellow gentry, served as a bridge between the more extreme factions, and
he enjoyed the confidence of both.

KING GEORGE III signed the Proclamation of 1763, restricting English
settlement west of the Appalachian Mountains, in October, only a few
days after Mason's hapless cousin George Mercer arrived in London to
lobby British officials on behalf of the Ohio Company. Technically, the
company's grant had lapsed during the French and Indian War, but Mason,
now a member of the company's five-person executive committee, hoped
Whitehall would reaffirm the original grant. Mercer proved wholly ineffective. Not until 1765 did he submit a petition to the king requesting that the
Ohio Company be compensated for its past losses or be awarded new lands
not located on the forks of the Ohio River, and even his halting efforts on
behalf of the company were interrupted by his ill-advised return to Virginia
as a stamp agent, a post he was soon forced to resign.[24]

Once he was back in London, Mercer apparently raised the Ohio Company's claim with the Board of Trade, to which his petition had been referred. In June 1767 the board asked the Earl of Shelburne, the secretary of state with jurisdiction over the American colonies, to request that the governor of Virginia provide it with a report on the history of the company and the origins of its grant. Two decades, after all, had passed since Thomas Lee and the original partners had organized the company. Shelburne waited until October before he forwarded the board's request to Governor Francis Fauquier. The request itself may have been unnecessary; the board already had a comprehensive file on the company's grant. British opposition to westward expansion was beginning to waiver, but the change in policy failed to benefit the Ohio Company. Shelburne reportedly favored expansion, but because the Ohio Company's initial grant contained a ten-year exemption from quitrents, Shelburne did not, at least one historian has speculated, want the company to spearhead the western movement. In any event, the Board of Trade, in March 1768, issued a report characterizing the 1763 proclamation line as a temporary expedient, and later in the year the Treaty of Fort Stanwick conveyed to the crown huge new tracks of Indian land, including territory between the Ohio and Tennessee rivers that the Ohio Company had long coveted. The Fort Stanwick treaty seemed to assume, however, that the Ohio Valley would end up in the hands of the so-called suffering traders, a group of Pennsylvania speculators led by Samuel Wharton and George Croughan, as compensation for losses they had allegedly suffered during the war.[25]

When Mason learned that the Ohio Company's petition had been referred to Fauquier, he wrote the governor to find out "what is expected from the Company." Mason also wrote Robert Carter, a shareholder in the company and a member of the council who lived in Williamsburg, asking for his assistance. Carter, who received a copy of Shelburne's inquiry two days after Mason's letter reached the capital, responded by sending Mason a summary of the document. Mason wrote back with confidence, telling Carter, "Most of the Interrogatories you mention may be easily answered," and Mason felt certain the company's records would show conclusively that the shareholders had received no compensation for "the Sums of Money actually advanced in the Prosecution of the Scheme." Mason, meanwhile, prepared a new set of terms for the company's grant in which he proposed the company be given immediately the entire 500,000 acres promised in its original grant or "greater Indulgencies"—a larger grant—in recognition of the losses the company had suffered and the services it had provided during the French and Indian War.[26]

John Mercer, the Ohio Company's attorney, died in October 1768 while Shelburne's request for information was pending before the governor. Mercer's death shifted even more responsibility onto Mason's shoulders. Mason would soon be expressing frustration with the other stockholders' apathy, claiming "it is absolutely more difficu[l]t to procure a Meeting of our Members than it is to assemble a German Diet."[27] In reality, the lack of interest was understandable. By the end of the decade, Mason could do little more than draw up boundaries for grants that would never be patented and plan surveys that would never be recognized. A powerful new rival, variously known as the Grand Ohio Company, the Vandalia Company, or the Walpole Associates, submitted a petition to the king in November 1769 for a huge grant on the Pennsylvania-Virginia frontier. With powerful political connections in Pennsylvania and London, its principals included Benjamin Franklin, Samuel Wharton, and Thomas Walpole, nephew of former prime minister Robert Walpole.[28]

Frustrated by a lack of directions from Virginia and intimidated by the Grand Ohio Company's political muscle, George Mercer surrendered to the blandishments of the Walpole group. In the spring of 1770, Mercer, acting on his own initiative, agreed that the Ohio Company would abandon its claims in exchange for two shares of stock in the Grand Ohio Company. Mercer himself received one or two shares—the accounts vary—in the Vandalia enterprise, and he was reportedly led to believe he would become governor of a new, interior colony.[29] Mercer wrote Mason in July 1770, "speaking," in Mason's words, "very doubtfully of the Ohio Company's affairs in England," but Mercer did not tell Mason about the merger. A year later, Mercer had still not made a full disclosure. When Mercer wrote Mason in August 1771, it was to complain about a lack of instructions and an absence of financial support. He had not, Mercer claimed, received "*one* clear answer to all the Letters I have wrote for eight years past to my Friends. . . . And I had warned them that I had strained my credit for them as far as it would strech." Mason apparently did not learn of the merger until Mercer's brother James wrote Gunston Hall several months later, and even then Mason did not know why George Mercer had come to terms with his rivals.[30]

Mason immediately repudiated the merger. Writing James Mercer in January 1772, Mason defended himself against George Mercer's charges of neglect. Saying that Mercer's letters had led him to believe that Mercer was returning to Virginia, Mason dismissed the 3,000 acres he stood to receive if the Vandalia colony succeeded as "so trifling as not to be worth our Regard." At a meeting later in the year, the Ohio Company's members voted to reject the merger and take their case to the governor's council. When the council informed the company that because "an Order in their Favour" had already been issued, no further action was necessary, Mason apparently concluded the company could begin surveying the land it wanted.[31]

In reality, the council had not explicitly reaffirmed the 1749 grant, and the company had new bureaucratic obstacles to overcome. At a meeting in August 1773 at the Stafford County courthouse, Mason and the other shareholders decided to stake their claim in what is today Kentucky. Mason may have acquired several hundred acres in Kentucky through headright claims as early as 1769. The Ohio Company persuaded the College of William and Mary to license William Crawford as a surveyor, and Mason hired Crawford, assisted by Hancock Lee, his brother Willis, and the soon-to-be famous frontiersman George Rogers Clark, to survey land for the company in Kentucky. The party surveyed hundreds of thousands of acres along the Licking River in 1774–75. But Kentucky was then part of Fincastle County, Virginia, and for their surveys to have legal standing, the surveyors had to be licensed by the county. The Fincastle County surveyor, William Preston, was close to the rival Loyal Company, and Preston made sure that the Ohio Company's surveyors never received the proper credentials. Not only were the company's surveys of doubtful legality, but even before they had begun, British policy had shifted once again. In April 1773 the privy council ordered colonial governors to make no new land grants pending a review of the western problem by the Board of Trade. The board announced its recommendations in January 1774: henceforth, western land should be auctioned off in small tracts.[32]

Probably out of frustration with the Ohio Company, and perhaps because he intended to challenge British policy directly, Mason changed his tactics. In June 1773 Mason purchased more than 18,000 acres in headright claims from Harry Piper for forty-seven pounds, two shillings, and six pence, and he continued to make smaller purchases for years thereafter.[33] To assert his headright claims, Mason wrote one of the longest documents he ever produced. Part legal brief and part revolutionary propaganda, Mason's "Extracts from the Virginia Charters" drew heavily on William Stith's *History of the First Discovery and Settlement of Virginia* (1747), and especially on Stith's appendix, which reproduced the Virginia charters of 1606, 1609, 1612, and 1621. Mason traced the practice of issuing headrights to Governor George Yeardley in 1616, and he noted that Charles II had confirmed the practice in 1676.[34] Mason went on to argue that the charter granted by Charles II had always been understood "to demonstrate that the Country to the Westward of the Allegheny Mountains, on both sides [of] the Ohio River, is part of Virginia." By virtue of the 1763 Treaty of Paris, Virginia's western boundary extended to "the Middle of the River Mississippi."[35] Both the Ohio Company's grant and Mason's headrights were, of course, worthless unless space for them could be found within the borders of Virginia. The Walpole group had challenged Virginia's claim and, Mason added, threatened to establish "a precedent of a very alarming & dangerous nature to the Liberties, Rights, & privileges of his Majesty's Subjects of this Colony."[36]

The "Extracts" may have been originally intended to serve as the basis for a legislative petition to the crown protesting the Grand Ohio Company's application for a land grant,[37] but the document deserves attention more as a statement of revolutionary political principles. Both Virginia's boundaries and Mason's legal claims depended heavily on the colonial charters, and the enforceability of those charters, issued as they were by the crown, rested on executive, as opposed to parliamentary, authority over the colonies. "The Disposition of Foreign or newly acquired Territory," Mason argued, "hath ever belonged to the Executive."[38] Mason's justification for the continued recognition of headrights fit neatly with the emerging American position that Parliament had no jurisdiction over the colonies' internal affairs, but the "Extracts" raised other issues that bore little relevance to Mason's land speculations. He criticized the council for exercising legislative, executive, and judicial powers and, when it sat as the General Court, in exercising original jurisdiction in cases in which there was no avenue of appeal. The good character of the council members had thus far prevented a serious abuse of power, but Mason wondered how long such virtue could survive in a slave society, where "habituated from our Infancy to trample upon the Rights of Human Nature, every generous, every liberal Sentiment, if not extinguished, is enfeebled in our minds." Mason realized he had ventured far afield from his original topic. "These Remarks may be thought Foreign to the design of the annexed Extracts—They were extorted by a kind of irresistable, perhaps an Enthusiastick Impulse; and the author of them conscious of his own good Intentions, cares not whom they please or offend."[39]

Mason ultimately condensed the "Extracts" into a petition, confined to the issue of headrights, that he submitted to the governor and council in June 1774. The petition requested warrants to take up land in Fincastle County and argued that long practice, sanctioned by the crown and the general assembly, had made the acquisition of headrights one of the rights and privileges of English citizens that could not be "Avoided, injured, invalidated, or in any manner affected by an Proclamation, Instruction, or other Act of Gover[n]ment." Mason appeared before the council in May and June to argue his case. The council recognized the merits of Mason's claim, and Governor Dunmore was sympathetic, but their hands were tied by the recent orders of the privy council, which were codified in the Quebec Act of August 1774. If British policy would soon be irrelevant, the legal and political battles for control of the frontier would go on for years.[40]

WHEN PARLIAMENT repealed the Townshend Duties, except for the tax on tea, it did "everything," in the words of the pseudonymous Whig pamphleteer Junius, "but remove the offense. They have relinquished the revenue, but judiciously taken care to preserve the contention."[41] Relative calm prevailed as Americans continued to drink English tea and to pay a three pence a pound duty at the same time they continued to smuggle into the colonies illegal, untaxed tea from the Netherlands. The Tea Act of 1773, which exempted the financially troubled East India Company from the tea tax, infuriated American merchants and shattered the uneasy truce in Anglo-American relations. It led directly to the Boston Tea Party. In response, the House of Commons, in the spring of 1774, began consideration of a bill to close Boston harbor. Americans saw the bill as part of a conspiracy to deprive them of all their liberties. Besides the Boston port legislation, Parliament passed a series of other bills that Americans castigated collectively as the "Intolerable Acts": the Quebec Act; the Massachusetts Regulatory Act, giving the crown control over the selection of most officials in the Bay Colony; the Impartial Administration of Justice Act, allowing for criminal trials of royal officials outside of the colony where the crime was committed; and legislation providing for the quartering of British troops in private homes. But it was the closing of the port of Boston that became the focus of American protest.[42]

In Williamsburg in May 1774 to present his headright claims to the governor and council, Mason soon became caught up in the debate over the port bill. On 24 May the House of Burgesses set aside 1 June as a day of "fasting, humiliation, and prayer . . . for averting the heavy calamity which threatens destruction to our civil rights, and the evils of civil war." Jefferson, Henry, Richard Henry Lee, and Francis Lightfoot Lee had drafted the resolution in the council chamber the day before; Mason may well have helped them. At some point, in any case, Mason conferred with Patrick

Henry, and the other "gentlemen concerned," and Mason wrote his neighbor Martin Cockburn to make sure Mason's three oldest sons and two oldest daughters attended church on 1 June. Mason expected the new governor, Lord Dunmore, to dissolve the assembly before the end of June, but Dunmore, who privately doubted his action would do any good, dissolved the burgesses on 26 May. Mason, in all likelihood, joined the burgesses when they reconvened the following day at the Raleigh Tavern, elected Peyton Randolph moderator, and formed an association to boycott all East India Company products, except for spices and saltpeter. Mason, although he pronounced himself "heartily tired of this town," was still in Williamsburg at the end of May, when a remnant of the defunct house issued a call for a meeting of all the counties on 1 August. It would be the first of five conventions that would provide Virginia with a provisional government in the early stages of the Revolution. Mason stayed in the capital until the middle of June to pursue his headright claims.[43]

Waiting on George Washington to return from Williamsburg, Fairfax County delayed its election for delegates to the upcoming convention until 5 July. Washington would run for one of the seats; he hoped Bryan Fairfax or George Mason would run for the other. "I think," Washington wrote Fairfax, "the country never stood more in need of men of abilities and liberal sentiments than now." But neither Fairfax nor Mason chose to run. The only other announced candidate was Charles Broadwater, and "Major Broadwater, though a good man," Washington lamented, "might do as well in the discharge of his domestic concerns, as in the capacity of a legislator." A storm forced the postponement of the election until 14 July, but Washington and an apparent handful of others, which presumably included Mason, met in Alexandria on the fifth and appointed a committee to draft a set of resolves that, in Washington's words, would "define our Constitutional Rights."[44] A meeting to discuss instructions to the newly elected delegates was scheduled for 18 July.

The committee essentially completed its draft, largely Mason's work, by 11 July, three days before Washington and Broadwater were elected to represent the county. Mason spent Sunday night, 17 July, at Mount Vernon; he and Washington may have polished the resolves and talked strategy for the next day's meeting. The two men rode to Alexandria on Monday, where the freeholders elected Washington to chair the meeting, and where Mason, as nineteenth-century Virginian historian Hugh Grigsby described it, "made his first great movement on the theatre of the Revolution."[45]

The twenty-four propositions Mason presented to the Fairfax County freeholders succinctly summarized the emerging revolutionary orthodoxy. There were conciliatory gestures. Mason denied any interest in independence, pledged the colonies to support the empire "in Proportion to their Abilities," and thanked America's friends in Great Britain for their "Efforts to prevent the present Distress." At the same time, however, he excoriated "a premeditated Design and System, formed and pursued by the British Ministry, to introduce an arbitrary Government into his Majesty's American Dominions." In order to justify oppression, the king's ministers had fabricated the notion that Americans were bent on independence.

The resolves criticized the Administration of Justice Act and the Massachusetts Government Act, but Mason focused his wrath on a broader target, Parliament's exercise of authority over the colonies. Virginia had acquiesced in Parliament's regulation of colonial trade, "altho' in some Degree repugnant to the Principles of the Constitution," as a matter of comity. But, in one of the earliest statements of the "dominion theory" of the British Empire, Mason argued Parliament had no legal basis on which to insist on American submission to its wishes. Virginia had been settled at private expense, and its charters represented contracts with the crown, not the legislature. "Our Ancestors" brought with them, and enjoyed under the charters, all the "Privileges, Immunities and Advantages" of English citizens, the most important of which was "the fundamental Principle of the People's being governed by no Laws, to which they have not given their Consent, by Representatives freely chosen by themselves." Parliament's attempt to make "all such Laws as they think fit" and "to extort from us our Money without our Consent," violated the English constitution, the colonial charters, "and the natural Rights of Mankind."[46]

Formally intended as instructions to Washington and Broadwater, not as a harangue of Lord North's administration, the Fairfax Resolves called for the appointment of county committees to collect provisions for the relief of the Boston poor, for a boycott of the East India Company, and for the convening of a continental congress "to concert a general and uniform Plan for the Defence and Preservation of our common Rights." The resolves also called on "Gentlemen and Men of Fortune to set Examples of Temperance, Fortitude and Industry" and to encourage local manufacturing and wool production. Mason anticipated a boycott of all English goods, except for a few necessities, to be enforced by local committees. Washington and Broadwater were also instructed to work for a suspension of the slave trade and an embargo on the shipment of American lumber to the West Indies. And if American grievances were not addressed by 1 November 1775, "we will not plant or cultivate any Tobacco after the Crop now growing." The freeholders approved the resolves and appointed Mason and Washington to a special emergency committee.[47]

Similar resolves from some thirty-one counties survive,[48] but the Fairfax Resolves were the most detailed, the most influential, and the most radical. Mason, for example, went beyond most other writers in calling for a continental congress.[49] Mason had reduced to writing ideas that were commonplace among colonial radicals, and somehow managed to do it in a way that was acceptable to most conservatives.[50] Washington took the resolves with him when he went to the 1 August convention in Williamsburg. The competing instructions differed on the timing and details of a nonimportation agreement, and one of Mason's proposals—to compensate the East India Company for tea lost in the Boston Tea Party if colonial grievances were addressed—failed to command majority support. The list of permissible imports was narrowed to include only medicine. Otherwise the nonimportation agreement approved on 6 August tracked the Fairfax Resolves, as did the instructions adopted for the Virginia delegation to the Continental Congress, a group that included Washington, Henry, and Lee.[51]

Mason undoubtedly remained interested in the fate of his work. After Washington had returned home from Williamsburg, Mason spent the night of 30 August at Mount Vernon, along with Patrick Henry and Edmund Pendleton; Washington, Henry, and Pendleton left for Congress the next day. In October Congress adopted a Continental Association patterned after the Virginia nonimportation plan.[52] As had the Fairfax Resolves, the Continental Congress rested American rights on the three-legged stool of colonial charters, the British constitution, and natural law, and the delegates recognized the primacy of the right of representation. Congress expanded on Mason's call for frugality by proposing a ban on gambling and by criticizing "expensive Diversions and Entertainments." He would have approved. Congress conceded Parliament's right to regulate American trade, and if the concession conflicted with the logic of the Fairfax Resolves, Mason himself had skirted the issue of trade regulations. In deference to South Carolina, Congress expressly permitted the export of rice, and it briefly delayed the effective dates of the various restrictions, postponing the start of the ban on imports from 1 November to 1 December 1774.[53] But the changes to the Fairfax Resolves and the Virginia plan were minor, which was a tribute both to the force of Mason's ideas and the strength of the Virginia delegation.

MASON MAY HAVE concluded by the fall of 1774 that war was inevitable. The Virginia Convention of that year had authorized each county to organize an independent militia company outside the control of the royal governor. On 21 September, while the first Continental Congress was still deliberating, Mason chaired a meeting of Fairfax County freeholders who pledged to raise a company of 100 men, who would, "each of us, constantly keep by us a stock of six pounds of Gunpowder, twenty pounds of Lead, and fifty Gun-Flints, at the least." The "Fairfax Independent Company of Volunteers" occupied much of Mason's time until the summer of 1775. By the middle of January, Washington was drilling a small force in Alexandria, and Mason had drafted a resolution, which was adopted by the county's Committee of Safety, to levy an assessment of "three shillings per poll" to purchase ammunition. In the meantime, Washington and Mason bought powder for the company on their own credit.[54]

Although Governor Dunmore reported to London that opposition to British policy enjoyed widespread support—"There is not," he wrote, "a Justice of the Peace in *Virginia* that acts, except as a Committee-Man"—he did not believe the colony could sustain an economic boycott of British goods; "the middling and poorer sort, who live from hand to mouth, have not the means of doing so."[55] For his part, Mason did not expect the North administration to retreat. Mason wrote Washington on 6 February 1775 that he thought "we have little Hopes of a speedy Redress of Grievances; but on the contrary we may expe[c]t to see coercive and vindictive measures still pursued." By the same letter, Mason sent Washington a formal plan to implement the September resolution to organize an independent militia company. More detailed and ambitious than the earlier resolution, Mason now envisioned the county raising an entire regiment. Consistent with his republican fears of a standing army, Mason would argue, when it came time to select officers, that they should be elected by their troops, which was not unusual among militia units, but serve a term of only one year and be ineligible to succeed themselves, which was less commonplace.[56]

The remarks Mason prepared in support of the periodic election of militia officers represented a classic statement of his republican philosophy. His arguments drew on Locke, Lucretius, Junius, the history of the Roman Republic, and even the Old Testament book of Exodus. Mason began with sentiments that would reappear almost verbatim in the Virginia Declaration of Rights. "We came equal into this world, and equals shall we go out of it. All men are by nature born equally free and independent." Men formed governments to "protect the weaker from the injuries and insults of the stronger," but they gave up no more rights "than the nature of the thing required." Unless political authority is exercised to promote "the general good and safety of the community," Mason wrote, "it may be called government, but it is in fact oppression."

Yet free governments were easily corrupted. Mason blamed, "the insidious arts of wicked and designing Men, the various and plausible pretences for continuing and increasing authority, the incautious nature of the many, and the inordinate lust for power in the few." Mason believed the most effective remedy for this tendency toward corruption was the frequent appeal to "the body of the people," by which he meant "some certain mode of rotation" that would ensure that authority was routinely "dissolved into and blended with that mass from which it was taken."[57]

A second Virginia Convention met in Richmond beginning on 20 March, with Washington and Broadwater again representing Fairfax County, and elected Washington to the Virginia delegation to the second Continental Congress scheduled for May. By the time Congress met, fighting had broken out in Massachusetts, and Washington, who would be named commander in chief of American forces in June, did not know when he might return to Virginia. On 16 May Washington wrote the Fairfax County Committee of Safety from Philadelphia to recommend a substitute be elected to replace him as one of the county's delegates should another Virginia Convention be called. Washington did not suggest a replacement, but Mason was an obvious candidate and by July at the latest a move was underway to draft him. On 11 July Mason wrote his friend William Ramsay, an Alexandria businessman and member of the Committee of Safety, that he could not accept the appointment. "I entreat you, Sir, to reflect on the duty I owe to a poor little helpless family of orphans to whom I now must act the part of father and mother both, and how incompatible such an office would be with the daily attention they require." But the freeholders presumably could find no other prospects of comparable stature and no one else who would be an appropriate replacement for Washington. At a meeting the day after Mason wrote Ramsay, the voters elected Mason to the third Virginia Convention, which was to meet in Richmond on 17 July.[58]

"THE AMERICANS WERE pretty unanimous before," Mason wrote his London agent William Lee in June 1775, "but the Acts of the present Session of Parliament, and the Blood lately shed at Boston have fix'd every wavering Mind; and there are no Difficulties or Hardships which they are not determined to encounter with Firmness & Perseverance."[59]

Why would a wealthy Virginia planter risk a comfortable life-style over a modest tax on a nonessential item like tea or be moved to support armed resistance by New England rebels he scarcely knew? There may be no single answer. But Mason's own writings, and the various crises Virginians faced in 1775, offer clues to his thinking that make his decision to help lead a rebellion explicable, however unlikely it may appear in hindsight.

To begin with, the problem of taxation without representation, with which Mason had struggled since the passage of the Stamp Act, was paramount. If the tax on tea seemed innocuous, Mason's republican political science taught him that it was the precursor of far more serious violations of American rights soon to come. Parliament's willingness to embark on such a scheme exposed, to his thinking, the corruption of the English system, and the colonial fear that England's political depravity might spread to America should not be underestimated.

Parliament's treatment of John Wilkes—the radical Whig leader who was four times elected to the House of Commons and four times denied his seat —outraged Mason and his fellow rebels. Up to a point, the colonial policies of George III, his ministers, and Parliament could be attributed to guileless ignorance. No such defense could be made of their treatment of Wilkes. In arguing for the annual election of militia officers, Mason had observed that the "suppression of the free voice of the people" leads to "the inevitable destruction of the state." In the Wilkes case, Parliament ignored the people's will. The British "constitution has strong symptoms of decay," Mason wrote. "It is our duty by every means in our power to prevent the like here." A sense of isolation and a belief "that North America is the only great nursery of freemen now left upon the face of the earth" heightened Mason's anxiety about the spread of British corruption to the New World.[60] In retrospect the American Revolution can be seen as the beginning of an age of democratic revolutions that produced the dominant political motif of modern times—liberal democracy. But to Mason's generation, Americans in 1775 were fighting a rearguard action to preserve a remnant of republicanism somewhere in the world.

The imperial relationship, moreover, encompassed a host of more mundane problems that, if individually insufficient to trigger a rebellion, must collectively have sapped Virginians' loyalty to the mother country. Thomas Jefferson believed that, in the words of one historian, "an accumulation of little things broke up the empire." George Washington complained repeatedly about British factors who sold his tobacco too cheaply, overcharged him for the goods he bought, and shipped him broken tools and out-of-date clothes. More widespread were complaints about huge debts owed to British lenders and, after the British economy slumped in 1772, the contraction of credit. Mason avoided the debt trap, and he believed Anglo-American trade could be mutually beneficial. At the same time, he appreciated the plight of Virginia debtors. The colony never had an adequate circulating currency, and even Mason, for all his affluence, sometimes suffered from a literal lack of hard cash.[61]

By 1774 Mason actually appeared to be making progress with local officials —even Governor Dunmore seemed sympathetic—in his long quest to make good on his efforts to acquire new land in the West, only to be stymied by another shift in Whitehall's land policies. The conflicting claims of Indians, squatters, small planters, and rival land companies might provide a partial excuse for British dithering, but under imperial rule, Virginia seemed unable to develop one of the prerequisites of a stable agrarian society, a coherent system of land titles. Conflicting grants, inaccurate surveys, squatters, and the gyrations of British policy made a mess of ownership records. George Washington complained, "no man can lay off a foot of land and be sure of keeping it."[62] Mason shared similar frustrations, telling Washington in 1769, "I have not an Acre of Land in the World for which I would give a general Warranty."[63] Colonial boundaries suffered from the same uncertainty; a small-scale war erupted between Pennsylvania and Virginia over their western border in the spring of 1774. When Dunmore sent a justice of the peace to assert Virginia's jurisdiction in Pittsburgh, he was promptly arrested by the Pennsylvania-appointed sheriff.[64]

The significance of tangible complaints, large and small, was likely exaggerated by less concrete tensions within Virginia society. Virginia's population had grown dramatically since Mason's boyhood; settlements had expanded in the West and the Southside. Religious dissenters, especially the Separate Baptists, had arisen to challenge the Anglican establishment. Small planters began to contest the political dominance of the landed gentry. Increased political competition produced charges of illegal "treating," bribery, and vote buying, and complaints about the election of "obscure and inferior persons" to the House of Burgesses. More and more disputed elections were coming before the burgesses' Committee on Privileges and Elections. Nothing suggests the new religious ferment disturbed Mason, but he may have seen the more contentious political climate as an early symptom of the British-style corruption he so deplored. Other Virginians saw the spread of slavery as a sign of a moral crisis, and we know Mason shared those fears.[65] Worse yet, perhaps, Mason must have known that despite all his arguments for the legal equality of white Americans within the empire, the British dismissed the Americans as crude provincials, culturally and intellectually inferior to more refined Europeans.[66]

By the spring of 1775, the existing political and economic system had proved inadequate to the demands of a growing colony. Mason had not yet embraced the goal of independence, but he had come to see British rule as an impediment to Virginia's natural and orderly development. It also presented a gathering threat to a new American concept of civil liberty.

THE HOUSE OF BURGESSES met in Williamsburg in June 1775 as royal government in Virginia collapsed about it. After the session had begun, Governor Dunmore, apparently fearful for his personal safety, retreated to the security of a British warship. Political power in Virginia was shifting to a series of extralegal conventions, the third of which met in the old Town Church, now St. John's, in Richmond on 17 July. George Mason's service in the third convention would soon be overshadowed by his work in the fifth, but few members of the July assembly contributed more to organizing the rebellion than did Mason. One study that assessed delegates based on their committee chairmanships and assignments ranked Mason behind only Edmund Pendleton and Archibald Cary, tying him in influence with Paul Carrington and ahead of Mason's allies Patrick Henry and Richard Henry Lee.[67]

On 19 July the Virginia Convention passed a resolution declaring "that a sufficient armed Force [should] be immediately raised and embodyed, under proper Officers for the Defence and protection of this Colony." Mason was appointed to a committee to draft an "ordinance" to implement the resolution. Only the House of Burgesses could pass "acts," and the convention was not yet ready to assume the House's duties.[68] The committee divided between those delegates who rightly anticipated a long war and those who, reasonably enough, doubted Virginia's ability, or willingness, to finance even a short one. Robert Carter Nicholas ambitiously envisioned an army of 10,000 to 20,000 men. Mason sided with the fiscal conservatives. When the convention voted to raise 3,000 men "as a Body of standing Troops," Mason complained to his friend Martin Cockburn, "We are getting into great Confusion here, & I fear running the Country to an Expence it will not be able to bear." Mason calculated the last Indian war had cost Virginia £150,000; its share of the Continental army's expenses were another £150,000; and the new army of Virginia, plus the militia, would cost an additional £350,000.[69]

Mason's objections to a large standing army were philosophical as well as fiscal. In classic republican fashion, Mason feared professional armies as a threat to liberty. He urged his son George Mason Jr. not to volunteer for the new army, but he had no objection to young George's service as a minuteman. "I look upon it to be the true natural, and safest Defence of this, or any other free country." George Jr. accordingly, served as a captain in one of the first minuteman regiments.[70]

Defense became the convention's principal concern, and Mason's committee assignment proved arduous. The committee, Mason told Cockburn, "meet every morning at seven o'clock, sit till the Convention meets, which seldom rises before five in the afternoon, and immediately after dinner and a little refreshment sits again till nine or ten at night. This is hard duty, and yet we have hitherto made but little progress."[71]

Mason, nevertheless, managed to reduce the final authorized troop level to 1,020 men, if he had only mixed success in putting the force on a solid financial footing. The convention voted to issue £350,000 in paper money to finance the war effort. The paper money would be redeemed with proceeds from taxes, but some of the delegates wanted to suspend tax collections until 1779. Issuing paper money on an empty treasury, Mason recognized, could produce runaway inflation that might doom the rebellion faster than defeat on the battlefield. He apparently wanted to start collecting the new taxes immediately; the best he could do was to persuade the convention to begin collections in 1777.[72] Mason's republican prejudices led him to exaggerate the military effectiveness of militia units, but experience would show his concerns about financing the revolution to be well founded.

Mason made his presence felt on other issues as well. He enjoyed only mixed results in his efforts to adopt a "test," or loyalty, oath for resident English and Scottish traders. To modern sensibilities, loyalty oaths have negative connotations, but Mason, rather than trying to initiate a witch-hunt, wanted to avoid one. He saw the oaths as a way by which apolitical merchants could immunize themselves from misguided patriot attacks. On 16 August the Virginia Convention appointed Mason and Josiah Parker, a delegate from Isle of Wright County, to prepare a test oath. Mason presented a draft to the convention three days later. A question may have arisen as to how an oath would be enforced; in any event, Virginia did not adopt one until 1777. But the third convention did pass a resolution calling for "lenity and friendship" toward "all natives of Great Britain, resident here" who did not engage in hostile acts.[73]

As always, Mason served reluctantly and longed to return to Gunston

Hall. Early in the convention, Mason feared he would be elected to Virginia's delegation to the Continental Congress, and by his count, "more than two thirds of the Members" urged him to run. Mason told them he could not go to Philadelphia, but he still received nineteen votes. The pressure on Mason increased in the middle of August after Richard Bland, citing his advanced age, resigned his seat. A faction led by Thomas Jefferson, Paul Carrington, and Patrick Henry wanted Mason to replace Bland. In an emotional speech on the floor of the convention, Mason explained his reasons for declining the office, presumably his poor health and his brood of motherless children. According to Mason's account, the performance brought a tear to the eye of Peyton Randolph, president of the convention. Mason endorsed Francis Lightfoot Lee, who defeated Carter Braxton by one vote in a runoff election. Much to Mason's dismay, however, he could not avoid election to the eleven-member Committee of Safety, which served as Virginia's provisional government between sessions of the convention. He finished second in the voting, behind only Edmund Pendleton.[74]

Mason's frustration at the convention went beyond the predictable response to stress or fatigue. His initial disgust at partisan bickering within the convention abated slightly after the first week of August when members of the current congressional delegation—Pendleton, Jefferson, Benjamin Harrison, and Patrick Henry—arrived in Richmond. Pendleton, Jefferson, and Harrison, at least, raised the level of the deliberations. But Mason battled bad health and shattered nerves throughout the convention. "I have been very unwell," he wrote Cockburn on 5 August, "& unable to attend the Convention for two or three Days." He continued to complain about the strain of the assembly even after he had returned home, confiding to George Washington in October 1775, "Mere Vexation & Disgust threw me into such an ill State of Health that before the Convention rose, I was sometimes near fainting in the House."[75] Mason did not attend the fourth convention, which sat in December 1775 and January 1776, and he appears to have met with the Committee of Safety only once before being replaced by the convention on 16 December. As he explained to George Washington the following spring: "Ill health, & a certain Listlessness inseperable from it, have prevented my writing you so often, as I would otherwise have done but I trust to your friendship to excuse it: the same cause disabled me from attending the Committee of Safety this Winter, and induced me to intreat the Convention to leave me out of it."[76]

Was a "certain Listlessness" depression? That diagnosis would be consistent with Mason's own confession in 1778 that, five years after Ann's death, he still suffered from "a Depression of spirits, & settled Melancholly." Undoubtedly his gout drove him to distraction. At least two of his contemporary fellow sufferers were clearly afflicted with serious mental illnesses: depression incapacitated William Pitt during his last term in the government, and the British-born American general Charles Lee experienced bouts of virtual insanity.[77] It is tempting to think that Mason's complaints about his health, his impatience with public service, and his skepticism about government may have had psychological origins. However remote the American Founders may seem, Mason and his contemporaries faced their own emotional struggles, including in his case his lingering grief over Ann's death. We can only guess at what really drove Mason, and little in his private life suggests a disordered mind.

DESPITE HIS VARIOUS ILLNESSES, Mason remained active in the revolutionary movement in Fairfax County during the winter of 1775–76, serving both on the county's Committee of Safety and on its Committee of Correspondence. When Mason learned the British agent John Connolly had been arrested by Maryland authorities, Mason wrote Maryland's council of safety urging it to take "proper measures" to prevent his escape. Connolly was widely believed to have been commissioned by General Gage to organize an Indian attack on Alexandria. Maryland surrendered Connolly to Congress, which imprisoned him as a spy in Philadelphia.[78] Congress, meanwhile, appointed Mason and several other luminaries from northern Virginia to a committee to purchase saltpeter "for the use of the united colonies," and Mason in turn, acting on behalf of the Fairfax County Committee of Correspondence, wrote Congress to lobby for an easing of the ban on the export of produce. Mason and his fellow Virginians wanted to be able to trade produce for salt, which was in increasingly short supply. Congress complied.[79]

Mason also helped to organize American defenses along the Potomac. In December the Fairfax County Committee of Correspondence sent nervous instructions to its convention delegates, Mason and Charles Broadwater; the committee may have assumed Mason would attend the fourth convention, but only Broadwater went. Although the early skirmishing had centered around Norfolk, the committee complained that Dunmore "still continues to pester us." Complaining as well of the inadequacy of "the Minute System," the committee asked for more regular troops and for the "fitting out a few vessels of war, to protect the Bays & Rivers, from Lord

Dunmore's Pirates." Trying to rally support for the Loyalist cause, Dunmore had horrified white Virginians in November when he promised freedom to slaves and indentured servants who joined the British army. As the Fairfax committee put it, "The Sword is drawn, the Bayonet is allready at our Brests."[80]

The Committee of Safety authorized Mason and John Dalton, another member of the Fairfax Committee of Correspondence, to raise two row galleys and three cutters for the defense of the Potomac. By April 1776 Mason and Dalton, who apparently advanced some of the costs, had the galleys under construction, and they had purchased "three Sloops for Cruisers." The largest of the sloops, the *American Congress*, mounted fourteen guns and carried a crew of ninety. Guns, powder, and shot were in short supply. Mason begged and borrowed what he could; supported the establishment of a munitions factory at Fredericksburg; and stockpiled tobacco to be traded in Europe for military supplies. Mason was also responsible for feeding 300 marines. A regiment of regular troops augmented the nascent naval force, and Mason felt "tollerably safe, unless a Push is made here with a large Body of Men." When Howe's British army abandoned Boston, Mason sent uncharacteristically enthusiastic congratulations to General Washington. The British withdrawal would render the general's "Name immortal in the Annals of America, endear his Memory to the latest Posterity, and entitle him to those Thanks which Heaven appointed the Reward of public Virtue." Mason correctly predicted Howe would regroup in Halifax, Nova Scotia, and he did not expect a major British campaign in Virginia before the autumn. "I think we have some reason to hope," he wrote Washington, "the Ministry will bungle away another summer, relying partly upon Force, & partly Fraud & Negotiation."[81]

Chapter Four

The Most Important of All Subjects

THE FIFTH Virginia Convention that would draft a constitution for the new state of Virginia assembled in Williamsburg on Monday, 6 May 1776. It would be dotted with familiar faces: Edmund Pendleton from Caroline County, Archibald Cary from Chesterfield, Patrick Henry from Hanover, Robert Carter Nicholas from James City, Richard Bland from Prince George, Thomas Ludwell Lee from Stafford, Dudley Digges and Thomas Nelson Jr. from York, and George Wythe from Williamsburg. At least two of the younger delegates, James Madison of Orange County and Williamsburg's ubiquitous lawyer-politician-historian Edmund Randolph, would soon rise to national prominence. Richard Henry Lee left his seat in the Continental Congress in June in order to participate in the Virginia Convention, a not unusual testament to the perceived importance at the time of local versus continental affairs. Peyton Randolph had once resigned the presidency of Continental Congress to preside over a short session of the House of Burgesses, and Thomas Jefferson tried unsuccessfully to get himself recalled from Congress so he could attend the convention.[1]

On a motion by Richard Bland, the Virginia Convention selected Edmund Pendleton as its president. Pendleton, who had also served as president of the fourth convention after the death of Peyton Randolph, believed it was time for the convention to assert itself. The crumbling facade of the old colonial administration could no longer be maintained. The House of Burgesses, its membership overlapping with that of the Virginia Convention, met for the last time on the day the convention assembled. As Pendleton reported to Richard Henry Lee on May 7, "We [in the House of Burgesses] met in Assembly yesterday, and determined not to adjourn, but let that body die —and went into convention."[2]

Although the fifth Virginia Convention is remembered for its contributions to American constitutionalism, the 1776 convention was very much a wartime congress. On the first day of the convention the delegates received a petition from Norfolk asking for advice on the selection of its representatives since the courthouse had been burned "and the place where it stood at present [was] in the power of the enemies of *America*." The next day the convention received a petition for relief from William Criddle, "a common soldier" who had served at Norfolk, where "his right arm was unfortunately taken off by a cannon ball." It would be the first of many such petitions the convention would receive. In Norfolk's case, the convention instructed local officials "to appoint some convenient place and time" for holding elections. William Criddle was voted an immediate bounty of ten pounds, plus a pension of ten pounds per annum for life.[3]

Fairfax County voters elected John West Jr. and Mason to represent them. Few details of the election survive, but one contemporary reported that Colonel Mason was elected only "with great difficulty." The historian Rhys Isaac has attributed Mason's close race to a popular revolt by small planters who felt empowered by military service. Or voters may have had doubts about Mason's ability, or willingness, to serve given his questionable health. He had, after all, missed the fourth convention and virtually all of the meetings of the council of safety. Indeed, Mason, delayed by what he called "a smart fit of the Gout," did not reach Williamsburg until 17 May and did not take his seat until the next day, almost two weeks after the convention had begun.[4]

On 15 May a unanimous convention passed a resolution drafted by Pendleton that instructed Virginia's congressional delegation to urge Congress to pass a declaration of independence. Virginians treated the convention's resolution as a declaration of independence itself. Williamsburg celebrated with cannon fire and parades, and its denizens finally hauled down the British flag from the cupola of the capitol.[5] Virginians had hesitated in transforming their rebellion into a full-scale revolution, waiting more than a year after the fighting had begun to make a formal move toward independence, but once the convention acted, the majority of the population, including Mason, readily embraced its decision.

Why, one might ask, did they wait so long? Undoubtedly men like Mason cherished their heritage as English citizens, and they tended to dismiss the imperial crisis as aberrational, the handiwork of corrupt or incompetent politicians, not the inevitable result of a flawed system. Nor did Virginians fully appreciate the chasm that existed between their idealized view of their rights as Englishmen on the one hand and English political and legal realities on the other.[6]

The appearance in early 1776 of Thomas Paine's *Common Sense*, attacking the monarchy as an institution, helped to undermine the American faith in the English constitution. But in Virginia—and for Mason—the cruelties and necessities of war played a larger role. As Edmund Randolph put it, "independence was imposed on us by the misdeeds of the British government." Mason himself dated his decision for independence to August 1775, when George III issued a royal proclamation declaring the colonies to be in a state of rebellion. If George III was only recognizing the obvious, other measures made independence seem almost inevitable. The Prohibitory Act of 1775 essentially declared war on American shipping. The British decision to employ foreign mercenaries, in particular the Hessians, and Governor Dunmore's efforts to recruit slaves for military service outraged white planters. The British were blamed for the burning of Norfolk, although American troops inflicted the bulk of the damage. Happenstance and personalities played their parts. Major General Charles Lee, appointed by Congress as commander of American forces in the South, arrived in Williamsburg in March 1776 and became a strong advocate for independence. In April a Virginia cruiser intercepted correspondence from Maryland governor Robert Eden: Virginia's moderates lost hope for a negotiated settlement when the letters revealed that Eden, generally respected in the colonies as a conciliatory influence, had been secretly urging London to suppress the Americans by force.[7]

Conventional wisdom, moreover, held that a declaration of independence would make it easier for America to attract foreign aid for its military efforts. In May 1776 Mason acknowledged America's need for "a regular Supply of Military Stores, and a naval Protection of our Trade & Coasts." Virginia, he believed, could trade tobacco for the former; the latter would require a foreign alliance, purchased perhaps by trade concessions. The demands of armed resistance led naturally, if not inexorably, to independence. Mason bristled at British charges that a cabal of American radicals had been bent on independence from the beginning of the imperial crisis. "The truth is," he wrote in 1778, "we have been forced into it, as the only means of self-preservation." Once the fighting began, the idea that Americans could have resisted Britain without taking into their own hands "the Reins of Government . . . is too childish & futile an Idea to enter into the Head of any Man of Sense." And once the fighting began, the passions aroused by the "Desolation & Blood" visited on the colonies made reconciliation impossible. Whenever Mason first embraced the goal of independence, he expressed his satisfaction to Richard Henry Lee that "the first grand Point had been carried" before reaching Williamsburg in mid-May 1776.[8]

On 10 May the Continental Congress had asked the individual colonies to organize new governments, and five days later, the Virginia Convention passed a resolution creating a committee to draft a bill of rights and a new constitution. The bill of rights, Edmund Randolph later wrote, was intended to serve two purposes. One was to bind the legislature, "the other, that in all the revolutions of time, of human opinion, and of government, a perpetual standard should be created, around which the people might rally and by a notorious record be forever admonished to be watchful, firm and virtuous."[9]

The committee, with thirty-some-odd members, proved unwieldy. Madison was added on 16 May. Mason was appointed on 18 May, his first day in the convention, when he was also named to the Committee of Privileges and Elections, the Committee of Propositions and Grievances, and ad hoc committees to prepare ordinances encouraging domestic manufacturing and the production of salt, saltpeter, and gunpowder. According to Randolph, many of the proposals circulated within the committee to draft a bill of rights and a constitution demonstrated an "ardor for political notice rather than a ripeness in political wisdom." Whatever its failings, the committee could boast of some distinguished names. Besides Madison, the membership included Randolph, Bland, and Thomas Ludwell Lee, but Mason took an instant dislike to the group as a whole. As he reported to Richard Henry Lee after his first day in the convention, "We are now going upon the most important of all subjects—Government: The Committee appointed to prepare a plan is, according to custom, over-charged with useless Members. You know our Conventions. I need only say that it is not mended by the late Elections. We shall, in all probability have a thousand ridiculous and impracticable proposals."[10]

Mason urged Lee to return to Virginia, but Mason did not wait to assert himself. Working in a room at the Raleigh Tavern, Mason immediately began drafting his own plan of government and his own bill of rights, apparently to forestall the host of frivolous efforts he feared would otherwise be put forward. The following week, an optimistic Edmund Pendleton, who had not seen Mason's draft, wrote Thomas Jefferson, who was still in Philadelphia, "the Political cooks are busy in preparing the dish, and as Colo. Mason seems to have the Ascendancy in the great work, I have Sanguine hopes it will be framed so as to Answer it's end, Prosperity to the Community and Security to Individuals." Edmund Randolph's later recollection that Mason's proposals "swallowed up all the rest" confirmed Pendleton's assessment of his "Ascendancy."[11]

The Declaration of Rights and the Virginia Constitution in their final forms were collaborative efforts, although Mason was the principal architect of both documents. For decades, however, their authorship was shrouded in confusion. Few records of the internal workings of the fifth convention and its committees survive, and much of what passes for evidence misled historians for years. Mason, it seems likely, worked closely with Thomas Ludwell Lee; the oldest surviving draft of the Declaration of Rights consists of ten provisions in Mason's handwriting and two, at the end, in Lee's. The committee as a whole expanded the twelve-article declaration by Mason and Lee into eighteen articles before the convention adopted a final version of sixteen provisions. Mason—we will never know exactly why—threw historians off the trail in October 1778 when he sent a correspondent what Mason claimed to be "a copy of the first Draught of the Declaration of Rights, just as it was drawn by me." In reality, Mason, presumably working with fragmentary notes and an imperfect memory, produced a composite draft that combined the Mason-Lee original, the committee version, and the final version as adopted by the convention. He even borrowed a word from the Declaration of Independence; the famous first phrase in the authentic original, which declares "that all men are born equally free and independent," became in the 1778 draft, "that all men are created equally free and independent."[12]

Other memories were little more reliable. Edmund Randolph wrongly attributed the last two articles of the Declaration of Rights to Patrick Henry. Article 15 called dutifully for "a firm adherence to justice, moderation, frugality, and virtue, and . . . frequent recurrence to fundamental principles." Henry would have supported the sentiments, but no credible evidence indicates he penned them; they appear in Mason's original draft. The final version of the more substantive Article 16, protecting religious freedom, came from James Madison. Beside contributing to the declaration, Madison also contributed to the confusion when, late in life, he acknowledged Mason's 1778 composite as the original draft of the declaration. Worse yet, although Madison largely credited Mason with securing the passage of the constitution, the ex-president resurrected a dubious oral tradition attributing authorship of the first draft to Meriwether Smith.[13]

Mason's first draft of the Declaration of Rights combined a succinct statement of the republican principles that underlay the Revolution with a smattering of constitutional doctrine and separate provisions designed to protect individual civil liberties. He began with language Thomas Jefferson would paraphrase in the second paragraph of the Declaration of

Independence: "That all men are born equally free and independent, and have certain inherent natural Rights, of which they can not by any Compact, deprive or divest their Posterity; among which are the Enjoyment of Life and Liberty, with the Means of acquiring and possessing Property, and pursuing and obtaining Happiness and Safety."

Mason's second article declared that magistrates derived their powers from the people, and in a third article Mason asserted the people's "indubitable, inalienable and indefeasible Right to reform, alter or abolish" any government that failed to provide "for the common Benefit and Security of the People, Nation, or Community." Mason's fourth article repudiated the notion of a hereditary aristocracy; "the Idea," he wrote, "of a Man born a Magistrate, a Legislator, or a Judge is unnatural and absurd." The fifth article called for the separation of legislative, executive, and judicial powers, and for "frequent, certain and regular Elections."

For the most part, Mason's last five articles more closely resembled a modern bill of rights. Without using the phrase "due process of law," Mason anticipated the concept: his sixth paragraph provided "no part of a Man's Property can be taken from him, or applied to public uses, without the Consent of himself, or his legal Representatives." Mason next recognized a series of procedural safeguards for criminal defendants, including a right to confront one's accusers, a right against self-incrimination, and a right to a speedy jury trial. Similarly, Mason's tenth article guaranteed the right to a trial by jury "in all controversies respecting Property, and in Suits between Man and Man." These provisions were—or have become—timeless, but Mason's eighth article employed the unique rhetoric of eighteenth-century republicanism: "no free Government, or the Blessings of Liberty can be preserved to any People, but by a firm adherence to Justice, Moderation, Temperance, Frugality, and Virtue and by frequent Recurrence to fundamental Principles."

Mason's republican obsession with political virtue led not illogically to his ninth article, perhaps the most important substantive provision of his original draft. Because, Mason argued, "the Duty which we owe to our divine and omnipotent Creator . . . can be governed only by Reason and Conviction," he embraced "the fullest Toleration in the Exercise of Religion, according to the Dictates of Conscience." Ironically, while Mason would move quickly toward a steadfast defense of the separation of church and state, at the same time that he was taking a dramatic step to enshrine religious pluralism into what Forrest Church has called "the American creed," Mason neither envisioned the complete deregulation of religion nor a wholly secular state. Initially, he would have permitted the state to intervene if, "under Colour of Religion, any Man disturb the Peace, the Happiness, or Safety of Society, or of Individuals," loosely worded language that might have supported a multitude of restrictions. And Mason concluded his ninth article with a pious admonition, "It is the mutual Duty of all, to practice Christian Forbearance, Love and Charity towards each other."[14]

The eleventh and twelfth articles, in the handwriting of Thomas Ludwell Lee, respectively ensured freedom of the press and prohibited ex post facto laws. Lee apparently sent the manuscript to his brother Richard Henry on 25 May, along with a revealing annotation. According to Thomas Ludwell Lee's note, the committee had already accepted the essence of their draft, but it intended to relax the prohibition of ex post facto laws "in cases of great, & evident necessity"; to add provisions banning the use of general warrants and "the suspension of Laws," a rebuke of the crown's practice of setting aside colonial legislation; and to make a few other "small alterations." Richard Henry Lee may have returned the manuscript to Mason when Lee reached Williamsburg in late June. In any event it ultimately came to rest among Mason's papers.[15]

The committee made further changes before it reported a draft declaration to the full convention on Monday, 27 May. Some were cosmetic. Others were subtle but significant. The committee aptly concluded Mason's article on criminal procedure by adding the phrase "that no man be deprived of his liberty except by the law of the land, or the judgment of his peers." The committee mildly strengthened Mason's ninth article (the eighteenth article in the committee version) protecting the free exercise of religion. Mason's "divine and omnipotent Creator" became simply "our Creator," and the committee deleted an offense to an individual, as opposed to an injury to society at large, as a basis on which religious freedom could be abridged.[16]

Even the changes made in committee, however, reflected Mason's influence. Mason later claimed authorship of all or parts of four new articles added by the committee, and to be sure, they bear marks of his rhetorical style and carry echoes of other statements that undoubtedly belong to Mason. A new sixth article, declaring "that all men, having sufficient evidence of a permanent common interest with, and attachment to, the community, have the right of suffrage," coincided with Mason's position in the 1787 Constitutional Convention.[17] Mason may have written the terse eleventh article, "excessive bail ought not to be required, nor excessive fines imposed, nor cruel and unusual punishments inflicted," which reappeared almost verbatim in the federal Bill of Rights. A new fifteenth article addressed one of Mason's characteristic fears in language reminiscent of his February 1775 "Plan for Embodying the People"; it condemned "standing armies, in time of peace," in favor of "a well regulated militia, composed of the body of the people, trained to arms."

The committee version, in language Mason may have drafted, outlawed the suspension of legislation without legislative consent, a provision, according to Randolph, "suggested by an arbitrary practice of the king of England before the Revolution in 1688." The committee draft also prohibited general search warrants, which Randolph believed was a reaction to the Wilkes case, but the committee did not relax the restrictions on ex post facto laws. Mason oddly considered the warrant provision to be immaterial, and he never claimed to have written it. Nor did he claim authorship of a new sixteenth article. Intended to maintain Virginia's sovereignty over its restless, far-flung western counties, it provided "that no government separate from, or independent of, the government of Virginia, ought . . . to be . . . established within the limits thereof."[18]

Archibald Cary, the committee's chair, presented its draft resolution to the full convention on 27 May, after which the proposed declaration received a second reading and was scheduled for debate two days later.[19] Thomas Ludwell Lee, in a letter to Richard Henry Lee, expressed frustration at the slow pace of the convention's deliberations, and given his impatient nature, Mason undoubtedly shared his coauthor's discontent. Yet keeping in mind the gravity of the task and their other responsibilities, the delegates acted with remarkable speed and unanimity. As the debate proceeded, three issues divided the convention. When the delegates, sitting as a committee of the whole, took up the declaration on 29 May, Robert Carter Nicholas objected to the first line of the first article. How could a slaveholding society declare that "all men are born equally free and independent, and have certain inherent natural rights"? Incorporating such language into the state's fundamental law, Nicholas worried, might have the effect of abolishing slavery or inviting a servile insurrection. The convention seemed to flounder on what became one of the fundamental dilemmas of the early republic. The convention shelved the declaration until 3 June, when Edmund Pendleton suggested that the offending clause be modified by adding the phrase, "when they enter into a state of society." It hardly resolved the paradox of African slavery in an ostensibly free republic; how after all could the exclusion of American blacks from civil society be justified? But Pendleton, adroit lawyer that he was, had found language the delegates could accept, and the revised article was tentatively approved.[20]

The delegates balked next at the ninth article of the committee draft, which prohibited ex post facto laws. According to Edmund Randolph, Patrick Henry rose to paint "a terrifying picture of some towering publick offender against whom the ordinary laws would be impotent," and who, without ex post facto legislation, would be beyond the reach of the legislature. If Randolph's memory was correct, and he occasionally erred, Henry may have been more interested in preserving the legislature's right to pass bills of attainder—acts punishing specific individuals—than in criminal statutes with retroactive effect, the classic ex post facto law. But the two were often lumped together, and Henry's reputation did not rest on a mastery of legal technicalities. In any event, Mason probably did not resist Henry's motion. The ban on ex post facto laws had not been part of Mason's original draft, and at the Constitutional Convention of 1787, Mason opposed a federal prohibition on state ex post facto laws. Henry's motion carried.[21]

The eighteenth article and the question of religious freedom proved more nettlesome to the convention. Mason's first draft essentially codified the principles behind the English Toleration Act of 1689: religious dissenters would be tolerated, but Anglicanism would remain the state religion and non-Anglicans could be relegated to second-class citizenship. If toleration had been a major step forward in 1689, a century later the more advanced reformers wanted to go farther. Thomas Paine would write before the end of the eighteenth century that "toleration is not the *opposite* of Intolerance, but is the *counterfeit* of it" because both assumed religious freedom depended upon the indulgence of the state. James Madison was thinking along similar lines in 1776.[22] Madison revised the article to delete the reference to mere toleration and substituted an affirmative guarantee of an equal entitlement of all citizens to "the full and free exercise" of their faith. More significantly, Madison added "no man or class of men ought, on account of religion to be invested with peculiar emoluments or privileges," language that would have effectively disestablished the Anglican Church.[23]

Madison, then a novice lawmaker and always an indifferent speaker, reportedly asked Patrick Henry to introduce the amendment, and whether he served as the sponsor, he did speak in its favor. A foe of the established church since the Parson's Cause a decade earlier, Henry seemed a natural choice, except that while Henry opposed religious discrimination, or at least discrimination among Protestant sects, he did not, as we shall see, oppose state aid to religion. When asked on the convention floor whether Madison's amendment constituted "a prelude to an attack on the Established Church," Henry hesitated, denied any such intent, and let the measure die.[24]

Dogged in his commitment to freedom of religion and the separation of church and state, Madison quickly drafted a second amendment. If he could not end state subsidies to the clergy, Madison would at least try to ensure the free exercise of each citizen's faith. Retaining, from his first amendment, language intended to substitute an entitlement to "the free exercise of religion" for mere toleration, Madison also attempted to limit the circumstances in which religious freedom could be restricted. The committee version had permitted restraints whenever "under colour of religion, any man disturb the peace, the happiness, or safety of society." Madison wanted to raise the standard, limiting restrictions to cases in which "the preservation of equal liberty and the existence of the state are manifestly endangered." According to Madison scholars, he prevailed on Edmund Pendleton to introduce the revised amendment. Pendleton, a respected lawyer as well as a conservative Anglican, was the perfect choice to make reform of church-state relations palatable to the great majority of the delegates. Indeed, if Virginians were not yet willing to end state support of the established church, the delegates had no stomach for persecuting Protestant dissenters and little appetite for harassing Catholics and Jews. In the course of the debate, the assembly voted to delete from Madison's revised amendment language suggesting any restrictions on the exercise of a citizen's religion might be appropriate and adopted as the sixteenth article a broader guarantee of religious freedom. It provided: "That Religion or the Duty which we owe to our Creator and the manner of discharging it can be directed only by reason and Conviction not by force or Violence and therefore all Men are equally intitled to the free exercise of Religion according to the Dictates of Conscience And that it is the mutual Duty of all to practice Christian Forbearance Love and Charity towards each other."[25]

The young delegate from Orange County had scored a signal triumph. Mason reportedly supported the revised amendment without reservation, and he later allied himself with Madison and Jefferson in the final, climactic battle to disestablish the Anglican Church and in the struggle to bar subsidies to religion in general. Their service together in the fifth convention marked the beginning of a relationship in which Madison considered the older Mason to be his political mentor.[26] The relative conservatism of Mason's first draft in all likelihood was an act of political caution or perhaps a failure of imagination, not a committed effort on his part to maintain the privileged position of his church.

On 10 June John Blair, on behalf of the committee of the whole, reported to President Pendleton that the committee had agreed on an amended Declaration of Rights. The convention accepted the amendments the following day and, after a third reading on 12 June, formally adopted the Virginia Declaration of Rights.[27] Before adoption, the sixth article, ensuring the voting rights of men with a "permanent common interest" in the community, and the seventh article, a prohibition in embryo of taking private property without due process of law, as they appeared in the committee draft, were combined by the convention into a single article. With the deletion of the clause prohibiting ex post facto laws, the convention thus trimmed the committee's eighteen-article declaration to a final sixteen. Of the sixteen, George Mason undoubtedly wrote all or part of twelve; Thomas Ludwell Lee may well have added the free-press provision at Mason's recommendation; and Mason created a placeholder for a provision ensuring the free exercise of religion that Madison filled with the sixteenth article. All but two of the final articles showed Mason's influence.

THE WORK OF THE FIFTH Virginia Convention assumed the doctrine of "constitutionality," or the belief that even popularly elected legislatures were subject to some higher law. Americans drew inspiration from Lord Coke's observation in *Dr. Bonham's Case* (1610), that the common law would not enforce an act of Parliament that was "against common reason and right." As the imperial crisis began, Americans invoked the idea of constitutionality to vindicate the prerogatives of their colonial assemblies against those of Parliament, as when the Stamp Act Congress proclaimed in 1765 "that only the representatives of the people of these colonies are persons chosen therein by themselves, and that no taxes ever have been, or can be constitutionally imposed on them, but by their respective legislatures."[28]

Constitutional considerations, however, could most often be used to limit the powers of legislatures over their own constituents. Coke's "common reason and right," of course, was unwritten, and hardly, in the American sense, constituted constitutional law of all. By the time the fifth Virginia Convention met, most Americans had come to the conclusion that a written constitution could better protect the rights of citizens from government abuse than could an uncodified collection of case law, statutes, and amorphous tradition. Arthur Lee had advocated the adoption of a written constitution as early as 1768. The American practice of reducing fundamental law to writing followed naturally from the American experience with colonial charters. Royal officials saw the charters as mere grants, revocable by the grantor, but to the Americans they resembled treaties or contracts that conferred on them certain legal rights that could not be abridged.[29]

In writing the Virginia Declaration of Rights, Mason drew on a variety of sources, including the Magna Carta, the Petition of Right of 1628, and the Bill of Rights of 1689. Virginia's ban on excessive bail or fines and on cruel and unusual punishment was taken from section 10 of the English Bill of Rights. The principle of no taxation without representation, the sixth provision of Mason's original draft, appeared in all of the three earlier English documents. The right to a trial by jury dated to the Magna Carta. Mason's draft also reflected the liberal political philosophy of the seventeenth and eighteenth centuries. Mason's strictures on equality, the citizen's inalienable right to life and liberty—he added the pursuit of happiness—and his idea that magistrates were trustees of the people's rights came directly from John Locke. Part of the genius of the Declaration of Rights lay in Mason's ability to combine Enlightenment political philosophy with the English legal tradition to express in scarcely two pages the ideology of the American Revolution.[30]

Mason could also draw on a long indigenous tradition, although he did not fully exploit it. On point after point, including the right to a grand jury indictment, the prohibition of double jeopardy, the right to counsel, and other substantive rights and procedural safeguards, American practice expanded on English precedent. The expansive Massachusetts Body of Liberties of 1641 protected freedom of speech, outlawed slavery and torture, and granted a host of rights to criminal defendants. Its provisions ensuring animal rights and public access to public records could be considered progressive even by twenty-first-century standards. The Rhode Island charter of 1663 provided that no citizen could be punished "for any differences in opinione in matters of religion." The Pennsylvania Frame of Government of 1682 and Pennsylvania's 1702 Charter of Privileges protected religious freedom and granted criminal defendants the right to testify on their own behalf, the right to counsel, and the right to bail.[31] The various declarations of the First Continental Congress recognized freedom of the press, the right of habeas corpus, the right to assemble, and the right to a jury trial by the "peers of the vicinage."[32]

In giving legal sanction to popular sovereignty, individual equality, and the right to revolt against an oppressive government, Mason codified basic liberal principles not then recognized in American and English law. Yet Mason omitted several more specific and traditional rights. The Virginia Declaration of Rights did not prohibit bills of attainder or double jeopardy, and it failed to guarantee the right to a writ of habeas corpus, the right to counsel, or the right to a grand jury proceeding. A few of the omissions simply reflected the practice of the time. Mason provided no protection for freedom of speech, but neither did the constitutions of ten other states.[33] After adopting its Declaration of Rights, Virginia passed legislation impos- ing fines up to £20,000 and prison terms of up to five years for defending the authority of the king. Mason may have believed freedom of speech was limited to freedom of parliamentary debate, which was a common view of the day.[34] He may not have intended his list to be exclusive, and perhaps he thought the addition of other provisions was unnecessary. Although Mason neglected it, the right to counsel was well established in Virginia law by 1776; likewise, he ignored habeas corpus, but Virginia courts recognized the writ nevertheless.[35]

However the omissions from the Declaration of Rights may be explained, it is a mistake to expect to find in Mason's work a modern theory of civil liberties. Mason was a transitional figure in a period during which liberal thought was shifting from an emphasis on representative government to a concern for individual rights. He recognized a collective right to resist an oppressive ruler, but he failed to articulate a theory of individual civil disobedience. Mason showed no interest in restricting the state's power to conduct searches, and his militia clause did not appear to recognize an individual right to bear arms. His right against self-incrimination, limited as it was to criminal defendants, was more narrow than actual practice and had little practical significance because criminal defendants were usually not allowed to testify. Mason either wrote or helped Thomas Ludwell Lee draft the article ensuring freedom of the press, but for Mason's generation freedom of the press usually meant nothing more than freedom from prior restraints.[36] In March 1777, when Mason heard reports of a story about a new British initiative to reach a negotiated settlement, he dismissed it as "a tory Invention to delay the raising [of] our Army," and complained to Richard Henry Lee, "such a Publication ought not to have been suffered, & I think that the author should be inquired after."[37]

Mason's treatment of religious freedom illustrates both the limits of his libertarianism and his willingness to expand the boundaries of individual liberty. His first draft of the ninth article, permitting restrictions on the free exercise of religion when necessary to preserve "the Peace, the Happiness, or Safety of Society, or of Individuals," was a little more conservative than the law in Rhode Island, a bastion of free thought that permitted beliefs that "doe not actually disturb the civill peace of our sayd colony." Similar language appeared in New York's almost equally progressive Charter of Liberties and Privileges. Yet the Virginia Convention deleted any basis for restricting religious exercises, with no recorded objection from Mason. And if Mason's first draft and the final version of the Declaration of Rights did not end state aid to Christian churches, Virginia was the only state to adopt a permanent constitution that did not include a religious test for holding public office. Ties between state and church would be hard to break. One of the last acts of the fifth convention was to order references to the king be deleted from the Book of Common Prayer. Nevertheless, in the area of individual rights, the convention's most substantive achievement may have been its endorsement of religious freedom.[38]

Its limitations notwithstanding, the importance of the Mason-Lee draft, as revised by the committee, in the evolution of American law and in the development of the modern concept of human rights, can hardly be exaggerated. Because of the vagaries of eighteenth-century communications, the committee version attracted more attention than did the declaration eventually adopted by the full convention. On 27 May the convention ordered the committee report printed prior to the beginning of the floor debate on 29 May. Dixon and Hunter's *Virginia Gazette* published the printed committee report on 1 June, and by 6 June it had appeared in the *Pennsylvania Evening Post*. Other Philadelphia newspapers reprinted the committee version of the declaration, and by the middle of June it had appeared in Annapolis in the *Maryland Gazette*. The report soon spread throughout the rest of the colonies. The final, official version of the Declaration of Rights was generally ignored outside Virginia.[39]

The Mason-Lee draft as revised by the committee became a model for other colonies. Benjamin Franklin copied from it in drafting Pennsylvania's new constitution; one historian has traced thirteen of its sixteen provisions to Virginia. John Adams used the committee report in Massachusetts. Others followed suit. Mason's assertion that "all men are born equally free and independent" reappeared in state constitutions in places as far removed from revolutionary Virginia as Wisconsin, South Dakota, and Montana. Thomas Jefferson paraphrased Mason in writing the second paragraph of the Declaration of Independence, simply repeating Mason's sentiments in more felicitous prose. The Virginia declaration anticipated most of the provisions of the federal Bill of Rights, and close parallels exist between the Mason-Lee draft and the French Declaration of the Rights of Man. As the legal historian Carter Pittman has written, with only slight exaggeration, "words, phrases, and sentences copied from the committee draft of May 27, 1776, may be found in every Declaration of Rights adopted in America since 1776, and in most other such declarations adopted elsewhere in the world." As the first bill of rights to be appended to a written constitution by a popularly elected convention, the Virginia declaration is usually regarded as the first modern bill of rights.[40]

That it could be largely the work of George Mason, a reluctant, part-time politician with no formal legal training and little formal education, in the words of one historian, "must remain a constant source of wonder."[41] But Mason had read widely in history, law, and political philosophy, and he seemed to have possessed an instinct for what would be acceptable to the colonial elite and to the masses. By 1776 Mason's ideas did not strike most Americans as truly revolutionary. Instead, he had skillfully reduced to writing a new ideological consensus.

MASON BEGAN WORK on a constitution for his newly independent state even before the convention had approved the Declaration of Rights. A few Americans may have doubted the need for a written constitution. As late as the 1780s Noah Webster wrote a series of articles attacking the concept. Americans, he believed, could trust their democratically elected legislatures to act responsibly without the restraints imposed by parchment charters.[42] But for Mason and most of his fellow citizens, by 1776 written constitutions were an essential part of the "American theory of constitutionalism."[43]

Perhaps a half dozen draft constitutions were circulating around Williamsburg in the summer of 1776, and Mason may have borrowed freely from two or three of them—he ever after showed less pride of authorship in the Virginia Constitution than he did in the Declaration of Rights. John Adams had sent Richard Henry Lee a brief outline of a plan of government the previous November; Lee apparently expanded on Adams's proposal in an article entitled "A Government Scheme" that was published on 10 May in Purdie's *Virginia Gazette*. Mason may have seen the Adams letter; he undoubtedly read Lee's article.[44] Adams, in the interim, had written a longer essay on constitution making at the request of George Wythe, who passed it along to Richard Henry Lee. Lee, with Adams's permission, published the essay in Philadelphia as "Thoughts on Government" and sent copies, we know, to Patrick Henry, Charles Lee, Robert Carter Nicholas, and, we can presume, George Mason.[45]

Lee and Adams were thinking along similar republican lines, eager to organize a government that rested on the civic virtue of its citizens. They both envisioned a brief constitution establishing a bicameral legislature and separate judicial and executive branches. If power was to be separated, however, it was not to be shared equally. As the people's body, the legislature was intended to be paramount among the three branches of government. That objective bedeviled a generation of American constitution makers. They did not want to stifle the voice of the people, but some restraints, they realized, needed to be put on the transient whims of popular majorities. In Great Britain, a system of checks and balances could be built on the divisions within British society—the monarchy, the aristocracy, and the people. The House of Lords, representing a distinct constituency, could, for example, check the Commons. But no such divisions existed in America, and Adams and Lee had no desire to create them.[46]

Rejecting the theory of "virtual" representation, Adams believed the popular assembly "should be in miniature an exact portrait of the people at large. It should think, feel, reason and act like them." Suffrage requirements and electoral procedures, however, would remain essentially unchanged. "At present," Adams wrote, "it will be safest to proceed in all established modes, to which the people have been familiarized by habit." A need to separate the powers of government resulted in part from the limitations of the assembly; it lacked the "secrecy and despatch" to function as the executive, and its members would be "too numerous, too slow, and too little skilled in the laws" to exercise judicial power. Adams feared, however, that the courts would lack the vigor to curb abuses of legislative authority, and after their experiences with George III and the colonial governors, patriot leaders were loath to confer real power on the new state executives. Legislative power could best be restrained by being divided between a lower and an upper house, although Adams's upper house, selected as it was by the lower house, would not necessarily represent distinct interests or points of view. And a constitution should embody two republican maxims that Adams shared with Lee and Mason. The first was frequent elections; as radical Whigs expressed it, "where annual elections end, there slavery begins." The second was "rotation" in office, the eighteenth-century equivalent of term limits, "if the Society has a sufficient number of suitable characters to supply the great number of vacancies which would be made by such a rotation."[47]

Carter Braxton, less sanguine about the people's virtue than was Adams or Lee, proposed checking the power of the representative assembly by strengthening the upper house and the governor and giving them lifetime appointments. If, as republican theorists believed, the preservation of virtue depended upon the maintenance of economic equality among citizens, virtue would not long endure in a state that offered as many opportunities to the ambitious as did Virginia. They would, Braxton predicted, "gather estates for themselves and children without regarding the whimsical impropriety of being richer than their neighbors." Braxton's much-abused "Address to the Convention of the Colony and Ancient Dominion of Virginia"—Lee called it a "Contemptible little Tract"—appeared while Braxton was a delegate in Philadelphia. His plan, an obvious attempt to replicate the British system, was too conservative to attract substantial support. At the other extreme, Thomas Jefferson, from his seat in the Continental Congress, forwarded the Virginia Convention a series of truly progressive proposals after Mason had begun his drafting work. As was his custom, Mason placed himself between the conservatives and the most advanced revolutionaries.[48]

By 10 June, if not earlier, Mason had submitted his proposal to Archibald Cary's committee on the constitution, and it became the committee's working draft. As did the rival plans, Mason's constitution established separate legislative, executive, and judicial departments, and a bicameral general assembly. All legislation originated in a popularly elected lower house. Except for "money bills," the upper house could accept, reject, or amend any bill sent to it, but it could only vote tax and appropriations bills up or down. The assembly, by a joint ballot, elected the governor, the attorney general, the treasurer, state court judges, and an eight-member privy council, or council of state. The governor could serve three consecutive one-year terms and then was ineligible to hold the office for three years. Two councillors would be replaced every three years and be ineligible to serve on the council for the next three years. The governor, with the advice of the council, appointed militia officers and justices of the peace. Most other local officials were appointed by the governor and the council upon nomination by the justices. All "officers of government" could be impeached "for maladministration, or corruption" by the lower house and tried before a supreme court. Commissions, writs, and indictments would be made in the name of the "commonwealth," nomenclature taken from John Locke that was intended to signify the supremacy of the legislature.[49]

Suffrage restrictions and legislative apportionment ranked among the most difficult issues facing the convention, and here Mason showed the most originality. His proposal that the lower house consist of two delegates from each county eliminated the rotten boroughs of Jamestown and William and Mary College and the almost rotten borough of Williamsburg. It also deprived Norfolk, Virginia's largest city, of its own representatives. Yet Mason failed to address a potentially more volatile issue, the overrepresentation in the House of Burgesses of the Tidewater. Mason's suggestion that members of the lower house possess estates of at least £1,000 essentially ratified existing practice in a legislature long dominated by the landed gentry. More progressive was Mason's proposal to extend the suffrage to landless men who were the parents of at least three children; one of Mason's more idiosyncratic prejudices was his belief that parenthood, as well as land ownership, gave citizens a sufficient stake in society to justify granting them the suffrage.[50] Most novel was Mason's idea for the creation of an electoral college. Twelve electors would be elected by the voters from each of twenty-four new districts to select members of the upper house. Anxious, as were others, to give the two houses of the legislature individual identities, Mason elected to give them different constituencies, and he saw other ways to make the upper house unique. Its members would be wealthier, possessing estates of at least £2,000, and slightly older. Mason would have set the minimum age for service in what would soon be known as the House of Senators at twenty-eight, as opposed to twenty-four for the lower house. And senators would be subject to rotation in office. Forced out of office every four years, they would be ineligible to return to the upper house for four more.

Otherwise, Mason drew from Adams's "Thoughts on Government" and the 10 May *Virginia Gazette* plan usually attributed to Richard Henry Lee. Mason also tried to adapt existing colonial practices to the needs of the new state. The sequence of articles in Mason's draft followed Lee; Mason's proposal that the privy council be chosen by both houses of the assembly "promiscuously from their members, or the people at large" echoed the 10 May scheme of government. Mason's proposal for a supreme court and courts of admiralty and chancery followed Lee, as did his decision to leave the process for selecting local officials essentially unchanged. On annual elections, rotation in office, and the election of the governor and other state officials by joint ballot of both houses of the legislature, Mason followed Adams. He omitted Adams's provisions for sumptuary laws and laws for the "liberal education of youth, especially of the lower class." Mason's treatment of "money" bills maintained the status quo. The House of Burgesses had controlled tax and spending legislation since 1689.[51]

With a draft constitution of his own, Thomas Jefferson, then a member of the Continental Congress, hoped to participate in the fifth Virginia Convention. Writing Thomas Nelson from Philadelphia in May, Jefferson suggested the Virginia delegation be recalled "for a short time." The organization of a new government, Jefferson believed, "is the whole object of the present controversy; for should a bad government be instituted . . . it [would have] been as well to have accepted at first the bad one offered to us from beyond the water without the risk and expence of contest."[52]

Although Lee and Wythe left Philadelphia on 13 June, Jefferson was not recalled. Dismayed but not deterred, Jefferson produced three drafts of a constitution, apparently mailing his third draft to Edmund Pendleton and sending another copy to Williamsburg via George Wythe, who reached the Virginia capital on 23 June. More detailed than the other drafts, Jefferson's constitution began with a long bill of particulars against George III that would soon reappear as the larger, if less memorable, part of the Declaration of Independence. Jefferson proposed to let small landowners and taxpayers vote and hold office in the lower house, which he styled "a house of Representatives." He also envisioned the periodic reapportionment of the house so that the "number of representatives for each county or borough shall be . . . proportioned to the number of it's qualified electors." Capital punishment was abolished except for murder and "offences in the Military Service," torture was prohibited "in any case whatever," and the importation of slaves into Virginia was outlawed. Jefferson championed the cause of land reform tirelessly, and he tried to encourage the convention to take up the issue. In his constitution, landless adults were guaranteed at least fifty acres of land. Jefferson's constitution abolished primogeniture, and in cases of intestate succession, Jefferson promised, "females shall have equal rights with males." Undoubtedly more liberal than Mason's draft on particulars, on the broader structure of the new government—the separation of powers, a bicameral legislature, the supremacy of the lower house, a weak governor, frequent elections, and rotation in office—Jefferson and Mason shared almost identical views.[53]

The committee began debating Mason's draft about 10 June, examining it, in the words of William Fleming, "clause by clause." As Fleming, a member of the committee, reported to Thomas Jefferson, the "progress of the business in convention is, according to custom, but slow." Edmund Pendleton suspected the work of the convention was being delayed "by intrigue and Canvassing to be uppermost in Offices of Power and Lucre."[54] As the deliberations went on past the middle of June, Edmund Randolph seemed almost beside himself. "We are in confusion beyond parallel," he wrote an associate, "no government is in existence but such as is vested in the hands of the Convention. . . . We are engaged in forming a plan of government. God knows when it will be finished."[55]

In reality, the committee was moving with a speed and consensus a modern convention would be hard pressed to match. On 19 or 20 June the committee ordered a revised version of Mason's draft to be printed. The committee had made numerous changes, some significant, others less so. Language in Mason's eighth article, providing that money could be "appropriated to" the privy council was amended to read "appropriated for." Other revisions possessed more obvious importance. In a likely bow to political expediency, representation in the lower house of the assembly was restored to Jamestown, Williamsburg, Norfolk, and the College of William and Mary. The committee rejected Mason's proposal to expand the franchise. Existing qualifications for voting would remain in place. It also rejected his proposals for property requirements for membership in the assembly and for an electoral college to select the úpper house. The ban on the governor remaining in office after serving three consecutive annual terms was extended from three years to four, and the governor's power to prorogue the assembly was eliminated. The committee made some improvements to the original draft and corrected one or two apparent oversights. The revised draft authorized the appointment of a secretary of state and creation of a system of superior courts, or local lawcourts, and it provided for the annual election of delegates to Congress. The changes must generally be attributed to the committee as a body. Mason, in all likelihood, suggested amendments himself in committee, but given the paucity of documents on the committee's deliberations, we cannot be sure.[56]

George Wythe arrived in Williamsburg with Jefferson's third draft of a constitution on 23 June. Wythe reported to Jefferson later that he had shown "the one you put into my hand" to "those who had the chief hand in forming" the new plan of government. "Two or three parts of this were, with little alteration, inserted," but Wythe told his young friend that, given the urgency of other matters, "I was persuaded the revision of a subject the members seemed tired of would at the time have been unsuccessfully proposed."[57] In fact, the committee adopted Jefferson's list of allegations against George III as a preamble to the constitution, and three of Jefferson's suggestions were combined by the committee into a single Article 14. Escheats, penalties, and forfeitures previously paid to the king would now go to the commonwealth, "save only as the legislature may abolish or otherwise provide for." The committee also accepted language from Jefferson prohibiting private purchases of Indian lands without legislative consent. Mason must have supported with alacrity Jefferson's proposal to reassert Virginia's boundaries under the charter of 1609; validation of the original charter was critical to enforcing the land claims of the Ohio Company. Jefferson's draft provided that territories "Westward of the Allegheny Mountains" be governed "on the same fundamental laws contained in this instrument" until made "free and independent of this colony and of all the world" by the assembly. The committee discarded the latter language and provided simply that the western territories would remain part of Virginia unless divested by the legislature.[58]

The Virginia Convention moved quickly once the committee completed its work. Archibald Cary presented the committee's report on Monday, 24 June. On Friday, the constitution received a third reading, which reflected a few amendments made by the convention, mainly after a debate in a committee of the whole on Wednesday and Thursday. Passage on Saturday, 29 June, was mere formality. In the final draft, the upper and lower houses of the assembly became, respectively, the House of Delegates and the House of Senators. The convention deleted the provision for superior courts from the committee report, but added a provision for a new General Court, which would be separate from the council. Jamestown and the College of William and Mary lost their seats in the House of Delegates, and the convention otherwise dealt with the problem of rotten boroughs in language that reeks of political compromise: a city or borough would lose its representative whenever the number of its eligible voters remained for "seven years successively less than half the number of voters in some one county in *Virginia*." Otherwise the inequality of representation in the lower house provoked little protest or debate. "Ministers of the Gospel of every denomination" were barred from serving in the general assembly or on the privy council.[59]

Patrick Henry, who undoubtedly saw himself as a likely candidate for the office, made a strong effort to give the governor the veto power, but it was a futile gesture, even for Henry. His impending candidacy may have made the veto unattractive even to conservatives who might otherwise have supported it. Of the first generation of state constitutions, only South Carolina allowed the governor to veto legislation, and South Carolina stopped the practice in 1778. Few principles were more firmly fixed in republican ideology than the fear that the executive, if allowed enough patronage and given a share of the legislative power, would corrupt and manipulate the popular assembly.[60] Henry's popularity did not suffer as a result of his association with an unpopular cause. Immediately after adopting the final version of the constitution, the convention began filling offices in the new state government and elected Henry governor by a vote of sixty to forty-five over Thomas Nelson.[61]

The essential structure of the government George Mason laid out early in June survived committee review and convention debate largely intact, yet the constitution, important as it was, contributed less to Mason's reputation than did the Declaration of Rights. Criticism began almost as soon as the convention adjourned in July. Richard Henry Lee approved of the document, pronouncing it, "very much of the democratic kind," but the more conservative Edmund Pendleton believed the constitution left the Senate too feeble. Pendleton's preference, he told Jefferson, was for the lifetime appointment of wealthy men who would be banned from holding other offices, "but this seemed so far removed from the temper of the times, I never mentioned it."[62]

Edmund Randolph complained of "the unreasonable exclusion of the Senate from the origination of *any* law." Jefferson and Madison, in particular, soon became outspoken critics of the 1776 constitution. It had not been the instrument of reform Jefferson had originally envisioned, and by allocating two representatives to each county, regardless of population, the charter left the House of Delegates grossly malapportioned. As did Pendleton and Randolph, Jefferson and Madison wanted to make the Senate stronger and more independent of the lower house, and Mason may have come to agree. He later regretted the convention's decision to give the county courts effective control over their membership. They remained self-perpetuating bodies that combined legislative, judicial, and executive powers in a way that itself seemed inconsistent with "the temper of the times."[63] Writing a few years after the Revolution, St. George Tucker, the eminent Virginia jurist, complained that the broad powers vested in the House of Delegates seemed inconsistent with the framers' professed commitment to the separation of powers.[64]

Perhaps the oddest defect of the 1776 constitution was its failure to provide for an amending process, which suggests the most serious objection made against it: was it truly a fundamental law superior to ordinary legislation, or was it a mere ordinance that could be amended by future legislatures? In 1656 Sir Henry Vane, a member of Parliament and opponent of Charles I, had argued that a constitution should be written by a convention elected specifically for that purpose. By 1776 the formal constitutional convention was becoming part of the American theory of constitutionalism. Of the thirteen colonies, only South Carolina and Virginia failed to hold special elections for a constitutional convention. During the fifth Virginia Convention, Edmund Randolph, at Jefferson's suggestion, had raised with Pendleton, Henry, and Mason the argument that a special convention was needed. But early in the summer of 1776 Americans were making constitutional theory almost overnight, and the concept of the special constitutional convention had not yet fully crystallized. Only twenty-three at the time, Randolph lacked the influence to carry the point, and Jefferson's eagerness to submit a constitution to the convention undermined his own credibility. Mason, on the other hand, believed that if the convention had authority to declare independence, which none of the Virginians doubted, it should have authority to organize a new government. Mason worried that if a special convention were to be called, questions would arise as to the validity of the colony's declaration of independence. His pragmatism carried the day, but criticism of the constitution continued. As Randolph later wrote, the defects and limitations of the 1776 constitution illustrated "that the most expanded mind, as that of George Mason was . . . cannot secure itself from oversights and negligences in the tumult of heterogeneous and indistinct ideas of government circulating in a popular body unaccustomed to much abstraction."[65]

Writing in October 1778, Mason himself expressed satisfaction with the work of the Virginia Convention and with the public's reception of its handiwork: "We have laid our new Government on a broad Foundation, & have endeavoured to provide the most effectual Securities for the essential Rights of human nature, both in Civil and Religious liberty; the People become every Day more & more attach'd to it; and I trust that neither the Power of Great Britain, nor the Power of Hell will be able to prevail against it."[66]

Whatever the defects of the constitution, sovereignty passed from the colonial government to the new commonwealth, as far as Virginians were concerned, with no crisis of legitimacy. "Happily," Edmund Randolph wrote, "practical utility will always exterminate questions too refined for public safety." Despite his own criticisms of the constitution, St. George Tucker ridiculed objections to the convention's lack of formal legal sanction; its power derived "from a higher source . . . namely the people in their sovereign, unlimited and unlimitable authority and capacity." The constitution was hardly a reactionary document. If the theory was mangled in execution, the Virginia charter was the first constitutional document in America to endorse expressly the separation of powers and the first to recognize the courts as a distinct branch of government. Virginia was one of the few states that did not impose a property requirement for service in the upper house of the state legislature. Jefferson himself would have acquiesced in the indirect election of senators because, as he told Pendleton, "a choice by the people themselves is not generally distinguished by its wisdom." In providing for a popularly elected senate, the Virginia Convention outdid Mason and even Jefferson in its liberalism. Subsequent Virginia legislatures considered themselves bound by the work of the fifth convention, and Mason's constitution, intended primarily to establish an interim, wartime government, survived until 1830, when according to proper constitutional theory, a special convention drafted a new fundamental law.[67]

Chapter Five

Growing from Bad to Worse

EORGE MASON followed the early stages of the Revolution with relative calm. In June 1776 American forces, led by the British-born general Charles Lee, repulsed a British attack on Charleston, and, a few weeks later, Lord Dunmore left Virginia for New York City. For the next two years, Virginia and the rest of the South enjoyed a measure of tranquillity as the opposing armies concentrated their efforts in the northern and middle colonies. If the war there went badly, the fall of Fort Washington, an American garrison on the Hudson River, and the capture of its almost 3,000 defenders in November 1777 illustrated the rebels' ability, which they would demonstrate time after time, to shrug off catastrophe. By contrast, the surrender of General John Burgoyne's British and Hessian army at Saratoga led eventually to French intervention on the American side, and if France's involvement did not ensure an ultimate American victory, it at least guaranteed that Great Britain would face a long and bloody struggle.

In the West, George Rogers Clark, his expedition sponsored by Virginia, seized Cahokia on the Mississippi River in May 1778, and in July he took the British post at the junction of the Mississippi and Kaskasia rivers. In the very same month, France declared war on Great Britain, and a French fleet commanded by Count Jean Baptiste d'Estaing arrived in the Delaware Capes. Peace feelers from London only bolstered American resolve. Confident from the beginning, George Mason, although "apt to wish for Peace," confessed fears in July 1778 that the war might end too quickly—before the new nation could secure Canada and West Florida.[1]

Mason had no reason to worry. During the winter of 1778–79, the British reoccupied Savannah and Charleston, and that spring they burned Portsmouth and Norfolk. The British abandoned Charleston in June 1779, but hundreds of Americans, as well as the gallant Polish nobleman Casimir Pulaski, died in a disastrous attempt to retake Savannah. Chasing what had become their American will-of-the-wisp, the British hoped to capitalize on purported Loyalist sentiment in the South. On 1 February 1780 General Henry Clinton arrived off the coast of Charleston with an 8,000-man army; by May he had forced the city's defenders, General Benjamin Lincoln and a 5,400-man garrison, to surrender. Before the end of summer, American forces would suffer another humiliating defeat when Lord Cornwallis routed General Horatio Gates, the hero of Saratoga, at Camden, South Carolina, destroying Gates's army and opening the way for a British invasion of North Carolina.[2]

George Mason spent these years in the Virginia House of Delegates, leaving before the tide of the war finally turned in America's favor. Less visionary than Thomas Jefferson, Mason supported Jefferson's reform agenda, but Mason concentrated his own efforts on immediate problems, primarily raising and equipping an army and placing the new state government on a sound fiscal footing. Mason could describe his own war aims eloquently: "If I can only live to see the American Union firmly fixed, and free Governments well established in our Western world, and can leave to my children but a Crust of Bread, & Liberty, I shall die satisfied."[3]

In reality, he remained focused on more prosaic issues. While trying to protect the interests of the almost moribund Ohio Company, Mason also pressed for settlement of the controversy among the states over control of unappropriated western lands, an issue that delayed ratification of the Articles of Confederation until 1781. He encountered his share of frustrations, especially with the almost intractable problem of American finances. Battling bad health and an ill temper, and dodging British raiding parties himself, Mason would succumb by the summer of 1781 to the malaise that had come to pervade a war-weary nation. But as long as he was in the legislature, he helped set its pace. When Mason's gout kept him from the spring 1778 session, John Augustine Washington wrote Richard Henry Lee, "It will be a short session, unless Col. Mason, who is not yet got down, should carve out more business for them [the delegates] than they have yet thought of."[4] After they had voted to move the capital from Williamsburg to Richmond, a move Mason opposed as an unnecessary expense, he complained about his fellow delegates wasting "time in Trifles & Whims, which ought to be applyed to the important Objects of restoring our Finances, & defending our Country." Yet Mason, his frustration notwithstanding, admitted to a friend that "he had some weight in our assembly."[5]

Merrill Peterson has written, quite correctly, that Mason "best represented the moderate element in the assembly," although the question arises, moderate compared with whom?[6] Divisions existed within the House of

Delegates, but in the absence of formal political parties, historians have struggled to identify them. Edmund Pendleton and Benjamin Harrison led a faction of what one historian has called "mercantile-conservatives" who were allied with the Pennsylvania financier Robert Morris and out-of-state land speculators. Opposing them was a liberal faction led by Thomas Jefferson. Land policy divided the two groups, but historians have disagreed about which faction truly embraced an aggressive program of westward expansion. Pendleton's biographer lumped Pendleton among a group of "seperationists" who favored independence but opposed fundamental social and political change, and Jefferson among a second group of committed revolutionaries.[7] John Alden proposed a tripartite taxonomy: conservatives, like Pendleton, who favored an established church, sound money, and strong governors; radicals or democrats, like Patrick Henry, who opposed the establishment and supported popular reforms from paper money to elected judges; and a moderate or liberal group, including Jefferson, Madison, and Mason, who shared the radicals' goal of a more democratic society but preferred more gradual tactics, among them the establishment of a system of public education.

The classifications, as Alden admitted, were crude approximations of political reality. On almost any issue at any given time, Henry might appear in any camp; Lee, whose liberal credentials could not otherwise be questioned, favored state aid to organized religion; and Mason, who fought to end state subsidies while defending the Anglican Church from more punitive measures, supported sound money as consistently as did the most rock-ribbed conservatives. Notwithstanding Mason's close ties to Jefferson, Madison, and Lee, Mason might better be seen as a faction of one than as a leader of a stable, sizable, and intellectually coherent bloc. As Jefferson said, in the legislature, Colonel Mason "was himself a host."[8]

Almost all the legislation Mason sponsored during half a dozen sessions of the general assembly was war related, involving efforts to raise troops or supplies or to cope with runaway inflation or shortages of vital commodities. There were a few exceptions, the most important being Mason's efforts to influence Continental land policy. Although sporadic attendance limited his effectiveness, he did his share, and more, of legislative work.[9] Mason nominated Patrick Henry to serve as Virginia's first governor; Mason's old ally would serve three consecutive one-year terms. Before the legislature adjourned in December 1776, Mason won passage of a resolution giving the governor and privy council broad powers to raise and dispatch troops during the legislative recess. Such resolutions became common as the war continued.[10] If Mason was not inordinately jealous of executive power in wartime, neither was he unduly parochial for an eighteenth-century state legislator. Among the resolutions Mason sponsored in the December 1776 session were measures calling for a temporary settlement of the long-standing Pennsylvania-Virginia border dispute, permitting recruiters from sparsely populated Georgia to enlist volunteers in Virginia, and dispatching cavalry to the North to assist General Washington.[11] In a day when Virginia slaveholders could not legally free their slaves, Mason sponsored one manumission bill, for a slave named Kitt who had exposed a counterfeiting conspiracy.[12] Fairfax County's other seat turned over quickly, from Charles Broadwater to John West Jr. to Philip Alexander to Jackie Custis, but Mason routinely won reelection.[13]

Mason's selection to the Committee of Revisers was evidence of his stature in the House of Delegates. In October 1776 the assembly passed Jefferson's bill to establish a committee to draft a new legal code appropriate for a newly independent republic. Edmund Randolph, John Blair, Paul Carrington, and Mason's brother Thomson were nominated to serve on the committee, but by a joint ballot of both houses of the assembly, Jefferson, Pendleton, George Wythe, Thomas Ludwell Lee, and George Mason were elected. The committee met at Fredericksburg on 13 January 1777. According to Jefferson, Pendleton, contrary to his generally conservative disposition, wanted to "abolish the whole existing system of laws, and prepare a new and complete Institute." Lee apparently concurred, but Jefferson, Wythe, and Mason favored retaining as much as possible of the old regime. Pendleton's more ambitious course, Jefferson believed, would exceed the committee's legislative authorization, would constitute a huge undertaking, and, by tampering with established legal constructions, would invite litigation.[14]

In reality, the committee members probably differed more over tactics and style than over substance, because they all saw their charge as involving more than a compilation of existing laws. Jefferson especially saw the committee as a vehicle to exploit the opportunity for reform that had been created by the Revolution: "The time for fixing every essential right on a legal basis is while our rulers are honest, and ourselves united. From the conclusion of this war we shall be going down hill." Once peace came, Jefferson feared, the people "will forget themselves in the sole faculty of making money."[15]

An aide-mémoire in Mason's handwriting has survived from the Fredericksburg meeting. Mason was assigned responsibility for the code provisions dealing with the establishment of land titles, with the caveat that "if he finds it too much, the other Gentleman will take off his Hands any part he pleases." In fact, Mason resigned from the committee shortly after the Fredericksburg meeting. "Mr. Mason," Jefferson recalled, "excused himself as being no lawyer . . . [and] felt himself unqualified for the work." Because Lee was not a lawyer, and his health apparently failing—he died in 1778—he also resigned.[16]

But Jefferson, Pendleton, and Wythe continued the work, and Mason continued to collaborate with Jefferson, coauthoring major bills to establish a land office and to settle disputed land titles and, from time to time, lending support in the legislature to the committee's recommendations. On 18 June 1779, the committee reported 126 bills to the House of Delegates. Four provisions, Jefferson believed, were essential to the eradication of "every fibre . . . of antient or future aristocracy" and to the establishment of "a government truly republican": the elimination of primogeniture, the abolition of entail, the separation of church and state, and the creation of a system of public education. Because primogeniture applied only in cases of intestacy and because entails could be set aside by court action or, in cases involving larger estates, by special legislation, Jefferson may have exaggerated the significance of their abolition, which the legislature approved in 1785. Adoption of the proposed Statute Establishing Religious Freedom took almost as long. Virginia did not authorize the creation of a system of common schools until 1796, and then they were to be established only at the discretion of local officials. Some 56 of the 126 bills, including a new criminal code, became law within seven years.[17]

Mason must have been pleased with the committee's final report. He had rejected primogeniture and entail in his own will, and he lent his prestige to the passage of the Statute Establishing Religious Freedom after he had left the general assembly. Jefferson considered Mason sympathetic to the cause of public education, and Mason served, in effect, as floor manager for several of the committee's bills, including one to establish criteria for Virginia citizenship. After Jefferson's election as governor in June 1779, Mason took charge of the citizenship bill and saw it passed by both houses of the assembly before the end of the month. Bill No. 55 of the revisers' report granted citizenship to native-born whites and residents who had lived in Virginia for two years prior to the passage of the act. It also provided for the naturalization of immigrants and, in its more liberal provisions, recognized a citizen's right of expatriation and guaranteed the "free white inhabitants" of other states the same rights of travel and trade in Virginia "as the citizens of the commonwealth."[18]

More routine matters occupied much of the assembly's time. The del-

egates retained most of their prewar duties, which extended to the lowest
levels of government. In October 1778 the House, for example, passed a
bill "to prevent swine going at large in the town of Mecklenburg." As in
peacetime, there were ferries to license, counties to organize, and vestries
to dissolve, and the legislature continued the grisly practice of reimbursing
masters for executed slaves. As do all legislatures, the wartime general assembly faced the chronic problem of financing basic social services. In June
1779 the "Keeper and Matron" of "the hospital for lunatics, idiots, and
other persons of unsound minds" threatened to resign "on account of the
lowness of their salaries." The Revolution increased the assembly's work-
load exponentially, and not merely with the great issues of foreign policy
and military strategy. Petitions for support from the victims of the fighting
inundated the House of Delegates during Mason's tenure. Thomas Trent
"lost both his arms in the battle of Monmouth"; he continued to receive a
soldier's pay, but found it "very insufficient to his support." Winnifred Johnson's son, John, was disabled by frostbite while fighting in the North. She
sent a messenger to bring John home, but the boy died before his mother's
emissary reached him. She asked the state to reimburse her for the cost of
the messenger. Thomas Trent and Winnifred Johnson were not atypical.
The petitions clogged the legislative process and must have taxed Mason's
patience, but he apparently supported legislative review of individual appeals. In late 1779 the House passed a resolution from its Ways and Means
Committee to refer the claims of military widows to the Committee of
Trade, which was then to "report each case specially to the House." Mason
served on the Ways and Means Committee, and the resolution has generally
been ascribed to him.[19]

By most accounts, the stature of the House of Delegates declined during
the war, perhaps because men of ordinary means were beginning to sup-
plant the old colonial aristocracy. Edmund Pendleton believed the loss of
members to the new state judiciary had "injured" the legislature, and, beyond question, the demands of the army, the Continental Congress, and the
diplomatic corps depleted Virginia's pool of political talent.[20] In October
1780, when Mason heard a rumor Thomas Jefferson might resign as governor, he urged Jefferson to stay on because, as he told Jefferson, he feared
the choice of a successor that the "present Assembly may make." Mason attributed the poor quality of his fellow legislators to low voter turnout. "An
ignorant or obscure Man may have considerable Influence within a narrow
Circle; but it will seldom extend thro' a County; unfortunately Elections
are so little attended to, that a factious bawling Fellow . . . may carry an

Election against a Man of ten times his Weight." Mason circulated privately a draconian proposal to deprive a county of representation if two-thirds of its eligible voters failed to vote, and he proposed fining nonvoters. Mason left the legislature before he could reduce his proposal to the form of a bill, but in 1785 the general assembly passed a measure drafted by James Madison that assessed on nonvoters a fine equal to one-fourth their normal tax assessment.[21]

For much of the war, Virginia's congressional delegation inspired no more confidence than did the House of Delegates, and Mason resisted repeated attempts to send him to Congress. In the spring of 1777, the legislature elected Mason, who was at Gunston Hall recovering from a smallpox vaccination, over Joseph Jones to fill the unexpired term of Thomas Nelson, who had resigned his seat. Mason's admirers lost an initial vote for a full term to supporters of Benjamin Harrison, but in balloting for a second seat, Mason easily defeated Jones a second time. Richard Henry Lee, one of the incumbent delegates, received two votes. Mason had declined a seat in Congress in August 1775, and two years later he still had no interest in Continental service. "My own domestic affairs are so circumstanced," he wrote the newly elected Speaker of the House George Wythe, "as not to admit of my continued absence from home, where a numerous family of children calls for my constant attention." In reality, something more than his children kept Mason at Gunston Hall. In electing Mason, the assembly had pointedly rebuked Lee, who was under fire for refusing to accept rent payments from his tenants in depreciated Virginia dollars. Mason wanted no part of the scheme to oust Lee, and Mason's letter to Wythe gave Lee an opportunity to come back to Williamsburg and vindicate himself. After convincing the House of Delegates that his lease agreements, calling for payments in produce, had been negotiated before the collapse of Virginia's currency, Lee won reelection to Congress.[22]

In private correspondence, Mason defended his refusal to serve. He had, he wrote, "constantly declined acting in any other public character, than that of an independent Representative of the People, in the House of Delegates; where I remain, from a consciousness of being able to do my country more service there than in any other Department." In the fall of 1778 Mason remained sanguine about Virginia's prospects, writing one correspondent, "We seem to have been treading upon enchanted Ground."[23]

At the very time Mason wrote those words, Cyrus Griffin was threatening to resign from Virginia's congressional delegation because of his colleagues' lack of principles. Less than a year later, Mason complained to

Richard Henry Lee, without a trace of irony, that the upcoming elections were "not likely to mend our Delegation in Congress" because "some of our best Men have refused to go, & others will not risqué their Reputation with Men in whom they can't confide." After the election of Patrick Henry, Gabriel Jones, Edmund Randolph, James Mercer, William Fitzhugh, Meriwether Smith, and Griffin, Mason reported the "disagreeable" news to Lee. Apart from Henry and Jones, "we never had so bad" a delegation. The group almost immediately self-destructed. Henry, as Mason had predicted, refused to go to Philadelphia, and neither would Jones. Mercer resigned in disgust after three weeks, telling Benjamin Harrison, "a still greater change must happen in men and measures to make it either honorable or safe to continue in Congress." Edmund Randolph returned to Virginia to become the state's attorney general. By December 1779 only Griffin remained in Congress, and the assembly was forced to hurriedly conscript replacements: James Madison, James Henry, Joseph Jones, and John Walker.[24]

As Virginia struggled to find delegates of stature, Mason's admirers again looked to him. In May 1779 Richard Henry Lee, who was resigning his seat, wrote Thomas Jefferson to express his hope that Jefferson, Wythe, or Mason would make themselves available. Only America's internal "distresses," George Washington believed, sustained Britain's resolve to suppress the rebellion. The states, he told Benjamin Harrison, should "compel their ablest men to attend Congress. . . . Where is Mason, Wythe, Jefferson, Nicholas, Pendleton, Nelson?" Washington wrote Mason directly: "Where are our men of abilities? Why do they not come forth to serve their Country? Let this voice my dear Sir call upon you—Jefferson & others—do not from a mistaken opinion that we are about to set down under our own Vine and our own fig tree let our heretofore noble struggle end in ignomy."[25]

But Mason continued to be distracted by poor health, business interests, his family, and, in all fairness, the wartime needs of the Northern Neck. He continued, for example, to serve on the Fairfax County Committee of Safety. After his fight with smallpox in 1777, two attacks of gout in the winter of 1778–79 left Mason threatening to "quit all public Business" had he not promised "some of my Constituents, that I would serve them another year." The gout struck Mason again in May 1779 shortly after he arrived in Williamsburg for another legislative session, and, he told Richard Henry Lee, "reduced me lower than I have been these twenty years." The House accommodated Mason's infirmities by allowing him to sit "when I have occasion to speak." Mason soon recovered, but he remained "in a very indifferent State of Health," to which, he believed, "Vexation has not a little contributed."[26]

Mason's far-flung business activities produced their own vexations. In May 1775 Mason had shipped 50,000 pounds of tobacco to William Lee, his London agent, shortly before the American tobacco embargo was scheduled to take effect. Mason hoped the impending embargo would inflate tobacco prices, but other planters had similar ideas and dumped enough tobacco on the London market to prevent a price spike. Disappointed with his returns, Mason believed Lee had disregarded his instructions and mishandled the shipment. Mason's suspicions produced a series of angry letters and eventually a lawsuit, which apparently dragged on until Mason's death. Mason's efforts to exploit the embargo, one historian has concluded, placed him "in a hypocritical and self-serving position," and his relentless pursuit of Lee suggests an unattractive tendency to try to squeeze the last dollar out of every transaction.[27]

The passage of time brought some easing of Mason's domestic responsibilities, if not of his worries. As his children reached adulthood, he described them proudly as "free from Vices, good-natured, obliging & dutiful." By 1778 his second daughter, Sally, had married the son of his neighbor Daniel McCarty. Mason's oldest daughter, Nancy, served, he said, as "Mistress of my Family, and manages my little domestic Matters, with a Degree of Prudence far above her Years." By 1780 Mason had recovered enough from his first wife's death to joke about the prospect of remarriage. In February, he wrote James Mercer that the "cold weather has set all the young Folks to providing Bedfellows." As a justice of the peace he had signed several marriage licenses, which made him wonder where he could find a wife himself, "for I find cold sheets extreamly disagreeable."[28] He listed his criteria to another correspondent: "She must be tolerable Handsome tho' goodnatured and Sensible."[29]

He may have already been courting Sarah Brent, because on 11 April 1780 he married the fifty-year-old daughter of his old family friend George Brent. It was Sarah's first marriage. Virtually no details of Mason's second marriage have survived, but it seems unlikely that he was as close to Sarah as he had been to Ann. According to family tradition, he continued to wear mourning clothes for Ann after he remarried and wore them until he died.[30]

Daily life, in other words, went on amid a revolution. In 1779 a late frost ruined the cabbage seed on Mason's Neck. Mason wrote James Mercer in Fredericksburg to send him some. Yet Mason could not escape the war. Years later John Mason recalled army officers, traveling north or south on the Post Road, who would spend the night at Gunston Hall. His sons' service brought the war even closer to Mason. George Jr. served as an ensign in the first militia company raised by the state and soon rose to the rank of captain.

His health proved even more fragile than his father's, and diagnosed with chronic rheumatism, he was forced to resign his commission. George Jr. went to Europe in a futile attempt to regain his health, dying in 1796 and outliving his father by only four years. Mason's second son, William, commanded a militia company in South Carolina, and his service gave Mason firsthand experience with Virginia's recurring inability to equip the troops it raised. Mason wrote Governor Jefferson to ask that William's company be provided with muskets and bayonets: "It is a most discouraging Circumstance to a young-fellow to lead Men into Action, without proper Arms."[31]

SUPPLYING AND EQUIPPING an American army proved to be more difficult than raising one because money was harder to command than men. In April 1776 Mason reported to Washington that Virginia's initial levy of troops had been made "with surprising Rapidity," but added ominously, "as to Arms," the new regiments were "very deficient." Taxes had been light during the colonial period, government was small, and officials were usually paid in fees. America's agrarian economy produced few liquid assets, and English law prohibited the importation of specie into the colonies. An unfavorable balance of trade drained away what little specie entered the colonies from Europe or the West Indies. An October 1778 congressional report explained the consequences of America's fiscal history after the Revolution began: "America having never been taxed . . . had no funds to support the war, notwithstanding her riches and fertility. And the question being upon the very question of taxation, the laying of imposts, unless from the last necessity, would have been madness. . . . A measure . . . familiar to the people was pursued. This was the issuing of paper notes representing specie, for the redemption of which the publick faith was pledged."[32]

The colonies had begun resorting to paper money in the late 1600s to provide a medium of exchange. Virginia used tobacco notes for most of its history, but the colony turned to paper money during the French and Indian War. British merchants disliked receiving paper money because of its questionable value, and after experimenting with more modest restrictions, Parliament, in 1764, prohibited future emissions of paper.[33]

However arcane government finance can be, paper money rested on a simple theory. The government would print money and spend it. At the same time, taxes would be imposed, to take effect in the not too distant future, to redeem the paper; indeed, the prospect it would be needed to pay taxes gave paper its worth. The value of the currency depended on the amount in circulation and on public confidence in the government's ability to collect the associated taxes. Political economists like David Hume and Montesquieu understood that the more money a government put into circulation, the less the money was worth. Politicians like James Madison understood that large emissions also undermined public faith in the state's commitment to redeem paper dollars through taxation. It was politically easier to print money than to collect taxes. By the end of 1776 Congress had issued $25 million in paper, and the decline in the value of the Continental dollar had begun. Inflation, of course, was a hidden tax, collected in the form of higher prices and falling most heavily on creditors and on those with fixed incomes. As Edmund Randolph described it, the Virginia General Assembly went down the same path as the Continental Congress: "Virginia, counting with certainty on the unquenchable spirit of America and buoyed up with hope, emitted large sums of paper money, without the pledge of adequate specific funds for its redemption. . . . We believed, because from enthusiasm we felt, what reason would have pronounced to be impossible, that good faith would at last redeem with an equivalent in specie every paper dollar, according to its nominal import, which the utmost industry of the printing presses and the extreme of public necessity would produce."[34]

By fall 1777 Virginia had issued £946,492 in paper money, and collected £91,246 in total revenue. Mason began work on a bill to curb the resulting inflation before the October session of the general assembly convened. Jackie Custis reported the heart of Mason's plan to George Washington: the redemption of £500,000 per year through the imposition of a modest property tax. Custis believed Mason's draft "will do him great credit," and Custis added, "He likewise has a plan for recruiting our Army, which I think a very good one." Unfortunately, the session had begun on 4 October, and Mason, his propensity for late arrivals aggravated by bad weather, remained at Gunston Hall as late as 26 October. Washington trusted Mason's judgment on financial matters and fretted about the delay. "It is much to be wished that a remedy could be applied to the depreciation of our Currency," he told Custis, and "I know of no person better qualified to do this than Colonel Mason." Nor could the assembly ignore his proposal for filling out the Virginia regiments in the Continental line. "I hope Col. Mason's health will admit his attendance on the Assembly, and no other plea should be offered, much less reced by his constituents."[35]

Mason arrived in Williamsburg on 14 November and immediately turned his attention to the most pressing needs of Virginia's troops. Washington, whose army had retreated to Valley Forge after a bloody defeat at Germantown, Pennsylvania, wrote Governor Henry the day before begging for a shipment of "cloathing of any kind." Even allowing for Washington's tendency to overstate his case in order to rouse his sometimes lethargic political superiors, the Revolution had entered a critical phase. Shortly before Christmas, Washington would write Henry Laurens of South Carolina that, unless its supply system could be reformed, "this Army must inevitably be reduced to one or other of these three things. Starve—dissolve—or disperse, in order to obtain subsistence in the best manner they can."[36]

Mason served as floor manager for a bill authorizing the governor to appoint commissioners to seize linens, woolens, leather, and clothing "proper for the use of the army." Passed as "An Act for Speedily Clothing the Troops Raised by This Commonwealth Now in Continental Service," the measure required the commissioners to issue certificates for goods they confiscated and authorized them to impress "so many workingmen as they shall judge sufficient to make up into wearing apparel such clothing and leather." Four "honest and reputable housekeepers of the neighborhood" were to be appointed by the commissioners to appraise seized items and regulate the wages of impressed workers. Passage of the act was accompanied by the fortuitous arrival from France of the *Congress*, laden with 1,500 blankets, 1,200 pairs of stockings, and parcels of linen and cloth. By 19 December Washington received word that nine wagonloads of supplies had been dispatched to Valley Forge and that £15,000 worth of wool clothing was being prepared for shipment.[37]

Apparently aimed at merchants who were allegedly hoarding supplies, Mason's bill reflected a widespread belief that the army's supply problems had been compounded by unscrupulous businessmen who were attempting to "engross"—or monopolize—markets and "forestall" commodities, or keep them off the market in the hope of selling them at a higher price. Rampant inflation encouraged such behavior. Mason and Jefferson drafted a bill early in the session to prohibit the engrossing of dried or salted beef or pork. After dealing with the clothing emergency, the House appointed Mason to a committee to consider legislation prohibiting the exportation from Virginia of pork or beef for civilian purposes. Mason quickly produced another bill that combined provisions on forestalling and engrossing with the export ban and, much as the clothing act had done, authorized the seizure from any person of "any livestock, or beef, pork, or bacon, more than is sufficient for the consumption of his family, and those in his employ." The bill became law in January 1778, and Mason may have been the author of a companion bill for the seizure of salt.[38]

Efforts to recruit new volunteers had gone badly, and the enlistments of all the Virginians in the Continental line were scheduled to expire by April 1778. In the summer of 1777 James Monroe reported that he had recruited fifteen men in and around Fredericksburg, but that he could not raise more without using "arts . . . which no man of honor would use." Virginia had originally hoped to woo volunteers with bounties of twenty dollars in cash and 100 acres of land. Neither proved effective. As all the states struggled to meet their quotas, Congress recommended they institute conscription. The general assembly had reluctantly enacted a limited draft in the spring of 1777, authorizing drafts from the militia in counties that failed to meet their quotas of volunteers by August. Richard Henry Lee expressed to Thomas Jefferson the prevailing sentiment, "I really believe that numbers of our lazy, worthless young men, will not be induced to come forth into the service of their Country unless the States adopt the mode recommended by Congress of ordering Drafts from the Militia."[39]

The defense measure Mason had been preparing since early fall evolved into "An Act for Speedily Recruiting the Virginia Regiments on the Continental Establishment," which was one of the most important pieces of legislation passed by the assembly in its 1777–78 term. An expanded draft made up the cornerstone of Mason's plan, and it drew prolonged debate. The delegates disagreed over who should be subject to the draft: all adult males, single men only, or "vagabonds and those who approach nearest to them." The final bill provided for drafting single men from the militia, although the delegates still hoped for new volunteers and reenlistments, offering additional bounties in both instances. The bill even authorized the enlistment of 5,000 volunteers for six-months service, a fairly grandiose proposal that does not sound like Mason and which may have been an amendment offered by Thomas Nelson. In addition to enacting penalties for desertion, the act authorized the county courts "to make a reasonable provision at the public expense" for the support of widows of men killed in action. Quakers and Mennonites with religious objections to military service would be excused, but their congregations would be assessed the costs of hiring substitutes. Baptists and Methodists, on the other hand, "may be adverse to serving in the same companies or regiments with others, and under officers of different principles." To accommodate them, the governor and privy council were authorized to organize separate Baptist and Methodist units.[40]

The other great issue before the assembly in the winter of 1777–78 was inflation. Mason's own constituents had submitted a petition to him and his colleague Philip Alexander complaining about the collapse of the currency and demanding "that a tax be immediately laid and collected." Their petition notwithstanding, additional taxes were no more palatable than conscription, but as Edmund Randolph observed, the "corroding tooth of depreciation had so deeply eaten into the credit of paper money . . . that the Assembly could no longer abstain from the delicate subject of taxation." The House of Delegates debated Mason's tax bill from the middle of November until the middle of January before finally adopting what was perhaps the most comprehensive system of assessments in Virginia's history. The final act imposed a tax of ten shillings per £100 of value on land, slaves, horses, mules, and plate. Carriages were taxed, and new fees were levied on ordinaries and on marriage licenses, in addition to an export tax on tobacco and an excise tax on distilled liquor and luxury items. Eager to shift more of the tax burden from planters to merchants, the assembly even imposed a tax on cash and, in its boldest move, assessed an income tax of half of 1 percent, which Thomas Jefferson later recalled was considered heavy at the time. With new taxes in place, Mason included a provision in the bill authorizing the emission of another $1.7 million in treasury notes.[41]

Neither the conscription act nor the tax bill produced the results Mason had sought. In some counties, the draft went smoothly, in others evasion was common. By May the act had produced 716 men for Washington's army, less than half the number Mason had anticipated, although the measure was scarcely given time to work. In May 1778, after the Franco-American alliance became public, the assembly, in an unbridled fit of unfounded optimism, ended the draft. Sound in theory, Mason's tax bill proved ineffective amid the inability of local officials to arrive at uniform, and politically tenable, property valuations. More to the point, the tax collectors could not keep pace with the ever accelerating printing presses and the growing costs of the war.[42]

After missing the spring session, Mason arrived more than six weeks late for the fall 1778 assembly. Little had been done in his absence, and the delegates enacted fewer major pieces of legislation than they had passed the prior year. Heavy rains had produced an insect infestation, appropriately named the Hessian fly, that had decimated wheat crops and exacerbated the problem of feeding the army. To conserve grain, Mason secured passage of a temporary moratorium on the production of "spirituous liquors," and he prepared a bill that banned individuals who violated the state's grain embargo from ever again doing business in Virginia. After abandoning the draft, Virginia had attempted to use a variety of inducements to persuade veterans to reenlist. They included payment in advance of six months' wages, a life pension for military widows, and the provision of scarce commodities like tea, coffee, chocolate, and sugar at fixed prices. But luxury items were prohibitively expensive, and Mason won passage of a measure permitting the governor and council, until the next legislative session, to "carry such act into execution, so far only as in their discretion it shall appear practicable to be done."[43] The general assembly also approved a new round of tax increases and ordered the county assessors to develop a uniform system of evaluation. Mason does not appear to have been deeply involved in drafting the bill. Pendleton believed the new tax was "deep" and likely to "ocassion distress to many individuals," but inflation continued unabated.[44]

Despite a severe attack of gout, Mason played a more active role in the session of late spring and early summer 1779, convinced then that the last election had "mended our House, in Point of Abilities," if not "in sound Whigism & Republican Principles." He also believed only three options remained open to the state "to prevent the further Depreciation of our Money, high & equal Taxation, Sale of the back Lands, & of British property." Mason expected "immense" revenues from an act he and Jefferson had sponsored for the sale of western land. Besides the land bill, the legislature approved the forced sale of Tory estates, which was one of Mason's projects, and levied a tax in kind to address the fiscal crisis. Neither measure enjoyed much success. The assembly also reinstated a limited draft.[45]

Through two sessions stretching from October 1779 into the summer of 1780, Mason and his fellow legislators continued to battle financial crisis. In May 1779 the assembly had authorized the printing of another £1 million of paper money; less than £110,000 remained in the state treasury by winter. With Mason acting as the driving force, new legislation was adopted authorizing the state to borrow up to £5 million. In order to attract large investors, interest payments and repayment of the principal would be adjusted to reflect increases in tobacco prices. A tax payable in tobacco and levied for eleven years would be imposed to fund the debt; existing taxes were raised and new taxes were laid on imports, inventories, and personal property. Intended in part to meet Virginia's own needs, the new loans and taxes were also intended to raise money toward the sums Congress had requisitioned from the state.[46]

Congress, of course, faced its own fiscal crisis. In May 1779 its treasury committee reported that, although $20 million would be "sufficient for a circulating medium," some $120 million in Continental currency was then in circulation and that, unless Congress acted, "a further depreciation of the currency . . . threatens a total Dissolution of the public credit." In September, with $160 million in circulation, Congress set a limit of $200 million on additional emissions, a limit it would reach within weeks. The leading historian of revolutionary finance has called the decision to stop the paper chase "a rational act of great courage," and it may have been, but it shifted more responsibility to the states to provide supplies to the Continental army.[47] As its monetary system collapsed, Congress, in February 1780, began requisitioning commodities rather than cash from the states. On 18 March 1780 Congress adopted a plan to redeem its outstanding currency. The states would continue to pay $15 million into the treasury, as they had been asked to do under a previous resolution, for thirteen months. Congress would accept the old money at a rate of forty to one against a Spanish milled dollar. New bills would be issued at one-twentieth of the nominal value of the dollars destroyed, would bear interest, and would themselves be redeemable in specie in five years. Sixty percent of the new dollars would be returned to the states; the rest would go to Congress. The states were called on to provide funds to redeem their shares of the new bills over six years.[48]

Cyrus Griffin, the only Virginian in Congress when the forty-to-one plan was approved, voted against it, and many southerners feared that efforts to curb inflation would depress farm prices and that the redemption plan would benefit northern investors who held large amounts of Continental currency. With Henry at the head of the opposition, the House of Delegates initially rejected the plan, but after Henry declared victory and left for home, Mason and Richard Henry Lee, who were now serving together on the Ways and Means Committee, won passage of a resolution endorsing it. Mason also secured passage of legislation authorizing the forced sale of commodities for the use of the Continental army.[49]

At the same time he was defending the congressional plan for sound money and the requisition of needed provisions, Mason proposed another emission of Virginia paper. He managed to fund the new scheme with taxes on glass windows, deeds, mortgages, tobacco exports, and rum imports. But both his initiative and that of Congress failed. The fall assembly delayed redemption of outstanding currency and issued yet more paper. The existence of a massive public debt in the form of negotiable certificates for impressed goods complicated efforts to rehabilitate the currency. More fundamentally Mason could attempt to fund paper emissions, but tax collections could not keep pace with the financial demands of war. Both Congress and the state of Virginia soon abandoned their own currencies, but not before the Continental, in April 1781, fell to 167 to 1 against specie, and $1,000 in Virginia treasury notes came to equal one Spanish dollar.[50] In the course of the debate, Mason showed himself to be a fiscal moderate, supporting paper money when he thought it could be properly funded, and something of a nationalist, supporting Congress's 40-to-1 plan in the face of strong, local opposition. If Mason was not able to control fiscal policy in the House of Delegates—and his fellow legislators delayed tax collections longer and issued more paper than Mason would have done—no one, when he chose to exercise it, had more influence in the House. Ultimately, only peace could end the financial chaos, and even peace would not ensure prosperity. If Mason fought a losing battle to maintain the public credit during the war, he does not seem to have been traumatized by the defeat. Presumably, Mason came to see the Virginia treasury note as a necessary casualty of the Revolution.[51]

THE DEBATE IN Virginia over the separation of church and state had little to do with the war effort, and a great deal to do with the Revolution itself. Legislation in Virginia and North Carolina "to give compleat Liberty of Conscience to Dissenters," John Adams believed, "is worth all the Blood and Treasure which has been and will be spent in this war." Or, as the Virginia Presbyterian Caleb Wallace put it, if the establishment were to continue, "what great advantage shall we derive from being independent of Great Britain?"[52]

The debate played out amid an obsession with the decline of public virtue that spanned the political spectrum and extended from the great to the obscure. "Speculation, Peculation, Engrossing, Forestalling with all their concomitants," George Washington complained, "afford too many melancholy proofs of the decay of public virtue." Washington raged furiously against the "monopolizers, forestallers, and engrossers" who, he believed, were keeping supplies from his army. William Fleming wrote Thomas Jefferson, "I have heard much, but seen very little, of patriotism & public virtue." Patrick Henry wrote Jefferson, "tell me, do you remember any instance, where Tyranny was destroyed and Freedom established on its ruins among a people possessing so small a share of virtue and public spirit?"[53] Edmund Pendleton rarely agreed with Henry, but he expressed similar sentiments on the question of American virtue: "Avarice, seems to have so pervaded our Vital principles, as to battle all hopes of a remedy but from peace and plenty." A Rhode Island delegate to Congress described American mores succinctly: in the United States, "the manners are generally corrupt, & the laws but feebly executed."[54] Americans often linked the apparent decline of public spiritedness with the rapid depreciation of paper money, which discouraged honest labor and prudent saving and rewarded currency speculation and the manipulation of commodity markets. Richard Henry Lee confided in Mason his fear that emissions of paper money had destroyed the nation's virtue and might ultimately destroy its liberties.[55]

In the absence of a professional civil service or a bureaucracy of any size, Congress and the states, including Virginia, relied on private merchants to procure supplies, arrange loans, and perform diplomatic assignments. William Aylett, for example, served as Congress's deputy commissary general for Virginia and as both director of public stores and overseas trade agent for the state of Virginia, while being a partner in a firm that did business with Virginia. Predictably, allegations of self-dealing became common. Robert Morris reportedly commingled personal cargo and Continental imports so that if the ship arrived in the United States, he treated the cargo as his, and if it was intercepted by the British, he assigned the loss to Congress. The widespread perception that the government was corrupt undermined public morale, and if the shenanigans did not prolong the war, American moneygrubbers placed undue hardships on Washington's army.[56] Even world-weary European observers saw the problem; as the French foreign minister Vergennes wrote in 1780, "In truth Congress has very sorry agents. I believe they are more concerned with their private speculations than with the interest of their principals."[57]

It is not quite accurate to say that the eighteenth century had no concept of a conflict of interest. James Madison privately resolved "never to deal in public property, land, debts or money, whilst a member of the body whose proceedings might influence those transactions." In 1779 the Virginia General Assembly passed an act prohibiting members of the state's congressional delegation from engaging in trade. Even in the absence of legislation some public officials knew enough to keep their self-aggrandizement secret. Despite complaining about the want of virtue himself, Patrick Henry, then serving as governor, told George Rogers Clark to bring him two stallions from Clark's western expedition, but to keep that assignment out of his public correspondence.[58]

A few Virginians connected the attack on the established church with the decline of public virtue, but most apparently did not. Mason, for his part, did not see state subsidies to organized religion as a bulwark of republican virtue. Less hostile to religious orthodoxy than was Thomas Jefferson —Robert Rutland has called Jefferson an arch liberal and Mason simply a liberal on church-state issues—Mason saw state entanglement as a threat, not a support, to the cultivation of the individual conscience. It is, nevertheless, somewhat remarkable that, in an age obsessed with virtue, a fence, if not a wall, could be erected between the government and the church.[59]

It is less surprising that a people who revolted against a tax on tea would also chafe under a parish levy, or that a religiously diverse society would end public support for its established church. Demographic trends were undermining the Anglican establishment, and its decline was hastened at the start of the Revolution by the departure or retirement of roughly a fifth of its clergy, including the president and most of the faculty of William and Mary, their pro-British sympathies presumably making their position in the American church untenable. Quakers had long been a presence in Virginia, and by 1776 Scotch-Irish Presbyterians formed a majority beyond the Blue Ridge Mountains. Because they had made inroads among the gentry, the Presbyterians were the most influential of the dissenting denominations. The Regular Baptists, Calvinists in theology, fanned out west and south from their stronghold in the Northern Neck, but the most dynamic Baptist faction was the Separate Baptists, evangelical refugees from New England who refused to seek licenses for their preachers and meetinghouses. The most unruly and plebian of all the major sects, the Separate Baptists were the most likely to attract actual persecution.[60]

In the fall of 1776 the dissenters flooded the general assembly with complaints and petitions, many of them arguing that Article 16 of the Declaration of Rights adopted that summer had effectively disestablished the Anglican Church. One Baptist petition quoted Article 4, which had been part of Mason's original draft. It prohibited "exclusive or separate Emoluments or Privileges from the Community, but in Consideration of public Services." If preaching was a public service, as it would have to be to receive public support, it could be regulated by the state, which would mean, the Baptists argued, "farewell" to religious freedom. The dissenters had much to challenge. English law did not, even as late as 1776, recognize the legality of baptisms and marriages performed by dissenting clergy, and dissenters were barred from public offices, military commissions, and the universities. In Virginia, each parish levied a tax on every household in the parish, and local priests were legally entitled to a rectory, a glebe of at least 200 acres, and a base salary of 16,000 pounds of tobacco a year. Thomas Jefferson said later that the dissenters' attacks on the privileged position of the established church "brought on the severest contests in which I have ever been engaged," for as he explained, "although the majority of our citizens were dissenters, a majority of the legislature was churchmen."[61]

Consideration of the dissenters' petitions began on 11 October when Speaker Pendleton appointed an eighteen-member committee on religion. Pendleton put Jefferson on the committee, but to check the reformers, Pendleton appointed Carter Braxton chair and gave Braxton at least one influential conservative ally, Robert Carter Nicholas. In one form or another, debate over the issue would continue almost daily until 5 December. Jefferson drafted a series of resolutions that would have repealed existing laws restricting religious freedom and that would have disestablished the Anglican Church. Jefferson proposed that ministers could retain life estates in their glebes, and the church could keep any property that had been privately donated to it. Otherwise all Anglican property would revert to the state on the theory it had initially been purchased with public funds. The committee apparently deadlocked because on 9 November it was relieved of responsibility for the petitions, and on 19 November the House took up the issue as a committee of the whole. Mason had not reached Williamsburg when Pendleton appointed the committee on religion, but he arrived at the capital in time for the debate. The committee of the whole passed a series of resolutions that both acknowledged the "reasonable" claims of the dissenters and asserted a need for state regulation of ministers and religious assemblies. The committee also allowed the church to retain all its property, a practical modus vivendi that at least hints at Mason's influence. Mason, Madison, and Jefferson were appointed to a new committee to draft implementing legislation.[62]

But majorities in the House were nothing if not fluid. By 30 November the churchmen had regained the ascendancy, and they won passage of a resolution endorsing simply the exemption of dissenters from the parish levy. In an obviously coordinated maneuver, the second committee on religion immediately produced a bill to that effect. The House took up the new bill on 5 December. With Jefferson having returned home, Mason assumed leadership of the reformers and persuaded the delegates to adopt an amendment repealing laws punishing religious opinions or worship and mandating church attendance. He did not attempt to go farther and disestablish the church; he probably did not think he had the votes, and he never supported confiscation of church property, however it had been acquired. Exempting dissenters from the parish levy would of course shift the costs of supporting the church to loyal Anglicans. In a move that suggested more concern for his co-religionists than for his church, Robert Carter Nicholas suggested the parish levy for the clergy be suspended in its entirety for one year, and the House agreed.[63]

The conservative alternative to disestablishment was a general assessment for the support of clergy of all denominations, but neither conservatives nor liberals had the votes to pass comprehensive legislation. In November 1778 the House ordered preparation of a bill to eliminate the Anglican clergy's monopoly on marriages; that modest measure survived two readings before finally being rejected. Meanwhile, the general assembly extended from year to year the suspension of tax collections for ministerial salaries.[64]

Jefferson had prepared his Bill Establishing Religious Freedom as part of the report of the Committee of Law Revisers. His election as governor on 1 June 1779, however, removed him from the legislative debate. On 4 June the House appointed Mason, John Harvey, and Jerman Baker to produce a bill to resolve the church-state controversy. On 12 June Harvey, on behalf of the committee, introduced Jefferson's bill, No. 82 of the law revisers' report. It passed a second reading on 13 June, but on a third reading it was tabled until the next session.[65]

In October Mason was appointed to yet another committee that produced, to his chagrin, a new general assessment bill. One dilemma state support to religion created was the need to define, for purposes of receiving state aid, what constituted religion. The conservatives in control of the committee produced a set of doctrinal criteria that would have appalled a freethinker like Jefferson.

> *First*, That there is one Eternal God and a future State of Rewards and
>   Punishments,
> *Secondly*, That God is publicly to be Worshipped.
> *Thirdly*, That the Christian Religion is the true Religion.
> *Fourthly*, That the Holy Scriptures of the old and new Testament are of
>   divine inspiration, and are the only rule of Faith.
> *Fifthly*, That it is the duty of every Man, when thereunto called by those
>   who Govern, to bear Witness to truth.[66]

"A Bill concerning Religion" barely passed on a second reading, and on 15 November the House postponed further consideration of it. The bill remained alive as long as it did because some of the dissenters who opposed the establishment did not necessarily oppose state aid to organized, or at least Protestant, religion in general. The Methodists, still operating in the

1770s as the evangelical wing of the Anglican Church, had few qualms about mixing church and state, and the Presbyterians largely abstained from the debate because of their internal divisions. Reverend Samuel Stanhope Smith, president of Hampton-Sydney Academy, wanted to form a coalition with the Anglicans, but the Hanover Presbytery, which represented Virginia Presbyterians, was already on record opposing state aid.[67]

On 18 November Mason introduced a bill making suspension of the parish levies for clerical salaries permanent. A few days later, he introduced legislation, which borrowed heavily from the law revisers' report, permitting the Anglican Church to retain its glebe lands. The House of Delegates finally agreed before the end of the session to make the suspension of the ministers' salaries permanent. Mason's companion bill failed, which in the absence of legislation confiscating church property left the future of that property in doubt. The uncertainty continued until the general assembly passed the Statute Establishing Religious Freedom seven years later.[68]

Neither modern advocates for an accommodation between church and state nor defenders of a wall of separation between the two will find their views vindicated in the Virginia debates of the 1770s. The House of Delegates found itself split among conservative Episcopalians and a few dissenters who hoped to establish Protestantism as the state religion, liberals who hoped to disestablish religion without doing irreparable damage to the Anglican Church, and others who favored more punitive measures. Deeply divided, the House could lurch from one extreme to the other in a single session.[69]

If the House left a mixed legacy, so too did the leading proponents of religious freedom. Skeptical of the tenants of orthodox Christianity, Jefferson, as governor of Virginia, dutifully issued a wholly conventional "Proclamation Appointing a Day of Thanksgiving & Prayer" when Congress recommended it. His Bill Establishing Religious Freedom must rank among history's great charters of intellectual liberty, but it is followed in the law revisers' report by a bill against "Sabbath Breaking." More enigmatic is Bill No. 86, which contemplates purely civil marriage, a radical concept in Jefferson's day, but bans marriages prohibited by "Levitical law." Jefferson's first draft of his Virginia Constitution required ministers to take a loyalty oath to the state and assumed state courts could decide questions of ecclesiastical law. A revised draft of 1783 was more liberal. At the same time, Jefferson struggled with the proper role of ministers in political society, and his revised constitution banned ministers from holding office until Madison persuaded him to drop the provision.[70]

George Mason's views may be equally ambiguous, not because Mason's thinking evolved, but because he tried to find a middle way toward a benign disestablishment that permitted some intertwining of church and state. When Congress set 6 May 1779 as a day of prayer and fasting, Mason made no objection: such "Solemnities, if properly observed, & not too often repeated, have a good Effect upon the Minds of the People." He believed "if ever there was a national Cause in which the supreme Being cou'd be safely & confidently appealed to, ours is one." Mason, however, did not trust in Providence alone; "no necessary Measure, on our Part," he wrote Richard Henry Lee, "shou'd be omitted." In a similarly pragmatic fashion, the state-church debate, to his mind, required a balancing of several interests. His 1779 bill allowing the Anglican Church to retain its property also proposed a procedure by which church members could fire their ministers for disloyalty, immorality, or neglect of duty. Whatever his commitment to freedom of conscience, and it was quite literally of historic proportion, Mason was willing to insert the state into matters of church polity in order to promote local control. His belief that churches ought to be supported by their own members may have been as much a matter of economic justice as intellectual freedom. Mason never showed quite the passion for religious liberty Jefferson demonstrated; admittedly few people did. Mason, in defending the church's property rights and in accepting such vestiges of the old regime as a parish levy for poor relief, approached the issue as a pragmatist, not an ideologue.[71]

BY VIRTUE OF ITS 1609 charter, Virginia claimed a vast western domain that extended west to the Mississippi River and that ran north from Kentucky to the Great Lakes. Despite the Proclamation of 1763, "multitudes of hardy adventurers," in Edmund Randolph's words, had infiltrated the area by the start of the American Revolution. Illegal though their homesteads were, "it was foreseen," Randolph wrote later, "that they could not be disturbed without some convulsion." The squatters' claims conflicted with those of veterans who had been promised land in exchange for military service, with the schemes of half a dozen land companies (including George Mason's own Ohio Company), and of course with the rights of the original Indian inhabitants. Out-of-state speculators, mainly from Pennsylvania and Maryland, dominated two of the largest land syndicates, the Indiana and Vandalia group, which held grants south of the Ohio River in what is today

West Virginia, and the interrelated Illinois and Wabash companies, which had purchased land to the north.[72]

The fifth Virginia Convention, in May 1776, had adopted a resolution, probably written by George Mason, promising to recognize the preemption rights of bona fide settlers. The convention also received a petition from Richard Henderson, a North Carolina judge and speculator, who wanted to organize the land between the Cumberland and Kentucky rivers as the new state of Transylvania. Henderson's Transylvania Company challenged Virginia's jurisdiction over the area around the falls of the Ohio, an allegation not likely to be seriously considered by the convention, but Henderson's title rested on purchases from the Indians, and that, as Randolph described it, raised "a great question in the law of nations. . . . whether a purchase of individuals of lands, to which the Indians claimed title, by their manner of occupancy was binding upon Virginia, within whose limits they lay." On 24 June the convention answered the question with another resolution, again attributed to Mason, declaring that private purchases of land would not be valid until approved by the Virginia legislature.[73]

As a purely legal matter, the convention reached the right result, although it was not able to put the issue to rest. Governor Dinwiddie had apparently blocked an effort by the Ohio Company to buy land directly from the Indians as "irregular or illegal." According to Jefferson's *Notes on the State of Virginia*, beginning "in the earliest times of our settlement" there arose in the "State a sole and exclusive power of taking conveyances of the Indian right of soil," a provision the 1776 constitution incorporated. Randolph supported the practice because he questioned the ownership claims of tribal leaders: "It was not less absurd to recognize the extravagant hunting rights of savages than the idle assumption of the Pope to grant the Western world between two nations." Even Edmund Pendleton, who represented out-of-state speculators whose would-be titles derived from the Indians, agreed in principle with the ban on private purchases. Principle, however, would not decide if a private purchase had, at some point, been ratified by the appropriate authorities, and it would not determine how far to the west and north Virginia law could be enforced.[74]

Mason and Jefferson worked together in the House of Delegates to promote comprehensive land legislation that would have encouraged westward migration. Jefferson envisioned in the Ohio Valley an "empire of liberty" populated by sturdy, yeoman farmers. Mason believed the sale of unappropriated land could fund Virginia's war effort, and he did not, apparently, see a new wave of settlers as a threat to the Ohio Company's claim to the

200,000-some-odd acres the company had already surveyed in Kentucky. Jefferson, in fact, believed Mason saw the pretensions of the land companies as a barrier to settlement and wanted to eliminate them. A powerful conservative bloc, including Pendleton, Archibald Cary, Carter Braxton, and Benjamin Harrison, abetted by Patrick Henry, stood in the way with a series of objections, some legitimate, others purely self-serving. Legislation to encourage settlement would drain population from the East, depress its property values, interfere with military recruitment, and, in all likelihood, aggravate already tense relations with the Indians. Many of Mason's opponents, as an additional incentive, were associated with out-of-state land companies that were wary of Virginia's hostility to Indian titles and, undoubtedly, of Mason's connections to the Ohio Company.[75]

In 1777 the general assembly passed legislation recognizing the preemption rights of western settlers and abolishing quitrents, except in the Northern Neck.[76] The claims of the land companies were left unresolved. On 13 December, however, Mason secured passage of a resolution calling for the sale of "unappropriated Lands" and for the creation of a state land office to manage the sales. The House appointed Mason and Jefferson to draft the appropriate legislation. Jefferson took the lead in preparing the land office bill while Mason drafted a related measure for settling land titles. Mason's bill would have recognized the legality of the Ohio Company's surveys, permitted the enforcement of headright claims, granted 400 acres to squatters who had settled their land prior to passage of the bill, and established a system of county land commissioners to decide title disputes. Mason introduced the land office bill on 8 January, and it survived two readings. Similarly, the bill to secure titles was read on 14 January and appeared headed for passage. It was not to be. Apparently bowing to rival land companies who felt their interests had not been adequately protected, the House postponed consideration of the land office bill until the next session and, on 24 January, the last day of the current session, voted to table the title bill.[77]

A deal may have been struck. On that last day, the general assembly also passed two resolutions, both drafted by Mason. One refused to recognize any new land claims until a land office was established, thus keeping alive Mason's hope of preserving the public domain until it could be sold to fund the public debt. The other resolution gave the various land companies until the twentieth day of the next legislative session to present their claims to the legislature. At the same time, the house appointed Jefferson and Mason to investigate the Henderson and Indiana Company claims. Henderson's title derived from a 1775 purchase from the Cherokees at Fort Watauga, and the Indiana Company's claim rested on a similar Indian purchase that had allegedly been ratified by the Treaty of Fort Stanwick. Given Jefferson's bias in favor of yeoman settlers, Mason's interest in the Ohio Company, and the hostility they shared toward Indian purchases, they were an odd selection, made stranger still by the failure of a divided house to appoint a conservative to assist them. Whether it was the product of a compromise or of shifting legislative majorities on a series of individual votes, the result was the same: the question of the western lands was deferred with, it seemed, minimal damage to Mason's long-range goals.[78]

Mason missed the short session of May 1778 and spent much of the year preparing yet another petition on behalf of the Ohio Company, which he submitted to the general assembly on 20 November.[79] Meanwhile, Mason gathered evidence to rebut the Indiana Company case—he made no pretense of being an impartial investigator—and he continued to tinker with the bills to establish a land office and to quiet western titles. The bills languished through another session of the legislature, to Mason's increasing dismay. "They have been too long delayed already," Mason wrote Jefferson in April 1779, "to the great Loss of the Public; and the Confusion among the People in the back Country will be every Day encreasing, until Laws are made to settle the present, & remove the Cause of future disputes."[80]

Despite Mason's frustration, the legislative logjam was dissolving as the assembly made peace with at least some of the land companies. Richard Henderson agreed to settle for 200,000 acres on the Green River in Kentucky, and the Loyal Company received 200,000 acres in southwestern Virginia. After a special hearing, Mason won passage of legislation rejecting the Indiana Company's claims. Conservatives, however, extracted amendments to the land office and title bills. As Mason told Richard Henry Lee after revised bills had won committee approval, "I understand both Bills are to be warmly opposed, & before they get thro' our Butcher's Shambles, the Committee of the Whole House, they will probably be mutilated mangled & chop'd to Pieces." Both bills finally passed in June 1779; the bill to quiet titles was substantially amended in the Senate, where the presiding officer, the "Old Bruiser" Archibald Cary, was hostile. Senate amendments made the bill more favorable to speculators. Ironically, none of the amendments benefited the Ohio Company. The legislature refused to cure the original defect in the company's title: that its survey had not been commissioned by the Fincastle County surveyor. The company was denied even the hearing extended to the Indiana Company, and although Mason groused, he seemed unashamed that the Ohio Company's petition to the legislature missed the deadline Mason himself had proposed in January 1778. The legislature struck Jefferson's proposal to grant seventy-five acres of land to native-born Virginians whenever they married, and the final version of the land office bill substituted a provision allowing county clerks to issue land warrants with one reserving that power to the registrar of the land office. The more centralized administration supposedly made it easier for speculators to collect warrants.[81]

The legislation meant little unless Virginia could enforce its expansive land claims, and they had yet to be established. Other states, perhaps most importantly New York, had sea-to-sea charters as well, but Virginia's claims were the most extensive, and they become the focus of the congressional debate over the future of the western lands. Maryland, one of the so-called landless states, went so far as to refuse to ratify the Articles of Confederation until Virginia ceded its western lands to Congress. "Their modest Claim to part of the back Lands," Mason wrote sarcastically, "after skulking in the Dark for several months, has at last made it's Appearance." Maryland feared an oversized Virginia would dominate the confederation, and its position reflected the influence of the Indiana Company and of the Illinois-Wabash group, whose Indian land purchases were worthless as long as the lands they coveted remained within Virginia's jurisdiction. Maryland was none too sure of its legal arguments, but Richard Henry Lee, writing from Philadelphia, warned Jefferson as early as August 1777 that Virginia's claims would be "strongly contested" on the theory that the Virginia Company's rights under the charter of 1609 had never been transferred to the people of Virginia. Because the western territories were being wrestled from Britain by the combined efforts of all the states, Maryland would argue, they should be the common property of all. After months of deadlock, Lee suggested to Patrick Henry in November 1778 that Virginia consider a compromise. Lee doubted that Williamsburg could effectively govern a domain stretching to the Canadian border, and he suggested a new state in the West might serve to buffer Virginia from Indian attack. It is impossible to believe Lee's proposal did not reach Gunston Hall.[82]

Meanwhile, the Indiana and Illinois companies, stymied in Virginia, lobbied the Continental Congress to assert jurisdiction and recognize their claims. In April 1779 Mason wrote Richard Henry Lee, who was nearing the end of his term in Congress, and suggested that Congress itself ought to recognize the invalidity of private purchases of Indian lands. If title to the trans-Appalachian West under the charter of 1609 had not passed from the Virginia Company to the people of Virginia, Mason thought, then the region must be part of Canada under a 1744 act of Parliament that extended Canada's border southward to the borders of the other English colonies. In that case, Americans had no right to the area apart from what they could claim as a military conquest.[83]

Virginia's protests notwithstanding, Congress decided in September 1779 to refer a memorial George Morgan had submitted on behalf of the Indiana Company to a committee for further investigation. In October, Maryland, with the support of seven other states, won passage, "after a great deal of heat and debate," of a resolution calling on Virginia to refrain from opening its land office or settling claims to unappropriated lands until the end of the war.[84] The resolution provoked a "Remonstrance" to Congress that Mason drafted on behalf of the general assembly. Mason criticized Congress for assuming jurisdiction over an issue of local concern. It was "a dangerous precedent" which might, he said, "subvert the sovereignty and Government of any one or more of the United States." Mason repeated the argument he had made to Lee: if the disputed territory was not part of Virginia, it belonged to Canada. But Mason left the door open to future negotiations. The assembly would "be ready to listen to any just & reasonable propositions for removing the *ostensible* causes of delay to the complete Ratification of the Confederation."[85]

Congress did not respond to Mason's invitation, but momentum was building for a settlement. Hoping to win support for its claim to Vermont, another hotly contested region, the New York legislature, in February 1780, offered to cede its western claims to Congress if the cession would expedite the ratification of the Articles of Confederation. Some members of Congress believed Virginia would have to surrender part of its claim to save any of it, and even members of Virginia's congressional delegation, in particular Joseph Jones, began to encourage a settlement. The broad outlines of a compromise had emerged by summer: Virginia would surrender its claims north and west of the Ohio River, where its control was most tenuous, in exchange for confirmation of its rights to the south.[86]

Jones sent Mason a copy of the New York cession proposal and asked Mason to recommend terms Virginia might be willing to accept. Mason too seemed eager to compromise. Jones's letter reached Mason shortly after he had pushed through the assembly a settlement of the long-standing Pennsylvania-Virginia border dispute. "I labored the ratification of the agreement, as heartily as I ever did any subject in my life," he told Jones. "I think it is the duty of a staunch whig, and friend to his country, to do every thing in his power to remove any cause of ill will or disagreement with a sister state."

Mason set out several conditions for Virginia's agreement to surrender the northwest territories. Virginia should be reimbursed for its costs in taking and administering Kaskaskia and St. Vincennes, and the heroes of the western expedition, George Rogers Clark and his men, should be provided with land. If land south of the Ohio proved insufficient for Virginia's veterans, they should be allowed to settle in the ceded territory. Most fateful was Mason's insistence that "the territory so ceded shall be laid out and formed into not less than two separate and distinct states or governments." Most controversial was Mason's insistence that lands not otherwise obligated "be considered as a common fund for the use and benefit" of those states that had joined the Confederation and that "all purchases and deeds from any Indian or Indians . . . shall be deemed and declared absolutely void and of no effect." Mason intended to retire from the House of Delegates after the next session, but he believed he could, as his "last act of service to the American union," persuade the assembly to agree to a cession.[87]

On 6 September 1780 the Continental Congress accepted a report from a committee it had appointed to investigate the western land issue. The report generally tracked Mason's conditions, and Congress called on Virginia and Maryland to follow New York's example and take the steps necessary to ratify the Articles of Confederation. Jones, who had been a member of the committee, then moved that the ceded territory be laid out in states, that Virginia be reimbursed for its military and civil expenses in the West, and that the ceded land be used for the common benefit of all the states. He also proposed the express nullification of the Indian purchases. Jones left Philadelphia a few days later for Richmond to lobby the general assembly to support a cession on Mason's terms. Jones's presence in the new state capital proved critical; gout kept Mason himself at Gunston Hall. On 10 October Congress passed Jones's resolutions, although it refused to reimburse Virginia for its civil expenses in the West, and on a five-to-five vote, repudiation of the Indian purchases failed. Paradoxically, Virginia voted against it, with Madison opposing the purchases but John Walker and Theodorick Bland supporting them. Nevertheless, Madison reassured Jones, "I do not believe there is any serious design in Congress to gratify the avidity of the land mongers." In large part through Jones's efforts, the general assembly, on 2 January 1781, passed a cession bill incorporating Mason's demands for reimbursement of the state; for land bounties for Virginia veterans and veterans of the Clark expedition, albeit giving Clark no special consideration; and for nullification of the Indian purchases. Virginia's conditional cession was enough to persuade Maryland to act. Under increasing pressure from the French minister La Luzerne, who believed his government could support a united ally better than it could a divided one, the Maryland legislature approved the Articles of Confederation in February, thus clearing the way to the implementation of a formal American union.[88]

Debate over the Indian land purchases and other details delayed congressional acceptance of Virginia's cession. The Virginia land legislation that Mason and Jefferson initiated proved disappointing, at least as it came out of the general assembly. The land office produced more litigation than revenue. Within a year the office had issued warrants for more land than existed in the public domain, and it was helpless against the continuing flood of squatters who dispensed with warrants altogether. Thomas Abernethy called the final act a "colossal mistake." Eric Hinderaker has offered a more recent assessment: the law favored "ambitious middling speculators" over both large land companies and ordinary settlers.[89]

What can be made of Mason's role given his ties to the Ohio Company and his own speculation in headright claims? A modern politician with so obvious a conflict of interest would be pilloried by his opponents and crucified in the press. Beyond question, Mason attempted, but failed, to exploit his political position to advance the interests of the Ohio Company, and he succeeded in winning legislative endorsement of his headright claims. Yet historians and biographers have treated Mason charitably. Recognizing the Ohio Company's contribution to the opening of the West, especially of Kentucky, students of the company have concluded that it deserved "better from the hands of fate" than it received. If, from a later ethical perspective, Mason was not the best person to press the company's claims, those claims were nevertheless defensible.[90] Indeed, Mason has usually been depicted as an opponent of the land companies, and he did show a striking solicitude for squatters and small settlers.[91] Mason's opposition to Indian purchases and his defense of Virginia's jurisdiction in the West reflected widespread sentiments in the state. By 1776 Mason appears to have abandoned his dream of patenting land north of the Ohio River for the Ohio Company; his connections to the company do not explain his initial reluctance to surrender that territory to the Confederation government. In both the boundary dispute with Pennsylvania and ultimately in his support for a settlement with Congress, Mason demonstrated a capacity to set aside parochial concerns in favor of the national interest. Mason hardly lacked a sense of honor. He refused, for example, to accept a commission on flour he purchased on behalf of the state of Virginia while he was acting as a member of the Fairfax County Committee of Safety. He walked an ethical fine line that distinguished between using his office to gain an advantage over private competitors and using it to exploit the public treasury. However unsavory the combination of politics and business may appear in hindsight, Mason's personal interests had little adverse impact on his public performance.[92]

MASON REMAINED optimistic about American prospects through five years of war, writing James Mercer in February 1780 that he believed "this approaching Spring will produce a Peace." Instead, the spring saw the fall of Charleston and the destruction of a Virginia regiment by Banastre Tarleton's cavalry at Waxhau, South Carolina. Summer brought Gates's humiliating defeat at Camden, and by September Cornwallis had launched his invasion of North Carolina. In October Mason received a gloomy assessment from George Washington: "Unless there is a material change both in our Military, & civil policy, it will be in vain to continue much longer."[93]

After British defeats at King's Mountain and Cowpens and a costly victory at Guilford Courthouse, Cornwallis retreated to Wilmington, North Carolina. But Virginia remained vulnerable to British raids up its many long, navigable rivers. Mason complained repeatedly about British attacks on private property and advocated adoption of a postwar duty on British imports to compensate the victims of British raiding parties. One band of British privateers, intercepted by patriots at Alexandria, had intended to burn Mount Vernon and plunder Gunston Hall. Virginians felt virtually and inexplicably helpless as Cornwallis prepared to move his main force into Virginia in the spring of 1781. "It is said we want Arms," Theodorick Bland wrote Richard Henry Lee, "Has not every peasant in Virginia & North Carolina a Gun?"[94]

Mason now put little faith in Virginia's "badly armed and appointed" militia. Only the arrival of a strong French fleet, he thought, could check the British, but Mason feared the French were extending the war in order to weaken America. On 31 May he wrote Pearson Chapman in Maryland to ask permission to store his furniture at Chapman's home until it could be moved to William Mason's plantation at the head of Mattawoman Creek. "Lord Cornwallis with the main body of the British army was at Hanover Court House (scarce fifty miles from Fredericksburg) on Tuesday morning. . . . I think if the winds permit we may expect their fleet up this river in a few days." Mason eventually moved his furniture two or three times to avoid the fate of other planters, especially on the James River, who had been "suddenly reduced from Opulence to Indigence" by British raids. His spirits probably reached their lowest ebb in June—it was the month Governor Jefferson had to flee Charlottesville to avoid capture by Tarleton's cavalry. Mason told his son, George, now settled in Europe, "Our Affairs have been, for some time, growing from bad to worse." Despite his own efforts on behalf of independence, Mason grimly concluded that, barring the arrival of a superior French fleet, popular support for the Revolution would soon collapse.[95]

Portrait of George Mason by John O'Toole, after a lost portrait by John Hesselius. The best-known likeness of Mason sadly fails to capture his forceful personality and commanding intellect. (Library of Virginia)

Portrait of Mason's first wife, Ann Eilbeck, by Domic W. Boudet, after a lost portrait by John Hesselius. George Mason believed that "in the Beauty of her Person, & the Sweetness of her Disposition, she was equaled by few, & excelled by none." (Virginia Museum of Fine Arts; gift of David K. E. Bruce)

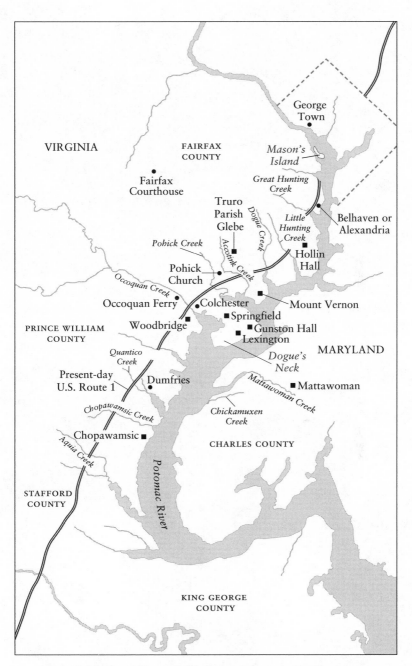

Mason's Neck, or Dogue's Neck, and the surrounding area.
One contemporary called it "a most delightful Country."

Gunston Hall. Mason much preferred "the happiness of independence & a private station" at Gunston Hall "to the troubles and vexations of Public Business." (Photograph by Dennis McWaters; courtesy of Gunston Hall Plantation)

The foyer of Gunston Hall showcased the skills of noted architect William Buckland and local carver William Bernard Sears. (Photograph by Jack L. Hiller; courtesy of Gunston Hall plantation)

Mason's desk occupied a small room that doubled as his office and
a family dining room. (Photograph by Hal Conroy; courtesy
of Gunston Hall Plantation)

"View on the Potomac, Virginia," engraved by J. Jeackes, after a painting by W. Roberts. Like many Virginia planters, Mason speculated in western lands throughout his life. (Library of Virginia)

A mural in an Alexandria tavern of Mason and a slave by an unknown artist. Mason waged a running battle with the Alexandria faction of the Fairfax County Court. He distrusted the "commercial classes." (Library of Congress)

A N.W. VIEW OF THE STATE HOUSE IN PHILADELPHIA taken 1778

A sketch of Independence Hall by J. Trenchard, after a painting by Charles Willson Peale. Independence Hall was the site of the federal Constitutional Convention that met in Philadelphia from May to September 1787. (Library of Congress)

Notice of a Charleston slave auction. The Philadelphia Convention's
decision to protect the foreign slave trade for twenty years
contributed to Mason's decision to oppose ratification of
the Constitution. (Library of Congress)

Chapter Six

Liberty and Independence

R AIDING ALMOST AT WILL throughout Virginia, Cornwallis had terrorized the civilian population and disrupted state government without winning a decisive military victory. In August 1781 Cornwallis withdrew to Yorktown and allowed himself to be trapped between a Franco-American army and de Grasse's French fleet. The British defeat at Yorktown did not bring the war to an immediate end. Skirmishes continued in the West, and privateers continued their raids along the coast and up the Chesapeake Bay. But Yorktown made independence inevitable. As soon as news of the American victory reached Gunston Hall, George Mason sensed that the surrender of Cornwallis's 8,000-man army would likely "lay the Foundation of a safe & lasting peace."[1]

Mason welcomed the Treaty of Paris, even supporting the controversial clause in which Congress agreed to recommend to the states that they allow British merchants to collect American debts incurred before the start of hostilities. "I hope every thing from Peace," Mason wrote Arthur Lee in March 1783. "I hope then to see our great National Council, as well as our different Assemblies, filled with Men of honest Characters, & of independent Circumstances and Principles," but he added ominously, "until this shall be the Case, our Affairs can never go well." Eight years of war had eroded American virtue and left Mason disillusioned: "I have seen that Lust of Power, so natural to the Mind of Man, prevailing in Congress, at a much earlier Period than cou'd well be expected. I have seen some of the States, from partial, local temporary Views, conniving at, and fostering Principles, which wou'd inevitably end in their own Destruction. I have seen our Legislatures trampling under foot the Obligations of Morality & Justice; and wantonly invading the Sacred Rights of their fellow-citizens."

Mason confided to Lee that he had once hoped Canada might join, or be forced into, an American union, but he now accepted the decision to leave Canada in British hands. Canada, Mason mused, might serve as a check on the more ambitious designs of Congress, and should either Congress or the Virginia General Assembly ever outdo the king and Parliament in corruption, Canada might become a place of refuge for a remnant of Patriots.[2] Writing Patrick Henry only a few weeks later, Mason seemed even more pessimistic. "Whether our Independence shall prove a Blessing or a Curse, must depend upon our own Wisdom or Folly, Virtue or Wickedness; judging the Future from the Past, the Prospect is not promising. Justice & virtue are the vital Principles of republican Government; but among us, a Depravity of Manners & Morals prevails."[3]

Historians have long debated the gravity of the perils facing the American republic in the 1780s. British restrictions on American trade, which included a ban on American bottoms in the British West Indies, hurt New England and the middle states, but had far less effect on Virginia. Tobacco markets boomed after the war, slumped in 1784, and by 1786 had begun to recover. Market fluctuations suggest little about the viability of the Articles of Confederation; cycles of boom and bust in commodity markets were hardly unique to the 1780s. Mason calculated that he had lost at least £10,000 during the war as a result of the depreciation of paper money and the disruption of the tobacco trade. He considered his losses "a cheap Purchase of Liberty & Independence." By "adopting Principles of strict Economy & Frugality," he managed to keep Gunston Hall debt free, and unlike Jefferson and so many of his fellow planters, Mason remained financially secure. Granting that Mason may have been atypical, little in his correspondence suggests that the 1780s were a period of economic crisis.[4]

On the other hand, Mason's concerns about the quality of the new nation's political life reflected the sentiments both of his contemporaries and of later generations. Congress, under the Articles, lacked an independent source of revenue and struggled simply to pay the interest on the national debt.[5] The war and the departure of perhaps 80,000 Loyalists disrupted traditional patterns of office holding. Members of the old aristocracy appeared less often in state legislatures—Mason himself had retired from the House of Delegates—and their replacements, James Madison complained, were often "men without reading, experience, or principle." By 1786 Madison had come to fear that the majority of state legislators, ill-informed political amateurs easily swayed by popular sentiment and parochial concerns, could not be expected to act consistently in the public interest. Madison's solution was to strengthen the central government.[6] Less nationalistic politicians preferred less drastic remedies. Edmund Pendleton expressed the hope to Richard Henry Lee in March 1785 that annual elections would eventually produce a better crop of legislators, but Pendleton admitted frequent elections had yet to "put a stop to every species of bribery . . . in the choice of our representatives."[7] Mason worried less about Congress's lack of power and more about the nation's lack of virtue.

The persistence of political factionalism aggravated a sense of malaise. Many historians have seen a conservative resurgence in 1781, when Thomas Nelson, who had opposed independence, succeeded Thomas Jefferson as governor. Richard Henry Lee and Patrick Henry, two of Mason's longtime compatriots, had begun to gravitate toward the conservatives while maintaining their own rivalry. Henry and Lee, for example, both supported the general assessment bill to subsidize Protestant churches, but in 1785 Henry blocked Lee's bid to become Speaker of the House of Delegates by promoting his own candidate, John Tyler. After the May 1784 legislative session, when Henry had helped defeat a proposed revision of the Virginia Constitution, thwarted a tax levy needed to pay Virginia's congressional requisition, and helped keep the general assessment bill alive, Thomas Jefferson shared with James Madison a plan for dealing with the great orator: "What we have to do I think is devoutly to pray for his death."[8]

Mason, nevertheless, remained on cordial terms with most of his old colleagues, and he remained a political force even in the privacy of Gunston Hall. In May 1783, as Henry began yet another term in the House of Delegates, Mason wrote him a friendly letter, full of legislative recommendations, that Henry's principal biographer has said, "came like a breath of fresh air, a salutory change from narrow provincialism."[9] Virginia struggled after the Revolution with a host of fiscal and economic issues, chief among them the payment of prewar debts to British merchants, the redemption of the state's own massive wartime debt, and tax levies to satisfy congressional requisitions. A legislative committee estimated in 1784 that of the state's annual expenditures of roughly £256,000, more than £207,000 went to pay the principal and interest on Virginia's revolutionary-era debt. Cash-strapped farmers opposed large tax increases and sometimes made their collection impossible; in the summer of 1787 they burned the jails and public buildings in King William and New Kent counties in a brief tax revolt. Mason used his influence with Henry and others to promote conservative fiscal policies. Virginia generally followed a middle-of-the-road approach, reducing taxes at least three times between 1785 and 1789, allowing the payment of taxes in hemp and flour, and on occasion extending the deadline for payment. The state, at the same time, paid large portions of its war debt, enjoyed a modest budget surplus in 1785–86, and rebuffed demands that it issue more paper money, a medium that terrified prudent liberals and fiscal conservatives alike.[10]

Yet despite the coming of peace and the relative prosperity of postwar

Virginia, Mason's letters reflect a deep anxiety, and they suggest an uncharacteristic ambiguity about his own intentions. "I quitted my Seat in the House of Delegates from a conviction that I was no longer able to do any essential Service," he wrote Edmund Randolph in October 1782. "Some of the public measures had been so contrary to my Notions of Policy and of Justice, that I wished to be no further concerned with, or answerable for them." A few months later, Mason told one correspondent, "they drove me out of the Assembly, with a thorough Conviction that it was not in my Power to do any Manner of Good." Mason would speak repeatedly of his intention "to spend the Remnant of my Life in Quiet Retirement" and then leave hints that he might return to public life. In April 1784, when he heard rumors that his name was to be put forward as a candidate in the upcoming legislative elections, he asked his friend Martin Cockburn, then Fairfax County sheriff, to stop the draft. Mason considered nomination to the House of Delegates to be "an oppressive & unjust Invasion of my personal Liberty; and was I to be elected under such circumstances, I should most certainly refuse to act."[11]

Mason continued to be plagued by intense pain in his hands and feet and by ailments he called "Gout in my Stomack" and "Convulsive Cholic," which must have contributed to his frequent bad temper. Nearing sixty at the end of the Revolution, Mason now wore glasses; the receipt of a new pair from his son, George, in Europe produced a rare trace of satisfaction about his physical condition. The "spectacles suit me as exactly as if I had chosen them myself, and have enabled me to read & write with much more Ease, than I could do with those I used before."[12]

Far more common were complaints, both about his health and about the performance of public officials. Mason had several specific concerns. He feared Congress, even under the Articles of Confederation, would exercise too much power, either by assuming it arbitrarily or as a result of amendments to the Articles. Mason opposed efforts to have Congress take jurisdiction over the states' western land claims, and he opposed allowing Congress to collect an impost. Distrustful of centralized political power, Mason also believed corruption was virtually endemic to any level of government. In Virginia, he thought he saw debtors attempting to escape their obligations to British merchants. There were legislators who wanted to dissolve the general assembly into a constitutional convention and rewrite the state's fundamental law without consulting the people. Others supported a new navigation act that would impose arbitrary restrictions on Virginia's trade. Even in Fairfax County, local officials attempted to oppress the people with excessive taxes. Everywhere the cause was essentially the same; self-serving politicians in league with stockjobbers, speculators, and profiteers.[13]

At times, Mason sounded like a common scold or an aging curmudgeon, leveling the same rhetorical blasts at minor bureaucrats that he had once used against George III or the British Parliament. Yet Mason retained his influence in Virginia politics and his capacity for constructive statecraft. Rather than fading into the obscurity of a "quiet Retirement," he was preparing, no doubt unwittingly, to step onto the national stage.

A PETITION MASON drafted for the freeholders of Prince William County in the fall of 1781 set the tone for much of his postwar writing. Intended to condemn a series of alleged offenses by state and local officials, Mason's petition is striking in its self-conscious parallels to earlier attacks on British tyranny and its readiness to equate the wartime miscues of a patriot government with the worst excesses of George III. "The good people of Virginia took up Arms, in the present Contest with Great Britain, in Defence of their Liberty and Property . . . [and] the same Principles which first induced us to draw the Sword will again dictate Resistance to Injustice & Oppression, in whatever Shape, or under whatever Pretence, it may be offered."[14] As one Mason biographer has written, "Not since the catalog of British wrongs in the Declaration of Independence had so harsh a condemnation of official excesses been published."[15]

Mason complained that "every petty-officer of Government . . . assumes a dispensing-power over the Laws; a Crime for which, even in a monarchial Government, King Charles the first forfeited his Life, and James the second his Crown," but Mason aimed his wrath primarily at Governor Thomas Nelson. Nelson had been elected governor in June 1781 at Stanton, where the state government had regrouped after British raids on Richmond and Charlottesville. At the time of his election, Nelson was commanding a militia brigade under Lafayette. Nelson was an unusually energetic governor, enforcing an embargo on the export of beef, pork, and other agricultural commodities and making liberal use of impressment to feed and equip Virginia troops. Nelson also took personal command of militia forces at Yorktown, which meant he could not act with the advice of the council, as required by the Virginia Constitution. Mason complained that Nelson's "Absence at the seige at York can be no just Excuse" for ignoring the council, "especially when it is considered that there were not less than fifteen or sixteen General-Officers there."[16]

Mason complained even more bitterly about the arbitrary use of the impressment power and, in particular, the seizure of provisions and forage for French troops who were prepared to purchase their own supplies with specie. "The Enormity & Tyranny of these Proceedings can hardly be parralled in the most despotic Governments." Some of his accusations suggested a trace of parochialism; he complained, for example, that "warrants have been issued for seizing horses to mount different Corps of Cavalry not belonging to the Virginia Line." Mason also believed the continued use of paper currency as legal tender, by encouraging speculation, had "corrupted and depraved the morals of the People." Experience, he now concluded, had demonstrated that it was impossible to maintain the value of paper currency, and he urged the assembly to redeem the existing paper and collect new taxes in specie.[17]

Little is known about the origins of the Prince William County petition, and although it bore fifty-eight signatures, Mason did not sign it. But his authorship has not been questioned. The document echoed his style, and it suggested a modest penalty be imposed on nonvoters, a remedial measure Mason had bandied about before he left the legislature. The draft presented to the House of Delegates on 10 December was in Mason's handwriting. John Hooe, one of the Prince William County delegates, may have brought the petition with him when he came to Richmond in November. Because we do not know when the petition first surfaced in Richmond, it is not certain that Mason influenced Nelson's decision to resign as governor, but at the very least Mason must have reflected and encouraged widespread discontent with Nelson's administration. Nelson, however, demanded a hearing to clear his reputation. At least one councillor, David Jameson, defended Nelson, and on at least one count, that of acting without consulting the council, Nelson could cite precedent in his defense. Previous governors had acted unilaterally and obtained the council's consent retroactively. By the end of December the assembly exonerated Nelson, "from a conviction," Edmund Pendleton reported to James Madison, "that what he did wrong was imputable to a mistake in his Judgment and not from a corrupt heart."[18]

Nelson's personal vindication hardly constituted a rebuff of Mason. The assembly responded to most of Mason's substantive complaints. The embargo was quickly repealed. New legislation established a procedure to adjust claims for impressed property: county courts were authorized to investigate complaints and report their findings to the assembly. Arthur Lee, who had visited Prince William County in the fall of 1781 and who may have discussed the petition with Mason, introduced a second bill to reform the impressment system. Lee's bill, which also became law, allowed county magistrates to arrest commissaries and quartermasters for wrongful impressments.[19]

Issues such as impressment were wartime measures destined for an early extinction, but the question of paper money would linger well into the 1780s. As a landlord, Mason felt an understandable dismay when paper collapsed: "I would almost as soon receive Payment for a Sum of Money in a Bundle of last Year's News-Papers." Gordon Wood has argued that critics of paper money failed to understand the need in an expanding capitalist economy for a fluid medium of exchange, but Mason believed paper undermined enterprise and initiative—and, as it was administered in Virginia, it probably did. Mason's views tracked those of James Madison, perhaps the most dogged opponent of paper money, who believed that only speculators benefited from the wild fluctuations of the currency. In part at Mason's urging, the assembly passed legislation requiring all currency be redeemed by 1 October 1782, at a paper-to-specie rate of 1,000 to 1, for certificates redeemable in specie in 1790. The certificates would accrue annual interest funded by a land tax or by the sale of western land. Yet paper money retained its defenders—especially among small farmers—and Patrick Henry led a rearguard effort to stall the new regime, persuading the legislature to delay tax payment deadlines for longer than Mason wanted and permitting payment in commodities.[20]

Mason complained to Arthur Lee in late March 1783 that he had "been a long Time disabled, by a very sore Finger, from holding a Pen," but Mason's fingers were well enough to allow him to join in the debate over the ratification of the Treaty of Paris. Mason criticized the general assembly's instructions to Virginia's congressional delegates to oppose the collection of debts owed British merchants, to seek the discharge of debts paid with depreciated paper currency deposited with the state, and to oppose the return of confiscated Loyalist property. Virginia planters owed over £2.3 million to British merchants and their factors. Under the law permitting debtors to discharge their obligations by paying paper money into the state treasury, Virginians retired £273,554 in debt with paper worth £12,035. With Patrick Henry championing the debtors' cause, the assembly in May 1782 had passed legislation baring British citizens from bringing debt actions in state courts and later prohibited British merchants from entering the state or acquiring Virginia citizenship. Mason considered efforts to avoid legitimate debts to be dishonorable, and recognizing the state's vulnerability—"a Frigate or two . . . [would] block up our Bay"—Mason feared continued obstructionism from the legislature might provoke British reprisals. He also feared the assembly might be tempted to use public funds to pay the difference between the real value of paper Virginia's debtors had paid into the treasury and the specie value of their debts.[21]

Mason's contributions to the debate over the treaty included a set of instructions he drafted to Fairfax County's delegates and two petitions to the general assembly, all on behalf of the county's freeholders. "We desire and expressly instruct you," the delegates were told, "that you not give your assent to, and on the contrary, that you oppose, to the utmost of your power, the smallest infraction of the late Treaty of Paris." More specifically, they were instructed to support legislation requiring repayment of British debts previously paid into the treasury according to their real value in specie and to oppose blocking the access of British merchants to Virginia's courts. Mason and the Fairfax County freeholders submitted a separate petition to the general assembly that also called for payment in full of prewar debts and condemned the proposal that the state assume responsibility for private debts in excess of the individual debtor's deposit in the treasury. "We shou'd be unworthy the name of Free-Men . . . If we submitted to Taxes imposed for paying the private Debts of a few individuals." The petitioners threatened to resist payment of such a tax "by every means in our Power." A second petition opposed attempts to repeal legislation, which Mason had helped write, prohibiting British merchants from extending credit for longer than six months. Apparently, some of the debtors who hoped to escape their old debts intended to accumulate some new ones. Mason, by contrast, believed that liberal British credit policies allowed British firms to monopolize local trade, discouraged self-sufficiency, and, worse in his eyes, encouraged the luxury and extravagance that undermined the virtue essential to republican government.[22]

Efforts to have the state bail out private debtors or to liberalize credit laws died in the House. The debate over the broader issue of allowing British creditors to use the state courts to attempt to collect what they were owed delayed implementation of the Treaty of Paris and agitated Virginia politics, to Mason's dismay, for the life of the Articles of Confederation. In December 1787 the general assembly finally repealed the statute obstructing debt collections, but even that action was conditioned on Great Britain abandoning its forts in the Northwest Territory and either returning slaves taken during the war or compensating their former owners. Not until the Constitution was ratified and the United States Supreme Court intervened were British merchants allowed access to Virginia's courts.[23]

The debate over the Treaty of Paris did not monopolize all of Mason's time. He saw other signs of corruption elsewhere: Mason engaged the Alexandria faction on the Fairfax County Court in a long-running war on several fronts. In June 1782 Mason drafted yet another petition to the assembly, this one objecting to a decision by a majority of the county court to impose a tax levy in excess of the county's budget. Because of their proximity to the courthouse, Alexandria merchants could dominate court proceedings. Yet the weight of the taxes they imposed fell on Mason and other planters. Mason proposed barring city officials from serving as justices of the peace, and he wanted to limit the level of taxes the county court could levy without a popular vote. The controversy must have left scars. More than a year later Mason moved successfully for a change of venue in a lawsuit he had brought in Alexandria. He believed he had "very little chance for common justice in the said County Court of Fairfax." In 1784 Mason wrote the state auditor's office alleging that Alexandria warehouse inspectors had overcharged planters by six shillings per hogshead on tobacco passing through the warehouses; the auditors agreed with Mason. But he did not necessarily believe that greater state control was always the preferred solution to his difficulties with local officials. Although he had complained in his 1782 petition on behalf of the Fairfax County freeholders that the county court was a self-perpetuating clique, a colonial practice the 1776 constitution had preserved, he joined his fellow justices in opposing Governor Benjamin Harrison's effort to appoint new justices in 1785.[24]

Mason's feud with the merchants of Alexandria and with their faction on the county court helps explain his opposition to efforts to restrict the number of foreign ports in Virginia. He mistrusted the urban, commercial class. In 1784 James Madison, as chair of the House committee on commerce, drafted legislation to make Norfolk the state's only port of entry; he later added Alexandria. Madison hoped to improve the collection of import duties and discourage smuggling, and he may have seen the port bill as a mechanism to stimulate the development of local commercial houses and one or two major seaports. On 17 June the House of Delegates passed Madison's bill by a narrow margin, with the future chief justice John Marshall among the opponents, and only after the addition of three new ports: Portsmouth, Tappahannock, and Yorktown. The Senate added Bermuda Hundred.[25]

Even in its diluted, final form, the port bill remained controversial. Madison confided in Jefferson in January 1786 that a concerted effort by its opponents would probably produce its repeal. Mason was understood to oppose the bill on the ground that "large cities corrupt good morals," and a rumor that a move was afoot to restrict foreign trade to a single port apparently persuaded a reluctant Mason to accept election to the House for the fall session of 1786. Although he complained of "the longest, & most severe fit of the Gout," he had ever experienced, he told one correspondent in late November that he still hoped to attend the assembly, "there being several things in Agitation there, which I think will be very injurious to the public." Presumably, the port bill was one of those things.[26]

Supporters and opponents alike believed Mason's attendance would prove decisive, but he never recovered sufficient strength to make the trip to Richmond.[27] Instead, as he had done so many times before, Mason entered the debate with a petition to the legislature, styled simply a "Protest by a Private Citizen against the Port Bill." Mason ridiculed the idea of depriving the public of the use of valuable, existing ports, which he believed would raise prices to consumers. Comparing the port bill with the odious British Navigation Acts, Mason asked rhetorically, "Is there any greater, or more dangerous error in government, than that of governing too much?" Mason argued that the port bill would encourage shippers bound for Virginia to detour to Maryland, and if the legislation succeeded in concentrating Virginia's shipping in one or a handful of ports, the state would become more vulnerable to attack.

The prospect of a great port city in Virginia worried Mason even more. "If virtue is the vital principal of a republic, and it cannot long exist, without frugality, probity and strictness of morals; will the manners of populous commercial cities be favorable to the principles of free government?" He went on: "Or will not vice, the depravity of morals, the luxury, venality, and corruption, which invariably prevail in great commercial cities, be utterly subversive of them?" Urban depravity had destroyed earlier republics: Athens, Carthage, Rome, Geneva, Venice, and Holland. As did other orthodox republicans, Mason believed that the tendency of rulers to augment their own power was so strong that the decline of free societies into tyranny was inevitable; measures such as the port bill would but accelerate the decay.[28]

With Mason ridden with gout at Gunston Hall, the port bill survived, but not unscathed. The assembly opened several more ports to navigation. A new Congress would soon assume jurisdiction over foreign and interstate commerce under Article I, Section 9, of the new federal Constitution, thus largely preempting state regulation. Mason's anti-urban rationale for his opposition to the port bill drew on a dominant strain in republican thought.

It appeared again in the famous line from Jefferson's *Notes on the State of Virginia*: "The mobs of great cities add just so much to the support of pure government, as sores do to the strength of the human body." Urbanization went hand in hand with extremes of wealth and poverty and, because most republican theorists believed "power follows property," economic inequality would undermine representative government by giving the rich too much influence and by robbing the poor of their independence. Mason, ironically, proved a better republican than did Jefferson, who reportedly supported the port bill. Mason's opposition also put him at odds with George Washington, as well as with Madison.[29]

Mason mistrusted government more than did Madison or Washington, and he lacked Jefferson's optimistic faith in the wisdom of the people. Their virtue was not inherent; it had to be cultivated. In actively supporting the Treaty of Paris, Mason had shown himself to be something of a nationalist. Frustrated with Virginia's political institutions and committed to conservative fiscal policies, Mason seemed to have much in common with the political elite who led the push for a new, far more powerful national government. In reality, however, Mason's local attachments, his fidelity to republican "first principles," and his fundamental suspicion of government at any level would lead him in another direction.[30]

WITH THE END OF hostilities, George Washington resigned his commission and returned to Mount Vernon on Christmas Eve 1783. A Miss Lewis, probably the daughter of Fielding Lewis, Washington's brother-in-law, recorded her impressions of Mason at Washington's homecoming: "Among the most notable callers was Mr. George Mason of Gunston Hall, who was on his way home from Alexandria. . . . He is said to be one of the greatest statesmen and wisest men in Virginia. We have heard much of him and were delighted to look in his face, hear him speak, and take his hand, which he offered in a courtly manner. He is straight in figure but not tall, and has a grand head and clear gray eyes. He has few white hairs, though they say he is about sixty years old."[31]

Washington and Mason resumed their relationship, exchanging social visits and fruit tree saplings. When Lafayette sent Washington seven French foxhounds, Mason loaned Washington two of his own dogs to teach the newcomers local ways.[32] Mason's influence rested in large part on his personal prestige and a network of similar relationships with Virginia's great and near great. Mason had his enemies. In 1783, when Charles Broadwater defeated David Stuart by three votes for a seat in the House of Delegates, Lund Washington, the general's cousin, blamed Mason for Stuart's loss. Mason had supported Broadwater, "a very ignorant man," because, Lund implied, Broadwater was more sympathetic to Mason's land schemes. Lund wrote George Washington that Mason's "whole mind is taken up with saving and accumulating wealth." Mason could, in fact, use his influence for purely personal objectives, as when he successfully lobbied the general assembly to impose a duty on imported snuff. Mason's son Thomson and Thomson's partner William Allison had decided to build a domestic snuff mill.[33]

More common than criticisms were expressions of a desire for Mason to return to the general assembly. Mason's decision in April 1786 to accept a seat in the House reportedly owned much to George Washington's entreaties.[34] Despite Mason's hostility to the port bill and his reluctance to give Congress greater powers, two of James Madison's pet projects, Madison welcomed Mason's return to state office. Madison considered Mason to be "an inestimable acquisition on most of the great points."[35] Madison saw Mason as his principal ally in the battle against paper money.[36] There were other issues as well where Mason's influence seemed decisive. In the spring session of 1784, Madison hesitated to press for a revision of the Virginia Constitution until he could be certain of Mason's support. Jefferson worried about what amendments Mason would accept, and whether "he is determined to sleep on, or will he rouse and be active?"[37] Mason remained noncommittal. James Monroe fretted about Mason's position on the proposed Jay-Gardoqui Treaty, which would have closed the Mississippi River to American shipping in exchange for certain commercial and territorial concessions from Spain. Henry Lee Jr., a member of Virginia's congressional delegation, wrote George Washington that if the treaty came before the general assembly, "much will depend on Mr. Mason's sentiments." Washington believed Mason would support demands for American navigation of the river.[38] Such was the power of Mason's mind and the force of his personality that his preoccupation with his heath, family, and business, his frequent absences from the assembly, and his penchant for petty controversies did not prevent him from wielding considerable political influence. In the early and middle 1780s, Mason exercised that influence on two issues of lasting significance, the final settlement of Virginia's western land claims and the disestablishment of the Anglican Church.

In June 1781 a congressional committee chaired by John Witherspoon of New Jersey recommended Congress deny the claims of the Illinois and

Wabash companies, which rested on purchases from Indian leaders, but accept the claims of the Indiana and Walpole groups. The Witherspoon committee also rejected the Connecticut, New York, and Virginia cessions, rejecting in other words the conditions Virginia had attached to its surrender of jurisdiction. The committee report encouraged Congress to assert its authority over the western territories on the theory that British sovereignty over the area had devolved upon the central government, such as it was, when the colonies declared their independence. Mason rejected the theory, writing Thomas Jefferson in September that should Congress act unilaterally to carve new states out of the disputed territories, it "will only change the name and place of Residence of our Tyrants." Faced with widespread opposition to the Witherspoon report, Congress appointed a second committee to reexamine the issue.[39]

Virginia resented the delay and considered withdrawing its offer, even with the attached strings, to surrender the area north and west of the Ohio River to Congress, but the general assembly elected, as had Congress, to pursue a temporizing strategy. At the spring session of 1782, the assembly appointed a committee consisting of Mason, Jefferson, Randolph, Arthur Lee, and Thomas Walker to prepare the state's rebuttal to Congress. Mason was the only member of the committee who was not currently a member of the assembly, but given his long interest in the West, he was a natural choice. According to Randolph, Mason's was the first name proposed. Randolph, for his part, had already decided to "say something in print upon the territorial rights of Virginia, if the legislature shall not adopt the better measure of forcing Mr. Jefferson and Mr. Mason to undertake the work."[40]

With Jefferson preoccupied with his wife's terminal illness—Martha Jefferson died in September 1782—the bulk of the committee's work fell to Mason and Randolph. Mason, in fact, had already suggested to several members of the general assembly that a committee be appointed. In the spring and summer of 1782, he was in no mood to make further concessions. Mason did not believe that Virginia would make Congress a more attractive offer, and he feared that without the appropriate restrictions, any territories transferred to congressional jurisdiction would be gobbled up by the various land companies. Too many members of Congress were members of the Indiana or Vandalia companies, or rival groups, "which is conceived to be as effectual as Bribery, as if they had received a round Sum in Guineas," in determining how they would vote. The Articles of Confederation did not, Mason argued, confer jurisdiction over the western lands to Congress, and if Congress ignored the lawful claims of an individual state, it might lead to the dissolution of the Union, "or . . . we are in Danger of establishing as tyrannical a Power in America, as that against which we have drawn the Sword."[41]

Mason sent "some valuable papers & remarks" to James Madison, then a member of the state's congressional delegation, that were intended to help Madison buttress Virginia's position. Mason also sent Randolph a long letter tracing the tortured history of the western land claims from the original colonial charters to the Treaty of Lancaster of 1743 through the 1749 grant to the Ohio Company and then to the Treaty of Fort Stanwick in 1768. Mason traversed little new ground, but no one was more familiar with the territory. Randolph assumed responsibility for producing a formal report, and "the Attorney," as he was generally known, did not finish the assignment until late in the summer of 1783.[42]

In the meantime, Randolph and Mason had been overtaken by events. In a decision entered on 29 April 1783, the Virginia Court of Appeals refused to recognize the Ohio Company's grant, thus eliminating whatever faint hope Mason may have still had of patenting land in the company's name north of the Ohio. In June the second committee appointed by Congress recommended acceptance of Virginia's conditions without expressly repudiating the land company claims. An informal agreement was reached. Congress would recognize no claims made prior to the date of cession if Virginia would pass a new, unconditional cession act. Jefferson, Madison, and Governor Benjamin Harrison were ready to compromise, and Mason remained committed in principle to a cession to Congress. On 8 December 1783 the House of Delegates ordered a bill be prepared accepting the congressional terms, save for the addition of a clause, drafted by Joseph Jones, to reserve land for the payment of military bounties. Congress accepted the new cession in March 1784.[43]

The resolution of the western land claims has been hailed as one of the signal achievements of the national government under the Articles of Confederation. Mason's July 1780 report to Joseph Jones laid the foundation for the Northwest Ordinance, which kept the region north of the Ohio in the public domain and provided for its eventual organization into new states, with a status equal to that of the original thirteen.[44] Mason seemed more interested in ensuring that proceeds from the sale of western land went into the national treasury than in advancing his own real-estate speculation. He apparently had little to lose. Nothing appeared likely to revive the Ohio Company grant, and he had "judiciously located" his headright claims so as to be unaffected by the cession. It was, however, critical to

Mason that the cession be negotiated and not imposed by Congress. He believed unilateral action by Congress would have violated the Articles of Confederation, which limited Congress to those powers expressly delegated to it. No issue—not even the debate over the ratification of the Constitution —threatened the sovereignty of the states more, in Mason's mind, than did the notion Congress could disregard Virginia's claim to its undeveloped western territories. Even in the early 1780s, Mason recognized Congress would likely need additional powers—but he would not agree to them until he could be confident that the Articles of Confederation would be strictly construed. A mutually agreeable resolution of the land claims also ensured the territorial integrity of the states, which, as Peter Onuf has suggested, was a prerequisite to state support of a stronger central government.[45]

If Mason, confined to Gunston Hall, played a limited role in the final resolution of the cession controversy, he, Jones, and Madison had begun the search for a solution before the end of the Revolution, and they had helped set the process of compromise in motion.

THE ISSUE OF THE proper relationship between state and church had also languished since the early days of the Revolution. In the fall of 1784 the general assembly took up two bills, supported by Patrick Henry and a powerful bloc of conservative churchmen, to incorporate the Episcopal Church and to levy a general assessment for the support of "Teachers of the Christian Religion." The measures seemed innocuous to Edmund Pendleton, but as he told Richard Henry Lee, "in both some very sagacious gentlemen, can spy designs to revive the former establishment." Madison led the opposition, and he agreed to accept the incorporation bill in order to win a delay in consideration of the assessment bill until the 1785 session. Incorporation affected mainly the internal affairs of the church and the balance of power between the clergy and the laity within the institution. More far reaching was the assessment bill, which levied a tax on all taxpayers for the support of Christian ministers and "places of divine worship." Individual payments would be appropriated to the denomination of the taxpayer's choice. Revenue collected from taxpayers who did not designate a denomination would be used "for the encouragement of seminaries of learning within the Counties whence such sums shall arise."[46]

The delay worked against the conservatives. Henry's election as governor removed him from the legislative debate. In October 1784 a group of Presbyterian ministers had submitted a petition in support of the assessment, but the laity generally disliked it, and by the fall of 1785 the church was firmly opposed to the measure. The Methodists, who had at one point officially endorsed an establishment, were by 1785 too divided to support the assessment effectively. And at least some Episcopalians began to see the assessment as a threat to lay control of the church because their ministers, if the bill passed, would no longer be dependent on purely voluntary contributions from their parishioners. The most noteworthy event in the course of the debate, however, was the appearance in June 1785 of Madison's famous "Memorial and Remonstrance."[47]

In private correspondence, Mason continued, as he had always done, to express traditional religious views, but he enthusiastically supported Madison's efforts to turn public opinion against the assessment bill. The "Memorial and Remonstrance" has been called "a virtuoso performance" and "the most powerful defense of religious liberty ever written in America." Mason told Washington that "the Principles it avows entirely accord with my sentiments on the subject." Mason sent copies to his friends, with mixed results; the assessment debate cut across traditional political alliances. Washington was noncommittal; Richard Henry Lee supported the assessment. Oddly enough, neither Lee nor Washington seemed to understand the bill. Lee defined "true freedom" of religion as supporting all faiths: Muslims and Hindus as well as Christians. Washington likewise professed little alarm at requiring "Christians . . . Jews, Mahomitans or otherwise" to support their respective sects. Yet the bill would have levied an assessment for the benefit of Christian churches only, and while the bill was not expressly limited to Protestant denominations, it is not certain Roman Catholicism was expected to fall within its ambit. Mason had Madison's petition printed as a broadside, with room for signatures at the end, by the Phoenix Press of Alexandria. In collaboration with George Nicholas, Mason circulated the broadside throughout the state. When the legislature reconvened in the fall of 1785, it had received thirteen petitions, each following the "Memorial and Remonstrance," with 1,700 signatures. Mason himself had apparently solicited four petitions from counties in the Northern Neck.[48]

The "Memorial and Remonstrance" quoted liberally from Mason's Declaration of Rights and began with a premise that was the foundation of Mason's commitment to freedom of conscience: liberty of religious belief was an unalienable right, existing before the individual entered into civil society. "What is here a right towards men, is a duty towards the Creator," and that duty, Madison wrote, quoting directly from Mason, "can be directed only by reason and conviction, not by force or violence." Madison attacked one specific provision in the assessment bill, an exemption for Quakers and Mennonites, for discriminating against the other sects, but his arguments transcended the immediate issue. As Madison wrote, in good republican fashion, "it is proper to take alarm at the first experiment on our liberties." Mason had used that argument many times. Who could not see, Madison asked, that "the same authority which can establish Christianity, in exclusion of all other Religions, may establish with, the same ease any particular sect of Christians, in exclusion of all other Sects?" Experience demonstrated that the church did not need state support and that religion had "both existed and flourished, not only without the support of human laws, but in spite of every opposition from them." By contrast, establishment had routinely corrupted true piety. "What have been its fruits? More or less in all places, pride and indolence in the clergy, ignorance and servility in the laity, in both, superstition, bigotry and persecution."[49]

Nor did the establishment of religion serve a legitimate secular purpose. "In many instances," Madison argued, ecclesiastical establishments "have been seen upholding the thrones of political tyranny: in no instance have they been seen as the guardians of the liberties of the people." Restrictions on religious freedom could discourage settlement in Virginia, and they threatened to aggravate political rivalries among the different denominations. On at least one point, Madison may have gone beyond Mason's earlier conception of religious freedom. Madison expressly recognized that right as an individual right, and he recognized the danger that "the majority may tresspass on the rights of the minority."[50] It is not altogether clear in Mason's earlier writings how far he was willing to extend any right to the individual citizen, as opposed to recognizing the people's rights in their collective dealings with the government.

Judging by the number of petitions to the general assembly, public sentiment had turned against the assessment bill by the time the legislature convened in the fall of 1785. In addition to the petitions based on the "Memorial and Remonstrance," Baptist, Presbyterian, and Quaker groups had submitted their own protests. Most numerous were copies of an anonymous, evangelical petition that came from central and southern Virginia. It argued that state support would sully the integrity of the gospel. Original, independent petitions sprang up around the state. There were dissenting voices, a few of which might have given the reformers pause. John Page told Thomas Jefferson that the assessment was needed to maintain the Episcopal Church as a middle way between no religion and the evangelical sects. Page, a liberal Episcopalian himself, defended the church's liberality and bemoaned the denomination's decline, "whilst some others of the most bigotted and illiberal are gaining ground." The alternative to state support was to see Virginia "divided between immorality, and Enthusiastic Bigotry." Notwithstanding such warnings, the assessment bill was not even brought forward for a vote. Instead, the legislature passed by a lopsided margin Jefferson's Bill for Establishing Religious Freedom, which had been proposed by the law revisers' committee almost a decade earlier. Jefferson's bill rejected the very principle of government aid to religion and prohibited the state from discriminating among citizens on the basis of their religious beliefs.[51]

The defeat of the assessment bill may be attributed in part to the jealousies of the dissenting denominations, especially the Presbyterians, who believed it would most benefit the Episcopalians. The incorporation of the Episcopal Church in 1784 revived fears that it might be reestablished. The assessment was also a tax, with all the political baggage of any tax.[52] But why did Mason enter the battle, or, more fundamentally, why did a thoroughly conventional Anglican become, with Jefferson and Madison, Virginia's staunchest advocate of the separation of church and state? Consistent with his interest in westward expansion and the development of Virginia's frontiers, Mason undoubtedly saw religious freedom as a magnet for immigration. Consistent with his suspicions of political power, Mason could not have trusted any government's capacity to regulate the individual conscience. Critical as virtue was to Mason's ideal of a republican society, he did not believe it could be achieved through state-supported churches.

CONGRESS LACKED THE power, under the Articles of Confederation, to impose taxes or to regulate foreign commerce, and the states, which retained those powers, proved unable to exercise them effectively. Immediately after the Revolution, Congress was forced to borrow money from private Dutch bankers simply to pay the interest on the national debt. By 1785 the United States was in default on its interest payments to France, and the new nation could not make the first principal payment when it came due in 1787. The state governments seemed to lack the will or capacity to collect taxes sufficient to pay their congressional requisitions. Meanwhile, the British privy council closed the British West Indies to American ships and to a variety of American products, including fish, which had been a major export before the war. Newfoundland and Nova Scotia were put off limits to American shipping. American fish, whale oil, and salted meats were banned from Great Britain itself, and other American exports faced high protective tariffs. State attempts at commercial retaliation against Great Britain proved ineffective; individual states, hoping to gain an advantage over their neighbors, were constantly tempted to relax trade barriers.

Congress itself generated more apathy than awe. "I am much grieved my dear friend, to observe the wonderful lassitude that prevails in public affairs," Richard Henry Lee wrote Sam Adams from Trenton in November 1784. Lee watched the national legislature struggle merely to obtain a quorum. "It is now eighteen days since Congress ought to have assembled here, and yet we have but five states." Feeble as Congress might have been, established political figures like Washington, Hamilton, Madison, and Mason worried even more about the "imbecility," to use a word they would have appreciated, of the state governments and, especially, the state legislatures. The popular assemblies, they feared, lacked a proper respect for property rights, sound money, and just debts.[53]

In the early spring of 1781, Congress proposed that it be given the power to levy a 5 percent duty or impost, payable in specie, on imports until the national debt was paid. Amendments to the Articles required a unanimous vote of the states, and Rhode Island rejected the impost. Even if Rhode Island had ratified it, the impost would have failed when Virginia, in December 1782, rescinded its earlier ratification. Virginians argued the impost would place a disproportionate burden on them because of the state's dependence on foreign trade. A federal impost would also drain the state customs office of the duties it collected on goods bound ultimately for North Carolina, a windfall the Old Dominion wanted to retain. Support for the impost in Virginia was limited largely to the Northern Neck and the James River Valley. In April 1783 Congress proposed a more modest impost, one that would be collected by state officials and that would expire after twenty-five years. The House of Delegates approved a version of the 1783 impost that gave the state credit for revenues it collected, but Washington's intervention helped defeat the measure and win passage of a bill essentially granting the request of Congress. By 1786 all the states had accepted the impost in principle, but they could not agree on the specifics. New York, for example, insisted that each state retain the duties it collected and that duties be payable in state paper money.[54]

Sectional jealousies helped kill the impost—Richard Henry Lee feared it would favor the North and "strangle our infant commerce in its birth"—and they helped to doom similar efforts to empower Congress to regulate foreign trade.[55] New York merchants and a few of the more nationally minded members of Congress supported giving Congress broad power over commerce, and in 1784 James Monroe proposed just such an amendment to the Articles. The general assembly, however, voted down a resolution with a similar purport. The only amendment that reached the states was more modest. It allowed Congress to tax and regulate trade, but the states themselves could collect and expend any duties Congress might levy, and the states retained the power to bar foreign imports as they saw fit. Many Virginians feared a northern majority in Congress would use a national commerce power to create a northern shipping monopoly. As had the impost, the commerce amendment drew significant support in Virginia only from the Northern Neck and Tidewater. Both votes foreshadowed later divisions between Federalists and Anti-Federalists over ratification of the Constitution.[56]

The debate over the impost and over a national commerce power also foreshadowed the sectional divisions that would loom large at the Constitutional Convention, divisions that would deeply trouble George Mason. Congressmen Rufus King of New York and Theodore Sedgwick of Massachusetts went so far as to suggest that the states north of the Mason-Dixon Line form a separate confederacy until the South agreed to congressional regulation of commerce. They may have been serious. The debate over American navigation of the Mississippi River further aggravated geographical rivalries and helped undermine support for strengthening Congress. In 1784 Spain closed the lower Mississippi, which gave western farmers their most viable outlet to foreign markets, to American shipping. Spain sent Don Diego de Gardoqui to New York to win American acquiescence in its decision. His government, which hoped to prevent Louisiana from being overrun by a burgeoning American population, was prepared to make concessions in the form of commercial privileges and territorial rights, perhaps to St. Augustine and West Florida south of the Tennessee River.

In turn, John Jay, the secretary of state for foreign affairs, asked Congress for permission to agree to the closing of the river for twenty-five years. After a rancorous debate along sectional lines, Congress granted Jay's request by a vote of seven states to five. Because nine votes were needed to approve a treaty under the Articles, Jay decided not to press the issue. Mason and most Virginians supported American navigation of the river; Mason reportedly believed the United States had a "natural right" to its use and predicted war with Spain in less than seven years if the port of New Orleans was not reopened. Patrick Henry had waffled on the impost; his principal biographer believes the North's indifference to the South's interest in the Mississippi, and the North's ability to assemble a majority in Congress, finally and permanently turned Henry against a stronger central government. Henry, as usual, was not alone. The controversy over Jay's instructions did incalculable damage to the relationship between New England and the South. In December 1786 James Madison told George Washington that unless Congress agreed to keep the Mississippi open, Virginia would not support a stronger union.[57]

Mason, in the Fairfax County Freeholders's Address of 1783, had opposed giving Congress an independent source of income because, he wrote, "when the same Man, or set of men, holds both the sword and purse, there is an end of liberty." The Mississippi controversy could only have compounded his reservations about conferring new authority on Congress.[58] Frustrated at the quality of Virginia's government and conscious of the inadequacies of the Articles, Mason would, however, gradually embrace a more nationalistic position.

James Madison, making a slow, rain-soaked journey home from Philadelphia in December 1783, spent an evening at Gunston Hall. Madison found that his host, six months after submitting the Fairfax County Freeholders's Address, had tempered his opposition to a federal impost, although Mason worried that it might "embarrass" efforts to retaliate against British commercial policies. Mason made clear that his earlier objections to a state constitutional convention had been procedural. He left Madison with the impression he would be willing to serve should the state call a convention. At the same time, however, Mason did not share Madison's concern about the fate of the union under the Articles. Mason may not have expected it to survive, and he probably expected Virginia, with Britain defeated, to exist as a virtually independent republic within the loosest possible confederation. "His [he]terdoxy lay chiefly in being too little impressed," Madison wrote Thomas Jefferson, "with either the necessity or the proper means of preserving the confederacy."[59]

On 28 June 1784 the general assembly adopted a resolution authorizing Mason, Edmund Randolph, James Madison, and Alexander Henderson to meet with representatives of Maryland to discuss "the jurisdiction and navigation of the River Potowmack." Mason had long been interested in the river as an artery of commerce, an interest that went hand in hand with his commitment to western expansion. In 1774 Mason had been elected trustee of a Potomac River canal company that hoped to make the river navigable to Fort Cumberland, Maryland. A year later, Mason drafted a bill granting the company a charter, but Maryland refused to cooperate, and with war looming, Mason abandoned the plan.[60]

The postwar conference might have enjoyed no more success. Governor Henry was responsible for notifying the Virginia delegates, which he failed to do. Mason learned of his appointment when two of the Maryland commissioners wrote him to ask if they could stay at Gunston Hall on their way to the meeting site in Alexandria. They had written Henry to suggest a meeting there in March 1785, and receiving no reply from the governor, they assumed the proposal was acceptable to Virginia. Mason proceeded to Alexandria to await the arrival of his colleagues, but when he received a letter from Randolph that did not mention the conference, Mason realized none of the Virginia delegates had been notified. By then, the Maryland delegates, Daniel of St. Thomas Jennifer, Thomas Stone, and Samuel Chase had arrived. Mason assumed, consistent with prior practice, than any two Virginia commissioners were empowered to negotiate on the state's behalf, and because Henderson, a local merchant, was nearby, Mason decided to proceed without benefit of instructions. In reality, the authorizing resolution specifically required three delegates to constitute a quorum. Mason also wrongly assumed that he and Henderson had authority to negotiate terms for the use and navigation of the Chesapeake and Pokomoke, as well as the Potomac.[61]

If Mason lacked unassailable legal authority, he had a powerful political ally. George Washington shared Mason's interest in the navigation of the Potomac and in a private canal company. Washington had loaned Mason his carriage for the trip to Alexandria, and Washington offered to host the meeting once all the expected delegates arrived. At about dusk on Thursday, 24 March 1785, the general's carriage brought Mason back to Mount Vernon in a fine mist of snow and rain. "The most amicable spirit" attended the negotiations, and the Mount Vernon Conference, as it came to be known among historians, completed its business the following Monday.[62]

The commissioners agreed to lift most duties on the ships of the two states and to create a free-trade zone for local shipments of produce. They agreed to share the costs of lighthouses and beacons and to divide criminal jurisdiction. One provision of the final agreement apportioned tonnage duties on vessels traveling to Virginia and Maryland. Other provisions recognized the fishing rights of both states.[63] The Virginia delegates had also been authorized by a resolution adopted by the general assembly in late 1784 to petition Pennsylvania for the right to use the Ohio River and its Pennsylvania branches without paying a duty, except for duties necessary to improve navigation. Mason and Henderson learned of the resolution from Washington, and the five delegates sent a brief communiqué to the president of the executive council of Pennsylvania proposing that goods moving on the Potomac and Ohio rivers not be taxed other than as necessary to defray the expenses of "Preserving the Navigation of the said Rivers."[64]

Before leaving Mount Vernon, Mason also drafted a cover letter for the copy of the compact that was sent to the House of Delegates. The letter addressed issues beyond the scope of the commissioners' appointment that Mason and Henderson, nevertheless, believed were "very important to the commerce of the two States." Mason proposed that Virginia ask Congress for permission to form a defensive compact with Maryland. He also recommended that foreign gold and silver circulating in the two states should be given the same value, and he advocated standardized rules for commercial paper and uniform import and export duties.[65]

The consequences of the Mount Vernon Compact overshadowed its specific terms. James Madison had been one of the chief advocates of the conference, and it is often seen as a first step on the road that led two years later to the Constitutional Convention in Philadelphia. Madison believed that the most important consequence of Mount Vernon was the decision that delegates from Maryland and Virginia should meet annually to discuss commercial issues. Maryland decided to invite Delaware and Pennsylvania to the annual conferences, at which point Virginia decided to invite all the states to the next meeting in Annapolis. The sparsely attended Annapolis gathering of September 1786 accomplished little, but it did propose that a constitutional convention be called, so in a sense the Philadelphia meeting was a progeny of the Mount Vernon Conference. But the evolution was not inevitable. Forrest McDonald has suggested that the conference was, in fact, an antinationalist enterprise, and the ability of a few states to deal with regional problems on an ad hoc basis would, as a purely logical matter, seem to mitigate against the need for a stronger national government. Politics, of course, has its own logic, and as more and more state delegations came together in better-attended meetings, nationalistic politicians gained a forum from which they could push for national reform. As far as Mason was concerned, however, the Mount Vernon Conference was what it appeared to be, an effort by two states to resolve common problems, not a first step to replace the Articles of Confederation.[66]

Mason's gout returned less than a week after the Mount Vernon Conference —while he was bottling apple cider and gathering watermelon seeds to send to Washington—and then he suffered terribly through the fall of 1785.[67] Sometime during the summer of that year, Mason had finally received a copy of the resolution authorizing the Mount Vernon meeting. When he realized he and Henderson had exceeded their instructions, Mason assumed "this blundering Business" would force on him "the Trouble & Expence of a Journey to Richmond, next Session, to apologize for, & explain our Conduct." Amid the controversy over the port bill, moreover, Fairfax County elected Mason to another term in the House of Delegates. Gout kept him from attending.[68]

He had also been one of eight delegates elected in January 1786 to represent Virginia at Annapolis. James Monroe, for one, hoped that Mason would go to Maryland: Monroe believed that exposure to the nationalists at Annapolis would cure Mason of his lingering "Antifederal prejudices." But as Edmund Randolph put it, "a journey from home ex gratia seems not to be a hobby-horse of his."[69]

While Mason was recuperating at Gunston Hall, the assembly named him to Virginia's delegation to Philadelphia, along with Washington, Madison, Randolph, George Wythe, and John Blair. Randolph informed Mason of his nomination and urged him to accept: "Give me leave to call to your mind the tottering condition of the United States, and to press you into this Service, if your health should permit." Rumor had it Mason would attend even though he had never in his life traveled farther than the distance between Gunston Hall and Williamsburg. Mason "will pretty certainly attend," Madison told Thomas Jefferson. "I am informed [he] is renouncing his errors on the subject of the Confederation, and means to take an active part in the amendment of it."[70]

Chapter Seven

One of the Best Politicians
in America

GEORGE MASON performed his duties as a member of the Virginia delegation to the Constitutional Convention with an unexpected stamina and a surprising vigor. Mason attended its daily meetings consistently, speaking frequently and serving on influential committees. Almost half of the fifty-five delegates, by contrast, appeared sporadically, or left well before the convention had completed its work. While Mason ultimately became the Constitution's most distinguished opponent, he left his mark on the document. Ironically, until he saw a central government emerging that, in his mind, failed to protect Virginia's economic interests, Mason was a more effective nationalist than many of the delegates who were more outspoken advocates of constitutional reform, among them James Madison, James Wilson, and Alexander Hamilton.

Mason went to Philadelphia because he believed the convention would do important work, because a near consensus existed among America's political elite that Congress needed new powers, and because he saw a stronger central government as a possible check on the state legislatures. In Philadelphia, Mason tried to draw a fine constitutional line between a few unabashed localists and a few, more ardent nationalists. He had less faith than did the nationalists in the capacity of ordinary politics, even at the national level, to produce good government. The possibility of corruption and the abuse of minority interests weighed more heavily on his mind.

Mason, like most of the other delegates, had his parochial concerns. The South Carolina delegates, for example, insisted on continuing the foreign slave trade and providing for the return of runaway slaves. They wrung concessions from the convention, and the South Carolinians signed the Constitution. Mason most feared congressional legislation that would make southern planters the captive customers of northern shippers. He came close to restricting the ability of Congress to pass a navigation law, but ultimately he failed, and he did not sign the Constitution.

Mason wanted to vest real power in a new central government without threatening vital local interests or opening the door to British-style corruption, avarice, and extravagance. Given his intelligence, his debating skills, and the personal prestige he brought to Philadelphia, it is not surprising that he cut a large figure in the convention. And given the difficulty of the task he had set for himself, his stubborn independence, and his lack, by 1787, of any concern for his own political future, it is not surprising that he left Philadelphia at odds with the great majority of his fellow delegates.

THE GENERAL ASSEMBLY, on 4 December 1786, had elected Washington, Madison, Randolph, Henry, Wythe, and James Blair, along with Mason, to represent Virginia in Philadelphia. Congress had placed no limits on the size of the state delegations; next to Pennsylvania's, Virginia's would be the largest. Richard Henry Lee and Thomas Nelson could have served, but they both declined the appointment. No delegates lived west of the Blue Ridge; otherwise the legislature had attempted to represent every political faction in the state. After the assembly adjourned, Henry, claiming he "smelt a Rat," resigned from the delegation. Governor Randolph appointed James McClurg, a prominent doctor whose patients included George Washington, to replace Henry.[1] Mason apparently did not know McClurg or Blair well, but he had served with Blair on the committee that had produced the Declaration of Rights and the new state constitution during the fifth Virginia Convention in 1776. McClurg and Wythe left the Philadelphia Convention early. Washington and Blair stayed, and remained largely silent, until the end.[2] Of the Virginia delegates, Randolph, Madison, and Mason—especially Madison and Mason—dominated the floor debates. When the two of them were in agreement, they formed a formidable alliance; when they disagreed, which they often did, the exchange could be electric.

The general assembly had appointed Mason and his colleagues, according to their instructions, "for the purpose of revising the federal constitution." A convention "was preferable to a discussion of the subject in Congress," the assembly tactfully suggested, "where it might be too much interrupted by the ordinary business before them." A convention could also enlist the "valuable counsel of sundry individuals" who did not serve in the national legislature. The assembly's instructions repeated a widespread belief that "the Crisis is arrived" in the affairs of the Confederation, and they authorized the delegates to consider "all such Alternations and farther Provisions as may be necessary to render the Federal Constitution adequate to the Exigencies of the Union."[3]

At the beginning of the convention, Mason seemed comfortable with the Virginia Plan, largely Madison's work, which called for a national executive and judiciary and for a bicameral legislature with a veto over state laws. The resumption of frequent contacts with George Washington after 1783 may have nudged Mason in a more nationalistic direction, but even the future Anti-Federalists among his correspondents were prepared, by 1787, to strengthen the Articles of Confederation. Richard Henry Lee believed that only Congress should be allowed to print money, and he believed state laws that were contrary to federal law should be treated as void. Arthur Lee sent Mason a list of proposed amendments to the Articles that included authorization of a federal impost for twenty-five years, federal regulation of interstate commerce, a national supreme court, and a constitutional convention to meet every five years.[4]

Money came closer to keeping the ever practical Mason from Philadelphia than did any philosophical reservations. In April 1787 Mason wrote Governor Randolph to request an advance against the £100 the assembly had appropriated for his expenses. Tobacco sales had been disappointing, and the advance, Mason told Randolph, was "of such Importance to me, that without it, I could hardly have attended." Acknowledging receipt of the money a few days later, Mason explained his concern to Randolph. "Considering the Number of Deputies from the different States, the great Distance of some of them, & the Probability that we may be obliged to wait many Days, before a full Meeting can be obtained, we may perhaps be much longer from Home than I at first expected." After arriving in Philadelphia with his son John, and at least two slaves, Mason complained to George Jr. that they had found "travelling very expensive, from eight to nine Dollars Per Day." Mason's per diem was six dollars. Fortunately their room cost only twenty-five shillings a day, in Pennsylvania currency, "so that I hope I shall be able to defray my Expenses with my public Allowance; & more than that I do not wish."[5]

The convention had been scheduled to begin on Monday, 14 May, but a quorum of seven states did not assemble until Friday, 25 May. Bad weather delayed several of the delegates. Mason, the last of the Virginians to reach Philadelphia, arrived on Thursday evening, 17 May. Madison, who had been early, hoped the entire Virginia delegation could stay at the House-Trist Inn, Madison's customary quarters at Fifth and Market streets, a block from the State House. Washington, instead, elected to lodge with Robert Morris in the Philadelphia financier's townhouse, and by the time George and John Mason reached the city, the House-Trist Inn was full. They stayed, with several other delegates, at the Indian Queen Tavern on

Fourth Street between Market and Chestnut.[6] Mason reported he and John were "very well accommodated" with "a good Room to ourselves." Manasseh Cutler visited Philadelphia later in the summer and described the Indian Queen as a large building "kept in an elegant style" with "numerous small apartments." It came to serve as the unofficial headquarters of the convention.[7]

While waiting for a quorum to form, the Virginians met together daily for two or three hours, and every day at three o'clock they assembled at the State House. There they visited with delegates from other states and with former army officers who were in Philadelphia for their own convention—a meeting of the Society of Cincinnati. Mason found broad support for the Virginia Plan, except among delegates from the smaller states. They objected to Madison's proposal to base representation in both houses of the national legislature on population. From the beginning, Mason himself worried about preserving viable state legislatures in a new, national political order. Despite his misgivings and those of the small states, Mason found more unanimity than he had expected. He believed that "with a proper Degree of Coolness, Liberality and Candor," a central government could be established that would reserve "to the State Legislatures a sufficient Portion of Power for promoting & securing the Prosperity & Happiness of their respective Citizens." He did, however, foresee a geographical division at the convention, and not one between large and small states. "We are likely to find Republicans, on this occasion, issue from the Southern and Middle States, and anti-Republicans from the Eastern," by which he meant New England. Mason explained the change as "a very common & natural Impulse of the human Mind." Having been the most radically revolutionary of them all, the New England states were now swinging to the other extreme. "Men disappointed in Expectations too hastily & sanguinely formed, tired and disgusted with the unexpected Evils they have experienced, & anxious to remove them as far as possible, are very apt to run into the opposite Extreme; and the People of the Eastern States, setting out with more republican Principles, have consequently been more disappointed than we have been."[8]

Mason's analysis echoed a 15 May letter from Richard Henry Lee. Lee had also expressed apprehension that the eight northern states would use their numerical superiority to enact legislation discriminating against the carrying trade of the five southern states. Once the convention began, nothing would worry Mason more.[9]

On his first Sunday in Philadelphia, Mason and the other Virginia delegates, save Washington, went to Mass, "more out of Compliment than religion, & more out of Curiosity than compliment." Mason found a large congregation with "an indifferent Preacher." The music and "the Air of Solemnity" that filled the chapel impressed him, although "I was somewhat disgusted with the frequent Tinkling of a little Bell, which put me in Mind of the drawing up [of] the curtain for a Puppet-Shew." More important perhaps than his critique of the service was Mason's willingness to attend, given the anti-Catholicism that pervaded English republicanism and much of American society. Mason's republicanism had never embraced religious prejudice.[10]

Mason's tolerance foreshadowed the convention's treatment of religion. Most of the delegates felt no need either to promote religion or to discourage it. Apart from Article VI—"no religious test shall ever be required as a qualification to any Office or public Trust under the United States"—the Constitution made no affirmative statements about state-church relations. Not everyone had kept pace with Mason in the transformation of republicanism from a Protestant ideology to a pluralistic, if not a secular, one. North Carolina proposed banning "Roman Catholics and pagans" from public office, which was a particularly ungracious suggestion since two of the delegates, Thomas Fitzsimmons of Pennsylvania and Daniel Carroll of Maryland, were Catholics. Almost every delegation floated a few ideas that received, deservedly, no support. There are, in the Constitution, two oblique references to religion. Article I, Section 7, exempts Sundays from the ten days the president has to veto legislation. Article VII dates the Constitution "in the year of our Lord one thousand seven hundred and eighty seven." When the convention neared an impasse in late June, Benjamin Franklin suggested a chaplain be retained to offer daily prayers, but with no money available to pay a minister, Franklin's motion never came to a vote. Unlike the French revolutionaries who rewrote the calendar to eliminate Sundays, Mason and the other Framers believed a secular government could peaceably coexist at a certain arm's length with a Christian culture. Some Anti-Federalists, but not Mason, would criticize the convention for its secular tone and disregard of religion.[11]

If within two weeks of his arrival in Philadelphia, Mason found a few reasons to complain, he also demonstrated an uncharacteristic optimism. He had never been so far away from home, never been in a large city, and never seen a real merchant aristocracy. He soon grew "heartily tired of the etiquitte and nonsense so fashionable in this city." At the same time, he viewed his fellow delegates charitably, finding many of them to be "men of firm Republican Principles." They were America's "first Characters," he wrote his son George; many of them were "of the most respectable Abilities; and so far as I can discover, of the purest Intentions."[12]

Mason enjoyed unusually good health in the summer of 1787, which may explain his improved disposition. In mid-July he would find time and energy for an early morning carriage ride, with John and several other delegates, across the Schuylkill River to visit the botanic garden of the noted naturalist John Bartram. The realization he was entering into a historic debate may have rejuvenated him; it did Washington. The general had complained that spring of "fever and ague" and "rheumatic pains," but he had completely recovered by the time the convention began. William Pierce, a Georgia delegate, profiled the other state representatives, and his sketch of Mason hardly sounds like the chronic invalid of Mason's letters. "Mr. Mason is a gentleman of remarkable strong powers, and possesses a clear and copious understanding. He is able and convincing in debate, steady and firm in his principles, and undoubtedly one of the best politicians in America. Mr. Mason is close to 60 years old, with a fine strong constitution."[13]

As did many of the other delegates—the taciturn Washington was more circumspect—Mason readily admitted he felt the eyes of history on the work of the convention. "I would not," he wrote, "upon pecuniary Motives, serve in this Convention for a thousand pounds per Day," but he clearly relished the assignment. Mason believed the creation of a new government to be far more important than the Revolution itself. The mind staggered, he wrote his son George, at "the Influence which the Establishments now proposed may have upon the happiness or Misery of Millions yet unborn."[14]

Mason ranked, quite literally, among the elder statesmen at the convention, although many of the other delegates could boast of a broader range of political experiences. The average age of the delegates was forty-three. At twenty-six, Jonathan Dayton of New Jersey was the youngest; eighty-one year old Benjamin Franklin was the oldest. Mason, by now almost sixty-two, was one of the most senior delegates. James Madison, for one, believed that the stature of the delegates suggested the states were taking the convention seriously. Many of the delegates knew one another from service in Congress or the Continental army, if not by happenstance. Thirty-nine of them had served in the Continental Congress. Wythe, Elbridge Gerry of Massachusetts, Roger Sherman of Connecticut, George Reed of Delaware, and Franklin and three other Pennsylvania delegates—James Wilson, Robert Morris, and George Clymer—had signed the Declaration of Independence. Gunning Bedford of Delaware and James Madison had been classmates at Princeton. Mason had no close personal acquaintances outside of Maryland and Virginia, but his reputation—as an early leader in the nonimportation movement, as author of the Virginia Declaration of Rights and Virginia Constitution, and as one of Virginia's most successful planters—had preceded him to Philadelphia.[15]

Mason would be forced, with mixed results, to navigate his way through a maze of competing factions and shifting alliances. Forrest McDonald has identified four broad interests in the convention: landless states jealous of neighbors with territorial claims in the West; commercial states anxious to protect their carrying trade; planters seeking to protect agricultural exports and, in South Carolina and Georgia, the foreign slave trade; and, finally, public creditors and investors who were concerned about the solvency of the central government.[16] The debate between large states and small states over the basis of representation in Congress would nearly deadlock the convention in its early stages. More ominous would be the division between North and South, and within the South, between southerners who wanted to abolish the slave trade and those who wanted to continue it. Battles raged within individual delegations. When James McHenry left on 1 June, to be replaced by Luther Martin on 9 June, Maryland slipped out of the large-state bloc. The Virginia delegation would eventually split, but the worst breakup came in New York. Robert Yates and John Lansing walked out on 11 July, convinced the convention was going too far in centralizing power in the national government. The only other New York delegate, Alexander Hamilton, had left near the end of June, convinced the convention was not going far enough. Hamilton later returned, but because he believed he could not in good conscience cast New York's vote alone, the state was essentially unrepresented for much of the convention.[17]

New York was not by itself. The New Hampshire delegation did not arrive until 23 July; the state legislature had refused to finance the trip. One of the New Hampshire delegates, John Langdon, the state's governor and a successful merchant, ultimately agreed to pay his own expenses and those of his one colleague, Nicholas Gilman.[18] Rhode Island boycotted the entire affair. Despite the absences, a quorum of seven states had formed by 25 May, only eleven days behind schedule.

"THIS IS A NOBLE BUILDING," one contemporary observed of Independence Hall. "The architecture is in a richer and grander style than any public building I have ever before seen." The Pennsylvania Supreme Court met on the first floor in the west wing. The state legislature sat in the east wing. The Constitutional Convention borrowed the legislative chambers for its own deliberations. The east room was forty feet by forty feet with twenty-foot ceilings, two fireplaces, and tall wide windows. A door to the right of the dais led to a room that served as both a library and a meeting place for the convention's many committees. Green baize covered the tables occupied by individual delegations. Contrary to legend, Philadelphia did not experience an unusually hot summer in 1787. The city's normal summers were hot enough, and the New Englanders undoubtedly chafed in their wool suits. Dressed in lighter camlet coats and accustomed to heat and high humidity, the southerners presumably fared better. In any event, Mason, who could usually find some cause for complaint, did not complain about the weather. When the supreme court convened in July, the convention retreated to the second floor to escape a rush of lawyers, litigants, and spectators. Throughout the convention's own meetings, sentries were "planted without and within—to prevent any person from approaching near."[19]

Closing its sessions to public scrutiny was one of several procedural decisions the convention made in its opening days. Almost inconceivable in a modern democracy, closed legislative sessions were not unusual in the eighteenth century. Access to the House of Commons had traditionally been limited, and the Continental Congress and the revolutionary-era assemblies had often met in secret. Mason supported the rule of confidentiality. He believed a constitution would evolve from a series of "crude and indigested parts" that, if disclosed individually, could only unsettle the public. He also concurred—the vote was unanimous—in the selection of George Washington as president of the convention. Much of the debate would be conducted in a less formal committee of the whole, and the convention selected Massachusetts's Nathaniel Gorham, president of Congress from 1786–87, as the committee's chair. Washington's election effectively removed him from floor debates and helped keep him above the political bickering that he abhorred. Washington's function was to be Washington, to legitimize the convention, and to lend his enormous personal prestige to the convention's handiwork, assuming the delegates could reach some agreement. Even when the convention dissolved into a committee of the whole, and Washington surrendered the speaker's gavel to Gorham, the general would not speak, except to say his role as presiding officer enjoined silence upon him.[20]

Mason proved far less reticent. On Friday, 25 May, George Wythe was appointed chair of a committee to draft standing rules for the convention.

After Wythe presented the committee's report on Monday, Rufus King of Massachusetts rose to object to a provision allowing any member to call for a recorded vote. Mason seconded the objection, arguing that "a record of the opinions of members would be an obstacle to a change of them" and might "furnish handles to the adversaries of the Result of the Meeting." The provision was deleted without dissent.[21] It was a foretaste of things to come. Only four or five other delegates would speak more frequently than Mason, and he won almost as many debates as he lost.

The convention took up its first substantive business on 29 May, when Edmund Randolph introduced the fifteen resolutions that constituted the original Virginia Plan. It provided for a two-house legislature in which representation was to be based on population or on a state's "contribution" to the national treasury. Soon to be known respectively as the House of Representatives and the Senate, the lower house was to be popularly elected, and the upper house would be selected by the lower from a list of candidates nominated by the states. Congress could veto state laws "contravening the articles of Union" and use force against recalcitrant states. The Virginia Plan provided for a national executive and judiciary, from which a council of revision would be drawn. The council would be empowered to veto acts of Congress, but Congress could override the council's veto. The plan left much to be decided. It did not define the length of the terms to be served by the executive or by members of Congress. Representatives were subject to term limits, but they were unspecified. Members were barred from holding other offices after leaving Congress, but the plan left the length of the ban to be decided. Robert Yates, who was not an entirely objective observer, described Randolph's presentation as "a long and elaborate speech" in which the Virginia governor expressed the idea the "states should be nearly annihilated." The initial debate focused on the first of Randolph's fifteen resolutions: "1. Resolved that the Articles of Confederation ought to be corrected & enlarged as to accomplish the objects proposed by their institution; namely, 'common defence, security of liberty and general welfare.'"[22]

Most of the delegates were prepared to go beyond "correcting and enlarging" the Articles of Confederation. The next day, Randolph, at the suggestion of Gouverneur Morris, an unabashed nationalist, proposed that debate on his first resolution be postponed to consider three principles. They expressed more clearly the nationalists' objectives.

> 1. that a Union of the States merely federal will not accomplish the objects proposed by the articles of Confederation, namely common defence, security of liberty, & genl. welfare.

2. that no treaty or treaties among the whole or part of the States, as individual sovereignties, would be sufficient.

3. that a *national* government ought to be established consisting of a *supreme* Legislative, Executive & Judiciary.

The third proposition provoked objections from two of the South Carolina delegates, Charles Pinckney and Charles Cotesworth Pinckney, and from Elbridge Gerry of Massachusetts. Morris attempted to alleviate their concerns. The difference, he said, between a federal system and a *"national, supreme"* government was simply the difference between "a mere compact resting on the good faith of the parties" and an irrevocable legal commitment.[23]

Mason seized the floor as soon as Morris relinquished it. His defense of Randolph's third proposition marked him early on as a nationalist. According to Madison's notes, Mason "observed that the present confederation was not only deficient in not providing for coercion & punishment agst delinquent states; but argued very cogently that punishment could not (in the nature of things be executed on) the States collectively, and therefore that such a Government, was necessary as could operate directly on individuals, and would punish only those whose guilt required it."[24]

Mason's speech also indicated that if he and Madison had similar objectives, they were moving toward them in different directions. Mason was not yet willing to subscribe to every provision of the Virginia Plan, in particular, the idea of using troops to enforce a congressional veto of a state law. Mason, by contrast, envisioned a national government that was both more effective and more palatable to state officials: more effective because it could act directly on individuals and more palatable because it would not directly challenge the authority of the states. Madison himself almost immediately abandoned his proposal to permit the use of force against state governments. The delegates tentatively agreed to allow Congress to overrule unconstitutional state laws, but on Madison's suggestion, they postponed consideration of language authorizing military force to implement federal law. On the question of patching or scrapping the Articles of Confederation, the states voted, with only Connecticut dissenting, to start from scratch.[25]

The convention spent the next several weeks wrangling over the apportionment of seats in the national legislature and a process for selecting its members. Mason consistently displayed moderate views, both in his nationalism and in his republicanism, defending, for example, the popular election of members of the lower house while supporting the indirect election of the upper house. Some delegates preferred an election by the state legislatures, not by the people themselves, even in the lower house. Elbridge Gerry, for one, complained that "the evils we experience flow from the excess of democracy." He believed that the people might be allowed to nominate candidates, but the state legislatures should make the final selection. Roger Sherman believed the "people should have as little to do as may be about the Government." Mason, by contrast, envisioned the lower house as "the grand depository of the democratic principle of Govert." The lower house ought to represent every faction and interest in society, which it would be more apt to do if its members were chosen by the people. Mason expressed on the floor of the convention the same concern that Richard Henry Lee had expressed privately to him, that the country was lurching from one extreme to another, rushing from an excess of democracy toward an aristocracy. It served the delegates self-interest, Mason argued, to "attend to the rights of every class." He had "often wondered at the indifference of the superior classes of society to this dictate of humanity & policy; considering however affluent their circumstances, or elevated their situations, might be, the course of a few years, not only might but certainly would, distribute their posterity throughout the lowest classes of society."[26]

If, as Mason envisioned, the new national government would act directly on citizens, they ought to be directly represented in its legislative assemblies. "Actual representation" required that representatives "sympathize with their constituents" and live among them. Mason admitted democracy had its "imperfections and evils . . . [and] improper elections," but he believed, as did Madison, that "there was a better chance for proper elections by the people, if divided into large districts, than by the State Legislatures." Paper money was the convention's great terror, and Mason charged that irresponsible state legislatures had issued paper money when the people opposed it. In a decisive vote on 21 June, with Maryland divided and only New Jersey dissenting, the convention settled the issue in favor of "election of the first branch by the *people*."[27]

The debate over popular elections was not simply a debate over the merits of democracy. Nationalists supported popular elections because they would bypass the state legislatures and make the new Congress answerable to the people, not the states. Roger Sherman expressed the opposing position: "If it were in view to abolish the State governts. the elections ought to be by the people." Popular elections provided a philosophical justification for giving the national government the power to act directly on individual citizens. Popular elections had the additional, political advantage of putting the states' rights delegates in opposition to popular rule. "States' rights delegates" is probably a misnomer to the extent it suggests any of the delegates held, or were motivated by, elaborate theories of state sovereignty. Practical politics were more important. Opponents of popular elections tended to be from small states. They were reluctant to give the national government much authority as long as the possibility existed that representation in both houses would be based on population. Delegates from the small states hesitated to surrender power to a national legislature likely to be dominated by Virginia, Pennsylvania, and Massachusetts.[28]

In the debate over the popular election of House members, Mason sided with Madison and James Wilson, two of the most extreme nationalists at the convention. He shares credit with them for the nationalists' victory. Yet Mason disagreed with both Madison and Wilson over the procedure for selecting members of the Senate, and their disagreement illustrates the limits of Mason's nationalism. Madison proposed, in the Virginia Plan, that senators be elected by the House from among candidates nominated by the state legislatures. Wilson preferred election by the people.[29] Convinced that the state governments needed a mechanism to protect legitimate state interests, Mason believed the state legislatures should be allowed to elect members of the Senate without the involvement of the House. Uncertain of how the debate over apportionment would be resolved, but personally willing to compromise, Mason sought a middle ground on the question of selecting representatives that would balance state and national interests regardless of what the convention decided on the question of apportionment. Defending the states on 7 June, Mason argued that every alternative presented some risks. The dangers posed by reckless state legislatures had been exaggerated because, under the Article of Confederation, "we have only seen the evils arising on the side of the state governments." Mason's views on selecting senators prevailed.[30]

Mason, however, did not want the state legislatures to have too much control over members of Congress, and he seconded a motion by Madison, which ultimately carried, to have Congress paid out of the national treasury and not by the individual states.[31] Having freed the national legislature from what he saw as undue state influence, Mason at the same time sought to guard the new Congress from corruption and an excess of democracy. Mason supported Madison's proposal for a council of revision that could strike down oppressive laws before they took effect. "Notwithstanding the precautions taken in the Constitution of the Legislature," Mason told the convention, "it would so much resemble that of the individual states, that it must be expected frequently to pass unjust and pernicious laws."[32]

Mason opposed efforts to restrict voting rights, but he did not believe every citizen was qualified to lead. He moved successfully on 22 June to make twenty-five the minimum age for service in the House of Representatives. He said he knew from personal experience that younger men were too immature for such responsibility. He added, according to Madison, "it has been said that Congress had provided a good school for our young men. It might be so for any thing he knew but if it were, he chose that they should bear the expense of their own education."[33] Mason also supported property qualifications for service in Congress. On 26 June he suggested a property requirement for senators because "one important object in constituting the Senate was to secure the rights of property." On 26 July Mason proposed that all members should own some amount of land and not be in debt to the United States. "Persons of the latter descriptions had frequently got into the State Legislatures, in order to promote laws that might shelter their delinquencies." Rumor had it, Mason said, that "this evil had crept into Congress." The proposal may have been intended as a jab at Robert Morris, who reportedly owed the central government $700,000. If it was intended to put control of the new government into the hands of the landed gentry, and not those of the financiers, it was halfhearted at best. Mason did not pursue the issue, and only his proposal that representatives be at least twenty-five years old became part of the Constitution.[34]

Mason recognized that the creation of an effective national government would require modification of a few republican principles. He concurred in the convention's decision to elect the House of Representatives biennially even though no axiom was more deeply rooted in republican thought than the idea that "when annual elections end, tyranny begins." He recognized that annual elections would put larger and more distant states at an unreasonable disadvantage. They would need several months to complete an election and get their delegates to Congress.[35]

Mason would not, however, compromise on the question of allowing legislators to hold other public offices, which good republicans saw as the principal device by which the executive could corrupt the legislature. The Virginia Plan, as revised by the middle of June, prohibited members of Congress from accepting any state or federal office during their terms in office, and in the case of national office, for one year after leaving Congress. On 22 June Gorham moved to strike the one-year restriction. Fearful of patronage, Mason objected: "I consider this clause as the corner-stone on which our liberties depend—and if we strike it out we are erecting a fabric for our destruction." Gorham's motion failed. Madison suggested another approach: members of Congress would be barred from assuming federal positions created, or given salary increases, during their terms of office. Leaving other offices open to them might serve "as an encouragmt. to the Legislative Service." The debate continued the following day, and Mason continued to support strict limits on legislative job hopping. If Congress made the appointments, it would favor its own members, he argued, and if the president made the appointments he could effectively bribe legislators. Mason ridiculed the argument that the prospect of future appointments would help lure the most talented politicians into legislative service. "Genius & virtue it may be said, ought to be encouraged. Genius, for aught he knew, might, but that virtue should be encouraged by such a species of venality, was an idea, that at least had the merit of being new." Mason's objection drew a personal and sarcastic rebuke from Madison, one aimed at Mason's well-known reluctance to accept public office. Madison admitted the failings of the legislatures, but he asked his fellow Virginian "to vouch another fact not less notorious in Virginia, that the backwardness of the best citizens in the Legislative Service gave but too great success to unfit characters." Madison's motion failed, but the issue would resurface later in the convention.[36]

Meanwhile, Mason's moderation and his commitment to the work of the convention would survive one more test—the battle over the apportionment of seats in the national legislature.

ON 9 JUNE two New Jersey delegates, William Paterson and David Brearly, had risen to challenge the concept of proportional representation. "It had been much agitated in Congr." when the Articles of Confederation were being drafted, Brearly said, but "rightly settled by allowing to each sovereign State an equal vote." Otherwise, the three largest states, Massachusetts, Pennsylvania, and Virginia, could "carry every thing before them." For his part, Paterson "considered the proposition for a proportioned representation as striking at the existence of the lesser states." The debate continued until 11 June, when the convention defeated, by a vote of six to five, a motion by Roger Sherman that each state be given an equal vote in the second branch of the legislature. Sherman warned that the small states would never agree to proportional representation in both houses of Congress. Even without New Hampshire and Rhode Island, the small states might have constituted a majority, but North Carolina, South Carolina, and even sparsely populated Georgia had large-state aspirations and voted with the large-state bloc. Immediately after defeating Sherman's motion, the convention passed, by an identical six-to-five vote, a motion by Wilson and Hamilton, "for making the ratio of representation the same in the 2nd as in the 1st Branch."[37]

On 13 June the committee of the whole reported a modified version of the Virginia Plan that proved for a two-house national legislature; representation in both houses would be based on population. Two days later, Paterson presented the New Jersey Plan as an alternative to the Virginia Plan. More modest than Madison's initial proposition, the New Jersey Plan illustrated the political consequences of the small states' opposition to proportional representation. They would resist a transfer of substantial power to a national government likely to be dominated by trio of large states. The New Jersey Plan contemplated amending the Articles, leaving in place a unicameral legislature in which each state had one vote. The New Jersey Plan failed to unite all the states' rights delegates; it did, after all, permit Congress to raise revenue and regulate foreign and interstate trade.[38] On 19 June the convention, by a vote of seven to three, with Maryland divided, elected to continue working from the modified Virginia Plan.[39]

The convention's action provoked a bitter response from John Lansing the following day. Lansing argued that the convention lacked the authority, or the popular support, to do more than amend the Articles of Confederation, and he attacked specifically Madison's proposal that the national legislature have a negative on the laws of the states. Mason was the first delegate to answer Lansing. He did not attempt to defend the congressional veto, and it would not survive the convention. He did, however, challenge the convention's alleged "want of power." The convention was not claiming a right to make law by "fiat." The final decision rested with the people. America, Mason said, now faced a crisis "in which the ordinary cautions yielded to public necessity." Mason went on to address the people's supposed hostility to a more energetic Congress. As Madison recorded his remarks: "He meant . . . to speak his sentiments without reserve on this subject; it was a privilege of Age, and perhaps the only compensation which nature had given for the privation of so many other enjoyments; and he should not scruple to exercise it freely."

The people had opposed conferring new powers on the old Congress because it would have meant a surrender of their rights. In the new, popularly elected Congress, they would "not part with power: they only transfer it from one sect of immediate Representatives to another sect." Deeply attached "to more than one branch in the Legislature," the people distrusted the unicameral Confederation Congress, but Mason believed the checks and balances inherent in a bicameral legislature would permit the new Congress to be entrusted with greater authority. Mason conceded the new government would not be "faultless," but he trusted "posterity" to make the necessary amendments.[40]

The nationalists fended off Lansing's challenge. In a vote later on 20 June, the New Yorker's motion to vest new powers in the Confederation Congress failed by a vote of six to four, with Maryland again divided. It was a narrow margin on which to rest a new government, and the convention had yet to resolve the thorny issue of representation. Indeed, it had been the small states, fearful of a legislature dominated by large states, that had supported Lansing. If New Hampshire and Rhode Island had been present on 20 June, they presumably would have voted with Connecticut, New York, New Jersey, and Delaware, and they would have deadlocked the convention. Connecticut, which voted to approve the revised Virginia Plan on 19 June, voted to abandon it the next day. Agreement, even within individual delegations, was proving to be elusive, and the end of the delegates' work was not yet in sight. The North Carolina delegation wrote Governor Richard Caswell to request an advance for another two month's service; "we are near the middle of June and though we sit from day to day, Saturdays included, it is not possible for us to determine when the business before us can be finished." Alexander Hamilton, who had returned to New York City, wrote George Washington to report growing support among the people at large for a vigorous and energetic government. Washington, stuck in Philadelphia, complained in reply of "narrow minded politicians" and others "under the influence of local views" who wanted to obstruct the convention.[41]

The slow pace took its toll on attendance. Among the first to leave had been George Wythe, who resigned to return home and care for his ailing wife. Wythe's departure left George Mason as the only member of the House of Delegates who was also serving in the convention. He worried that when the time came for a report to the state legislature, "the whole weight of explanation must fall upon me." On 30 June Mason wrote Beverly Randolph, who was serving as acting governor while Edmund Randolph was in Philadelphia, to recommend that Francis Corbin, a member of the assembly who was then in Philadelphia, be appointed to replace Wythe. Mason's request went unheeded. Mason believed that the convention had reached a critical stage, that the next two or three days would decide if it could continue, and that if it could, the convention was likely to last until September.[42]

Conceding defeat after Lansing's motion to amend the Articles was voted down on 20 June, the small-state delegates accepted the existence of a bicameral legislature, and they did not attempt to resurrect the New Jersey Plan. But critics of the Virginia Plan could agree on one issue: the states should enjoy equality in at least one house. On 29 June Connecticut's Oliver Ellsworth renewed Sherman's earlier motion that each state be given a single vote in the Senate. The convention debated the motion and then voted on 2 July. The vote resulted in a five-to-five tie. Georgia, which had previously sided with the large states, now found itself divided. One Georgia delegate, the Connecticut-born and Yale-educated Abraham Baldwin, had not come to Georgia until 1783. His ties to Connecticut apparently pulled him into the small-state camp and helped produce a stalemate. "We are now," Sherman observed, "at a full stop."[43]

MASON HAD NOT participated in the debate over Sherman's motion, but he must have indicated privately a willingness to compromise. After the 2 July vote, the convention did what organizations typically do when they confront seemingly intractable problems; it appointed a committee, in this case a Grand Committee, consisting of one delegate from each state. The composition of the committee seemed to indicate the direction the convention hoped to take. Small-state delegates, and large-state delegates who had not staked out positions against compromise, dominated its membership. In selecting Pennsylvania's representative, the outspoken James Wilson was passed over in favor of the more conciliatory Benjamin Franklin. The convention selected Mason to represent Virginia in lieu of James Madison, who along with Wilson, had opposed Sherman's motion. Franklin and Mason were the committee's most prestigious members. The convention named Elbridge Gerry, another large-state delegate known to favor compromise, to chair the committee.[44]

The Grand Committee deliberated over the convention's Fourth of July recess. The earlier decision for a bicameral legislature with an upper house elected by the state legislature—and in a sense representing the individual states as distinct constitutional entities—helped push the committee toward the eventual compromise. So did the inability of the large states to agree on a system of proportional representation that would not make the Senate larger than any of the delegates thought proper.[45] The committee found itself as deeply divided as the convention had been, but Franklin eventually proposed a compromise, along the lines earlier suggested by Sherman, that was acceptable to a majority of the members. The dissenters agreed, in the interest of keeping the convention together, to acquiesce in the majority report.[46]

On 5 July Gerry submitted the committee's proposal to the convention. What became known as the Great Compromise provided that in the House of Representatives each state would have one representative for every 40,000 inhabitants; money and salary bills would originate in the House; and each state would have an equal vote in the Senate. No records exist of Mason's activities within the committee, but it seems certain the originating clause was either his idea or, at the least, the price of his acquiescence to state equality in the Senate. Mason had himself inserted a similar clause in the Virginia Constitution, and he vigorously defended House control of appropriation bills once debate began on the committee report. Mason spoke after Gerry. The convention might elect not to adopt the specific proposals made by the committee, Mason admitted, but "there must be some accommodation on this point, or we shall make little further progress." He went on: "It could not be more inconvenient to any gentleman to remain absent from his private affairs, than it was for him: but he would bury his bones in this city rather than expose his country to the consequences of a dissolution of the convention without anything being done."[47]

The convention debated the committee's report for the next two weeks, with Madison, Wilson, and Charles Pinckney of South Carolina leading the opposition. The issue of the origination of money bills was critical to Mason and became almost as contentious as the question of representation. Conceding a monopoly over revenue measures to the House was intended to be a concession to the large states, and it conformed to Mason's republican ideology. Since 1407, the House of Commons had enjoyed the sole right of initiating money bills; the House of Lords could approve or disapprove a revenue measure, but the Lords could not amend it. As the representatives of the people, only the House of Representatives, the Commons' American equivalent, should be allowed, in Mason's mind, to initiate a tax on the people.[48] The issue divided the Virginia delegation. Madison saw the originating clause as a trivial concession to the large states and feared the Senate's veto would become a blunt instrument to use against the House, perhaps even on unrelated legislation. Mason and Randolph, on the other hand, warmly embraced the clause.[49] Should the Senate, Mason argued, "have the power of giving away the people's money, they might soon forget the source from which they received it. We might soon have an aristocracy."[50]

Madison and Wilson, loath to acknowledge the sovereignty of the states, fought hard against opposition to state equality in the Senate. A desperate Madison suggested an alternative compromise in which Senate seats would be distributed unequally, but not quite on the basis of population. It went nowhere. The small-state delegates stood adamantly behind the Great Compromise, and Mason was one of several large-state delegates—Franklin, Caleb Strong, and Elbridge Gerry of Massachusetts, John Rutledge of South Carolina, most of the North Carolinians, and perhaps even Gouverneur Morris—who were open to compromise. However Mason might have described the legal status of the states, he seemed to see them as political and geographical realities that could not reasonably be ignored. When the final vote came on 16 July, the small states and the large-state moderates won a deceptively decisive victory, passing the Great Compromise by a vote of five to four, with one state divided. Franklin and Mason had not been able to deliver the votes of their states in favor of the compromise, but Gerry and Strong produced an even split in the Massachusetts delegation, removing a critical vote from the large-state bloc. Three small states, New York, New Hampshire, and Rhode Island, were unrepresented in the vote; if they had participated, the compromise would have passed easily.[51]

The Great Compromise carried the convention over its first great hurdle, but in light of the visceral opposition of most of the large-state delegates, the term "compromise" seems a misnomer, although Madison himself used it. The vote of 16 July was less a compromise among competing interests than it was a victory of small states that were operating from a position of strength because of the convention's decision to give each state one vote in its own deliberations. The large-state delegates reconvened at the Indian Queen that evening and held a formal caucus the next morning before the convention reassembled. They could not agree on a strategy. A few at least were willing to abandon the small states and to take a competing constitution to the people. Others urged their colleagues to accept defeat. It is hard to believe Mason was not among the group urging reconciliation, and he may well have contributed the most to the Great Compromise by reminding men like Madison and Wilson that if they attempted to act without unanimity among the states, they would not enjoy unanimous support within their home states. In any event, the vote of 16 July resolved the single most contentious issue before the convention and converted the small states, now satisfied they would be fairly represented, into enthusiastic supporters of national power.[52]

Mason had helped broker the compromise, and it represented the apex of his career as a nationalist. But in some respects, it was a Pyrrhic victory.

The Great Compromise diluted Virginia's influence within the national legislature, created new strains within the Virginia delegation, and may have left Mason less, not more, committed to framing a new constitution.

THE CONVENTION FACED three especially contentious issues: the basis of legislative representation, the right to initiate revenue measures, and the nature of a republican presidency. As an exercise in political theory, the presidency may have been the most difficult. One overriding consideration colored the perspective of the delegates. Virtually everyone agreed that George Washington would be the nation's first chief executive. Whatever defects might unwittingly be written into the office would temporarily be remedied by his monumental character. But after Washington transferred power to a successor, how could the delegates prevent the office from becoming an instrument of tyranny? And how could the Constitution restrict the presidency without giving affront to Washington, and perhaps even alienating him from the new government? The delegates had no successful models on which to draw. Almost all agreed that the new state governors created by the revolutionary-era constitutions had been too weak. Yet, except for Alexander Hamilton, Gouverneur Morris, and a handful of extreme nationalists, no one wanted a chief executive as strong as the British monarch or the prewar royal governors. The debates over the presidency cut across sectional lines, produced a wealth of proposals, generated a series of indecisive votes, and left fundamental issues—such as the need for an electoral college—unresolved until almost the end of the convention.[53]

Mason, nevertheless, lost one battle at the very beginning. The Virginia Plan had not specified whether the "National Executive" would consist of one individual or several. In the course of debate on 2 June, it was proposed that the executive power be vested in "one person." Randolph opposed the suggestion "with great earnestness," according to Madison's notes. The "permanent temper of the people," Randolph said, "was adverse to the very semblance of monarchy." Franklin agreed with Randolph, and so did Mason. With Mason off the floor, however, the convention voted seven to three on 4 June to establish "a single Executive." The issue split the Virginia delegation: Randolph and Blair voted against it; Madison, Washington, McClurg, and Wythe, who had already left the convention, and who cast a vote by proxy, supported the single magistrate.[54]

Mason feared the power of a solitary official equipped with the power to veto legislation and to appoint federal officeholders. The president could use his patronage to corrupt Congress the way the British monarchy had used a similar power to manipulate Parliament. According to the notes he made for himself in the course of the debate, Mason believed, "If strong extensive powers are vested in the Executive, and that executive consists of only one person, the government will of course degenerate (for I will call it degeneracy) into a monarchy—a government so contrary to the genius of the people, that they will reject even the appearance of it."[55]

He saw a three-person executive as a partial remedy for the lack of a council of revision, which he had envisioned as an advisory panel of elder statesmen who could serve as a check on the executive. Councils had been common in the colonial governments, and the Virginia Plan initially called for one, but the idea had limited support in the convention. More importantly, Mason's three-member presidency would have consisted of representatives chosen by region—one each from the northern, middle, and southern states—thus ensuring a sectional balance. Randolph favored a similar arrangement, but neither man pursued the issue in the early stages of the convention. It must have been discussed informally. Hugh Williamson of North Carolina was apparently the first delegate to raise the issue on the record when, during the debates of 24 July, he proposed that "the Executive power . . . be lodged in three men taken from districts into which the States should be divided." Williamson's suggestion attracted no support. The tripartite presidency was only one of several probably unworkable ideas that surfaced briefly in Philadelphia; Martin and Gerry, for example, wanted to fix the size of the army in the Constitution.[56]

Mason's interest in a multiple executive is early evidence of his sensitivity to sectional differences. From the very start of the convention, Mason saw the South as a separate region and feared that southern interests would not be adequately protected in the new government. Despite these fears he did not aggressively pursue his goal of a co-presidency, perhaps because he saw other ways to protect southern interests and perhaps because he thought the effort would be futile.[57]

Mason fared better, at least initially, in the debate over selecting the president and fixing the term of the office. On 1 June James Wilson suggested the president be elected directly by the people; Mason liked the idea and suggested Wilson be given time to prepare a formal proposal. But the Virginia delegate questioned the practicality of a national, popular election. For much of the convention, the delegates assumed the national legislature would choose the president, as provided for in the Virginia Plan. As the debates went on, Mason's opposition to popular election seemed to harden.

On 17 July he complained "it would be as unnatural to refer the choice of a chief magistrate to the people, as it would, to refer a trial of colors to a blind man." In a country the size of America, the people would know too little about candidates for national office. Nine days later, he was even more specific. A popular election would be dominated by the nation's only organized interest group—former Continental army officers. "A popular election in any form . . . would throw the appointment into the hands of the Cincinnati, a Society for the members of which he had a great respect; but he never wished to have a preponderating influence in the government."[58]

Most of the delegates agreed with Mason, but they struggled throughout the convention to find an alternative to direct elections. Almost equally elusive was agreement on the president's term. In the debates on 1 June, Wilson and Sherman had proposed three years. Mason favored a seven-year term with no opportunity for reelection. Assuming that Congress would select the president, Mason believed an incumbent seeking another term would be too submissive to the legislature. The convention approved a seven-year term by a vote of five to four with one state divided. On 2 June the delegates voted to limit the executive to a single term. Hamilton and a few of the more extreme nationalists continued to support tenure during good behavior, which Mason denounced as "a softer name only for an executive for life . . ., an easy step to hereditary monarchy." In mid-July the delegates reduced the executive's term to six years but lifted the ban on a second term. The convention returned to the issue on 26 July when Mason moved to reinstate language limiting the executive to a single seven-year term. "Having for his primary object, for the polestar of his political conduct, the preservation of the rights of the people, he held it as an essential point, as the very palladium of Civil liberty, that the great officers of State, and particularly the Executive should at fixed periods return to that mass from which they were first taken." The motion passed seven to three with Massachusetts off the floor.[59]

Mason also supported making the president subject to impeachment, but he helped defeat a motion by John Dickinson to allow the national legislature to impeach the president upon the petition of a majority of state legislatures. Mason rarely talked during the convention in terms of checks and balances or the separation of power, but he believed that every agency of government, including the states, needed some mechanism to protect its domain from encroachment by the others. Impeachment should be available to curb abuses of executive power, but it should not be so easy as to provide Congress with a device by which it could dominate the president. Many of the delegates believed federal judges would be called upon to decide impeachment cases, and, in part to maintain their independence, Mason opposed presidential appointment of the federal judiciary. He would have allowed Congress to pick judges. He feared the president would be too apt to select nominees from the small group of lawyers the president would know in the nation's capital. Mason put little faith in Senate confirmation as a barrier to bad presidential appointments. "The false complaisance which usually prevails in such cases will prevent a disagreement to the first nominations."[60]

ON 26 JULY the convention voted to adjourn for ten days to permit a Committee of Detail to prepare a report of the convention's decisions as of 23 July. Mason did not serve on the committee. Despite his misgivings about the presidency, Mason had been an effective advocate of a moderate, republican nationalism during the first half of the convention. Mason said he considered the Articles of Confederation government to have been effectively dissolved by the Philadelphia assembly, and he urged his fellow delegates to agree on a design for a new government as quickly as they could.[61]

Mason had played a pivotal role in the passage of the Great Compromise, the convention's most impressive accomplishment by late July, and a constructive role on a host of other issues. Mason opposed discrimination against new states and advocated a regular reapportionment of the lower branch to reflect changes in population. He fought repeated efforts to base representation on a state's wealth or its share of the national tax burden.[62] Mason even opposed a motion by Pierce Butler of South Carolina to count slaves for purposes of determining representation "notwithstanding it was favorable" to Virginia. He thought it "unjust" to use a species of property to inflate the political influence of white southerners.[63] He supported giving the national government the power to suppress revolts against state governments as necessary to prevent a general rebellion. He supported submitting the Constitution, once it was completed, to popular conventions for ratification, not the state legislatures, which were likely to be less amenable to strengthening the national government. It was Mason who first suggested that the national capital not be located in a state capital. He anticipated conflicts over jurisdiction otherwise, and he feared "the intermixture of the two Legislatures" would give "a provincial tincture to . . . Natl. deliberations."[64]

Mason was not, however, a man who was easily pleased, and when the convention resumed its deliberations, his commitment to a powerful, new national government would be severely tested.

Chapter Eight

The Sanction of Their Names

THE COMMITTEE OF DETAIL consisted of its chair, John Rutledge of South Carolina, and members Edmund Randolph, Nathaniel Gorham, Oliver Ellsworth, and James Wilson. When the convention reassembled on Monday, 6 August, Rutledge placed the committee's report on the secretary's table. The report, a draft constitution of twenty-three articles, was read aloud, and each delegate received a seven-folio-page printed copy with ample margins for notes and revisions. After hearing the report, the delegates adjourned for the day. The only other business on the sixth was the arrival of Mason's cousin, John Francis Mercer of Maryland, who made his first appearance at the Constitutional Convention.[1]

The committee's report provided the outline and much of the language of the convention's final product. Rutledge and his colleagues had attempted to reduce the convention's various resolutions to a coherent form, filling in gaps not yet addressed by the rest of the delegates and borrowing freely from handy sources—among them the Articles of Confederation, the state constitutions, the Paterson plan, and another plan prepared by Charles Pinckney. On balance, as a tentative document, it was acceptable to George Mason. There was a two-house national legislature—now denominated a Congress—consisting of a House of Representatives and a Senate. There would be one house member for every 40,000 citizens and two senators for each state. Money bills were to originate in the House and could not be amended in the Senate, which was a critical point with Mason. Senators served six-year terms; representatives served for two years. House members could not hold additional offices during their terms in Congress; senators were banned from other positions during their terms and for one year thereafter. Mason would have preferred even stronger restrictions on the power of the executive to purchase influence with patronage. In recommending that the states, not the national government, pay members of Congress, the Committee of Detail ignored the previously expressed will of the convention. The change was one concession to the states that Mason opposed.[2]

Especially in light of the decision to give the states equal votes in the Senate, the body was stronger than Mason thought appropriate. The Senate could make treaties and appoint ambassadors and Supreme Court justices. The longest and oddest section of the committee's constitution—Section 2 of Article VIII—authorized the Senate to supervise the resolution of conflicts among the states "respecting jurisdiction or territory." The committee surely anticipated disputes over western lands. The delegates from the smaller states, represented by Ellsworth, presumably insisted that those conflicts be resolved by the Senate, where Connecticut and Delaware would have an equal vote with Pennsylvania and Virginia. Mason believed new states should be admitted into the union with the same rights as the original states, but notwithstanding his lifelong interest in western land, he no longer showed much interest in rivalries among competing land speculators.[3]

In the committee's report, the nation's highest judicial tribunal became the Supreme Court, and the chief executive was now the president, elected by the legislature for seven years and ineligible for reelection. Mason would have preferred a multimember executive. The committee made no provision for a council of revision, and however archaic the institution may appear in hindsight, Mason and several other delegates considered its absence to be a serious omission.[4]

The political scientist Clinton Rossiter has said that the committee's "most important contribution" was its decision to enumerate specifically the powers of Congress. They included eighteen separate provisions, beginning with "the power to lay and collect taxes, duties, imposts and excises" and continuing through the power "to call forth the aid of the militia in order to execute the laws of the Union, enforce treaties, suppress insurrections, and repel invasions." To give the new government some flexibility, the committee added, portentously, the power to "make all laws that shall be necessary and proper" for executing the other powers vested in it by the Constitution. With delegates present like Mason who were fundamentally skeptical of political authority and who were jealous of the rights of the people, the necessary and proper clause generated surprisingly little debate.[5]

One purpose of the convention had been to curb the state legislatures; granting broader power to the national government and imposing limits on the states were different sides of the same coin. The decision on 17 July to reject Madison's proposed congressional veto on state legislation forced the Committee of Detail to consider other alternatives. In addition to conferring a range of functions on Congress, the committee took two specific

steps to rein in the states. First, the committee either removed certain powers from the states altogether or conditioned their exercise on congressional approval. The states could not, in any instance, "enter into any treaty,
alliance, or confederation" but they could, with the consent of Congress,
issue paper money or "lay imposts or duties on imports." Rossiter called the
restrictions the "second most important contribution of the committee."
But the committee's other effort to subordinate the states to the national
government was arguably as far reaching. Borrowed from Paterson's New
Jersey Plan, what became known as the supremacy clause made federal law
supreme in areas subject to federal jurisdiction and required state courts
to respect legitimate federal authority, notwithstanding state law to the
contrary. Mason had no great confidence in the state legislatures, but he
preferred the supremacy clause to a heavy-handed congressional oversight
of all state laws.[6]

The committee draft also limited the power of Congress. Four provisions
in three sections—Sections 4, 5 and 6 of Article VII—showed the hand
of John Rutledge. They would occupy much of the rest of the convention
and prove decisive to Mason. Under Section 4, "no tax or duty shall be laid
by the legislature on articles exported by any state; nor on the migration
or importation of such persons as the several states shall think proper to
admit; nor shall such migration or importation be prohibited." The protection of the right to transport "such persons as the several states shall think
proper to admit" was the committee's ingenuous, or disingenuous, way of
protecting the slave trade without putting the word "slave" in the Constitution. South Carolina and Georgia, more dependent on slavery than were the
states of the upper South, refused to surrender control over their labor supply to Congress. Mason had a mixed response to Section 4. He opposed the
taxation of exports. As a planter, Mason feared it would make his tobacco
less competitive in European markets. At the same time, he found the slave
trade morally offensive.[7]

Section 5 provided that a federal "capitation," or poll, tax if levied by
Congress had to be "in proportion" to the federal census. Intended to prevent discrimination among the states, it provoked little debate. Section 6
of Article VII was a different matter. "No navigation act," it stated, "shall
be passed without the assent of two thirds of the members present in each
House." To Mason, Section 6 would protect the South from an American
version of the British Navigation Acts. He feared that the South, at least
initially, would be a minority in the House of Representatives, and he could
easily see that Virginia would be only one among equals in the Senate.

Mason feared that the North would use its numerical superiority to force southern planters to carry their staples to European markets in American bottoms, thus eliminating foreign competition for the carrying trade and raising shipping costs. The two-thirds requirement in Section 6 was intended to give the southern states a veto over a new navigation act. Mason considered it to be the single most important provision in the Constitution, and it would tie the convention in knots for weeks.[8]

THE TWO WEEKS of debate following the introduction of the draft constitution from the Committee of Detail showed, as clearly as did any other comparable period, Mason's commitment to both republican virtue and the interests of Virginia. The rhetoric of the country opposition, expressing the radical Whig suspicion of commerce and centralized political power, had served Americans well during the Revolution, and for Mason it proved equally useful at the Constitutional Convention. Before the Revolution, Americans had been, within the British Empire, a political minority that could not compel Parliament to respect its unique interests. Mason feared, far more than most of the other southerners, that Virginia planters might come to occupy a similar position in the new Congress.

Mason would readily debate procedural as well substantive issues. When the convention resumed its deliberations on 7 August, Mason helped to defeat an effort by Gouverneur Morris and Rufus King to eliminate a provision in Article III requiring annual meetings of Congress. King argued that, once a system was established to regulate commerce and collect revenue, "alterations would be rarely necessary & easily made." Congress would have little else to do. Mason disagreed. Congress would have ample opportunities to make law, and its responsibilities extended beyond legislation. "The extent of the Country will supply business. And if it should not, the legislature, besides legislative, is to have *inquisitorial* powers, which can not safely be long kept in a state of suspension."[9]

Mason's views on issues of procedure offer a glimpse of his temperament and philosophy; he wanted the convention to succeed and he did not object to strengthening the national government, but his belief that fine points mattered created repeated opportunities to object. He helped win approval of committee recommendations that one-fifth of the members of either house could request a record vote, that Congress periodically publish a journal of its proceedings, and that a majority of the members of either house be required to constitute a quorum. Mason "liked" the one-fifth rule "as a middle way between the two extremes" of allowing an individual member to request a record of yeas and nays and making no record at all. Congressional proceedings ought to be published because he "thought it would give a just alarm to the people to make a conclave of their legislature." More telling were his remarks on the simple matter of defining a quorum. His defense of the committee's proposal that a majority of members be present before Congress could pass a bill reflected the fiscal conservatism that pervaded the convention. In Virginia, he told his fellow delegates, an emission of paper money had been avoided by a similar requirement in the House of Delegates. The quorum debate also revealed Mason's cautious support for the committee's work. The "Constitution as now moulded was founded on sound principles, and [he] was disposed to put into it extensive powers. At the same time, he wished to guard agst. abuses as much as possible."[10]

Mason defended the liberal suffrage requirements recommended by the committee. During the first day of debate on the committee's report, Gouverneur Morris moved to strike language in Article IV, Section 1 that made the suffrage qualifications for congressional elections the same as the states' requirements for electing "the most numerous branch of their own legislatures." Morris wanted to "restrain the right of suffrage to freeholders," and he minimized the number of potential voters who might be disenfranchised. Several delegates, including Mason, objected, and the convention defeated Morris's motion. A majority of the states, Mason pointed out, had abolished the freehold requirement; citizens in those states would resent being denied the right to vote in federal elections. He admitted the "Freehold is the qualification in England," but he believed "We . . . view things too much through a British medium." Republican philosophers had long seen property as essential to the economic independence that they believed was a prerequisite to responsible citizenship. Mason, by contrast, took a more modern view, basing a right to vote not on the citizen's independence, but on a legitimate interest in the welfare of the community. As he asked the convention, "does nothing besides property mark a permanent attachment" to society? "Ought the merchant, the monied man, the parent of a number of children whose fortunes are to be pursued in his own Country, to be viewed as suspicious characters, and unworthy to be trusted with the common rights of their fellow Citizens."[11]

Mason, however, balked at the prospect of electing recent immigrants to public office, a sensitive matter since at least a handful of delegates, including the outspoken Scotsman James Wilson, were foreign born. Article

IV, Section 2, of the Committee of Detail's draft imposed a three-year citizenship requirement for service in the House of Representatives. Mason wanted to extend the requirement to seven years. He "was for opening a wide door for emigrants; but did not chuse to let foreignors and adventurers make laws for us & govern us." Morris seconded the motion, and it passed with only Connecticut dissenting. John Rutledge wanted to impose a separate, seven-year state residency requirement for House members. Mason and the majority of delegates believed seven years was too long, but Mason worried aloud that "Rich men of neighboring States," if they failed to win office at home, might go shopping for a more favorable political climate. He and Oliver Ellsworth lost by a close vote of six to four, with one state divided, a motion to adopt a one-year residency requirement.[12]

The question of a citizenship requirement for senators triggered, for a seemingly minor issue, one of the convention's most heated debates. Article V, Section 3, required a senator to "have been a citizen of the United States for at least four years before his election." When the section reached the floor on 9 August, Gouverneur Morris moved immediately to extend the requirement to fourteen years. The ensuing debate cut across normal alliances. Mason supported the motion; had it not been for the service of foreign-born patriots during the Revolution, "he should be for restraining the eligibility into the Senate, to natives." But Ellsworth, who had fought along side Mason to impose a residency requirement on House members, opposed the motion, as did Edmund Randolph, who was otherwise Mason's closest collaborator. The convention ultimately settled on a compromise of nine years.[13]

Morris, who had been an advocate of more stringent requirements on office holding by immigrants, moved a few days later to adopt a clause providing that the limitation approved by the convention would not affect the rights of any person who was then a citizen. Morris's attempt at a conciliatory gesture provoked an even more acrimonious debate. Morris had raised, perhaps unwittingly, a question that went to the nature of the American union. Citizenship, Roger Sherman argued, was a matter of state law; the United States had made no representations to the foreign-born that the new government was bound to respect. Sherman's argument enraged James Madison: "It was a subtilty by which every national engagement might be evaded." Madison's response drew Mason into the debate once more. He opposed an exception for immigrants who were already nationalized because the new government would be most vulnerable to foreign influence in its early years. "All the great objects wd. be then provided for.

Every thing would be set in motion." Madison carried the Virginia delegation with him, but Mason better reflected the views of the convention, and Morris's motion failed by a vote of six to five.[14]

Mason had fared well in what were relatively minor skirmishes. More ominous was a discussion on 8 August when, to his mind, the Great Compromise began to unravel. Article IV, Section 5, provided that "all bills for raising or approximating money . . . shall originate in the House of Representatives, and shall not be altered or amended by the Senate." The clause was an anomaly. The small-state representatives had agreed to it in the Grand Committee in an effort to win the support of the large states for state equality in the Senate, but it had failed to pacify the majority of the Virginia and Pennsylvania delegations. After the debate on the provision resumed, Charles Pinckney moved to strike it. Mason spoke against Pinckney's motion, warning that it would "unhinge the compromise of which it made a part." Allowing the Senate to initiate money bills would further enhance the power of an institution that, because of its small size and the extended terms of its members, threatened to become a dangerous aristocracy. Despite support from Mercer, Butler, and Ellsworth, Mason could not defeat the motion. It passed on a seven-to-four vote.[15]

The following day, Edmund Randolph announced his intention to seek reconsideration of the origination clause, and when moments later the convention reached Article V, Section 1, giving each senator one vote, he moved to postpone discussion pending a final decision on the treatment of money bills. Several delegates responded. Benjamin Franklin said he "considered the two clauses, the originating of money bills, and the equality of votes in the Senate, as essentially connected by the compromise which has been agreed to." Mason supported delay; if the origination clause was not revived and the Great Compromise collapsed, "each state may have two members, and yet have unequal votes." He added "that unless the exclusive originating of money bills should be restored to the House of Representatives, he should, not from obstinacy, but from duty and conscience, oppose throughout the equality of Representation in the Senate." Randolph's motion was defeated, with only Virginia and North Carolina supporting postponement.[16]

On 13 August Randolph introduced an amended version of Section 5 which required money bills to begin in the House but which allowed the Senate to correct clerical errors and initiate bills that might have the incidental effect of raising revenue. Randolph and Mason were now acting clearly in concert. After the Virginia governor presented the amendment, Mason rose to support it with one of his longest and most important speeches of the convention. Because, he said, the Senate represented the states, not the people, it should not tax the people. No reason existed to give the Senate equal weight with the House in the business of raising revenue. He admitted "the Republican form . . . had its evils," chief among them the majority's tendency to trample on the rights of minorities and the opportunities it offered to charismatic but unscrupulous politicians. Yet Mason, in the high tide of his own nationalism, believed the central government could protect minority rights without augmenting the power of an undemocratic Senate. He went on to explain "the evils of our Republican system. . . . The chief ones, were the danger of the majority oppressing the minority, and the mischievous influence of demagogues. The Genl. Government of itself will cure these. As the States will not concur at the same time in their unjust & oppressive plans, the general Govt. will be able to check & defeat them, whether they result from the wickedness of the majority, or from the misguidance of demagogues." After a long debate, Randolph's motion failed on a seven-to-four vote, but Randolph and Mason had managed to win over the Virginia delegation. Washington, hoping a concession on the originating clause would make Randolph and Mason more conciliatory on issues that the general considered to be more important, gave them his vote. Madison and Blair remained adamantly opposed to the provision.[17]

The issue refused to disappear. On 15 August the convention reached Article VI, Section 12, of the committee's report, which provided simply that "Each House shall possess the right of originating bills, except in the cases beforementioned." The last clause gave Mason and his allies another opportunity. Caleb Strong of Massachusetts now proposed an amendment to Section 12 that would recognize the House's exclusive right to initiate money bills but give the Senate broader amending powers than Randolph had proposed. Mason seconded the motion, adding forebodingly that "he wished the motion to be decided now, that the friends of it might know how to conduct themselves." Despite his plea, the convention voted, six to five to postpone further debate.[18]

By the middle of August, Mason seemed to be growing more skeptical of the emerging Constitution. He objected during the third week of August when Charles Pinckney attempted to weaken the ban in Article VI, Section 9, preventing members of Congress from accepting other offices. Pinckney proposed they merely be required to vacate their seats. Mason responded sarcastically: the entire section might well be stricken to help complete "that Aristocracy which was probably in the contemplation of some among us." Given "the present state of American morals & manners," Mason feared "few friends will be lost to the plan, by . . . giving premiums to a mercenary & depraved ambition." Pinckney's motion failed, but the convention postponed a final decision on the ban on legislators accepting other positions.[19]

Mason had more objections. He expressed concern about the ability of the Senate to use the treaty-making power to surrender American territory without the consent of the House.[20] He wanted Congress's general taxing power to include a specific prohibition against taxes on exports, but he could not force a vote on the issue.[21] The Committee of Detail draft gave Congress the power to "emit bills on the credit of the U. States." Morris wanted to delete the provision and foreclose the possibility of another national emission of paper money. Mason claimed a "moral hatred" of the medium but opposed an absolute prohibition; "the late war could not have been carried on, had such a prohibition existed." Few issues united the delegates more than their hostility to paper emissions—only the inconsequential John Francis Mercer confessed himself a "friend of paper money"—and Morris's motion passed easily.[22] Mason also met defeat on one of his pet causes, sumptuary laws to limit extravagant spending and lavish entertainment. He proposed Congress be given the power to pass sumptuary legislation. "No government can be maintained unless manners be made consonant to it." Mason believed a republican government, dependent as it was on the virtue of its citizens, needed to be able to give "proper direction" to the "love of distinction." A clear majority of the delegates thought otherwise.[23]

Yet Mason continued to participate, influencing the course of the debates, winning small victories, and leaving his mark on the very words of the Constitution. Some triumphs were fleeting. In mid-August Mason defeated a proposal to have the president, as opposed to Congress, appoint the new government's treasurer, only to see the delegates reverse themselves near the end of the convention.[24] He won approval of a resolution calling for a prohibition on "perpetual revenue," or a permanent tax, but it never found its way into the Constitution.[25] On the other hand, it was Mason who suggested the phrase "giving aid and comfort" to the enemy in the Constitution's definition of treason.[26] He favored giving Congress, not the president, the authority to commit the nation to war, and he supported modification of Congress's war-making power from the right to "make" war to the power to "declare" war. The chief executive, the delegates realized, would have to take responsibility for actual military operations.[27]

As the convention neared the end of its debate on the enumerated powers of Congress, Mason raised the issue of federal regulation of the militia. He hoped, he said, "there would be no standing army in time of peace, unless it might be for a few garrisons." Yet Mason recognized the need for some coordination of military forces. Republicans like Elbridge Gerry saw federal regulation as a threat to the security of the states themselves. On a more philosophical level, the militia embodied republican virtue and the duty of the citizen to sacrifice for the common good. The convention elected Mason to another grand committee to draft language establishing an appropriate level of federal control. The convention also grappled in mid-August with the question of national assumption of the states' wartime debts, and it referred that issue to the committee. On 21 August the committee recommended Congress be given the discretion to assume the states' debts, and it recommended Congress be authorized to regulate that part of the militia "as may be employed in the service of the U.S." The states would retain the right to select officers and to train the militia "according to the discipline prescribed by the U. States." The convention skirted the assumption issue, but the militia clause, with a few modifications, became part of the Constitution.[28]

ON TUESDAY, 21 AUGUST, shortly after William Livingston delivered the report of the committee on state debts and the militia, Mason called for a decision on the long-delayed Article VI, Section 12, requiring money bills to begin in the House of Representatives. To Mason's dismay, the convention again postponed debate on the issue, again by a vote of six to five. More substantive was the beginning of debate on a proposed ban, contained in Article VII, Section 4, on a federal tax on exports. Dickinson, Madison, and Wilson spoke against the ban. Mason supported it. He cited "a principle often advanced & in which he concurred, that 'a majority when interested will oppress the minority,'" and he did some quick political arithmetic. The North would outnumber the South in the new House by thirty-six votes to twenty-nine, and by eight states to five in the proposed Senate. A compromise measure to permit duties solely to regulate trade failed seven to three. Attempting unsuccessfully to placate Mason, James Madison and James Wilson proposed permitting a federal tax with a two-thirds vote of both houses of Congress; even it failed. They lost, but the vote had been close, six to five. The Virginia delegation split again. Randolph and Blair supported Mason; Washington sided with Madison.[29]

Luther Martin then suggested that Section 4, to the extent it protected the slave trade, be amended to authorize Congress to tax or prohibit the importation of slaves. It was, he said, "inconsistent with the principle of the revolution and dishonorable to the American character to have such a feature in the Constitution." Martin drew a predictable response from South Carolina. "Religion & humanity had nothing to do with this question," John Rutledge replied. "Interest alone is the governing principle with nations," and South Carolina's interest would not permit it to accept congressionally imposed restrictions on the slave trade. Charles Pinckney warned, "South Carolina can never receive the plan if it prohibits the slave trade." The state did not necessarily want to guarantee itself an unlimited supply of slaves. The South Carolina legislature routinely imposed temporary moratoriums on the importation of slaves when the demand for them faltered, but the state's great planters insisted on maintaining local control over their labor supply. Oliver Ellsworth of Connecticut supported Rutledge and Pinckney. "The morality or wisdom of slavery are considerations belonging to the states themselves," Ellsworth argued. "What enriches a part enriches the whole, and the states are the best judges of their particular interest."[30]

When debate resumed the following day, Roger Sherman continued in a similar vein. His personal disapproval of the slave trade notwithstanding, Sherman argued that an explicit ban would generate more objections to the Constitution. The abolition of slavery had already begun, and he reassured the convention "that the good sense of the several states would probably by degrees compleat it." Mason responded with a bitter attack on the institution of slavery itself, the most bitter of the convention, and one of the convention's most frequently quoted speeches. Mason began by condemning the British government and British merchants for forcing slavery on Virginia, a bit of a revisionist history popular among southern planters. Mason's speech echoed arguments from Jefferson's *Notes on the State of Virginia*. Slavery stifled industrialization and economic modernization, discredited otherwise honorable manual labor, and discouraged the immigration of whites, "who really enrich & strengthen a Country." But Mason saw slavery as more than a failing economic system. He saw it as a moral evil, debasing the souls of slave owners and storing up wrath against the entire nation for a final day of judgment. Slaves, Mason said, "produce the most pernicious effect on manners, every master of slaves is born a petty tyrant. They bring the judgment of heaven on a Country. As nations cannot be rewarded or punished in the next world they must be in this. By an inevitable chain of causes & effects providence punishes national sins, by national calamities."[31]

Charles Pinckney answered Mason: "If slavery be wrong, it is justified by the example of all the world." Few of the delegates attempted to defend the morality of slavery. The other Pinckney at the convention, Charles Cotesworth, said plainly, "S. Carolina & Georgia cannot do without slaves." John Dickinson dismissed southern threats to reject the Constitution if it permitted Congress to regulate the slave trade. James Wilson and John Langdon pointed to the inconsistency in opposing congressional regulation while arguing, as some delegates did, that slavery was a decaying institution and that the states themselves would eventually stop the traffic in human beings. The most strident retort to Mason came from Oliver Ellsworth. "As he had never owned a slave [he] could not judge of the effects of slavery on character," but the Connecticut delegate suggested, "if it was to be considered in a moral light we ought to go farther and free those already in the country." He preferred not to "intermediate."[32]

With the convention divided and tempers short, Gouverneur Morris suggested the slave trade, the taxation of exports, and the number of votes required to pass a navigation act all be referred to a new grand committee. "These things," Morris hoped, "may form a bargain among the Northern & Southern States." Because the clause prohibiting an export tax had already been decided, it could not be recommitted, but the delegates readily agreed to send the other two issues to committee. Madison was chosen to represent Virginia.[33]

The new Committee of Eleven submitted its recommendations on 24 August. Section 4 of Article VII of the Committee of Detail's report would be amended to prohibit Congress from outlawing the slave trade before 1800. A tax "not exceeding the average of duties laid on imports" would be permitted. Section 5, requiring the apportionment of capitation taxes based on population, would be retained. To Mason's dismay, the committee struck Section 6, requiring a two-thirds vote of both houses of Congress to pass navigation acts. Mason believed, as he later told Thomas Jefferson, that South Carolina and Georgia had "struck up a bargain with the 3 N. Engld. States, if they would join to admit slaves for some years, the 2 southernmost states wd join in changing the clause which required $2/3$ of the legislature."[34]

The convention passed the slave trade provision with relatively little debate, even agreeing to Charles Cotesworth Pinckney's motion to extend the trade's constitutional protection from 1800 to 1808. Morris suggested limiting the provision to North Carolina, South Carolina, and Georgia—the states that wanted slaves the most. Mason disagreed, fearing "it should give offence to the people of those States." Morris withdrew the motion. The convention moved next to the question of taxing the slave trade. Mason thought "not to tax, will be the equivalent to a bounty on the importation of slaves." It was a practical observation, but not an inevitable product of Mason's antislavery sentiments. Madison, who also wanted to stop the slave trade, thought "it would be wrong to admit in the Constitution the idea that there could be property in men," which taxing slaves "like merchandise" seemed to imply. Nevertheless, the convention voted to treat slaves like merchandise at a rate "not exceeding ten dollars for each person."[35]

The South Carolinians, or at least Charles Cotesworth Pinckney, doubted the sincerity of those delegates who wanted to restrict the foreign slave trade.[36] Virginia had a surplus of slaves. Foreign competition complicated the efforts of Virginia's slave traders to market that surplus in the Deep South and farther west. Mason's objection to limiting the international trade to North Carolina, South Carolina, and Georgia, as Morris suggested on 25 August, could be seen as an effort to stifle competition. Would not a partial ban on the slave trade have been better than no ban at all? Perhaps not. Mason had already rejected the concept in his speech of 22 August. Maryland and Virginia had prohibited the importation of slaves, and North Carolina discouraged it, he had said then, but "All this would be in vain if S. Carolina & Georgia be at liberty to import." White farmers in the West wanted slaves and "will fill that country with slaves if they can be got thro' S. Carolina & Georgia."[37]

Protecting the interstate slave trade and stopping the foreign traffic would, presumably, encourage the dispersal of the slave population and hasten the day of eventual abolition since the institution would be of declining economic importance in any particular region. Relatively small local populations of African Americans would also make emancipation less threatening to whites. Yet when the vote came on the slave trade compromise, Mason did not speak out against it. According to a letter Madison wrote Washington a few weeks later, Mason apparently agreed to allow the importation of newly enslaved Africans to continue for another twenty years. If so, it was an abrupt change in position, especially since the Virginia delegation voted against the compromise.[38]

What then did Mason think about slavery in 1787? Kate Mason Rowland denied emphatically that he was "an *abolitionist* in the modern sense of the term." From a sympathetic white southerner writing during the heyday of

Jim Crow, the disclaimer seems as predictable as it does unnecessary. Row-land even asserted that Mason "insisted that the rights of his section in this species of property should be protected, and he wished for a guarantee in the Constitution to protect it," which is apparently a reference to Mason's observation at the Richmond convention of 1788 that the Constitution did not explicitly protect the slave owner's investment. In the hands of recent historians, Mason has become an abolitionist—"openly and urgently abo-litionist," no less.[39] Openly perhaps, but not urgently. Mason consistently voiced his disapproval of slavery. His 1787 attack on slavery echoes a simi-lar speech to the Virginia Convention of 1776. His conduct was another matter. Washington freed his slaves in his will. Jefferson freed a few.[40] Mason freed none, either during his lifetime or in his will.

Yet Mason never seemed defensive about his glaring inconsistency. He made no excuses, and he expressed no remorse. In all likelihood, Mason believed, or convinced himself, that he had no options. Mason would have done nothing that might have compromised the financial futures of his nine children. Racial prejudice reinforced economic self-interest. Mason must have shared the fears of Jefferson and countless other whites that whites and free blacks could not live together. Emancipation could not proceed until a way acceptable to whites could be found to segregate the two races. Mason could rise above interest and prejudice, which was a feat in itself, to see the evil of slavery, but he could not rise far enough to move effectively against it.

The poll tax provision passed easily, but the convention postponed con-sideration of navigation acts as Mason and the rest of the delegates turned their attention to other issues. Mason, who owned continental paper him-self, objected at the start of the 25 August session to a requirement that the new government assume the debts of the old. Mason feared the wording of the provision would require the national government to pay off existing debt at face value and provide a windfall to speculators who had purchased the securities at severely deflated prices. The issue would convulse the poli-tics of the early republic far more than most of the issues that had divided the convention. A motion by Edmund Randolph simply to recognize the continuing validity of continental securities passed ten to one.[41]

Relatively minor issues remained to be decided as the convention wound down. Mason was appointed to another grand committee; it was asked to draft language ensuring that the collection of customs duties would not discriminate among ports. The committee's report, filed 28 August, was tabled. Mason and Madison worked together to add the phrase "and will to the best of my judgment and power preserve protect and defend the Constitution of the United States" to the president's oath of office. They failed in an effort to prevent Congress from raising the salaries of sitting Supreme Court justices; Mason undoubtedly saw the increases as a way for the legislature to influence the court. Mason and Madison clashed over allowing the states to enforce embargoes or tax imports with the consent of Congress. Madison favored an absolute ban. Mason won both votes. He also objected to an absolute ban on a state's power to impair contracts, and he won a temporary concession from the convention: the contract clause was shelved in favor of a ban on bills of attainder and ex post facto laws.[42]

Mason, Elbridge Gerry, Luther Martin, Charles Pinckney, and a handful of other delegates began meeting in mid-August to plan a strategy to derail the committee recommendation that the two-thirds requirement for navigation acts be dropped. When the proposal to delete Section 6 of Article VII of the Committee of Detail report reached the floor of the convention on 29 August, Pinckney proposed an alternative amendment that would have required a two-thirds vote for all commercial regulations. Rather than trying to win constitutional protection for the South's unique interests, the dissenters hit upon a clever strategy. Appealing to the distinctive characteristics of each region, Mason and his compatriots would attempt to convince a majority of the states that they were all potentially endangered minorities. New England, Pinckney said, was interested in coastal fisheries and the West Indian trade; New York in free trade; the other middle states in wheat and flour; Maryland, Virginia, and North Carolina in tobacco; and South Carolina and Georgia in rice and indigo. Martin seconded Pinckney's motion, and Hugh Williamson and Mason spoke in its support. "The Southern states are the minority in both houses," Mason warned. "Is it to be expected that they will deliver themselves bound hand & foot to the Eastern states?"[43]

But Mason could not convince all of his fellow southerners that the rule of a simple majority in matters of economic regulation presented a threat to southern interests. The rest of the South Carolina delegates—Charles Cotesworth Pinckney, Pierce Butler, and John Rutledge—all spoke against Charles Pinckney's motion, and James Madison offered a long rebuttal. Permitting a minority to thwart economic legislation would invite foreign intervention in Congress, and the system of checks and balances being written into the Constitution made the two-thirds requirement unnecessary. If, Madison argued, Congress did decide to encourage American shipping through a navigation act, a national maritime industry would be a nursery for the officers and crew of a new American navy, and a strong navy would benefit southern exports. Madison differed from Mason most fundamentally in his vision of the likely sectional alliances in the new republic. Madison believed, as did others, that the South and West, and perhaps Connecticut and New Jersey, would form a natural agricultural majority. Mason, by contrast, seemed more fearful that the South's commitment to slavery might make it a discrete minority.[44]

Pinckney's motion failed by a vote of seven to four, winning support only from Maryland, Virginia, North Carolina, and Georgia. The committee recommendation to delete the two-thirds rule completely then passed without dissent. Finally, Pierce Butler introduced an amendment requiring the return of fugitive slaves, and it too passed unanimously. Some historians have seen the fugitive slave clause as part of the bargain that secured South Carolina's support for striking the two-thirds rule, but it could not have been a very hard fought part. Few of the delegates wanted to encourage runaway slaves.[45]

Much has been written about what might be called the convention's second Great Compromise, which extended the slave trade and repealed the two-thirds rule, but the details of the transaction remain murky. Why, for example, did South Carolina agree to an apparent "compromise" that represented a substantial retreat from the Committee of Detail's report, which protected the slave trade indefinitely and required a two-thirds majority to regulate navigation? The South Carolinians presumably realized, no doubt correctly, that the full convention would not agree to an arrangement so favorable to the South. The evidence suggests a deal between Sherman of Connecticut and Rutledge of South Carolina. Rutledge's biographer claims, without citing his sources, that a deal was made as early as 30 June.[46] If it was, Sherman did not have the Connecticut delegation in line; it voted against referring the two-thirds issue to the Committee of Eleven, which was a critical step in reaching the final agreement.[47]

It seems more logical, and it is consistent with the testimony of Luther Martin, who was on the committee, to conclude that the Sherman-Rutledge deal took shape in the committee itself.[48] Even at that stage the terms of the agreement are not obvious today, and they apparently remained subject to change. Forrest McDonald has gone so far as to argue that South Carolina's real concession and Sherman's real objective was the Palmetto State's support for federal jurisdiction over Connecticut's western lands claims. Mason and his contemporaries had a different impression.[49] More likely than the McDonald thesis is the possibility that the principals themselves did not have a final agreement and that a bargain evolved over time. Note, for example, the decision on the convention floor to extend the life of the slave trade for eight years beyond the 1800 deadline recommended by the Committee of Eleven. Presumably Georgia, South Carolina's junior partner in the bargain, supported the compromise in committee, but Georgia voted for Charles Pinckney's effort to upset the deal by proposing a two-thirds requirement for all commercial regulations. Georgia's vote was not critical in the full convention, and ironically neither was South Carolina's. Pinckney's motion lost by a three-state margin.

Why then would New England make concessions on the slave trade that failed to deliver one state on a crucial vote and which delivered another state that New England did not need? To begin with, most of the New Englanders seemed to be morally indifferent to slavery and saw the slave trade as a bargaining chip.[50] For antislavery delegates, ending the slave trade in 1800 or even 1808 represented progress over the perpetual slave trade envisioned by the Committee of Detail. The New Englanders may not have wanted to win the navigation issue on a purely sectional vote; close tallies had a way of coming undone. They may have expected the vote on the two-thirds requirement to have been closer than it was. Connecticut and its New England allies on the one hand and South Carolina and Georgia on the other apparently swapped other concessions, especially the odd Article V of the final draft of the Constitution. It put two provisions beyond the reach of future amendments: the equality of the states in the Senate and the maintenance of the slave trade for twenty years.[51]

To summarize, Sherman and a majority of the South Carolina delegation reached some accommodation on the slave trade and navigation laws, but Mason probably overstated the case when he told Jefferson that New England, South Carolina, and Georgia had conspired to revise "the great principles of the constn . . . in the last days of the Convention." The events of the third week in August, nevertheless, constituted a crushing blow to George Mason. By sizable majorities the convention had rejected one provision that he considered essential to the economic security of Virginia while accepting one he considered morally indefensible.[52] Yet Mason had not, even at the end of August, given up completely on the Constitution.

ONE OF THE CONVENTION'S most dramatic moments came on Friday, 31 August, when Article XXII of the Committee of Detail report reached the floor. It provided that the Constitution, if approved by Congress, would be

sent to the states for consideration by conventions called by the state legislatures. After the convention deleted the requirement for express, congressional "approbation," Elbridge Gerry moved to postpone further debate
on Article XXII. Mason seconded the motion. He would "sooner chop off
his right hand than put it to the Constitution as it now stands. He wished
to see some points not yet decided, before being compelled to give a final
opinion on this article. Should these points be improperly settled, his wish
would then be to bring the whole subject before another general Convention." Mason did not elaborate, and the motion failed, but he set out a list
of objections in a memorandum to the Maryland delegation that he wrote
the same day. His reservations included the lack of an independent council
of state, the absence of a two-thirds requirement for navigation laws, the
prospect of a "permanent" federal revenue, the Senate's discretion over appropriations bills, the president's eligibility for reelection, and a half dozen
other objections.[53]

Despite his obvious frustration, Mason refused to try every available tac-
tic to delay or defeat the Constitution. Seemingly still convinced the document could be salvaged, Mason, at the end of August was no more a threat
to the Constitution than some of its staunchest promoters. Alexander Hamilton, for example, had supported the requirement for explicit congressional
approval of the new charter. As one historian has observed, congressional
ratification could not be assumed; Hamilton's plan "might have destroyed
the new government in the womb." On 31 August, before taking up Gerry's
motion—and before Mason's threat to cut off a hand—the delegates had
wrangled over the number of states to be required for ratification, an issue
the Committee of Detail had avoided. Charles Carroll and Luther Martin
lost overwhelmingly on a motion to require unanimous consent. Madison
and Wilson got nowhere with a proposal to require "a majority both of the
people and of the States." Roger Sherman and Jonathan Dayton proposed
ten states and got four votes. Mason spoke in favor of a lower hurdle: nine
states, which would be "familiar to the people" since nine states "had been
required in all great cases under the Confederation." The nine-state requirement passed by a vote of eight to three.[54]

Later in the day, the convention appointed a new Committee of Eleven
to consider, among other items, what James Wilson called "in truth the
most difficult of all [the questions] on which we have to decide," a process
for electing the president. David Brearly, the chief justice of the New Jersey
Supreme Court, reported for the committee on 4 September. The Brearly
committee recommended that an electoral college be established in which

each elector would cast two votes, at least one of which would be for a candidate from another state. If no candidate received a majority of the electoral votes, the Senate would select from among the top five vote getters. The first runner-up would become vice president. The ensuing debate created strange bedfellows. Mason agreed with Gouverneur Morris that, because the electors would vote in their home states, "the danger of cabal and corruption" had been greatly reduced. But Mason feared "that nineteen times in twenty the president would be chosen by the Senate." In an era before national political parties or an effective national media, most of the delegates apparently assumed that few candidates would ever win a majority in the electoral college. A national election seemed likely to produce a stalemate among several regional candidates. Mason feared collusion between the Senate and a presidential candidate, and he distrusted the Senate. He would, he said, "prefer the Government of Prussia to one which put all power into the hands of seven or eight men, and fix an Aristocracy, worse than absolute monarchy." Mason suggested making a plurality of electoral votes sufficient for victory, as did Alexander Hamilton, but the convention disagreed. An alternative proposal by Mason to restrict the Senate's discretion by limiting its choice to the top three candidates won no support.[55]

In a speech given the next day, James Wilson suggested the House of Representatives select the president when no candidate received a majority in the electoral college. Madison objected, arguing that the large states would be encouraged to run stronger candidates—in other words, candidates who could appeal to the small states that would dominate the Senate—if the Senate was likely to decide the election. In truth, the obstacle to a compromise was another agreement that had been reached in committee. The large states had agreed in Brearly's committee to allow the Senate to resolve electoral college stalemates if the House of Representatives could retain the exclusive right to originate money bills.[56]

On 6 September, after three days of deliberations, the delegates, Mason included, reached a near consensus. Elbridge Gerry began the day's debate by reviving the idea that the House, not the Senate, select the president when no candidate received an electoral college majority. Roger Sherman and Hugh Williamson suggested that if elections went to the House, each state should be given one vote. Mason liked the suggestion "as lessening the aristocratic influence of the Senate." At the same time, it preserved the influence of the small states, and it passed with only Delaware dissenting. A few details remained. Madison observed that since a majority of House members constituted a quorum, Virginia and Pennsylvania could elect the president if they were the only states present. Rufus King suggested raising the quorum requirement to two-thirds of the states. Mason agreed and the convention accepted King's amendment.[57]

Mason must have been encouraged by the debate over the presidency, which included a definition of the grounds for impeachment. Failing to persuade the convention to make "Maladministration" a basis for removal from office, Mason next suggested "high crimes and misdemeanours" as an alternative. Borrowed from English law, the phrase went into the Constitution. Despite opposition from Washington, Madison, and Blair, and the other large-state delegations, Mason helped pass a resolution reducing the number of votes needed to override a presidential veto from three-quarters of both houses to two-thirds. Despite his mounting reservations about the direction of the convention, Mason was still winning critical votes and hearing unlikely allies articulate some of his own concerns. The convention finally agreed that revenue measures would originate in the House. During the debate over the presidential election process, James Wilson confessed he considered the draft constitution "as having a dangerous tendency to aristocracy; as throwing a dangerous power into the hands of the Senate." The president "cannot even appoint a tide-waiter without the Senate." As late as 12 September, even Alexander Hamilton, a self-confessed "friend to a vigorous Government," worried openly, as did Mason, about collusion between the president and the Senate. Hamilton feared, as did Mason, "that the House of Representatives was on so narrow a scale as to be really dangerous, and to warrant a jealousy in the people for their liberties." It has been suggested that the convention removed the Senate from a role in selecting the president in an effort to appease Mason and an emerging bloc of Anti-Federalist obstructionists. At least equally plausible is the conclusion that on broad issues of republican theory, especially in their commitment to independent representative assemblies and in their fear of an executive-legislative cabal, Mason and most of his colleagues shared similar views.[58]

They did not, however, share his concerns for sectional minorities in general or for Virginia in particular. Important issues remained to be decided, but after a summer in Philadelphia, the convention was moving quickly toward its end, leaving Mason little time in which to influence the other delegates. On 5 September Brearly's Committee of Eleven reported a new version of the origination clause: revenue measures would begin in the House of Representatives but be subject to amendment in the Senate. A critical issue to Mason, the convention postponed consideration of it. Nevertheless, on 8 September the convention named a Committee of Style—consisting of

Johnson, Hamilton, Morris, Madison, and King—to put the Constitution in near final form.[59]

Even though he had some formidable allies, Mason could not win majority support for a council of state, which he saw as another mechanism to protect sectional interests. He raised the issue again on 7 September in an unlikely context—during debate over the proposal to make the vice president the ex officio president of the Senate. Gerry and Mason believed the proposal violated the principle of separation of powers. Gerry wanted no vice president at all. Mason took the "occasion to express his dislike of any reference whatever of the power to make appointments to either branch of the legislature." He preferred referring appointments to a "privy council" chosen by the Senate and consisting of two members from the North, two from the middle states, and two from the South. A council would, he argued, "save the expense of constant sessions of the Senate." Constant sessions, moreover, would allow the Senate to expand its own influence. Mason failed to make the obvious point: his council would give each section a veto over presidential appointments. Instead he appealed to history. In rejecting a council to the president, "we were about to try an experiment on which the most despotic governments had never ventured—the Grand Signor himself had his Divan." James Wilson expressed support for a purely advisory council; Franklin, Dickinson, and Madison supported Mason without reservations, but his motion lost badly, going down to defeat by a vote of eight to three. Even Virginia opposed it, one of the few times in which Mason and Madison found themselves together on the losing side within their delegation.[60]

ON 10 SEPTEMBER Edmund Randolph, leveling a long bill of particulars against the emerging Constitution, moved that the states be given the opportunity to propose amendments to the document in a second convention. Still trying to forge a constitution he could accept, Mason managed to have Randolph's motion tabled for a few days to see "what steps might be taken" to alleviate Randolph's objections. Undoubtedly, Mason hoped the threat of a second convention could be used to force further concessions.[61] Besides the ill-fated executive council, Mason would make two other major efforts to protect minority rights in the waning days of the convention: a temporary requirement of a two-thirds vote in both houses of Congress to pass any commercial regulations and the addition to the Constitution of a bill of rights. Like the council, both would fail.

After a rare Tuesday recess, during which it waited for the Committee of Style to complete its work, the convention, on Wednesday, 12 September, took up the committee's report. As soon as William Johnson, chair of the committee, had "reported a digest of the plan," Hugh Williamson moved that a two-thirds vote of each house, as opposed to the three-fourths required in the report, be sufficient to override a presidential veto. The committee recommendation conflicted with an earlier vote, and Mason joined with Sherman, Gerry, and Charles Pinckney to pass Williamson's motion over the objections of Morris, Hamilton, and Madison. Williamson next proposed that some provision be made for ensuring the right to a jury trial in civil cases. Nathaniel Gorham replied that the issue might best be left to the legislatures; it would be difficult for the convention to distinguish between cases at law, which required a jury, and cases in equity, which did not. Gerry supported Williamson, urging "the necessity of juries to guard agst. corrupt Judges."[62]

Mason spoke next. He conceded the difficulty of specifying when juries should be required, but he thought a "general principle laid down on this and some other points would be sufficient." And he added, "He wished the plan had been prefaced with a Bill of Rights, & would second a Motion if made for the purpose—It would give great quiet to the people; and with the aid of the state declarations, a bill might be prepared in a few hours."[63]

Gerry so moved, and Mason seconded the motion. Only Roger Sherman spoke against it, briefly making two points. First, the state declarations of rights remained in force and were sufficient to protect the liberties of the people. Second, the "Legislature may be safely trusted" to determine when jury trials were proper. Mason responded with the observation that the "Laws of the U.S. are to be paramount to State Bills of Rights." With no more debate, the convention defeated Gerry's motion by a vote of ten states to none. Massachusetts abstained.[64]

Conventional wisdom, with good reason, has long held the omission of a bill of rights to have been the convention's greatest political blunder. It handed the Anti-Federalists a popular argument against the Constitution, and it made ratification much more difficult than it otherwise would have been. "Mason's point that a bill of rights would quiet the fears of the people," Leonard Levy has written, "was unanswerable." Madison considered it a "fatal objection" as far as Mason was concerned. Federalists later argued that because the new national government was a government of delegated powers and could do only what it was expressly authorized to do, specific limitations on its powers were unnecessary. The argument was a triumph of bad logic over common sense. The Pinckney Plan, which had been referred to the Committee of Detail, had contained a rudimentary bill of rights. It had been largely ignored, but the delegates had repeatedly seen the need to insert other safeguards into the text of the Constitution. The Committee of Style report contained numerous proposals protecting civil liberties, including freedom of speech and debate in Congress, a requirement that a conviction for treason rest on the testimony of at least two witnesses, bans on bills of attainder and ex post facto laws, a right to a jury trial and a writ of habeas corpus in criminal cases, a guarantee that citizens of all states would enjoy the same privileges and immunities, and a prohibition on religious tests for national office. In reality, the omission of a bill of rights may have owed as much to the delegates' desire to go home as it did to constitutional theory. Mason undoubtedly could have provided a draft within a matter of hours; how long it would have taken the convention to agree on a draft is another matter. Madison wrote later that a "number of little circumstances arising in part from impatience which prevailed towards the close of business conspired to whet" Mason's "acrimony."[65]

We do not know why Mason waited until near the end of the convention to propose that the Constitution include a bill of rights. Was he laying the foundation for a campaign against ratification? Could a charter of the people's liberties have been an afterthought for the celebrated author of the Virginia Declaration of Rights? It might have been; until Mason raised the issue on 12 September, no one else appears to have given it much thought. Richard Henry Lee said later that the rights of the people were so well understood that it was "not uncommon for the ablest men" to assume they did not need to be "constantly kept in view . . . in bills of rights."[66]

Posterity, of course, has its own priorities. However elemental the Bill of Rights may seem to American democracy in retrospect, Mason and the convention spent more time debating a state's right to tax exports. Immediately after the convention rejected his offer to draft a bill of rights, Mason moved to ensure a state's right to levy export duties to finance its inspections of outgoing goods. Mason wanted to protect Virginia's tobacco inspection program, and he gave a longer speech in defense of state export fees than he did in support of a bill of rights. He also provoked more discussion. Debate over the export duties continued intermittently over four days until the convention agreed to permit state duties if they were approved by Congress and if the "nett" proceeds went to the national treasury.[67]

Mason, moreover, had his own understanding of civil liberties, which did not preclude state regulation of behavior that threatened republican virtue.

The day after volunteering to draft a federal bill of rights, Mason made another plea for sumptuary legislation, and on 14 September he moved to strike the Constitution's ban on ex post facto laws. The convention made Mason chair of a committee to draft enabling language for a sumptuary law, but the convention adjourned before the committee could submit a report. The delegates rejected Mason's effort to strike the ex post facto ban.[68]

Mason remained active to the end of the convention, but by its last week, he had too many objections to be listed among the Constitution's likely supporters. He found himself reduced to arguing about trivia, with little hope of prevailing on major issues. He and Gerry lost in an attempt to require the House of Representatives to publish a record of all its proceedings. He and Madison lost in an attempt to empower Congress to charter canal companies, and the convention rebuffed Mason's suggestion to insert a warning "against the dangers of standing armies in time of peace" into the Constitution. His motion to require annual publication of public expenditures failed, but the convention did agree they should be published "from time to time."[69] On Saturday, 15 September, the convention's last day of substantive business, he lost a debate over allowing states to collect duties for harbor improvement, which he supported, and he lost again in a debate over the president's power to pardon treason, which he opposed. Mason and others complained that the process of constitutional amendment was too cumbersome; he won a minor victory when the delegates decided to allow two-thirds of the states to call a convention for purposes of considering amendments.[70]

Only two major votes remained. Toward the end of the debate on Saturday, Mason moved that "no law in the nature of a navigation act be passed before the year 1808, without the consent of 2/3 of each branch of the legislature." Otherwise, "a few rich merchants in Philada N. York & Boston . . . [would] monopolize the Staples of the Southern States & reduce their value perhaps 50 per ct." It was not an unreasonable proposal—the foreign slave trade had received comparable protection—but it failed seven to three with one abstention. Edmund Randolph moved immediately that the state conventions be allowed to submit proposed amendments to a second federal convention. Mason seconded the motion. The people, he argued, had taken no part in framing the Constitution as it now stood. A second convention could take account of their sentiments. "It was improper to say to the people, take this or nothing. As the Constitution now stands, he could neither give it his support or vote in Virginia; and he could not sign here what he could not support there. With the expedient of another convention as proposed, he could sign."[71]

Gerry supported the motion with his own list of objections, most of which reflected either the parochialism—"Massachusetts has not a due share of Representatives allotted to her"—or the paranoia—"The vice president being made head of the Senate"—that would do so much to discredit the Anti-Federalist cause. Only the irrepressible Charles Pinckney spoke against a second convention, which is strong evidence the more sagacious delegates knew further debate was not needed. No state voted for Randolph's motion.[72]

When the convention reconvened on Monday, 17 September, James Wilson read a long, eloquent speech by Benjamin Franklin calling on the recalcitrant delegates to sign the Constitution and to at least acknowledge their states', if not their own, approbation. Randolph replied: his refusal to sign "might be the most awful [decision] of his life, but it was dictated by his conscience." Gerry replied as well; he feared the Constitution would only aggravate the division in Massachusetts between "two parties, one devoted to democracy, the worst of all political evils, the other as violent in the opposite extreme." For once, Mason was silent. In light of the investment he had made in the Constitution and what he could imagine of the fight that lay ahead, it must have been a glum and bitter silence. After the convention decided to entrust its journal and papers with George Washington, the members proceeded to sign the document. As the last delegates signed, Franklin made his famous observation: of the sun painted on the back of the president's chair, "I have the happiness to know . . . is a rising and not a setting sun." James Madison then made his last notes: "The Constitution being signed by all the members except Mr. Randolph, Mr. Mason, and Mr. Gerry, who declined giving it the sanction of their names, the Convention dissolved itself by an Adjournment sine die."[73]

ON 28 SEPTEMBER 1787 George Mason submitted his expense account for service at the Constitutional Convention; it consisted of 138 days work from 13 May to 27 September, travel time included, and it totaled £248, 8 shillings.[74] What did the state of Virginia receive for its investment?

By any measure, Mason must rank among the most influential delegates at the convention. Despite James Madison's sobriquet as the "Father of the Constitution," neither Madison nor any other single delegate dominated the proceedings in Philadelphia. Mason was one of perhaps a dozen, among the fifty-five delegates, who made a substantial impact on the final text of the document. Only four delegates—Madison, Gouverneur Morris, James Wilson, and Roger Sherman—spoke more frequently than did

Mason. Madison's principal biographer placed Mason alongside Madison, Wilson, Benjamin Franklin, Rufus King, William Paterson, and Edmund Randolph in the first tier of the convention's leadership. If nothing else, Mason and the other future Anti-Federalists in Philadelphia, along with Franklin, helped check the aristocratic tendencies of men like Morris and Alexander Hamilton.[75]

More specifically, Mason left his fingerprints on issues great and small. He pushed successfully for payment of members of Congress by the national government, reducing their economic dependence on the states. He led the fight for citizenship requirements for senators and representatives. Although he was not fully satisfied with the final results, the constitutional provisions requiring revenue measures to begin in the House and allowing Congress to prohibit the slave trade after 1808 resulted in part from Mason's efforts. Likewise, Mason wanted tighter restrictions on the eligibility of lawmakers to accept positions in the executive branch, and he helped defeat efforts by Alexander Hamilton, James Wilson, and Gouverneur Morris to leave the practice unregulated. He helped place the Great Compromise before the convention even if he could not persuade Virginia to support it. He provided critical support to the cause of a popularly elected House and formidable opposition to the proposal for a congressional veto over all state laws. His influence is also seen in the Constitution's relatively liberal suffrage requirements, in the role given to the House in resolving Electoral College stalemates, and in the procedures for overriding a presidential veto. When the convention was floundering over how many states would be required to ratify the Constitution before it could take effect, Mason spoke up for nine, and the delegates quickly agreed. He cast the critical vote to ban a federal tax on exports, carrying the Virginia delegation with him by a vote of three to two and thereby prevailing on the convention floor by a vote of six to five. And who knows when, or if, a bill of rights would have eventually been added to the Constitution if Mason had not raised the issue?[76]

Having accomplished so much, why then did Mason refuse to sign the Constitution? All his objections cannot be given equal weight. A few of the battles he lost in Philadelphia were never refought. At the same time, he raised some objections for the first time after the convention had adjourned. Anti-Federalists complained incessantly, for example, that Congress would abuse its power to regulate "the time, manner, and place of elections," but congressional oversight had not been an issue in the convention.[77] Mason can be made to appear a hero or a crank depending on which objections receive the most attention. The heroic Mason ought not to be overdone; the absence of a bill of rights worried Mason less than his most enthusiastic admirers might want to admit. On the other hand, despite a strange fetish for ex post facto legislation, Mason was no crank. Mason distrusted the Senate as an incubus of aristocratic influence, he believed too much power had been conferred on the president, and he lamented the absence of some kind of advisory council to serve as an independent check on the executive. As time went on, Mason seemed to regret more and more the continuation of the slave trade, if only for another generation. He complained, however, most consistently about Congress's ability to pass navigation acts by a simple majority. Madison thought it was Mason's principal complaint, and Madison was in a position to know.[78]

Economics played a large part in Mason's opposition to the Constitution, but in a more obvious sense than Charles Beard suggested. Mason opposed ratification despite holding debt likely to appreciate under a stronger central government. Nor did his western land holdings appear to have influenced his position on the Constitution, although a connection can be made between his land speculation and his support for admitting new states into the Union on the same footing as the original thirteen. One historian of the convention has gone so far as to write that, of the critics of the Constitution, "Mason appears as the most disinterested, [and the] purest in his motives."[79] Yet the sincerity of his republicanism did not blind him to the economic interests of his class and region. His hostility to paper money, which was less intense than that of the convention as a whole, was consistent with his position as a creditor. His opposition to the foreign slave trade, which was more intense than that of the convention as a whole, was consistent with his position as a representative of a state with a surplus of slaves. His opposition to navigation laws reflected the self-interests of planters who stood to benefit from vigorous competition for their carrying trade.

Republicanism, more than states' rights, provided the rationale for Mason's opposition. Mason's support for a popularly elected House of Representatives, with the exclusive power to initiate money bills, illustrates his willingness to elevate the rights of the people, and hence the power of the central government, over the rights of the states. As had many revolutionary-era leaders, Mason had come to fear the tyranny of majorities, especially local majorities manipulated by demagogues. The delegates in Philadelphia saw a stronger national government as an antidote for a new, democratic form of corruption. Mason opposed the Constitution not because he objected to any consolidation of political power, but because the document did too little to protect the minority closest to his own heart—Virginia's planters. Mason stands out among his colleagues for his prescient recognition that the South was likely to remain a minority, mainly because of its dependence on slavery and plantation agriculture, within the new Union. Mason's advocacy of a regionally selected executive or council of state and his support for a two-thirds requirement for navigation laws were obviously intended to protect southern interests. Indeed, his solicitude for minority rights provides the common thread between Mason's commitment to the two-thirds rule and his proposal for a bill of rights. Mason ultimately convinced himself that the Constitution combined the worst features of two different political worlds. The presidency, the Senate, and the federal courts would replicate the corruption of the old regime. At the same time, the democratic elements of the new system, he feared, would not protect legitimate minority and individual rights.[80]

Chapter Nine

That Paper on the Table

GEORGE MASON had left Philadelphia, James Madison reported, "in an exceeding ill humor." Mason believed the Constitutional Convention, in a rush to conclude its work, had given his objections too little attention. The trip home did nothing to improve his mood. Mason enjoyed the company of his traveling companion, the Maryland delegate James McHenry, but as they neared Baltimore, their carriage overturned. Mason's injuries required medical attention, which only made matters worse. Local doctors bled him. By October Mason was home and recovering, although he complained his neck and head were "at times still uneasy."[1] His humor, by contrast, only grew worse. Mason soon faced one of the busiest legislative sessions of his career, and one that played out against the background of politics high and petty—the ongoing debate over the ratification of the Constitution and his long-standing feud with the town of Alexandria. Mason would run for a seat in the Virginia ratifying convention and encounter unprecedented opposition from his Fairfax County neighbors. For the first time in his career, Mason found himself the frequent target of public criticism. The attacks only increased his hostility to the Constitution. Yet even as his hand could be seen in the document he so strenuously opposed, he would also leave his mark on the Virginia Convention.

CONGRESS, THEN SITTING in New York City, took up the proposed Constitution on 20 September 1787. The Federalists, as the advocates of ratification would soon be called, wanted to send the Constitution to the states with a recommendation that it be approved. Richard Henry Lee and a few other lawmakers objected. Because Article 13 of the Articles of Confederation required the consent of all thirteen states to amend the Articles, Lee did not believe Congress could endorse a constitutional revolution dependent on the votes of only nine states. As a compromise, Congress agreed to recommend unanimously that the states simply consider ratifica-tion, thereby giving the appearance, without the substance, of widespread support for a new national government.

By a letter dated 1 October, Lee advised Mason of the proceedings in Congress. Lee shared Mason's concerns about the Constitution's aristocratic features and its failure to protect southern interests. "The greatness of the powers given, & the multitude of Places to be created, produces a coalition of Monarchy Men, Military Men, Aristocrates, and Drones whose noise, impudence & zeal exceeds all belief—whilst the commercial plunder of the South stimulates the rapacious Trader." As did Mason, Lee found in the Constitution "many excellent Regulations," and he believed "if it could be reasonably amended [it] would be a fine system." Lee urged Mason to con-tact sympathetic acquaintances in South Carolina and Maryland to develop a set of amendments southern Anti-Federalists could support, and he sent Mason some draft amendments of his own. Lee's amendments included pro-visions to protect civil liberties—among them freedom of religion, freedom of the press, and the right to trial by jury—and proposed structural changes to the new government. Lee wanted to add a council of state, restrict the powers of the Senate, abolish the vice presidency, increase the size of the House of Representatives, and require more than a simple majority to adopt a "Monopoly of Trade."[2]

If Lee's fears and remedies paralleled Mason's, it seems certain that Lee had seen a copy of "Objections to this Constitution of Government," a draft that Mason had begun before he left Philadelphia.[3] Mason had warned Lee that the Federalists would attempt to rush the Constitution through Congress; Mason's "Objections" apparently inspired Lee's amendments. George Washington told James Madison that "the political tenets" of Lee and Mason were "always in unison." Washington believed Mason "gives the tone" to the pair because Mason "will receive it from no one." In ad-dition to corresponding with Lee, Mason had also met with Pennsylvania Anti-Federalists to try to agree on a coordinated strategy for the ratification debate.[4]

The early draft of the "Objections" first circulated privately, but it was published, without Mason's consent, by a Philadelphia printer early in Oc-tober. Madison complained that Mason's "Objections" went well beyond the reservations he had expressed on the floor of the convention, but mainly Mason's tone had changed. The "Objections" found no redeeming qualities in the Constitution and gave no indication that Mason himself wanted to strengthen the national government. Mason lamented the lack of a bill of rights or a council of state, the small size of the House of Representatives, and the broad powers of the Senate. The vice presidency "dangerously" blended legislative and executive powers, and Mason objected to giving the president unlimited power to pardon treason. Litigation in the federal courts, he warned, would be "tedious, intricate and expensive," thus "enabling the rich to oppress and ruin the poor." The longest paragraph in the "Objections" was a plea for a two-thirds majority to adopt commercial regulations. Mason raised at least one new issue: the "necessary and proper clause" would allow Congress to grant monopolies, invent new crimes, inflict cruel and unusual punishments, and generally "extend their powers as far as they think proper." Before closing with a brief objection to the continuation of the foreign slave trade for another twenty years, Mason offered a dire prophecy of the nation's future under the new Constitution: "This government will set out a moderate aristocracy: it is at present impossible to foresee whether it will, in its operation, produce a monarchy, or a corrupt, tyrannical aristocracy; it will probably vibrate some years between the two, and then terminate in the one or the other."[5]

Mason sent copies of his "Objections" to Anti-Federalist leaders in New York and New Hampshire and to his neighbor George Washington. In his correspondence with Washington, Mason minimized the significance of his "Objections" and promised his support, as a member of the House of Delegates, for transmitting the Constitution to a popular convention. At the same time, Mason's "Objections" were one of the two or three most influential pieces of Anti-Federalist writing produced during the ratification struggle. Mason's opening line— "There is no Declaration of Rights" —gave the Anti-Federalists their most effective slogan. Succinct and to the point, the "Objections" required little space in a newspaper and were widely reprinted.[6]

Mason readily provided copies of his "Objections" for local distribution, but he hesitated to publish them in a Virginia paper. His reluctance drew criticism from Federalists spoiling for a newspaper debate. Writing Elbridge Gerry in mid-October, Mason said that his original draft had been "written in a hurry, & very incorrect." Mason had made a few changes in the version sent to Washington, suggesting for example that the chair of the council of state might serve as president should the chief executive be incapacitated. Mason presumably considered his early draft to be a preliminary effort not ready for the newspapers. He may have wanted to solicit the views of some of his regular correspondents before releasing the "Objections" to ordinary Virginia voters. One Anti-Federalist, writing in the *Virginia Journal* as

Philanthropos, defended Mason: as a delegate to the Philadelphia Convention, Mason was properly restricting his public comments until he could make a formal report to the legislature that had appointed him.[7]

Ironically, it was a Federalist, Tobias Lear, who was responsible for the first publication in Virginia of Mason's "Objections." Lear, who was Washington's secretary, disliked Mason, and he wanted the "Objections" published so he could rebut them more effectively. Publication also allowed the Federalists to point out that northern papers, when they printed Mason's comments, generally deleted his argument for a two-thirds majority for commercial regulations. They could gloat over the exposure of Anti-Federalist duplicity and divisions within Anti-Federalist ranks. Writing as Brutus, allegedly without Washington's knowledge, Lear also criticized Mason for allowing himself to be identified as the author of the "Objections." Eighteenth-century etiquette demanded that political tracts be published under pseudonyms so the author's reputation would not prejudice debate over the substance of the work. Whatever the merits of the "Objections," no one questioned Mason's authorship. Some of his criticisms of the Constitution "are raised on so slender a foundation as would render it doubtful whether they were the production of *Col. Mason's* abilities," Brutus wrote, "if an incontestable evidence of their being so could not be adduced."[8]

As the Brutus essays would suggest, Mason's public opposition to the Constitution made him a frequent target of Federalist opprobrium. At a public rally in Philadelphia on 6 October, James Wilson pointedly refuted Mason's "Objections." The most widely circulated rebuttal came from another delegate, Oliver Ellsworth of Connecticut. In his *Landholder Essays*, Ellsworth excoriated the Anti-Federalist leadership, in particular Mason and Richard Henry Lee. Ellsworth blamed opposition to the Constitution on the Lees' hatred of George Washington—tension between the Lee family and Washington went back to the early days of the Revolution when there were widespread doubts about Washington's military competence—and on what Ellsworth called "the madness of Mason." If Washington had not endorsed the Constitution, Lee would have embraced it, Ellsworth claimed, "and Col. Mason would have vented his rage against his own negroes and to the winds." Ellsworth chided Mason for raising objections he had not pressed on the convention floor, and he exploited, for northern readers, Mason's fears of an American navigation act: "Mr. Mason would prefer the subjects of every foreign power to the subjects of the United States who live in New-England."[9]

The public debate produced a private rancor. Tobias Lear believed Mason's opposition to the Constitution had cost him "much of his popularity" in the predominantly Federalist Northern Neck. Lear thought Mason "piqued" that he had not been able to dominate the Constitutional Convention the way he had influenced "those publick bodies where he has acted heretofore." Tench Coxe believed Mason's "conduct appears to be resented." The debate permanently ruptured his ambiguous relationship with Mount Vernon. Washington believed Mason had "rendered himself obnoxious in Philadelphia by the pains he took to disseminate his objections." Washington arranged for the publication in the Alexandria and Richmond papers of James Wilson's rejoinder to Mason. The general dismissed Mason's "Objections" as an effort to incite needless fears among the people, and he privately ridiculed Mason's hope that the northern and middle states would agree to give the South a veto over commercial regulations.[10]

Hostility in Fairfax County to Mason's refusal to sign the Constitution quickly assumed a mythic quality. According to a widely reprinted newspaper account, when Mason reached Alexandria on his way from Philadelphia to Gunston Hall, town officials warned him to leave within the hour. His Anti-Federalism had provoked such popular animosity that they could not guarantee his physical safety. The story seems implausible, and in November 1787 the *Massachusetts Gazette*, which had helped spread the tale, printed a retraction. By other, more creditable accounts, Mason had the town crier assemble a crowd to hear an impromptu report on the convention, and Mason received a peaceful, if unsympathetic, hearing.[11]

The abuse directed toward Mason reflected the division of public opinion on the question of ratification, and Mason had his defenders. The *Philadelphia Independent Gazetteer* praised the sage of Gunston Hall: "His manly conduct will be attended with a growing fame." Most newspapers, by contrast, supported ratification and articulated the views of the urban merchants and financiers who made up a large part of their readership. Little evidence exists that a majority of Americans affirmatively supported the Constitution; large majorities in Rhode Island, New York, South Carolina, and North Carolina opposed it. Anti-Federalists in Virginia may have had a slight edge in public sentiment, and the question of ratification produced a rare split among a political elite that had usually agreed on the great issues of the Revolution. Washington, who favored ratification, feared that most voters opposed it. Mason, who opposed ratification, feared that most voters supported it. Mason expected the state convention, however, to propose some amendments. He hoped that if the state conventions could meet at about the same time, the states could exchange proposed amendments, reach a consensus, and, "without Danger of public Convulsion or Confusion, produce a general Adoption of the new Government." Mason saw reasons for optimism. He believed the tactics of Federalists in Pennsylvania, where Anti-Federalist legislators had been dragooned to form a quorum so the Federalist majority could set an early date for a state convention, would create a backlash against ratification. Mason felt confident the unamended Constitution could not withstand careful scrutiny.[12]

Divisions within their own ranks, however, hamstrung the Anti-Federalist opposition. Anti-Federalist strongholds were scattered throughout the country from Rhode Island and the fringes of New England to the Hudson River Valley and western Pennsylvania and down through Virginia's Southside, North Carolina, and the South Carolina upcountry. The historian Saul Cornell has further divided Anti-Federalists by class into a relatively conservative elite, "middling" democrats, and plebian radicals. Each faction held differing degrees of commitment to popular democracy. Diversity of section and class helps explain why Mason's fears of a federal navigation law failed to mobilize an Anti-Federalist majority. Samuel Chase in Maryland, Rawlins Lowndes in South Carolina, and most Anti-Federalists in Virginia and North Carolina supported an amendment requiring a supermajority to pass commercial regulations, but the idea never took hold in the North. A trace of the rivalry between large and small states remained. When Anti-Federalist Luther Martin reported to the Maryland legislature in November 1787, he complained that Gerry and Mason had initially supported efforts to empower the large states to dominate the small. In other words, they had at first supported the Virginia Plan.[13]

Only in Virginia did the Anti-Federalists enjoy leadership that rivaled their Federalist opponents in ability and prestige, but even among Anti-Federalist leaders in Virginia important divisions existed. Mason has been described as an "unregenerate radical" in his devotion to the egalitarian principles of the American Revolution, but Mason was far more moderate than Patrick Henry. Madison divided Virginia's Anti-Federalists into two camps: a moderate faction led by Mason and Edmund Randolph that did "not object to the Substance of the Governt. but contend for a few additional Guards in Favor of the Rights of the States and of the People," and a more extreme group, led by Henry, that seemed willing to divide the Union rather than accept the Constitution. Divisions existed even among the moderates. Mason, Randolph, and Richard Henry Lee all supported the creation of a council of state to advise the president; disagreements over how it should be constituted apparently prevented them from making a comprehensive, coherent proposal.[14] Randolph published a pamphlet in December 1787 that explained his reasons for not signing the Constitution. Randolph's arguments did not mesh well with Mason's. As did Mason, Randolph disliked the new institutions created by the Philadelphia Convention—the presidency, the Senate, and the federal judiciary. To Mason's certain dismay, however, Randolph confessed his opinion that it was too late to add a provision requiring a two-thirds vote for navigation acts. Randolph would prove to be a feckless ally. According to Herbert Storing, the leading student of Anti-Federalist thought, Anti-Federalists most feared the creation of an American aristocracy; Federalists by contrast, worried about the dangers of "majority faction" and the abuse of minorities by popular majorities. Yet the common thread in Mason's advocacy of the two-thirds rule and of a bill of rights was his fear of majority rule, an anxiety not uniformly shared by his fellow dissenters.[15]

If Anti-Federalist ideology was not a model of clarity and consistency —and few ideologies forged in a real-world political struggle are—there were at least three positions that constituted the core of the critique of the Constitution, and Mason subscribed to them fully. First, conventional political theory, best expressed by Montesquieu, held that republican government was possible only in a small territory with a homogeneous population. America's size, diversity, and almost unlimited potential for expansion made the notion of a national, republican government problematical for Anti-Federalists such as Mason. Worse yet was the prospect that the United States would become a commercial republic in which extremes of wealth and poverty would destroy any concept of a common good. Expanding the size of the House of Representatives was a partial solution, but the Senate, with its long terms of office and its monopoly over the fearsome treaty-making power, only made the national government less responsive to public sentiments.[16] Second, most other Anti-Federalists agreed with Mason on the need for a bill of rights, especially for amendments protecting the right to a jury trial, freedom of the press, and freedom of religion. Living in a less litigious age, as far as political questions went, Anti-Federalists saw bills of rights less as judicially enforceable restrictions on government than as tools of public education; bills of rights put both the ruled and the rulers on notice of the freedoms enjoyed by the people. A few Anti-Federalists doubted the efficacy of "parchment barriers," but the demand for a bill of rights was the Anti-Federalists' most appealing argument.[17] Finally, Anti-Federalists condemned the transfer of power from state and local governments to a new central government.[18]

Indeed, their opposition to the consolidation of authority in a national government is often seen as the distinguishing characteristic of Anti-Federalist thought.[19] Mason in particular warned that the federal judiciary would largely supersede the state courts. Yet it may well be that because questions of states' rights loomed so large in subsequent American history, their importance to the ratification debate of 1787–88 has been exaggerated. As we have seen, Mason had no reason to romanticize Virginia's government, and his complaints about Fairfax County officials continued throughout the ratification struggle. Mason appeared to distinguish between an institution that represented the people, as he thought Congress should, and an institution, such as the county court, that was simply close to the people. At the very least, questions of federalism should not be allowed to overshadow Mason's conviction, and that of other Anti-Federalists, that however badly the Constitution divided sovereignty between the federal government and the states, power was also malapportioned within the federal government.[20]

Besides their common ground on several fundamental issues, Anti-Federalists shared a common voice. It was the rhetoric of the Whig opposition, honed through years of imperial conflict. Directed at Parliament and George III, it had served the patriots well. Directed at Washington, Madison, and Franklin, it could seem overwrought. Anti-Federalist propaganda tried to raise the alarm against leaders who would attempt to hide the most enormous crimes behind the flimsiest of constitutional technicalities. Mason, for example, claimed the president might manipulate the Senate's quorum requirement to circumvent the need for a two-thirds vote to ratify a treaty. Other Anti-Federalists suffered from more acute cases of paranoid legalism: the assumption that popularly elected representatives would establish an autocracy if they could find any legal authority, no matter how farfetched, to justify it. The rhetoric proved ineffective, if not counterproductive. Early in the debate, Washington privately accused Mason and Randolph of searching for excuses to justify their refusal to sign the Constitution, and he predicted they would present their reasons "in terrific array, with a view to alarm the people." As the debate went on, Washington claimed the opponents of ratification made arguments "upon principles which do not exist in the Constitution—which the known & literal sense of it, does not support." Nevertheless, Mason and other Anti-Federalists, by participating in the ratification process, helped give legitimacy to the Constitution by ensuring that its adoption would come only after a vigorous public debate.[21]

GEORGE MASON REACHED Richmond on 24 October, the day before the House of Delegates took up the question of calling a convention to consider ratification of the Constitution. On 2 October better than two dozen Fairfax County freeholders had signed instructions to Mason and his colleague David Stuart calling for the "speedy Adoption" of the new Constitution and directing them to support "the immediate Convocation of a Convention . . . for the said Purpose." The list of freeholders included several familiar names—Charles Broadwater, Lund Washington, Daniel McCarty, Thomas West, and Robert T. Hooe. Stuart supported the Constitution; the instructions were aimed at Mason. They apparently had their intended effect. On 7 October Mason assured George Washington that he supported submitting the Constitution "to a Convention chosen by the People . . . and should any attempt be made to prevent the calling such a convention here, such a Measure shall have every Opposition in my Power to give it."[22] It may have been a small concession; a convention would be needed to propose the amendments Mason wanted.

On 25 October Francis Corbin introduced a resolution in the House of Delegates to call a convention. Patrick Henry moved that the convention be empowered to propose amendments; Mason seconded the motion. He would, "at a proper season," explain his refusal to sign the Constitution. No one, he told his fellow delegates, was "more fully convinced of the necessity of establishing some general government," but "I thought it repugnant to our highest interests. . . . I would have lost this hand, before it should have marked my name to the new government."[23]

The unamended Constitution enjoyed less support in the general assembly than it did among the electorate at large, which was partly because of Henry's success in exploiting on the House floor what Edmund Randolph called "the most vulnerable and odious part of the Constitution"—its provision for a federal judiciary. More specifically, debt-ridden Virginians feared that the federal courts would offer British creditors a friendly venue where collection suits could be brought far from the debtor's home and tried without a jury of the defendant's peers.[24] Federalists, led in debate by George Nicholas, opposed Henry's motion because it seemed to imply the Constitution ought to be amended before its final ratification. Mason's relative moderation undercut the more radical Anti-Federalists. In the course of the debate, Mason conceded he would not risk everything to defeat the Constitution; he would remain in the Union even if amendments were not adopted.[25]

John Marshall came forward with compromise language the House of

Delegates could accept: the convention would be vaguely authorized to engage in "free and ample discussion." The House also adopted a series of procedural rules. All freeholders could be candidates for convention seats without regard to the residency and other requirements applicable to legislative races. Qualifications and procedures for voting would be unchanged. Each county could elect two delegates; each town could elect one. Convention delegations would be elected in March 1788 for a May convention; the Senate wanted to postpone the convention until June. The House agreed and ordered 2,000 copies of the resolutions be printed.[26]

As the result of an apparent oversight, the convention issue resurfaced later in the session. The resolution of 25 October made no provision for paying convention delegates. On 30 November Samuel Hopkins Jr. introduced a resolution to pay the delegates' expenses and the expenses of a second national convention, should one be necessary. Federalists objected to the implied endorsement of a second convention. Mason aligned himself with the Federalists to defeat a resolution explicitly approving a second convention, but he supported Hopkins's motion. Mason denied it expressed a preference for a second convention, but some Federalists were unconvinced. Archibald Stuart wrote James Madison, "Mason on the subject was less candid than ever I knew him to be." Despite their reservations, Hopkins's motion passed, and the House appointed Mason to a committee to draft implementing legislation. Mason's committee reported a bill on 4 December, but debate continued until the House agreed to reimburse delegates to the state convention and, in another vague compromise, authorized the convention to communicate with other states.[27] Their compromises notwithstanding, the debates indicated most House members favored amendments of some kind. Robert Rutland has called the "implicit endorsement" of a second convention "the first clear-cut Antifederalist victory."[28] Perhaps more telling, given the outcome of the ratification struggle, is the fact that Mason and many of his allies felt compelled to make concessions.

Mason's fiscal conservation may have tempered his opposition to the Constitution. He shared some common ground with his Federalist adversaries. Despite breaking ranks on the question of ratification, Mason's fiscal views generally reflected the prevailing sentiment in the Northern Neck, where the large planters who dominated the region's political life were as likely to be creditors as debtors. Early in November the assembly debated petitions from Albemarle, Pittsylvania, and Washington counties for an emission of paper money. When the House of Delegates, as a committee of the whole, debated the petitions, Mason introduced a series of resolutions opposing a paper emission and, in the words of Archibald Stuart, "preached the funeral sermon of paper money." Mason believed the petitions were "founded upon Fraud & Knavery"; paper money, among its many ill effects, would induce "moneyed-men to lock up their Gold and Silver, preferring the loss of Interest to the Risk of Lending or putting it out here." As he recounted the debate to George Washington, Mason dared the supporters of the petitions to step forward; when no one spoke up, the House passed Mason's resolutions unanimously.[29] Mason also supported efforts to prevent the receipt of public securities in payment of taxes, and he tried unsuccessfully to block the payment of taxes with tobacco.[30]

More relevant to the ratification debate was the matter of prewar British debts. Most observers assumed a stronger federal government would be more effective than the Confederation Congress had been in enforcing the nation's obligations under the Treaty of Paris of 1783. The debate over the payment of debts owed by Virginians to British merchants put Mason at odds with Patrick Henry and in the camp of Federalists such as George Nicholas. The House took three recorded votes on 17 November. Mason voted with the majority to defeat a resolution sponsored by Henry that would have kept Virginia's courts closed to British creditors until Britain complied with all its treaty obligations. Mason also helped defeat a proposal to permit the payment of British debts in installments. A third resolution repealed all laws inconsistent with the treaty; Mason supported the measure, and it passed with a popular caveat that it would not take effect until similar laws had been adopted in the other states. Despite its defeats, the debtors' party would not surrender. No installment bill passed, but before the session ended, the delegates voted eighty to thirty-one, with Mason in the minority, to make repeal of laws inconsistent with the treaty dependent on a British evacuation of forts on American territory around the Great Lakes. Mason's many reasons for opposing the Constitution did not include a desire to escape responsibility for money owed to British creditors.[31]

At least one other issue arose that had implications for the ratification debate, and here Mason found himself in more familiar company. In August 1786 the American diplomat John Jay, then engaged in negotiations with Spain, had asked Congress for permission to trade American rights to use the Mississippi River for commercial concessions from the Spanish. A predominantly northern majority granted Jay's request, but it was a Pyrrhic victory because the proposal failed to garner the nine votes necessary to approve a treaty under the Articles of Confederation. Nevertheless, the vote enraged southerners and westerners, who saw the Mississippi as the economic lifeline of the expanding frontier. Southern Anti-Federalists could argue that the effort of a majority in the Confederation Congress to surrender American navigation rights had been defeated, but would the South fare as well under a new government? On 12 November the House of Delegates passed resolutions asserting America's right to the "free use and navigation of the western streams and rivers" as a matter of both natural and international law. Mason, Henry, and James Monroe, another Anti-Federalist, were appointed to draft instructions to Virginia's congressional delegation reminding it that the "Continental Congress . . . had no power to cede or suspend American rights on the Western Waters." It was an indirect jab at the Constitution. The issue would reappear in the Virginia ratifying convention.[32]

As was typical, of course, Mason spent much of his time during the legislative session on matters that had little to do with international relations, national politics, or constitutional reform. His colleagues appointed him to a committee to draft a bill "giving Richard Towns and John Woolfolk the exclusive right of conveying persons in stage carriages to and from certain places for a limited time." In the same session that granted Jon Fitch a steamboat monopoly on Virginia waterways, Mason was asked to draft legislation providing for highway construction and the organization of fire companies.[33] Mason supported an unsuccessful effort to require newly freed slaves to leave Virginia within twelve months, and he sponsored an amendment to an existing statute that prevented the fraudulent gift of slaves.[34] He served on a committee to draft a bill regulating the fees of Potomac River pilots, and at Washington's request, Mason pushed through the assembly a bill to expedite collections from delinquent subscribers to the Potomac Navigation Company.[35]

Mason's most time-consuming project in the 1787 session appears to have been his service as chair of a three-member committee appointed to examine the proceedings of a commission established by Congress to audit Virginia's claim for reimbursement for expenses associated with George Rogers Clark's conquest of the Northwest Territory. Intimately familiar with Clark's expedition and one of the architects of the cession of the territory to Congress, Mason was the obvious choice to head the committee. Frustrated with the slow pace of the audit and with a lack of information, Mason submitted a memorandum on Virginia's behalf to the commissioners on 31 December, and he provided a written report to the House a week later. Virginia eventually received $1.25 million from the federal government.[36]

Mason's most impressive display of political influence in the 1787 legislative session came as part of his long-standing feud with the Alexandria faction on the Fairfax County court. Mason submitted two petitions to the House of Delegates on 24 November. The first petition, which bore 617 signatures, accused the county's "overseers of the Poor" of "improper and improvident Management." The county poorhouse had been located near Alexandria, to the distress of poor residents in other parts of the county. The selection of the Alexandria site raised the cost of poor relief because, near the city, "the Charges of Rent, Fire-wood & Provisions are much dearer than in other Parts of the County." The poor there could do less to feed themselves "for want of Ground, upon which they might raise Vegitables for [a] great Part of their Subsistance." Mason alleged that the overseers had ignored residency requirements, allowing "vagabonds" without a residence in the county to enter the poorhouse, where they were maintained in "such Idleness, Ease and Plenty, as cannot fail continually to encrease their Number." The result was an oppressive tax burden that fell disproportionately on rural residents because there were relatively more tithables, especially slaves, in the countryside than in Alexandria. Yet Alexandria residents dominated the county court. Mason's solution was to separate municipal and county administration and to prohibit municipal officials from serving on the court. "The custom of uniting different & distinct Officers of Power and Authority in the same Men tends to create an undue Influence in particular Individuals, naturally subversive of Liberty, and productive of oppression; incompatible with the Genius of Republican Government, and inconsistent with the Principles of our own Laws and Constitution."[37]

Mason's second petition, which had been signed by 638 residents of the county, complained about a 1785 highway act and its administration by the county court. The 1785 act had imposed a levy of sixty pounds on the entire county for the maintenance of two roads that Mason claimed served Alexandria almost exclusively. Worse yet, the county had placed turnpikes, the eighteenth-century equivalent of toll booths, to collect tolls from travelers using only a small strip of the roads supported by the tolls. Justices of the county court, acting in their capacity as road commissioners, had arbitrarily conscripted "Hands at several miles Distance from the said Roads" to work on them. Public funds had been used to build private roads, "a man who keeps a disorderly tippling-House" had been placed in charge of one turnpike, and most of the county's road fund had been squandered on extravagant salaries and "in frequent meetings of the Commissioners." Mason and the other petitioners asked for a public accounting of the commissioners' finances and for a revision of the state's road laws.[38]

The general assembly responded quickly to the petitions. On 28 December the House of Delegates passed a bill sponsored by George Nicholas that required towns to assume responsibility for their own needy and required a freehold in the county for service as an overseer of the poor.[39] The House made Mason chair of a committee to draft amendments to the 1785 and 1787 road laws; his amendments had passed both the House and Senate by the middle of December.[40] Most far reaching was a bill Mason presented on the House floor on 24 December; it barred most municipal officials from serving on any county court, and it limited the jurisdiction of municipal courts to cases between citizens of the town or to controversies arising within the town. The restrictions on municipal authority obviously appealed to a mostly rural legislature, and Mason's bill became law on 8 January 1788.[41]

Why would a man of Mason's stature enter a debate over the location of poorhouses or toll booths? In the context of local politics, his strictures about the "Genius of Republican Government" seem overblown. It may have been the only language he had, but it suggests to the modern ear a lack of proportion and a suspicion of all levels of government that borders on paranoia. Yet complaints about Virginia's county courts and their part-time, amateur justices were common.[42] Mason's petitions enjoyed widespread popular support, and they found a receptive audience in the general assembly. For his part, Mason showed scant concern for his own status or his place in history, and he never considered local politics beneath him. Were those politics relevant to national issues? Given the time and energy Mason spent on Fairfax County politics, it is difficult to believe they meant little to him. They may help explain Mason's reservations about the Constitution. Of the major political figures in Fairfax County, Mason was one of the few who opposed ratification without prior amendments; he was also the one who was the most estranged from the Alexandria merchants, who generally supported the Constitution. Could it be that Mason's opposition, and especially his fear that northern commercial interests would exploit the South, owed something to the injustices he believed the Alexandria merchants had perpetrated on the countryside?

By the end of the 1787 session, Mason was nearing sixty-two, a fairly advanced age for the late 1700s. Still plagued by gout and other ailments, Mason had, for the most part, been away from Gunston Hall since May. He must have been tired. He seemed satisfied with the arrangements made for the Virginia ratifying convention, he had won an easy victory over the advocates of paper money, he had kept pressure on the Illinois commissioners to settle Virginia's claims, and he had scored a series of signal triumphs over the Alexandria faction on the Fairfax County Court. But he had only mixed success in his efforts to do justice to British creditors. He suffered an embarrassing defeat when he supported an effort to repeal the port bill, which had created several authorized ports of entry for foreign goods. Archibald Stuart, who watched Mason during the port bill debate, confided to James Madison that "the Effects of Age have sometimes been discoverable" in Mason. Besides the press of public business and periodic episodes of gout, Mason had other reasons to be distracted. Crop yields in the fall of 1787 were one-third to two-thirds of a normal year. Mason worried about finding a career for his son John. In October Mason was planning to send John to London for experience in a mercantile house, with the thought he would return to Alexandria or Georgetown. Those plans soon changed. By the spring, John was planning to enter trade in Bordeaux. Mason would write letter after letter promoting John's new firm.[43] Mason would also join in one more great debate.

DELAWARE, PENNSYLVANIA, and New Jersey ratified the Constitution in December 1787; on the second day of the new year, Georgia endorsed the Constitution with a unanimous vote; and a week later, Connecticut's state convention approved it by a three-to-one margin. But as the race for seats in the Virginia ratifying convention began, the drive for ratification seemed to lose momentum. Federalists in Massachusetts faced strong opposition from John Hancock and Samuel Adams. On 6 February the Massachusetts Convention approved the Constitution but by a relatively narrow vote of 187 to 168. Proponents of ratification cobbled together a majority only by agreeing to support nine amendments, which included protections for civil liberties and a reservation to the states of all powers not expressly granted to the federal government. In March a popular referendum in Rhode Island rejected the Constitution by a more than ten-to-one margin; the state's beleaguered Federalist minority boycotted the election. Public opinion in North Carolina opposed ratification. New Hampshire, New York, and Virginia were bitterly divided, and their conventions were not scheduled to meet until June. In the early spring of 1788, it seemed possible that the Constitution might not win ratification in the nine states needed to make it effective, or if it did, defeats in New York or Virginia would cripple the new government.

Many of the members of the House of Delegates would seek seats in the Virginia Convention, and the convention races began as soon as the general

assembly adjourned. Federalists conceded the Southside, long dominated by
Patrick Henry, to the Anti-Federalists. The Piedmont was more competitive.
James Madison had to fight to win a seat in Orange County. Federalists
enjoyed substantial majorities in most of the counties along the Rappahan-
nock and in the Northern Neck. In some areas, Anti-Federalists failed to
field candidates; George Mason's biggest disappointment of the campaign
may have been Richard Henry Lee's decision not to run in Westmoreland
County. Henry was an ally; Lee was a confidant. Lee cited ill health in
explaining his decision not to run.[44] Mason knew before the legislature
convened that he would face strong opposition in Fairfax County. As one
correspondent reported to James Madison in October, "The freeholders
of Fairfax have on the most pointed terms directed Col. Mason to vote
for a convention, and have as pointedly assured him he shall not be in it."
The legislative session did not improve his political position at home. John
Hughes wrote Horatio Gates in November that if Mason ran for a convention seat in Fairfax County, "he would hardly see twenty votes in the whole
county for, he has made himself odious by an illiberal abuse of the Commissioners of the Turnpike, & an attempt, to divide the Town, from the
County." The regulations governing the convention elections gave Mason
some flexibility in shopping for a constituency, and admirers in nearby Stafford County persuaded him to enter the race there.[45]

Without modern public opinion surveys, or even modern news reporting,
neither Mason nor any one else knew what to expect from the convention
elections. At the start of the year, Washington expressed optimism; a month
later he felt less confident. Others detected shifts in public opinion. Madison believed the Constitution enjoyed broad support until the "tide next
took a sudden and strong turn in the opposite direction." By the middle of
February, Madison thought the Constitution was regaining lost ground.
Despite his unpopularity at home, Mason heard reports he would win in
Stafford County, and that he could have been elected in Prince William
or Fauquier. All agreed that Mason, Lee, Henry, and Randolph formed
a formidable phalanx against ratification, but Tobias Lear believed they
would have less influence on the voters than normally. The subject "is an
important one upon which they chuse to think for themselves."[46]

The attacks on Mason triggered by his "Objections" to the Constitution
continued throughout the spring campaign. The North Carolina lawyer
James Iredell, a future Supreme Court justice, wrote a point-by-point rebuttal to the "Objections" that appeared as a series of essays in the Norfolk
and Portsmouth newspapers. The *Petersburg Virginia Gazette* responded

to Mason's critique of the necessary and proper clause: "Nothing can be more groundless and ridiculous than this." His construction of the clause was "absolutely puerile." Other writers dismissed Mason's demand for a two-thirds requirement for navigation laws; why, they asked, would the agricultural middle states support New England's efforts to oppress southern planters? Mason's dogged defense of ex post facto laws, one antilibertarian measure banned by the Constitution, drew scorn. Can anything, the Petersburg newspaper asked, be more "demonstrative of the imbecility of human nature than to mistake a virtue for a defect?"[47]

Mason's patriotism and even his sanity came under scrutiny. Rumors circulated privately that Mason and Henry supported creation of a southern confederacy.[48] In a widely reported, but probably apocryphal story, Mason supposedly attacked his fellow delegates to the Philadelphia Convention. At a campaign stop in Stafford County, Mason allegedly said that "you may have supposed that they were an assemblage of great men—There is nothing less true. From the Eastern States there were knaves and Fools from the States southward of Virga. They were a parcel of coxcombs and from the Middle States office hunters not a few."[49]

Another story of questionable authenticity had Mason encountering a heckler in Stafford: "Mr. Mason, you are an old man, and the public notices that you are losing your faculties," to which Mason reportedly replied, "Sir, the public will never notice when you lose yours."[50]

Mason continued to say he would not risk disunion to defeat the Constitution, and he undoubtedly heeded Richard Henry Lee's advice that they not lose "the good part of the plan proposed."[51] By all accounts, however, Mason was becoming more strident in his opposition to the unamended Constitution. Madison believed Mason was "growing every day more bitter, and outrageous." Madison feared "the violence of his passions" would eventually carry Mason into Henry's radical Anti-Federalist camp. Federalist George Nicholas, who remained on friendly personal terms with Mason, believed two considerations fueled his passions. Mason thought Virginia could extract concessions from the other states, and Mason believed he could lead Virginia. Mason had also become, according to Nicholas, increasingly embittered by "the hard things that have been said of him."[52]

As always Mason had more than politics on his mind, and by modern standards, his campaign for a convention seat could not have been very grueling. He would not have been expected to campaign daily or to raise large sums of money. Among his many business interests, he had private legal matters to resolve; John Francis Mercer assisted Mason with a debt action in Maryland and a title dispute involving an old Ohio Company claim in Walnut Bottom. Mason tried to help his son John, who was entering a mercantile partnership with Marylanders Joseph and James Fenwick in Bordeaux. Mason wrote Thomas Jefferson that he would find John "a modest, cheerful, sensible Young Man" whose "Integrity & Diligence will merit the confidence of those, who may favour the copartnership." As was the custom of the great planters, Mason undoubtedly entertained a steady stream of visitors at Gunston Hall. An account from Dumfries merchant George Walker of his visit strikes several familiar notes. Walker had dinner at Gunston Hall, where Mason assured him that his unsettled account with Walker's firm "was purely owing to the want of money . . . and the first cash that came to his hand he would pay it." Mason's assurance was apparently good enough for Walker, but Mason detained his guest "so long on the subjects of politics and the forming of a harbour here that I could not get further than Alexa. that night."[53]

On 10 March, election day, "old G. Mason & attorney Buchanan, [were] returned before Chas. Carter & B. Fitzhugh."[54] Mason was apparently the only delegate who did not live in the county he was elected to represent. The Federalists carried the Tidewater north of the James River and the Northern Neck. According to one report, one of Mason's sons cast the only Anti-Federalist ballot in Fairfax County. Anti-Federalists carried the area south of the James. The two sides divided the Piedmont. The Great Valley and the Ohio Valley leaned toward ratification. More generally, Federalists did well along the coast and in the mountains; Anti-Federalists dominated the center of the state and Kentucky. At least a half dozen counties, distributed widely across the state, split their votes, electing a Federalist and an Anti-Federalist. Commercial areas tended to vote for candidates who supported ratification, but class differences do not appear to have been of overriding importance. Many frontier voters favored the Constitution in the hope that a new government could finally expel the British from their Great Lakes forts.[55] The gravity of the issue and the passion of the debate can give a distorted view of public interest in the convention elections. Many Virginians lived beyond the reach of Virginia's few newspapers and knew little about the Constitution. Probably no more than a quarter of eligible voters participated in the election.[56]

Newspaper assessments gave the Federalists about a ten-vote lead in elected delegates, but a few delegates, especially in Kentucky, remained undecided or undeclared. The vote was a close but imperfect barometer of public opinion. A few delegates, notably Edmund Pendleton and George Wythe, may have been

elected on the basis of personal prestige, not because they accurately represented the views of their constituents. In part because Richard Henry Lee had
not run and because Edmund Randolph's commitment to Anti-Federalism
was suspect, the Federalists had the advantage in the quality of their delegates, but not by much.[57] Mason believed the convention was too evenly
balanced for anyone to predict its end result, but he believed the great majority of the delegates would support amendments to the Constitution. The real
issue would be whether amendments would be a condition of ratification,
or whether Virginia would follow Massachusetts's example and ratify the
Constitution and then recommend amendments be adopted. "This Idea,"
Mason told Thomas Jefferson, "appears to me so utterly absurd, that I can
not think any Man of Sense candid, in proposing it."[58]

THE CONVENTION CALLED to consider ratification of the Constitution
met in Richmond on 2 June 1788, near the end of a dry, hot spell. Drought
had killed the young tobacco plants, but in an era before paved highways
—or even raincoats and umbrellas—it made travel a little easier. The convention assembled in Virginia's temporary capitol, a fifty-foot square wooden
building at the corner of Fourteenth and Cary. One of Mason's first contributions to the convention was to suggest it move to the largest building in town,
the newly established Academy of Sciences and Fine Arts, better known as
the New Academy, on Shockoe Hill. It was large enough to accommodate
the 170 delegates, but it could not hold everyone who came to watch the
daily debates. Far larger than the Philadelphia Convention, the Richmond
meeting, as an earlier Mason biographer has said, was "essentially an ad-
versary proceeding." Elected, in most cases, because of their position on the
single issue of ratification, the delegates were unlikely to change their minds
and little interested in compromise. The convention produced few intellectually creative exchanges, and no more than twenty delegates participated in
the debates.[59]

Mason, predictably, was among the more active delegates. William Wirt,
Patrick Henry's nineteenth-century biographer, thought Mason displayed
"Roman energy and Attic wit." Virginia historian Hugh Blair Grigsby described Mason's "once raven hair white as snow, his stalwart figure, attired
in deep mourning, still erect, his black eyes fairly flashing. . . . His voice
deliberate and full." John Marshall recalled years later that Mason "spoke
from very copious notes & spoke very slow and distinct." Mason stayed
at the famous Swan Tavern; as Grigsby described Mason's daily walk to

Shockoe Hill, he "was remarkable for the urbanity and dignity with which he received the courtesies of those who passed by him." The Mason of 1788 may have seemed more measured and circumspect in hindsight as a later generation of white southerners found the antecedents of the doctrine of states' rights in the philosophy of Anti-Federalism. In reality, Mason's rhetoric was much more strident than it had been in Philadelphia, and unfounded rumors circulated that Mason and Henry might resort to force to prevent the convention from ratifying the Constitution.[60]

Mason was often described as the "first man in every assembly in which he sat," but he took a secondary role to Patrick Henry in the Richmond debates. "The powers of Henry," in a large assembly, one contemporary observed, "are incalculable." Another put the matter less charitably: "In such as Assembly he must to be sure be better adapted to carry his point & lead the ignorant people astray than any other person upon earth." Henry, whose great speeches of the past had typically been short, spoke for hour after hour in Richmond. Mason and Henry tried to work together. No evidence exists that Mason resented Henry's preeminence as an orator, and Grigsby describes them as "walking arm in arm" from the Swan to the New Academy, but Henry was more opportunistic in his arguments and more extreme in his objectives.[61]

By a unanimous vote, the convention elected the venerable attorney Edmund Pendleton, permanently reduced to crutches by a riding accident, to serve as its presiding officer.[62] On the second day of the convention Mason surprised both friend and foe by moving that the convention consider the Constitution clause by clause. He also supported a motion by John Tyler to dissolve the convention into a committee of the whole. Mason wanted to delay any substantive vote until the debate was concluded. Mason's support for a clause-by-clause debate was widely seen, then and later, as a tactical blunder because it put a premium on the technical skills of Federalists like James Madison and John Marshall, and threatened to make Patrick Henry's soaring oratory irrelevant. In reality, the rules of debate made little difference. Mason believed a narrowly focused debate would expose the Constitution's defects, and he was certainly prepared to argue specifics. Uncertain that the Anti-Federalists had the votes to prevail at the outset of the convention, Mason may have decided he needed the time a meticulous debate would require to persuade the wavering and the undecided. More importantly, the rules could not restrain Henry—or others of the more loquacious members—and debates over fine points of constitutional law frequently degenerated into rambling speeches.[63] As early as 5 June Edmund

Randolph complained that "if we go on in this irregular manner, contrary to our resolution, instead of three or six weeks, it [will] take us six months to decide this question." Complaints continued until about midway through the convention, when the debate seemed to become more focused.[64]

The deliberations started badly for the Anti-Federalists. News arrived on the first day of the convention that South Carolina had ratified the Constitution. Because Maryland, which voted in April, had already endorsed the document, it was only one state short of the nine needed to make it effective. More damaging was the defection of Edmund Randolph, who announced his support for ratification on 4 June. Insisting on previous amendments so late in the ratification debate, Randolph said, would cause "inevitable ruin to the Union." After Randolph made public his change of heart, Mason was reportedly heard to murmur, "Young Arnold, Young Arnold," comparing Virginia's governor to America's most notorious traitor, Benedict Arnold.[65] Randolph not only withdrew from the Anti-Federalists ranks; he became an active proponent of the Constitution. Mason made his first substantive speech on 4 June, opposing congressional power to tax the people directly, complaining that the House of Representatives was too small, and raising the question whether "one general national government can exist in so extensive a territory as this?" Randolph joined Pendleton in rebutting Mason, and Randolph suggested the Northern Neck might secede from Virginia and join Maryland if the convention did not approve the Constitution.[66] Randolph's conduct has been ascribed to different motives. John Randolph of Roanoke called his cousin "a chameleon on an aspen: always quaking, always changing." Edmund Randolph may have succumbed to Washington's influence, or he may have had reason to expect a high position in the new government if he supported ratification.[67] In any event, Mason and his remaining allies never fully recovered from the loss of Randolph.

Mason's remarks on the convention floor did not necessarily follow his published "Objections." Old issues, like a council of state, were dropped. New issues, like direct taxation, were raised. As the ratification contest had dragged on, Mason found more and more faults with the Constitution, and he was trying to appeal to undecided delegates. At Richmond, the treaty-making power assumed new significance; trade regulations took on less.[68]

Mason also argued in his 4 June speech that allowing Congress to tax citizens directly would transform the confederacy into a consolidated, national government. Besides the familiar problem of "a general national government extending over so extensive a country," Mason complained that the

House of Representatives, because of its small size, would be too ignorant of local economic conditions to draft tax policies appropriate for the entire nation. After missing several days of debate, Mason returned to the tax issue on 11 June, when he read a 1782 letter from Robert Morris, then the Confederation's secretary for finance, recommending adoption of a land tax, a poll tax, and a liquor tax. Mason said he read the letter "to show that taxes would be laid by those who are not acquainted with our situation, and that the agents of the collection may be consulted upon the most productive and simple mode of taxation." Mason also feared a federal tax on slaves that would place a disproportionate share of the tax burden on the South. He proposed Congress be allowed to impose a tax only if a state failed to comply with a federal requisition. The Federalist argument that the South had nothing to fear because taxes and representation were to be kept in proportion left Mason unimpressed: "I am one of those unhappy men who cannot be amused with assertions. A man from the dead might frighten me, but I am sure he could not convince me without using better arguments than I have yet heard."[69]

All the delegates recognized the importance of the tax question, and Mason's speeches on the issue, especially his invocation of Morris's aging letter, provoked some of the most partisan debates of the convention. Federalist Henry Lee rebuked Mason directly. Mason, Lee said, "has endeavored to draw our attention from the merits of the question, by jocose observations and satirical allusions. He ought to know that ridicule is not the test of truth. Does he imagine, that he that can raise the loudest laugh is the soundest reasoner?"[70]

Mason next turned his fire on federal control of the state militia—in two long speeches on 14 and 16 June, Mason warned that Congress might attempt to make militia service unattractive in order to create a pretext for establishing a standing army. "If that paper on the table gets no alteration," he feared the militia "may be confined to the lower and middle classes of the people," and, if so, Congress would show little concern for their rights.[71] The debate over the treaty-making power soon overshadowed everything else. After the abortive Jay-Gardoqui Treaty, southerners and westerners feared another attempt might be made to surrender American rights to use the Mississippi River. Access to the Mississippi was critical to the development of the frontier, which was in turn critical to ensuring agricultural states like Virginia would constitute a majority in the new government. "I look upon this," William Grayson said, "as a contest for empire."[72] Opponents of an unamended Constitution hoped the prospect of another

Jay-Gardoqui Treaty would tip a few undecided western delegates into the Anti-Federalist camp, and they hit the issue hard. George Nicholas called the debate "their scuffle for Kentucky votes."[73] Anti-Federalists argued repeatedly that the Articles of Confederation, which required the votes of nine states to approve a treaty, better protected western interests than did the Constitution. As Grayson explained the arithmetic, five states, with ten senators, could constitute two-thirds of a quorum and pass a treaty. Mason proposed a three-fourths vote of both houses of Congress to approve a treaty surrendering territorial rights.[74]

The debate over the treaty clause may have caused some discomfort for Mason. His pet project had been a two-thirds vote for commercial regulations, but he found himself arguing in Richmond that a two-thirds requirement failed to adequately confine the treaty-making power. The Anti-Federalist strategy assumed Virginia, because of its size and prestige, could virtually dictate amendments to the other states. As Grayson, holding up a tiny snuff box, told the convention, most of the states that had ratified the Constitution, "When compared to Virginia . . . are no more than this snuff box is to the size of a man." Yet the image of a majestic Virginia demanding amendments was not entirely consistent with the notion of an embattled South unable to rally a majority of Congress against a navigation act or even unable to assemble the votes—one-third plus one—to defeat an oppressive treaty. Federalists, by contrast, could say simply the staple states represented an expanding majority and had nothing to fear from the new Union. In any event, Mason's proposal to limit the ability of Congress to regulate trade, which may have had scant appeal to the Kentucky delegates he wanted to impress, attracted little attention.[75]

One of Mason's longest speeches was an attack on the federal judiciary on 19 June, toward the end of the convention. He entered the debate with "reluctance," he said, "as it lies out of my line." Mason feared the broad scope of federal jurisdiction would not only render the state courts superfluous, but he claimed "it will destroy the state governments." Mason returned to the issue the next day and again on 23 June. Federal jurisdiction presented practical objections beyond the more general matter of consolidating power in a national government. Hapless defendants could be forced to litigate in distant and expensive venues. Mason offered examples calculated to alarm a Virginia audience. British creditors might abuse federal process, the Fairfax estate might attempt to collect Northern Neck quitrents abandoned during the Revolution, or the Indiana Company might challenge the land titles of the 20,000 Virginia families beyond the Blue Ridge. Mason objected in particular to the prospect of federal courts hearing cases between a state and the citizen of another state.[76] Randolph, Pendleton, and John Marshall tried to reassure Mason. Marshall told him he was wrong: the Supreme Court did not have jurisdiction to hear a suit by a citizen against another state. Ironically, the Supreme Court rejected the future chief justice's interpretation in *Chisholm v. Georgia*, which led to the adoption of the Eleventh Amendment.[77] Everyone made mistakes. Patrick Henry expressed concern the federal courts would not strike down unconstitutional laws. From New York, Alexander Hamilton opined in *Federalist Papers* 77 that Senate approval would be needed to dismiss presidential appointees.[78]

Mason proposed limiting federal courts to matters of international law, admiralty jurisdiction, suits involving the United States, or suits involving two or more states, including competing land grants from different states. He also wanted to limit federal appellate jurisdiction to questions of law and leave most cases arising before ratification with the state courts.[79] Most striking about Mason's jurisprudence was his willingness to let state judges decide ordinary matters of federal law.

Judging from the attention they gave the issue in debate, Mason and his fellow Anti-Federalists believed the Constitution was especially vulnerable in its treatment of the federal executive. Mason first objected to the president's unlimited eligibility for reelection: "Nothing is so essential to the preservation of republican government as a periodical rotation." James Monroe predicted "that the Gentleman who will be first elected, may continue in the office for life."[80] Mason and Grayson feared European intervention to keep a favored puppet in office; Mason warned of "the horrors and calamities of an elective monarchy."[81] Given the localism that then dominated American politics, Mason could envision few candidates who could win a popular majority. The mode "of election was a mere deception." The people had been led to believe they would elect the president "whereas it would not be once out of fifty that he would be chosen by them." The House of Representatives, he thought, would normally select the president. Mason feared collusion between the Senate and the president, mutually interested as they were in presidential appointments and the negotiation of treaties. He believed congressional approval should be required before the president should be allowed to take personal command of the army. The vice president, with the office's ill-defined duties mixing legislative and administrative functions, was "not only an unnecessary but a dangerous officer."[82]

Other issues that loomed large in Philadelphia, and in later American history, received less attention in Richmond. In a speech on 16 June, Mason suggested the necessary and proper clause might give Congress warrant to suppress free speech and freedom of the press; he proposed an amendment reserving to the states all powers not expressly delegated to the national government. Otherwise Mason said little about civil liberties, other than to express the objection that the Constitution's ban on ex post facto laws would require the federal government to pay speculators holding depreciated public securities for the face value of their notes.[83] Mason made one speech condemning the slave trade—he could not let a great occasion pass without making an antislavery speech—but this speech lacked the moral force of earlier efforts. It was undercut by Mason's simultaneous complaint that the Philadelphia Convention had done nothing to protect slavery except adopt what Mason believed would be an ineffective clause calling for the return of fugitive slaves.[84] Issues ranging from the mundane to the surreal gained as much consideration as civil liberties and slavery. Mason complained of the lack of a mandate for regular financial reports from Congress and about federal preemption of the inspection of exports.[85] He raised a concern that Congress might abuse its authority to regulate the time, place, and manner of federal elections.[86] He suggested the federal district that was to be the permanent capital of the new government could "become the sanctuary of the blackest crimes," its juries dominated by the federal toadies who would populate the district.[87]

As his criticism of the federal district suggests, he feared corruption at any level of government more than he feared the consolidation of power in a national government. James Madison observed toward the end of the convention that the opponents of ratification "suppose, that the General Legislature will do every mischief they possibly can, and that they will omit to do every good which they are authorized to do." Madison disagreed. "I go on this great republican principle, that the people will have virtue and intelligence to select men of virtue and wisdom."[88] Mason began from a different premise: Congress, "like all other assemblies, will be composed of some bad and some good men; and considering the natural lust for power so inherent in man, I fear the thirst of power will prevail to oppress the people." Warnings of potential corruption appear repeatedly in his convention speeches. Comparing the British House of Commons with the much smaller House of Representatives, Mason asked: "Are 65 better than 550? Bribery and corruption, in my opinion, will be practiced in America more than in England; in proportion as 550 exceeds 65; and there will be less integrity and probity in proportion as 65 is less than 550."[89]

Legislators were corrupted, he believed, primarily by executive appointments; the Constitution's ban on members of Congress accepting "civil offices" created or given salary increases during their terms of office was, in Mason's opinion, inadequate. Mason lamented the absence of some institution to try impeachment cases against senators—their role in ratifying treaties made them obvious targets for foreign intrigue. He had no more faith in the president, and he opposed giving the chief executive the power to grant pardons "because he may frequently pardon crimes which were advised by himself."[90] If Mason crossed a line between healthy skepticism and virtual paranoia, he was contemplating a government that was novel, remote, and theoretically supreme within the scope of its authority. It seemed to him sure to degenerate into faction and cabal.

MASON PLAYED HIS most productive role off the convention floor, helping to draft the amendments his fellow delegates would ultimately endorse. Richard Henry Lee wrote Mason in May to suggest a meeting of a small group of Anti-Federalist leaders to consider amendments. Lee believed the amendments proposed by the Massachusetts convention could be used as a model, and he suggested Virginia condition its ratification on the approval of amendments within two years. Lee may have envisioned a meeting before the convention began. No evidence of any such meeting exists, or at least none has survived, but shortly after the delegates assembled, the Anti-Federalist caucus made Mason chair of a committee to draft amendments. He was apparently off the floor from 5 to 10 June. In all likelihood, Mason spent his time writing and meeting with Anti-Federalist leaders, including the printer Eleazar Oswald, a representative of New York Anti-Federalists. Oswald's presence reflected their interest in coordinating their efforts with Virginia's Anti-Federalists—New York's convention was also in session—and it betrayed their lack of confidence in the security of the regular mail. By about 8 June Mason had prepared a rough draft of thirteen structural or procedural amendments to follow a Declaration of Rights, which he had not completed. Most of the amendments addressed Mason's familiar complaints. Mason proposed a council to advise the president on treaties and appointments, and he also wanted to require a two-thirds majority to pass navigation laws. A few of the amendments raised less familiar issues. He proposed a three-fourths vote of both houses be required to ratify a commercial treaty and that no military enlistment extend beyond four years or the duration of hostilities.[91]

On 18 May John Lamb, chair of the New York Federal Republican Committee, which had been organized to oppose ratification, had written Mason to propose "a free Correspondence on the Subject of Amendments." Mason replied to Lamb on 9 June. Mason expressed confidence the Virginia ratifying convention would support amendments, but because "the members were so equally divided with respect to the Time and Manner of obtaining them," Mason indicated any official communication between the two states would be premature. In fact, Virginia's Anti-Federalists had not reached agreement among themselves, and they may not have even discussed amendments to curb the federal courts, police the federal capital, or protect the state militia.[92] By 11 June, however, the committee had completed its work, adding a twenty-article Declaration of Rights to the structural amendments Mason had composed a few days earlier. About half the new declaration came from Mason's 1776 draft of the Virginia Declaration of Rights, but the committee made several additions. It recognized the rights of assembly and petition, prohibited the quartering a soldiers in private homes during peacetime, and permitted a conscientious objector to avoid military service "upon payment of an equivalent, to employ another to bear Arms in his stead." Oswald took a copy of the 11 June draft with him when he returned to New York.[93]

Anti-Federalist strategy called for Patrick Henry to introduce the amendments near the close of the convention, and, for once, Henry struck observers as more moderate than Mason. On 23 June Mason raised the specter of "popular resistance" should the Constitution be approved in its current form; he "trusted gentleman would pause before they would decide a question which involved such awful consequences."[94] The next day George Wythe moved that the committee of the whole ratify the Constitution and propose amendments to be considered by Congress pursuant to the amending process established by the Constitution. In response, Henry proposed fifteen amendments, in addition to a bill of rights, to be accepted by the other states before the Constitution would be given effect. Despite some revisions, Henry's amendments were essentially those drafted by Mason's committee, with additions suggested by Mason in the course of the debates. Only one of his major projects—a council of state—fell by the wayside.[95]

As George Mason had understood from the beginning, the real issue was the timing, not the substance, of amendments, and the omens looked bleak for the Anti-Federalists. On 25 June two previously undeclared western delegates, Adam Stephen of Berkeley County and Zachariah Johnston of Augusta County, endorsed the Constitution. Mason remained silent and watched Patrick Henry enjoy his finest moment of the convention. Sensing defeat, Henry thanked the assembly for its patience, promised to be "a peaceable citizen," and pledged to seek reform of the new government by constitutional means. "I shall therefore patiently wait in expectation of seeing the Government changed so as to be compatible with the Safety, liberty, and happiness of the people." A motion by John Tyler to submit Henry's amendments to the other states prior to ratification lost eighty-eight to eighty. It was the climatic vote of the convention, making the vote on Wythe's motion that afternoon a foregone conclusion. Between two and three o'clock an angry Mason voted with the minority as the convention accepted the unamended Constitution, eighty-nine to seventy-nine.[96] As one historian has written, "There is no evidence that the lengthy debate changed a single vote."[97]

Following the ratification vote, the convention appointed a committee consisting of eleven Federalists and nine Anti-Federalists, including Mason, to prepare a final set of amendments. George Wythe served as chair. On 27 June the Wythe committee reported a bill of rights and twenty structural amendments to the full convention. They showed Mason's influence. The bill of rights came almost verbatim from the Anti-Federalist proposal of 24 June, with one noteworthy change. Article 20 of the Mason committee's declaration, which protected the free exercise of religion, also prohibited discrimination in favor of any "particular religious Sect or Society of Christians." The Wythe committee deleted "of Christians." Likewise, the structural amendments repeated the final draft of the Anti-Federalist caucus report with a few minor additions that could not have been objectionable to Mason. He failed in the Wythe committee to resurrect his coveted executive council, but the committee revived a proposal Mason had made on 11 June to prohibit Congress from adopting regulations for congressional elections "except when the legislature of any state shall neglect, refuse, or be disabled by invasion or rebellion to prescribe the same." The convention accepted the Wythe committee report without a recorded vote.[98]

Mason's success in shaping the amendments left him unappeased. He apparently convened a meeting of Anti-Federalist delegates for the evening of 27 June in the chambers of the Virginia Senate. His ostensible purpose was to "prepare an address to reconcile the minds of their constituents to the new plan of government." Mason's petition has not survived, but by all accounts it was more inflammatory than conciliatory. One newspaper called it a "fiery, irritating manifesto." Benjamin Harrison, John Tyler, and John Lawson objected to Mason's tone, and with what must have been considerable embarrassment, Mason withdrew the address.[99] Mason also considered attempting to censure his erstwhile ally Edmund Randolph. On 8 May Governor George Clinton of New York had written Governor Randolph a letter implying New York would support a second federal convention. Randolph showed the letter to the council of state, which advised him to share it with the general assembly. The assembly was not in session, but Randolph seemed content to dawdle; he sent the letter to the legislature on 24 June, as the convention was winding down and as legislators were trickling into Richmond. Before he left for Gunston Hall, Mason drafted resolutions calling for an investigation of Randolph's tardiness in making the Clinton letter public. Chastised by his defeat in the Anti-Federalist caucus, Mason decided against introducing the resolutions.[100] Yet tempers remained hot. Shortly after returning home, Mason felt compelled to publish a notice in the *Maryland Gazette* denying allegations that his cousin John Francis Mercer had said "the people of Maryland were so adverse to the new constitution . . . that they would take up arms against it."[101]

Patrick Henry could take defeat with good grace because, as a professional politician, he needed to reposition himself to compete in the new area. Always disdainful of ordinary politics, Mason had none of the ambitions that might have tempered his resentments. The reasonableness of his position, in his own mind, must explain much of his frustration. Unlike Henry, Mason supported a stronger national government, as did a majority of convention delegates, and they supported most of Mason's amendments. Operating from a position of considerable strength, he could not convince a majority of the convention to hold out until the Constitution was amended. Divided among themselves, Virginia's Anti-Federalists never explained in convincing terms how a national consensus behind previous amendments could be reached, and it hurt their cause. Washington's influence, the pace of ratification in other states, and the Federalists' willingness to support subsequent amendments created a pro-ratification majority. Bitter as defeat was to Mason, he played a pivotal role in the process that produced the Bill of Rights, and in the greatest irony of his career, by participating in the ratification debate as part of a loyal and peaceful opposition, he helped establish the legitimacy of the Constitution he had so vigorously opposed.[102]

Chapter Ten

I Am Grown Old

IT WOULD BE tempting, and misleading, to portray George Mason's last years as an unhappy period of steady decline. Defeated in the greatest political battle of his career, estranged from many old allies, and tormented by frequent fits of gout, Mason had reasons to be embittered. Yet even without a public position he remained active. Opinionated as ever, Mason dabbled occasionally in politics, but he spent more time on the family matters that had always been his first love. John Mason recalled years later that his father "kept up constantly during his retirement, an active correspondence with many of the prominent of that day." He rarely traveled, but Mason remained "hospitable, cheerful, and fond of conversation."[1]

As always, health complaints appear repeatedly in Mason's letters, and they began as soon as he returned home from the Richmond convention. Writing Thomas Jefferson in July 1788: "I have had so severe an Attack of the Gout in my Stomach, for two or three Days past, that I have not been able to set up." Writing Beverly Randolph in March 1790: "I have been confined by a severe fit of the Gout, ever since the Second Week in January." Writing Robert Carter in September 1791: "I am at present very unwell, from a late fit of Gout in my Stomach."[2] Despite his complaints, Mason did not consider himself disabled. Recovering from another episode of gout in the summer of 1789, he confessed to his son John that, for his age, his health was "tolerable." As late as January 1792, in the last year of his life, Mason told John that, apart from gout, "in every other Respect, thank God, I am in good Health."[3]

He was less sanguine about public affairs. Back at Gunston Hall after the ratifying convention, Mason complained to Jefferson, then American minister to France, of "the present gloomy state of American Politics."[4] Mason still entertained "hopes of proper & safe Amendments," and he was encouraged by the fall 1788 session of the Virginia assembly. Dominated by an Anti-Federalist majority, the assembly petitioned Congress to call a second constitutional convention, and it passed legislation barring federal officials from simultaneously holding state office. Mason also endorsed legislation, considered favorable to Anti-Federalists, that divided Virginia into districts for purposes of electing members of the House of Representatives and established a one-year residency requirement for congressional candidates.[5] The fall elections produced mixed results. Federalists won seven of Virginia's ten House seats, including the race in the hotly contested Fifth District, where James Madison defeated James Monroe. But the assembly elected two Anti-Federalists, Richard Henry Lee and William Grayson, to the Senate, and Mason was pleased to see Beverly Randolph replace Edmund Randolph in the governor's office.[6] Rumors persisted that Mason still opposed the new government. When the debates of the Virginia ratifying convention appeared in print, Mason criticized the reporter, David Robertson, as a "Federal Partizan" who had "garbled" Anti-Federalist speeches. In August 1789 Mason resigned from the Fairfax County Court rather than comply with a new federal law requiring public officials to take an oath to support the Constitution.[7]

William Grayson died shortly after his election to the Senate, and the state legislature asked Mason to replace him. Mason declined the appointment, which was no surprise given his health problems and antipathy to travel—Congress was meeting at the time in New York. "In such a situation," he wrote Beverly Randolph, "even if I was in New York it wou'd not be in my Power to render our Country any essential Service, and I can't reconcile myself to the Idea of receiving the Publick's Money for Nothing." Poor health prevented him from accepting a Senate seat even "if I had no other Objection." Presumably the other objection was his opposition to the new government, and according to one story, Mason had actually been offended by the appointment. Whatever his own misgivings about federal service, he was pleased to see the Senate seat go to his Anti-Federalist protégé, James Monroe.[8]

The adoption of the Bill of Rights and the rise to national prominence of men like Monroe mollified Mason even if he was never fully reconciled to the Constitution. A second constitutional convention was, of course, never called, and Mason initially had no faith in the ability of Congress to produce adequate amendments. In July 1789 he called Madison's efforts to secure amendments a "Farce." Mason wrote his son John that "perhaps some Milk & Water Propositions may be made by Congress to the State Legislatures by way of throwing out a Tub to the Whale; but of important and substantial Amendments, I have not the least Hope." Mason may not

yet have seen Madison's proposals because by September he was expressing "much Satisfaction" at what eventually became the Bill of Rights. He
remained concerned about the broad jurisdiction of the federal courts, the
power of Congress to regulate elections, the ability of a simple majority to
adopt navigation laws, and the lack of an executive council. If those issues
could be addressed, he told one correspondent, "I cou'd cheerfully put my
Hand & Heart to the new Government."[9]

Notwithstanding the bitterness of the ratification debate, most Americans quickly came to see the new government as legitimate. Thomas Jefferson, who had watched the debate from France, shared many of Mason's
reservations, but he subtly encouraged Mason to accept the Constitution.
Mason left a few hints of a softening attitude. During the debate over Gouverneur Morris's nomination to be United States minister to France, James
Monroe asked Mason for his opinion on the Senate's prerogatives under
its power to "advise and consent." Could the Senate, Monroe asked, make
its own selection if it rejected the president's nominee? It could not, Mason
replied, although the "Constitution . . . wisely & Properly directs" that ambassadors had to be approved by the Senate. Earlier Mason had condemned
the Senate's role in the confirmation process.[10]

Mason's criticisms of the Constitution receded as his disillusionment with
the pro-Federalist policies of the Washington administration grew. Mason
objected to Alexander Hamilton's proposals to refinance the national debt,
repay outstanding securities at face value, and have the federal government assume the states' wartime debts. Nor did he approve of the treasury
secretary's plan to establish a Bank of the United States. "Our new Government is a Government of Stock-jobbing and Favourtism," he wrote Monroe
in February 1792. "It required no extraordinary Degree of Penetration, to
foresee that it wou'd be so, from it's Formation."[11] Some of his criticisms
were personal; the Morris appointment particularly troubled him. "I don't
think a more injudicious Appointment could have been made . . . to appoint
a Man of his known Monarchial Principles has rather the Appearance of Insult, rather than of Compliment." Mason reportedly bemoaned "the Pomp
& parade" in New York, which he blamed on John Adams and, somewhat
curiously, on a coterie of wives and daughters of unnamed Federalist politicians. He saw the president as a check on their aristocratic pretensions. As
long as Washington stayed in office, "It would be out of the Power of those
Damned Monarchial fellows with the Vice President, & the Women to ruin
the Nation."[12]

Mason did not necessarily personalize political disagreements, which undoubtedly made it easier to accept defeat. Mason considered John Marshall, the most durable of Federalists, to be a "very worthy" man, and he ranked Marshall among his "intimate Friends." Political differences did not prevent Mason from hiring Marshall, and another Federalist lawyer, George Nicholas, to represent him. Mason complained about Marshall's inattention to business, but he did not question the intelligence or the integrity of the future chief justice. Despite their differences, Mason's respect for James Madison never wavered. Mason expressed a fear to Jefferson that the ratification debate had caused a "Coolness" with Madison. "He is one of the few Men, whom from a pretty thorough Acquaintance, I really esteem." Jefferson tried to reassure him of Madison's continuing admiration. More importantly, their mutual opposition to Hamilton's fiscal policies soon returned Mason and Madison to the same political camp. The funding scheme assumed sectional as well as philosophical overtones and drove a wedge between what Jefferson called "Monarchial Federalists" and "republican Federalists." Mason and "republican Federalists" like Jefferson and Madison shared a similar commitment to protecting southern agrarian interests.[13]

Mason and George Washington, by contrast, only drifted farther apart. Mason visited Mount Vernon in November 1788, but social contacts between the two men virtually ended after the Richmond convention. Writing about his relationship with Washington in March 1789, Mason told his son John, "I believe there are few men in whom he placed greater confidence; but it is possible my opposition to the new government, both as a member of the national and of the Virginia Convention, may have altered the case."[14] An unrelated issue further strained the relationship. Lund Washington told the general that acquaintances in Stafford had heard reports that John Travers Cooke, Mary Mason's husband, had been complaining that Washington had purchased a tract of land from Mason with worthless paper money. Mason had not complained at the time, Lund told the president, but "your secret enemy," as Lund called Mason, was now accusing Washington of virtual fraud. Lund Washington's story was hearsay on hearsay, and no other evidence exists that Mason ever spoke unfavorably of Washington. Washington, on the other hand, came to attribute Mason's refusal to accept the Constitution after the new government began operating to "Pride on the one hand, and want of manly candor on the other." Mason could not admit a mistake, and unfortunately, there were those in Virginia who would "tread *blindfold* in his steps." Visiting Mount Vernon in July 1792, the president wrote Hamilton that since returning home he had heard numerous complaints "from sensible & moderate men" and from "others, less friendly perhaps to the Government . . . (among whom may be classed my neighbor & quondam friend Colo. M.)." Washington listed twenty-one specific allegations, most of which involved Hamilton's funding plan. Whatever his private frustrations, Washington never attacked Mason publicly.[15]

MASON RETAINED HIS influence in local politics and with the general assembly. He used it to continue his war with the Alexandria faction on the Fairfax County Court, a faction composed, he told Martin Cockburn, of "Merchants & Men totally unacquainted with the Laws & Constitution of the Country," by which he surely meant Virginia. In December 1788 the court had indicated its intent to levy a tax to construct a new courthouse. As the presiding judge when the court met on 19 January 1789, Mason adjourned the proceedings to prevent passage of the tax; Mason opposed it because the Alexandria group wanted to build the new courthouse in the city. Mason favored a more central location. When the court reconvened the next day with the "country" faction temporarily in control, they passed a resolution stating that the court could not impose a tax "for any purpose whatever." It was an odd decision, probably wrong as a matter of law, and the court reversed itself a month later.[16]

Mason's next move was to draft a petition to the general assembly for authorization to move the county seat to the center of the county. Alexandria could retain its own corporation court, but the "partiality of Town Jurys," Mason argued, "has already begun to create a prejudice in the minds of many good citizens" from outlying parts of the county. He conceded moving the courthouse might adversely affect Alexandria merchants, but "compelling the People to spend their money and their time in tipling houses and Taverns, is not worth encouraging." With 550 signatures, Mason's petition quickly produced the legislation he requested, but by the next legislative session Mason was back, complaining now that the court was stalling in its selection of a new courthouse site. The courthouse flap led Mason to admit one flaw in the 1776 Constitution: "the unfortunate, and ill-judged clause in our Constitution of Government, investing the County Courts with the dangerous Power of filling up their own Vacancys." Mason won a posthumous victory; a 1798 act finally forced Fairfax County to build a new courthouse at a central location. It was completed in 1801.[17]

Mason lobbied the legislature on other issues as well. When he heard a rumor Fairfax County was to be combined into a new congressional district with the larger Loudoun County, he responded with a petition that was a classic republican jeremiad. Redistricting would reduce the freeholders of Fairfax County to the status of slaves because they would effectively be denied the most basic of all rights—the right of representation. An offense as minor as a poorly drawn congressional district ought to be resisted because every affront becomes a precedent for a more serious attack on the people's freedom. Districts "shou'd be Fairly and justly made; and not with a view of serving any temporary, local Party-Job whatever," in other words, the reelection of incumbent Richard Bland Lee. It was a false alarm; the legislature later adopted a new redistricting plan more advantageous to Fairfax County.[18]

Other disputes were real. Mason blocked an attempt by the merchant John Hooe to get permission to operate a ferry at Colchester. Hooe's ferry would have competed with one the Masons had operated for years. When the Indiana Company petitioned the general assembly for compensation for western lands it had been promised but had never received, Mason advised legislators to deny the request. When a dozen immigrants from Maryland violated a Virginia law requiring them to register any slaves brought into the state within ten days, Mason procured passage of exculpatory legislation.[19]

Is there any broader significance to Mason's often self-serving forays into local politics in the last years of his life? Experience had taught Mason that he could wield power more effectively at the local level than he could nationally, thus reinforcing a tendency toward provincialism. At the same time, what he saw as the malfeasance of the Fairfax County Court surely reinforced his republican predilection to distrust government in general and, more particularly, any government that was dominated by commercial interests.

A VIOLENT STORM struck Gunston Hall in mid-August 1789 and brought with it several days of rain. Mason assessed the damage in a letter to his son John. Too much rain would make the tobacco crop "unusually bad this Year." The wheat had "suffered some Damage, & our Hay a great deal." Omens for the corn "looked pretty good."[20]

In retirement at Gunston Hall, Mason endured the vagaries of the weather, as farmers always have, but if living well is the best revenge, Mason had his revenge on his critics. He refused to overextend himself. Mason had an opportunity to buy Marlborough, the Potomac plantation built by his uncle, John Mercer, but he refused. "There is no estate in Virginia which I should prefer to it," he told John Francis Mercer. He had, however, "Made it a Rule thro' Life, never, on any consideration whatever, to embarrass, or subject myself to Difficulties." He could not, consistent with that rule, and his financial obligations to his children, buy another plantation.[21]

Mason apparently settled his own debts with his British creditors before he died, although he grumbled about having to pay interest that had accrued during the American Revolution. He won a partial judgment against William Lee for Lee's alleged mishandling of a tobacco shipment at the beginning of the war. It was one of several lawsuits spawned by Mason's extensive agricultural operations and land speculations. He often complained about "all my ill luck with lawyers."[22] Robert Carter asked Mason to serve as a mediator in one of Carter's own legal squabbles. Mason tried to resist. "I am grown old & infirm, and find Business grow[s] fatigueing and irksome to me." In reality, Mason continued to do a good bit of his own legal work, and his letters suggest he eventually agreed to help Carter.[23] Mason had inherited a large estate, and with enterprise, frugality, and political connections, he made it a larger estate. By the time of his death in 1792, Mason had paid off his own debts, and his holdings included 15,000 acres along the Potomac, 60,000 acres in Kentucky, $50,000 worth of personal property, $30,000 in accounts receivable, and 300 slaves.[24]

By the late spring of 1789, the family at Gunston Hall had been "reduced," in Mason's words, "from a very large to a small one." Besides Mason's wife Sarah, only his second son, William, and his youngest daughter, Elizabeth, remained at home. Ann, at thirty-four the oldest daughter, had just married Rinaldo Johnson of Maryland. Elizabeth would marry William Thornton before the end of the year. William Mason did not marry until 1793, when he wed Ann Stuart, the daughter of an Anglican minister. Mason's daughter Sarah had been the first to leave home, marrying Daniel McCarty Jr. in 1778. In 1784 Mary married John Travers Cooke, Thomson married Sarah McCarty Chichester, and George Mason V, the firstborn, married Elizabeth Hooe. Cooke later bought Marlborough. George Mason V established his own plantation, which he christened Lexington. Thomson and his wife Sarah lived at Gunston Hall until 1787; Mason helped them build Hollin Hall. In 1788 the youngest son, Thomas had been sent to Fredericksburg Academy, along with George Graham, who was Sarah Brent's nephew. Graham had moved into Gunston Hall after Sarah and Mason married.[25]

Although George Mason V inherited his father's gout, Mason worried most about Thomas. Mason had expected Thomas to make a career in trade, but the boy waffled, and Mason lamented "a fickleness of Disposition, & want of Steadiness, that may prove highly injurious to him." Mason's fourth son John, as we shall see, flourished in a mercantile house in France, but fearing Tom would develop "a Distaste for his own country," Mason hesitated to send him abroad for a similar experience. "In my Opinion, there can hardly be a greater Misfortune, that a Man's having a Distaste to that Country, in which all his connections are, and in which he is to spend his Life."[26]

Mason's hyperbole, when he declined John Francis Mercer's offer to purchase Marlborough, is understandable: "The Payment of my Daughter's Fortunes, the building for; & settling two of my sons, and raising Capitals in Trade for two others, had required, & will require, all the money I am able to commend, and puts any large Purchase, at present, out of my Power."[27]

Mason may have been closest to John, and their correspondence forms the single most important source of information about Mason's final years. John had worked under the Quaker merchant William Hartshone in Alexandria. John accompanied his father to Philadelphia in 1787, but he returned to Alexandria before the convention adjourned. In 1788 John formed a partnership with James and Joseph Fenwick of Maryland. They hoped, among other things, to market American tobacco in France after the expiration of an exclusive contract between Robert Morris and the French Farmers' General. John Mason left for Bordeaux on 22 June 1788; Joseph Fenwick had arrived in France the previous year. John Mason impressed the older man: "He is *industrous* attentive *frugal* & *reasonable*,—he has courage to form resolutions & spirit to adhere to them."[28] Mason began sending his son advice even before John left for France. Mason wrote one letter from Richmond during the ratifying convention: "Confide as little as possible in the Merchants of the Place; at least never so far, as to give them the Power of hurting you; for they will look on your Success with a jealous & an evil Eye." He went on: "Live in a frugal Style, without parade or Ostentation, avoid all unnecessary Expence, & do as much of your Business your selves, as you can; when it exceeds this Compass, look narrowly into the Conduct of those you employ. Attend with Diligence & strict Integrity to the Interest of your Correspondents & enter into no Engagement which you have not the almost certain Means of performing." If you follow "these Maxims," Mason wrote John, "you will deserve to be rich; and you will be rich."[29]

More advice followed after John reached Bordeaux. Beware of borrowing money and "stick to your first Principles of giving no credits yourselves; especially in America, where large credits must infallibly ruin you, and small ones are not worth the charge of collecting. . . . Diligence Frugality & Integrity will infallibly increase your Business. . . . Content yourselves with moderate things at first." And resist the temptation to confide too freely in other English-speaking émigrés. Avoid the Irish—they were a bad influence—and watch the Scottish merchants—"they wish your House the Devil." Mason's letters even included home remedies for "convulsive cholic," which consisted of vile concoctions of bark, rhubarb, wine, castor oil, and a half dozen other ingredients, plus a little common sense. "You shou'd use exercise, & eat moderately, always rising from Table, with some little remaining Apetite."[30]

Mason provided more than advice. He patronized the firm himself. He shipped wheat and tobacco to Bordeaux to satisfy John's £1,000 capital subscription to the firm. He wrote letter after letter soliciting business for Mason, Fenwick, and Fenwick. He wrote James Monroe, for example, to suggest state-owned tobacco be marketed through John and his associates.[31] Mason's major undertaking was a lobbying effort to have Joseph Fenwick named American consul in Bordeaux, although he warned John that "I have no reason to expect my Interest will have much weight in the new Government, having, as you know, warmly opposed it." His strained relationship with George Washington notwithstanding, Mason remained on the best of terms with the new secretary of state, Thomas Jefferson. Mason candidly admitted to Jefferson that Fenwick's appointment would exempt the firm from certain regulations, "add to their Respectability as Merchants, and probably increase their Consignments." Fenwick got the appointment. John Mason had originally been interested in the position, but his father believed Fenwick, who had more commercial experience overseas, was better qualified.[32]

John Mason's venture in France—he returned to America in the summer of 1791—had a political significance beyond allowing his father to exploit his political connections. George Mason always believed in doing well by doing good. When he placed an order for "coarse goods" from France with John's firm, Mason told his son the slave clothing, nails, and axes he wanted were "of much greater Importance than you may at first conceive." Mason saw it as the opening salvo in a campaign to wean America from its economic dependence on Great Britain and to expand trade with France. The quality of French goods, however, proved disappointing, and if John did well selling tobacco in France, he was not able to ignite a commercial revolution.[33]

John witnessed a political revolution instead and provided his father with eyewitness accounts of the collapse of the Old Regime. When Mason learned John had been in Paris during the meeting of the Estates-General that triggered the revolution, Mason wrote back excitedly, "Pray give me the best Description you can of their Appearance; their Proceedings, & what is likely to be the Result. I am anxious to hear all I can about them."[34] As did most republicans in America, George Mason enthusiastically supported the French Revolution in its early stages. "These People seem to have catched the Flame of American Freedom," he wrote Samuel Griffin in September 1789. Mason supported John's decision to take an oath to support the new French government, and he took pride in John's appointment to the constitutional convention for the city of Bourdeaux.[35] As early as May 1790, however, Mason expressed concern about the inability of the relative moderates who had begun the revolution to consolidate their power and restore stability to France. Yet he remained uncharacteristically optimistic, expressing the belief as late as July 1792 that "Affairs there will soon be settled on a firm and safe Establishment." By October his confidence in the revolution began to waver. Mason did not live long enough to see the execution of Louis XVI and Marie Antoinette and France's descent into the chaos of the Jacobin Reign of Terror.[36]

EVEN IN RETIREMENT, George Mason remained in frequent contact with many of his old allies. Jefferson visited Gunston Hall, perhaps at Washington's request, to hear Mason's views on the site of a permanent location for the national capital. An agreement to build a capital in the South was part of the compromise made to pass Hamilton's funding and assumption plan, but an exact location remained to be decided. Jefferson detected in Mason "a shyness not usual in him," which the secretary of state attributed to Mason's ownership of land near Georgetown. Mason said enough to indicate his preference for a Georgetown site over Alexandria, a rival candidate. Mason may have had an interest in the federal district that went beyond a possible real-estate windfall. In January 1791 Mason wrote Jefferson to ask if a decision had been made. John Mason wanted to open an office in the capital and wanted to know where it would be. His father thought Congress would probably stay in "the whirlpool of Philadelphia . . . for half a century to come." Congress eventually selected the location Mason preferred, and

2,000 acres of Mason land were included within the final borders of the District of Columbia. He could not, however, control the location of a Potomac River bridge; he wanted it to cross Analostan Island, which Mason owned, but the bridge was built elsewhere.[37]

Mason corresponded frequently with Senator James Monroe. One of Mason's last letters to the future president contained an extended critique of American Indian policy. Mason warned against headlong westward expansion. It was strangely cautious given Mason's own history of land speculation and the expansionist tendencies of the emerging Democratic-Republican party, of which Mason was an intellectual godfather. At the same time, however, what had the Ohio Company been if not an attempt to provide for the orderly settlement of the West? In November 1791 a force commanded by General Arthur St. Clair had been defeated by a group of Ohio Indians near Fort Wayne. Mason believed a full-scale Indian war was now a necessity, mainly as a result of white mistakes. The Blue Ridge Mountains had been a boundary between white settlement and Indian country until the Treaty of Fort Stanwick pushed it back to the Ohio River. Mason believed whites should have stayed east of the river until that area was thoroughly settled. In earlier years, he told Monroe, whites had negotiated for small tracts and developed them before pushing west. Intensive settlement drove game from the fringes of white communities, and as the game left, Indians would abandon an area, which created an opportunity for a negotiated sale. Gradual settlement, Mason told Monroe, could prevent bloodshed.

Unfortunately, in Mason's view, speculators and the federal government's desire for money from public land sales prevented systematic expansion. The publication of maps showing the West divided into new states, a project Jefferson had supported, further unnerved the Indians. Mason hoped whites would be more moderate in their territorial demands, and he wished the Indians could live "by cultivating the Ground."[38] Mason romanticized early European-Indian relations—settlement had never been tidy or entirely peaceful—and he exaggerated the willingness of whites to live alongside even sedentary Indian farmers, but for Mason's day, his views were humane and enlightened.

Mason's health complaints seemed to multiply in the summer and early fall of 1792. The gout returned, accompanied perhaps by pneumonia or influenza. In August he described to John "Fevers" that left him "very weak & low." In September he complained of "an exceeding troublesome Cough." Meanwhile, Sarah was confined to bed with a broken leg. Mason had forty-nine slaves and several of his grandchildren inoculated for smallpox; the inoculations generally went well, but Betsy, William, and many of the household slaves were incapacitated by other ailments. "I hardly remember so sickly a season," he wrote John.[39]

Mason managed somehow to produce his last state paper, a petition to the general assembly to encourage "the Manufacture and Sale of Flour." He proposed a series of reforms intended to make inspections less burdensome on wheat producers. Progressive farmers in the Northern Neck had long seen wheat as an alternative to tobacco, but by the early 1790s Mason, Washington, and others were becoming concerned that Virginia wheat was no longer competitive, in part because of a 1787 inspection law. The assembly made only a few limited changes, but the petition was vintage Mason despite its lack of republican rhetoric—he did not claim the inspection system was the handiwork of a corrupt cabal of stockjobbers intent on reducing free farmers to slavery.[40] To the very end, Mason worried about the practical details of public policy, especially its economic consequences. If Mason occasionally sounded like an advanced libertarian, he never condemned outright the concept of a regulatory state with broad, coercive powers. Instead, Mason strove to make government less arbitrary, less burdensome, and more respectful of the most basic of human rights.

Thomas Jefferson visited Mason on Sunday afternoon, 1 October, when Mason seemed to be "recovering from a dreadful attack of the cholic." Mason reminisced about the Constitutional Convention. He "could have set his hand and heart" to the Constitution before the infamous deal between New England and "the 2 Southernmost States," which continued the slave trade and permitted a simple majority to adopt navigation laws. He also recalled the deep divisions within the New York delegation: Yates and Lansing, he told Jefferson, "never voted *in one single instance*" with Hamilton. And Mason recalled exposing Gouverneur Morris's effort early one morning near the end of the convention to slip past a half-empty chamber an amendment depriving the states of the power to call a convention to consider constitutional amendments.

Jefferson and Mason also discussed more current issues. Hamilton's plan for funding the national debt, Mason said, had "done us more injury than Gr. Britain and all her fleets and armies." According to Jefferson's notes, Mason had his own funding plan, which called for giving priority to the creditors who had kept their original certificates of indebtedness. Speculators would be paid as funds became available. Mason may have anticipated redeeming their certificates at a market price if they did not want to wait until the "unalienated certificates" were redeemed at face value. Jefferson left only the sketchiest outline of Mason's proposal, but Mason clearly did not want to reward speculation. Mason, Jefferson wrote James Madison, "was perfectly communicative, but I could not in discretion let him talk as much as he was disposed."[41] Mason died quietly at Gunston Hall, reportedly of "Gout in the Stomack," the following Sunday afternoon. He was sixty-six.

JEFFERSON CALLED IT "a great loss." Monroe believed Mason's "patriotic virtues thro the revolution will ever be remembered by the citizens of this country." In reality, apart from obituaries in the Maryland newspapers, Mason's death attracted little immediate attention.[42] Irritable and acerbic, yet independent and incorruptible, Mason had always inspired more respect than affection. His opposition to the Constitution probably cost him less support than his refusal to accept defeat graciously or to accept a position in the new government.

He would eventually enter the pantheon of Virginia heroes. As much as anyone—literally—George Mason helped to make a respectable revolution. From the nonimportation movement and the Fairfax Resolves to the Virginia Declaration of Rights and Virginia's first state constitution, Mason stood at the center of the revolutionary movement.[43] He contributed to its success partly by pursuing limited objectives. The rebellion against British rule was a movement for political independence, not social revolution, although few American leaders saw more clearly the implications of what Gordon Wood has called the "republican assault on patrimonialism." Mason knew "our own children will in a short time be among the general mass."[44] His revolution expanded the political rights of free white men. That objective seems wholly inadequate today, but Mason's conservatism, by modern standards, avoided the failures and excesses of many of the revolutionaries who came after him, especially in France and Russia, while laying the foundation for further reform.

Mason's most obvious legacy is in his contribution to America's founding documents: the Declaration of Independence through the Virginia Declaration of Rights, the Constitution through his role at the Philadelphia Convention, and the Bill of Rights through his dogged opposition to a Constitution without one. Mason may have taken a circumscribed view of the rights he advocated—limiting the right of representation to white men or restricting freedom of the press to a ban on prior restraint—but he put words on paper that could be given more expansive meanings by later generations.

In 1787 and later, Mason identified the fundamental fault line in American politics—the sectional rivalry between North and South. James Madison conceded before the new government was a year old that southern Anti-Federalists had been right about the threat the northern majority in Congress posed to the South. The "Antifederal champions," Jefferson wrote Washington in May 1792, "are now strengthened in argument by the fulfillment of their predictions."[45] Mason misdiagnosed the ultimate problem. The expansion of slavery, not navigation laws, would become the great flash point. Troubled as he was by slavery, he would have been appalled to see future generations of white southerners defend the institution as a positive good.

Nor did he foresee the informal, or extraconstitutional, political arrangements, such as the two-term tradition for presidents or the Senate filibuster, which would limit both majority rule and federal power. Practical considerations he did not predict also played a role in stemming the tide of what he would have seen as corruption. The unattractiveness of congressional service in the early Republic, for example, created de facto term limits. During the 1790s, few representatives served more than three terms in the House.[46] Mason would have approved.

More fundamentally, Mason failed to anticipate the extent to which Anti-Federalism would evolve to become one of the main currents of American political life. Opposition to the new Federalist regime extended beyond the South. During the ratification debate, Anti-Federalists forced the Federalists to defend the Constitution as creating a government of delegated, and therefore, limited powers. After ratification, Anti-Federalists used that argument to limit the expansion of the central government. They made strict construction and original intent staples of political and constitutional debate, and by taking their arguments from the history and text of the Constitution, they helped to elevate the document to near sacred stature.[47]

Anti-Federalists and moderate Federalists — Jefferson's "republican Federalists" — combined in the 1790s to create the Democratic-Republican Party, which elevated Mason's friend Jefferson to the presidency in 1800.[48] One of Mason's fellow nonsigners, Elbridge Gerry, would serve as vice president of the United States, as would Anti-Federalists Aaron Burr and George Clinton. By 1817 an old Anti-Federalist and another Mason ally, James Monroe, would be president. As Gordon Wood has written, the Anti-Federalists lost the battle over the Constitution, "but by 1800 they and their Jeffersonian-Republican successors eventually won the larger struggle over what kind of society and culture America was to have, at least for a good part of the nineteenth century."[49] Writing in the middle of that century, Martin Van Buren concluded that the Anti-Federalists "had won the struggle for America's political soul."[50]

And what of Mason's soul? He was not a modern-day libertarian, but he doubted any government could promote the public interest consistently. Mason harbored deep suspicions of the capacity of democracy, and even local government, to resist corruption. His advocacy of a two-thirds majority for navigation laws offers an insight into his way of reconciling majority rule and minority rights: those rights are not absolute, but they should not be abridged by simple majorities. Mason hoped the people's virtue would sustain a republican government, but he feared it would not, and so he sought safeguards to contain corruption and to protect minority interests.

If the Bill of Rights was Mason's direct legacy, and if he contributed to the enshrinement of the principle of limited government as part of the American political tradition, states' rights, a persistent canard in American politics until relatively recent times, is part of Mason's legacy only by mutation. Mason never made a major philosophical or constitutional defense of state sovereignty. He saw the states as existing political entities, each with unique interests and a special relationship with its citizens, and he assumed, more as a matter of common sense than political theory, that they ought to continue to be major forces in American political life. States' rights can be linked to Mason's brand of Anti-Federalism primarily by way of a shared objective—the desire to protect regional majorities that are minorities within the nation at large.

This is a refinement on a larger theme. George Mason's opposition to the ratification of the Constitution was not the protest of an isolated dissenter, and it was not an aberration in a career otherwise spent in the revolutionary mainstream. Mason's fear of the abuse of political power and the inevitability of political corruption was grounded in the ideology of the American Revolution, and because that fear was so deep-rooted, essential elements of his philosophy have echoed throughout American history.

NOTES

Abbreviations

DGW Donald Jackson and Dorothy Twohig, eds., *The Diaries of George Washington*, 4 vols. (Charlottesville: University Press of Virginia, 1976–78).

DHRC Merrill Jensen et al., eds., *The Documentary History of the Ratification of the Constitution of the United States*, 20 vols. (Madison: State Historical Society of Wisconsin, 1976–).

GM George Mason

JCC Washington C. Ford, ed., *Journals of the Continental Congress, 1776–1789*, 34 vols. (Washington, D.C.: U.S. Government Printing Office, 1931–44).

JHB *Journals of the House of Burgesses of Virginia*

PGM Robert A. Rutland et al., eds., *The Papers of George Mason*, 3 vols. (Chapel Hill: University of North Carolina Press, 1970).

PGW-ColS W. W. Abbot and Dorothy Twohig, eds., *The Papers of George Washington: The Colonial Series*, 10 vols. (Charlottesville: University Press of Virginia, 1983–95).

PGW-ConfS W. W. Abbot, ed., *The Papers of George Washington: Confederation Series*, 6 vols. (Charlottesville: University Press of Virginia, 1992–).

PGW-PS Dorothy Twohig, ed., *The Papers of George Washington: The Presidential Series*, 11 vols. (Charlottesville: University Press of Virginia, 1987–).

PGW-RWS Philander D. Chase, ed., *The Papers of George Washington: The Revolutionary War Series*, 14 vols. (Charlottesville: University Press of Virginia, 1985–).

Preface

1. Pacheco, *The Legacy of George Mason*, 7. See also Rutland, *George Mason and the War for Independence*, 2–3; Mapp, *The Faiths of our Fathers*, 110–11.

2. Schwartz, "George Mason, Forgotten Founder," 143; H. Miller, *George Mason: Constitutionalist*.

3. Morison, Commager, and Leuchtenburg, *The Growth of the American Republic*, 1:258. See also Brinkley, *American History*, 127; Goldfield et al., *The American Journey*, 207, 225; Roark et al., *The American Promise*, 228, 248. *The American Promise*, an otherwise excellent text, wrongly asserts that Mason agreed to support the Constitution once the Federalists agreed to support a bill of rights. Mason receives a more thorough treatment in Tindall and Shi, *America*, 216, 280–94. Mason fares well in the popular history of the Philadelphia Convention. See Collier and Collier, *Decision in Philadelphia*, especially chap. 32, "George Mason and the Rights of Man."

4. See Ellis, "The Persistence of Antifederalism after 1789," 295–314; Siemers, *Ratifying the Republic*, 215–27; Lienesch, "In Defense of the Anti-Federalists," 65–87.

5. See Senese, "George Mason," 147–52; Rutland, *George Mason: Reluctant Statesman*; Rowland, *Mason*, 1:272–73.

6. Rossiter, *Seedtime of the Republic*, 437.

7. Ellis, *Passionate Sage*, 227–28.

8. Quoted in Stourzh, *Benjamin Franklin and American Foreign Policy*, 5.

9. Carter Braxton, "An Address to the Convention of the Colony and Ancient Dominion of Virginia; on the Subject of Government in General, and Recommending a Particular Form to Their Consideration," in Van Schreeven et al., *Revolutionary Virginia*, 6:522.

10. Ibid., 522.

11. See Kramnick, "'The Great National Discussion,'" 3–32; Wood, *The Creation of the American Republic*, 96–97.

12. GM to John Mason, 14 May 1789, *PGM*, 3:1150.

Chapter One

1. Mason's nineteenth-century biographer, Kate Mason Rowland, listed George Mason along with George Washington, Thomas Jefferson, and other revolutionary-era patriots as descendants of Cavaliers. Rowland, *Mason*, 1:1. For most of them, the truth was less romantic. Jefferson's English roots, for example, are wholly obscure. See Malone, *Jefferson*, 1:4–8. Washington, by contrast, could trace his lineage to some prominent Royalists, but the first Washington in the colonies had been "a merchant adventurer," not an aristocrat. Randall, *George Washington*, 10. For an introduction to the historiographical debate, see Fischer and Kelly, *Bound Away*, 35–43, 311 (n. 44). The best history of the Mason family is Copeland and MacMaster, *Five George Masons*, upon which the following account draws heavily.

2. "Headright" refers to the practice, begun by the Virginia Company, of awarding fifty acres to any individual who paid for the transportation of an immigrant to the colony. Because headrights were sometimes traded and because patents were not always sought in a timely manner, it is impossible to determine whether George Mason I personally brought eighteen settlers to Virginia and, if so, when. See Morgan, *American Slavery*, 94, 171–73, 219, 405–6.

3. Moxham, *The Colonial Plantations*, 5–8; Copeland and MacMaster, *Five George Masons*, 19–49.

4. Jones, *Present State of Virginia*, 87. See also Rowland, *Mason*, 1:30–39; and Copeland and MacMaster, *Five George Masons*, 50–52.

5. Rowland, *Mason*, 1:39–47.

6. See Copeland and MacMaster, *Five George Masons*, 62–66.

7. Jones, *Present State of Virginia*, 85–86.

8. H. Miller, *Gentleman Revolutionary*, 25; Copeland and MacMaster, *Five George Masons*, 81–86; Rowland, *Mason*, 1:51; Moxham, *Colonial Plantations*, 9–10; Guardian's Report to Prince William County Court, ca. 1740, Mason Papers, Gunston Hall, Lorton, Virginia.

9. *Maryland Gazette* (Annapolis), 23 December 1762.

10. William Blathwart, as quoted in Morgan, *American Slavery*, 240.

11. As quoted in Copeland and MacMaster, *Five George Masons*, 78. On Mercer, see H. Miller, "John Mercer of Marlborough."

12. See Copeland and MacMaster, *Five George Masons*, 75–78; H. Miller, *Gentleman Revolutionary*, 31–33; Rowland, *Mason*, 1:52–53.

13. Quoted in Roeber, *Faithful Magistrates and Republican Lawyers*, 77. See also *PGM*, 1:64. Dumas Malone considered Thomson Mason to be "comparable with George Wythe in legal erudition." Malone, *Jefferson*, 1:121. George Mason is wrongly identified as "a highly respected lawyer" in Briceland, "Virginia: The Cement of the Union," 208.

14. Philip V. Fithian to Rev. Enoch Green, 2 November 1773, in Farish, *Fithian Journal and Letters*, 21; Fischer and Kelly, *Bound Away*, 86. On the Fairfax proprietary and the evolution of Fairfax County, see Sweig, "1649–1800," 6–11. The quitrents were not, apparently, overly burdensome: one shilling per fifty acres, collected haphazardly. See Sosin, *The Revolutionary Frontier*, 25; Bond, "The Quit-Rent System in the American Colonies."

15. Rowland, *Mason*, 1:55–58; Mason Family Bible Entries, 4 April 1750–11 April 1780, *PGM*, 1:480–83.

16. Endorsement on William Buckland's Indenture, 8 November 1759, *PGM*, 1:45–46; Copeland and MacMaster, *Five George Masons*, 96–100; Dunn, *Recollections of John Mason*, 47 (n. 30); Sobel, *The World They Made Together*, 100–105.

17. See Beirne and Scarff, *William Buckland*, 26–27; Beckerdite, "William Buckland and William Bernard Sears"; GM to George Mason Jr., 1 June 1787, *PGM*, 3:890–94.

18. H. Miller, *Gentleman Revolutionary*, 47–54; H. Miller, *George Mason of Gunston Hall*, 13–14.

19. See generally H. Miller, *Gentleman Revolutionary*, 55–56.

20. Dunn, *Recollections of John Mason*, 60–61, 78–80; *PGW-ColS*, 7:191 (n. 5); GM to George Washington, 16 May 1758, *PGM*, 1:43–44. On the education of the Mason children, see also Henri, *George Mason of Virginia*, 37.

21. Randolph, *History of Virginia*, 202. See also Jones, *Present State of Virginia*, 77–78; and H. Miller, *Gentleman Revolutionary*, 21–22.

22. *Animal Husbandry* (1775), in Jensen, *American Colonial Documents to 1776*, 329.

23. Ragsdale, *A Planters' Republic*, 9–10; Kulikoff, *Tobacco and Slaves*, 118–19; Copeland and MacMaster, *Five George Masons*, 105–6, 157; McCusker and Menard, *The Economy of British America*, 117–143.

24. GM to Alexander Henderson, 18 July 1763, *PGM*, 1:56–57.

25. Philip V. Fithian to Rev. Enoch Green, 1 December 1773, in Farish, *Fithian Journal and Letters*, 26–27.

26. Dunn, *Recollections of John Mason*, 77–80; Rutland, *George Mason: Reluctant Statesman*, 21–28.

27. Dunn, *Recollections of John Mason*, 69; Grigsby, *The Virginia Convention of 1776*, 154–55; Henry, *Henry*, 1:311; GM to George Washington, 6 May 1758, *PGM*, 1:42–43.

28. Dunn, *Recollections of John Mason*, 67–68.

29. See B. Brown, "The Library of George Mason."

30. GM to George Washington, 21 August 1755, *PGM*, 1:31–38; Copeland and MacMaster, *Five George Masons*, 114.

31. See generally Porter and Rousseau, *Gout*.

32. *Encyclopedia Britanica* (1771), as quoted in H. Miller, *Gentleman Revolutionary*, 43.

33. Dunn, *Recollections of John Mason*, 68; Reiss, *Medicine in Colonial America*, 146–150, 291–96. See generally Porter and Rousseau, *Gout*, 42–65, 101–14.

34. *Minutes of the Vestry*, 158; H. Miller, *Gentleman Revolutionary*, 33–34.

35. GM et al. to Thomas Waite, 21 June 1754, *PGM*, 1:36–37; *Minutes of the Vestry*, 79; Syndor, *American Revolutionaries*, 83–84. R. E. Brown and Brown, *Virginia, 1705–1786*, 243; Nelson, *A Blessed Company*, 43, 273–81. Nelson, arguing that Anglicanism has been unfairly judged by the standards of New England Puritanism and evangelical Protestantism, concludes that the established church was a more vigorous institution than commonly believed.

36. Rakove, *Madison*, 226–27; Rakove, *Declaring Rights*, 22.

37. W. Meade, *Old Churches*, 1:151–52; Wood, *Radicalism of the American Revolution*, 330; Kulikoff, *Tobacco and Slaves*, 233–34; Fischer and Kelly, *Bound Away*, 103–7, 132. See also Lambert, *The Founding Fathers and the Place of Religion in America*, 98–99.

38. An early historian of Truro Parish called Mason "the Father of Religious Liberty" for both defending the separation of church and state and for opposing punitive treatment of the Episcopal Church after it was disestablished. P. Slaughter, *The History of Truro Parish in Virginia*, 143–50. Robert A. Rutland, has suggested that, of all the Framers, Mason may have been the most consistent opponent of an established church. Rutland, "George Mason and the Origins of the First Amendment," 87–100.

39. Thomas Jefferson to Peter Carr, 10 August 1787, in Boyd et al., *The Papers of Thomas Jefferson*, 71:14–19; Jefferson, *The Jefferson Bible*.

40. W. Meade, *Old Churches*, 1:99. Although he was politically closer to Patrick

Henry and personally closer to Richard Henry Lee, Mason may have been intellectually more in tune with Madison, with whom he was almost invariably allied until the climatic struggle over the ratification of the Constitution toward the end of Mason's career. See Rutland, *George Mason and the War for Independence*, 5; and Rutland, "George Mason and the Origins of the First Amendment."

41. "Last Will & Testament," 20 March 1773, *PGM*, 1:147; Mapp, *Faiths of Our Fathers*, 113–19.

42. H. Miller, *Gentleman Revolutionary*, 84; Montagu, *Reflections on the Rise and Fall of the Ancient Republicks*, 295–97, 307–8; Nelson, *Blessed Company*, 205–7. Brent Tarter provides a useful introduction to the relevant literature in "Reflections on the Church of England in Colonial Virginia."

43. "Recusant convicts," Catholics who refused to attend Anglican services, were disenfranchised. In 1762 the right to vote of Mason's Catholic neighbor George Brent was challenged, but Brent was allowed to vote apparently because, whatever his personal beliefs, he was not a "recusant convict." Kennedy, *JHB, 1761–1765*, 126–30. See generally Hening, *Statutes*, 3:172, 238; 4:133–34, 477; Syndor, *American Revolutionaries*, 35–37; Dinnerstein and Palsson, *Jews in the South*, 5; Kolp, *Gentlemen and Freeholders*, 43–49. For support for an 85 percent level of eligibility, see R. E. Brown and Brown, *Virginia, 1705–1786*, 142. See also Greene, *The Quest for Power*, 186.

44. Kolp, *Gentlemen and Freeholders*, 43–58. For slightly lower rates of voter turnout, see Griffith, *The Virginia House of Burgesses*, 54–60.

45. Roeber, *Faithful Magistrates*, 75. See also Wood, *Radicalism of the American Revolution*, 115–21.

46. Main, "The One Hundred." On the rise of the small planter and the political consequences of slavery, see Morgan, *American Slavery*, 345–47, 364–71.

47. Sweig, "1649–1800," 28–36; Kolp, *Gentlemen and Freeholders*, 133–64. Fairfax County's population increased from the late 1740s to Mason's death in 1792 even though Loudoun County was carved out of it in 1757. Trends in Fairfax County reflected a colony-wide pattern: a relatively small population growing at a rapid rate. Between 1730 and 1760, for example, Virginia's population increased from 115,000 to 340,000, and twenty-two new counties were created. Billings, Selby, and Tate, *Colonial Virginia*, 252–53.

48. Syndor, *American Revolutionaries*, 76–78; Roeber, *Faithful Magistrates*, 42–43; Sweig, "1649–1800," 51, 60–61.

49. As quoted in Isaac, *The Transformation of Virginia*, 133–34. See also Roeber, *Faithful Magistrates*, 141–42.

50. Roeber, *Faithful Magistrates*, 172–73. For the more conventional view of the role of the courts, see Isaac, *Transformation of Virginia*, 133–34.

51. Mason's service on the county court, or his lack thereof, is detailed in Horrell, "George Mason and the Fairfax County Court."

52. Proceedings of the Constitutional Convention, 22 June 1787, *PGM*, 3:192. See also Kolp, *Gentlemen and Freeholders*, 146–49; Syndor, *American Revolutionaries*, 96; Countryman, *The American Revolution*, 32–33.

53. John Kirkpatrick to George Washington, 21 July 1758, *PGW-ColS*, 4:314–15; Kolp, *Gentlemen and Freeholders*, 153–54.

54. See generally Greene, *Quest for Power*, 28–30; Griffith, *Virginia House of Burgesses*, 8–15, 46–48, 129–40; Henry, *Henry*, 2:73–77. See also Egnal, "The Origins of the Revolution in Virginia: A Reinterpretation," which argues for the existence of a cohesive, expansionist Northern Neck clique and an opposing Tidewater faction that, although it included members who speculated in western land, had little real interest in developing the frontier.

55. McIlwaine, *JHB, 1758–1761*, 8, 12, 50, 104.

56. Ibid., 7, 80, 84; Rowland, *Mason*, 1:72–73.

57. McIlwaine, *JHB, 1758–1761*, 50; Copland and MacMaster, *Five George Masons*, 107–9; Rowland, *Mason*, 1:77.

58. *PGM*, 1:159; H. Miller, *Gentleman Revolutionary*, 32–33.

59. Randall, *George Washington*, 68. See also Bailey, *Ohio Company*, 103.

60. James, *Ohio Company*, 7–18.

61. Mulkearn, *George Mercer Papers*, 3–4; James, *Ohio Company*, 13; Philyaw, *Virginia's Western Visions*, 49.

62. Mulkearn, *George Mercer Papers*, 174–75; GM to Lawrence Washington, 27 May 1750, *PGM*, 1:11–12; Agreement with Christopher Gist, 11 September 1750, ibid., 12–13; Bailey, *Ohio Company*, 73–78; James, *Ohio Company*, 36–37.

63. As quoted in James, *Ohio Company*, 13. See also Bailey, *Ohio Company*, 116–22.

64. H. Miller, *Gentleman Revolutionary*, 37–39; *PGM*, 1:5–6. The other investors included nineteen-year-old George Washington.

65. Randall, *George Washington*, 72–73; Robert Dinwiddie to Thomas Cresap, 23 January 1752, in Brock, *The Official Records of Robert Dinwiddie*, 1:17–18.

66. Bailey, *Ohio Company*, 147–49; James, *Ohio Company*, 81–82; Koontz, *Robert Dinwiddie*, 172.

67. GM to Christopher Gist, 28 April 1752, *PGM*, 1:15–18.

68. Morton, *Colonial Virginia*, 2:618–19; Hinderaker, *Elusive Empires*, 134–37; Ward, *Breaking the Backcountry*, 26–29.

69. "Proposal to Settle Foreign Protestants," 6 February 1753, *PGM*, 1:28–30; Marshall, "A Nation Defined by Empire, 1775–1776," 208–21.

70. Philyaw, *Virginia's Western Visions*, 61; Hinderaker, *Elusive Empires*, 39. The story of the beginning of the French and Indian War has been told many times, but useful accounts from the Ohio Company's perspective include Abernethy, *Western Lands and the American Revolution*, 5@13; and Bailey, *Ohio Company*, 152–59, 179–80. See also Anderson, *Crucible of War*, 25–29.

71. James, *Ohio Company*, 99–103; Bailey, *Ohio Company*, 213–17.

72. GM to George Washington, 13 September 1756, *PGM*, 1:39–40; Fairfax County Minute Book, 1756–1763, 17B, Fairfax Co. (Va.) Public Library; George Washington to Thomas Waggoner, 8 October 1755, *PGW-ColS*, 2:89, George Mercer to John Carlyle, 10 October 1755, ibid., 96.

73. Edward Kimler, as quoted in Isaac, *Transformation of Virginia*, 109.

74. See generally Sosin, *Whitehall and the Wilderness*, 48–78. See also H. Miller, *Gentleman Revolutionary*, 65–68.

75. "Petition to King George III," 9 September 1761, *PGM*, 1:47–49.

76. GM to Robert Dinwiddie, 9 September 1761, *PGM*, 1:46–47; GM et al. to Capel and Osgood Hanbury, 10 September 1761, ibid., 50–51.

77. For contrary views of Dinwiddie as an aggressive representative of the Ohio Company, see Ward, *Breaking the Backcountry*, 26–29; and Royster, *The Fabulous History of the Dismal Swamp Company*, 52–60.

78. Jennings, *The Creation of America*, 88. See also Bailey, *Ohio Company*, 222–30; James, *Ohio Company*, 115–18; and Sosin, *Whitehall and the Wilderness*, 42–43.

79. "The Royal Proclamation on North America," 7 October 1763, in Morison, *Sources and Documents*, 1–4; Sosin, *Whitehall and the Wilderness*, 48–49.

80. John Mercer to Charlton Palmer, 17 April 1764, in Mulkearn, *George Mercer Papers*, 185.

81. As quoted in Sosin, *Whitehall and the Wilderness*, 122–23. See also *PGM*, 1:5–8; Bailey, *Ohio Company*, 36, 204–19; and Philyaw, *Virginia's Western Visions*, 67.

82. GM et al. to Capel and Osgood Hanbury, 10 September 1761, *PGM*, 1:50–51.

83. See Holton, *Forced Founders*, 7–8.

Chapter Two

1. GM to Committee of London Merchants, 6 June 1766, *PGM*, 1:65–73.

2. "Proposal to Settle Foreign Protestants," 6 February 1753, ibid., 1:29; Morgan, *American Slavery*, 345.

3. See Alden, *American Revolution*, 36–37; Middlekauff, *The Glorious Cause*, 143; and Rutland, *George Mason and the War for Independence*, 16.

4. Morgan and Morgan, *The Stamp Act Crisis*, 21–23; Middlekauff, *The Glorious Cause*, 57.

5. Ragsdale, *A Planters' Republic*, 48–49; Middlekauff, *The Glorious Cause*, 61. The various acts are reprinted in Jensen, *American Colonial Documents*, 351–64, 643–50.

6. James Otis, "The Rights of the British Colonies Asserted and Proved" (1764), in Morison, *Sources and Documents*, 6; Daniel Dulany, "Considerations on the Propriety of Imposing Taxes in the British Colonies" (1765), ibid., 30. See also Morgan and Morgan, *The Stamp Act*, 38–39, 272–74.

7. Quoted in Middlekauff, *The Glorious Cause*, 111–12. See also Peters, *The Elder Pitt*, 155–56.

8. Morgan and Morgan, *The Stamp Act*, 38–39, 152–53; Alden, *American Revolution*, 66–67; "The Stamp Act," in Jensen, *American Colonial Documents*, 655–56.

9. Francis Fauquier to the Board of Trade, 3 November 1765, in Reese, *The Of-*

ficial Papers of Francis Fauquier, 3:1290–96. See also Alden, *American Revolution*, 70–72.

10. Edmund Pendleton to James Madison Sr., 11 December 1765, in Mays, *Pendleton Papers*, 1:20–21; Edmund Pendleton to James Madison Sr., 15 February 1766, ibid., 21–24. See also Morgan and Morgan, *The Stamp Act*, 170–79.

11. H. Miller, *George Mason: Constitutionalist*, 93; "Scheme for Replevying Goods," 23 December 1765, *PGM*, 1:61–65.

12. "Scheme for Replevying Goods," *PGM*, 1:61; Rutland, *George Mason and the War for Independence*, 13.

13. GM to George Washington and George William Fairfax, 23 December 1765, *PGM*, 1:60–61.

14. Chitwood, *Richard Henry Lee*, 17–21; Ragsdale, *A Planters' Republic*, 115–16, 119–22; Isaac, *Transformation of Virginia*, 247; Berlin, *Many Thousands Gone*, 280; "Address of the House of Burgesses to the King in Opposition to the Slave Trade," 1 April 1772, in Van Schreeven et al., *Revolutionary Virginia*, 1:85–88.

15. Henry, *Henry*, 2:152–53.

16. Dunn, Gunston Hall Liberty Lecture, 18 February 2004, Gunston Hall; George Washington to John Posey, 11 June 1769, *PGW-ColS*, 8:211–16; Farish, *Fithian Journal and Letters*, 37–39, 84–85, 129.

17. Jones, *Present State of Virginia*, 130–32. See also ibid., 75–76. See generally *PGM*, 3:50–55. Ira Berlin argues, to the contrary, that slave working conditions deteriorated in the early 1700s as slavery became more entrenched. Berlin, *Many Thousands Gone*, 116–17.

18. Franklin, "Observations Concerning the Increase of Mankind" (1751), in Labaree, *The Papers of Benjamin Franklin*, 4:225–34; Thomas Jefferson, *Notes on the State of Virginia* (1785), in Peterson, *The Portable Jefferson*, 192–93.

19. See Davis, *The Problem of Slavery*, 41, 210.

20. Jordan, *White over Black*, 44.

21. Ibid., 20–24, 187–90, 213 (n. 74).

22. Branchi, "Memoirs of the Life and Voyages of Doctor Philip Mazzei, Part II," 251; Marchione, *Philip Mazzei*, 223–24; Jordan, *White over Black*, 552; Davis, *The Problem of Slavery*, 179, 212.

23. Hening, *Statutes*, 4:132; R. E. Brown and Brown, *Virginia, 1705–1776*, 285. When private manumissions produced a notable increase in the number of free blacks in Virginia, the legislature responded by increasing restrictions on them until, by 1806, it required all newly freed blacks to leave the state within twelve months. Jordan, *White over Black*, 348. Hostility toward free blacks was hardly unique to Virginia. At the same time that Massachusetts, in 1788, banned the slave trade, it also banned voluntary immigration from Africa. Ibid., 410–11.

24. Jefferson, *Notes on the State of Virginia* (1785), in Peterson, *The Portable Jefferson*, 186.

25. Henry, *Henry*, 1:112–16. Indeed, David Brion Davis has expressed doubts about the competence of early American governments to have managed a program of general emancipation even if it did not include colonization. *The Problem of Slavery*, 256–57.

26. Quoted in Breen, "Ideology and Nationalism," 33.

27. Locke, *Two Treatises*, 105–6, 236–37, 284–85, 322–23, 350–51. See also Katz, "Thomas Jefferson and the Right to Property in Revolutionary America," 467–88. To view the matter from a slightly different angle, Winthrop Jordan has argued that, after about 1740, Americans increasingly understood natural rights to mean political rights, and few white Americans wanted to extend political rights to blacks. Jordan, *White over Black*, 294–301.

28. Katz, "Thomas Jefferson and the Right to Property," 469–75, 483–84. Despite the embarrassment slavery caused many of the Virginia Founders, outspoken popular support for the institution existed even during the revolutionary era. See Schmidt and Wilhelm, "Early Proslavery Petitions in Virginia," 133–46.

29. Morgan, *American Slavery*, 381–87; Davis, *The Problem of Slavery*, 261–62; Sobel, *The World They Made*, 45.

30. See Freehling, "The Founding Fathers and Slavery," for a relatively sympathetic assessment of the Founders' contribution toward the abolition of slavery. Freehling's later work, "The Founding Fathers, Conditional Antislavery, and the Nonradicalism of the American Revolution," 12–33, is more critical, but still concludes that the abolition of the slave trade weakened slavery in the border states. Reducing the growth of the slave population diverted slaves to the Deep South, Freehling suggests, where slavery was most profitable. Ibid., 28–29. For a more critical assessment, see Finkelman, "Slavery and the Constitutional Convention: Making a Covenant with Death," 188–225.

31. Morgan and Morgan, *The Stamp Act*, 159–60, 264–65; Alden, *American Revolution*, 76–77.

32. *Virginia Gazette* (Purdie), 16 May 1766; Morgan and Morgan, *The Stamp Act*, 282; Greene, *Quest for Power*, 372; Middlekauff, *The Glorious Cause*, 138–39.

33. GM to Committee of Merchants in London, 6 June 1766, *PGM*, 1:65–66.

34. Ibid., 66–67.

35. Ibid., 69–70. American irritation at the Navigation Acts should not be minimized. Woody Holton believes taxes were "only the straw that broke the camel's back." According to this interpretation, Americans thought they were subsidizing British industry but hesitated to call for repeal of the Navigation Acts, which were popular in Britain. Because of the subsidies already flowing to Britain, even a minor tax could seem unduly burdensome. "Historians," Holton writes, "have focused on the straw and ignored the enormous burden the camel already carried." Holton, *Forced Founders*, 56 (n. 24).

36. *PGM*, 1:68, 70–71. See also Morgan and Morgan, *The Stamp Act*, 284–89; and, "The Declaratory Act," in Jensen, *American Colonial Documents*, 695–96.

37. Randolph, *History of Virginia*, 176; Lee, *Memoir of the Life of Richard Henry Lee*, 1:45; Middlekauff, *The Glorious Cause*, 190.

38. Morgan and Morgan, *The Stamp Act*, 295–96; DePauw, "The Roots of American Federalism"; Ganter, "The Machiavellianism of George Mason"; Rossiter, *Seedtime of the Republic*, 352–56; Isaac, *The Transformation of Virginia*, 49.

39. Countryman, *The American Revolution*, 60–63; Murrin, "Can Liberals Be Patriots?," 35–65; McDonald, *Novus Ordo Seclorum*, 66–77; Lutz, "Relative

Importance of European Writers on Late Eighteenth Century American Political Thought," 189–197.

40. Locke, *Two Treatises*, 138–39, 156, 350, 357–58, 398–402. For an accessible introduction to Locke, see Ebenstein and Ebenstein, *Great Political Thinkers*, 425–54.

41. Trenchard and Gordon, *Cato's Letters*, 2:804. For a skeptical view of the republican influence, see Diggins, "Comrades and Citizens: New Mythologies in American History," 614–49.

42. Trenchard and Gordon, *Cato's Letters*, 2:121; Maier, *From Resistance to Revolution*, 43–45. On Jefferson's fear of luxury, see Colbourn, *The Lamp of Experience*, 168–69.

43. Middlekauff, *The Glorious Cause*, 46–48, 130–35, 238–39; Bailyn, *The Ideological Origins of the American Revolution*, 34–54; Wood, *The Creation of the American Republic*, 16–17; Wood, *Radicalism of the American Revolution*, 102–3.

44. Countryman, *The American Revolution*, 57.

45. GM to George Brent, 6 December 1770, *PGM*, 1:127; Wade, *The Letters of Junius*, 1:153–62.

46. Trenchard and Gordon, *Cato's Letters*, 1:188. On Sidney's pervasive influence on the American revolutionaries, see Robbins, *The Eighteenth-Century Commonwealthman*, 46.

47. Trenchard and Gordon, *Cato's Letters*, 2:556; 1:105.

48. GM to Richard Henry Lee, 7 June 1770, *PGM*, 1:118; Rossiter, *Seedtime of the Republic*, 389; Maier, *From Resistance to Revolution*, 137–38. As an example of an eighteenth-century view of civil liberties, Mason may have valued free speech less as an exercise of self-expression or an abstract search for truth, but as a check on the abuse of government power. See Schauer, "Free Speech and Its Philosophical Roots," 132–55.

49. Trenchard and Gordon, *Cato's Letters*, 2:648–49.

50. Ibid., 1:103.

51. As quoted in Robbins, *The Eighteenth-Century Commonwealthman*, 122. More specifically, "the people" did not include the urban poor. Ibid., 116, 321.

52. Ibid., 15; McDonald, *Novus Ordo Seclorum*, 15–17; Colbourn, *The Lamp of Experience*, 130–31; Pangle, *The Spirit of Modern Republicanism*, 93; Middlekauff, *The Glorious Cause*, 238–39; Proceedings of the Constitutional Convention, 20 August 1787, *PGM*, 3:962–63.

53. Trenchard and Gordon, *Cato's Letters*, 1:xxxvii; Sidney, *Discourses on Government*, foreword; Pangle, *The Spirit of Modern Republicanism*, 29–35; Houston, *Algernon Sidney and the Republican Heritage in England and America*, 223–31, 277.

54. See Pocock, "Between Gog and Magog: The Republican Thesis and the *Ideologia Americana*," 325–46. Maier, *From Resistance to Revolution*, 39, points out Sidney's and Locke's mutual commitment to the right of armed resistance to an arbitrary government, a highly salient point, to say the least, to the American revolution-

aries. On Locke's contribution to modern notions of individual rights and equality, see Breen, "Ideology and Nationalism," 34–39.

55. The cliché was inspired by Countryman, *The American Revolution*, 57, commenting on the colonists' tendency to exaggerate their policy differences with the British government.

56. Malone, *Jefferson*, 1:89. Bland has been neglected by historians, but he is deftly profiled in Rossiter, *Seedtime of the Republic*, 247–80. See also Tarter, "Richard Bland," 2:10–13.

57. Richard Bland, "The Colonel Dismounted" (1764), in Bailyn, *Pamphlets of the American Revolution, 1750–1776*, 293–354.

58. Ibid., 319–20.

59. Ibid., 321.

60. Bland, "An Inquiry into the Rights of the British Colonies" (1766), in Hyneman and Lutz, *American Political Writing during the Founding Era*, 1:67–87.

61. Ibid., 73.

62. Ibid., 74–80.

63. Henry, *Henry*, 1:112–16. Ironically, the revolutionary-era commitment to religious tolerance rested in part on an aversion to slavery. Henry's comments, for example, were made in the course of ruminating on the need to attract white farmers, as opposed to black slaves, to Virginia. See also Robbins, *The Eighteenth-Century Commonwealthman*, 116–18; Locke, *Two Treatises*, 55, 405; Trenchard and Gordon, *Cato's Letters*, 2:797–803; R. E. Brown and Brown, *Virginia 1705–1786*, 251; *PGM*, 1:28–29.

64. As quoted in Chitwood, *Richard Henry Lee*, 73. The relevant portion of the Quebec Act appears in Morison, *Sources and Documents*, 103–4. For the entire act, see Force, *American Archives*, 1:216–20. Holton, *Forced Founders*, 208–9, questions the sincerity of Lee's anti-Catholicism. Holton suggests Lee may have seen anti-Catholic rhetoric as a politically popular way to attack a bill he opposed for other reasons, including its expansion of Quebec's boundaries into territory claimed by Virginia.

65. GM to Committee of London Merchants, *PGM*, 1:70; see generally R. E. Brown and Brown, *Virginia, 1705–1786*, 243–70. Mason's second wife, Sarah Brent, was a Catholic. Steiner, "The Catholic Brents of Colonial Virginia."

66. Rossiter, *Seedtime of the Republic*, 448; Bailyn, *Ideological Origins*, 19, 283–84. This is not to deny that the Revolution triggered social changes that transformed American society; it is to say simply that the Founders did not intend to bring about widespread social change. See Wood, *Radicalism of the American Revolution*, 169–73.

67. Peterson, *Thomas Jefferson and the New Nation*, 76; Wood, *The American Revolution*, 43, 58–60. John Phillip Reid, in *Constitutional History of the American Revolution*, develops at length the argument that America's challenge to Parliament's authority was seen by many English politicians as a threat to constitutional government in Great Britain.

68. On the passage of the Townshend Act, see Alden, *American Revolution*,

84–94; and Middlekauff, *The Glorious Cause*, 136–52. See also Peters, *The Elder Pitt*, 172–83; and Brooke, *The Chatham Administration*, 93–94, 134–38.

69. Ragsdale, *A Planters' Republic*, 72–73; Dickinson, "Letters from a Farmer in Pennsylvania," in Morison, *Sources and Documents*, 34–54.

70. George Washington to GM, 5 April 1769, *PGM*, 1:96–98. The Philadelphia agreement is reprinted in ibid., 100–102.

71. GM to George Washington, 5 April 1769, ibid., 99–100.

72. *DGW*, 2:142; GM to George Washington, 23 April 1769, *PGM*, 1:102–3, 94–96.

73. Recent scholarship tends to confirm Mason's authorship of the nonimportation agreement. See Ragsdale, *A Planters' Republic*, 73–76; Holton, *Forced Founders*, 86 (n. 20). H. Miller, *George Mason: Constitutionalist*, 100, goes so far as to credit Mason with drafting the Maryland resolves against the Townshend Duties, but does not document the claim.

74. *PGM*, 1:103–6. The essay Mason told Washington he was writing to popularize nonimportation may have appeared in the Virginia papers as two letters from "Atticus" in May 1769. Certainly the points made in the second letter—for example, that the abolition of the slave and tobacco trades would encourage domestic industry and the immigration of English workers—could have come from Gunston Hall. Otherwise little more than tradition identifies Mason as Atticus. Conceivably, Atticus could have been two people: Mason, who wrote the second letter, and another writer, perhaps the unknown copyist who helped Mason with the nonimportation agreement, who drafted the first. But the theory is largely conjecture. See ibid., 106–9. Ragsdale believes Mason was Atticus. Ragsdale, *A Planters' Republic*, 77.

75. Kennedy, *JHB, 1766–1769*, 214–18; *DGW*, 16–18 May 1769, 2:151–53; *PGM*, 1:109–13.

76. Rutland, *George Mason and the War for Independence*, 21; Ragsdale, *A Planters' Republic*, 87; Wood, *The American Revolution*, 35–36; *Historical Statistics of the United States*, part II, 1176, 1192.

77. As quoted in Alden, *American Revolution*, 104.

78. GM to Richard Henry Lee, 7 June 1770, *PGM*, 1:116–19; George Washington to George William Fairfax, 27 June 1770, *PGW-ColS*, 8:353–54; Ragsdale, *A Planters' Republic*, 91–92.

79. GM to George Brent, 6 December 1770, *PGM*, 1:127–30; GM et al. to Peyton Randolph, 18 July 1771, ibid., 132–33; Sweig, "The Virginia Nonimportation Association Broadside of 1770," 316–325; Ragsdale, *A Planters' Republic*, 101, 107–9, 176.

Chapter Three

1. GM to Committee of Merchants in London, 6 June 1766, *PGM*, 3:71.

2. The assessment is Forrest McDonald's in his *E Pluribus Unum*, 265. Ralph Ketcham offers a similar opinion in *James Madison*, 71, arguing that Mason, by 1776, was generally acknowledged as Virginia's premier republican theorist.

3. Thomas Jefferson to A. B. Woodward, 3 April 1825, in Lipscomb, *The Writings of Thomas Jefferson*, 16:166–67; Rowland, *Mason*, 1:248–49; Randolph, *History of Virginia*, 192; Henry, *Henry*, 1:311; Rutland, *George Mason and the War for Independence*, 25, 28.

4. Morgan and Morgan, *The Stamp Act*, 293–94; Peterson, *Thomas Jefferson and the New Nation*, 41–42; "The Representation of John Robinson's Administrators," 22 November 1769, in Mays, *Pendleton Papers*, 1:49–53.

5. See generally Maier, "A Virginian as Revolutionary: Richard Henry Lee," in Maier, *The Old Revolutionaries*, 164–200.

6. Chitwood, *Richard Henry Lee*, 234.

7. Lee, *Memoir of the Life of Richard Henry Lee*, 1:136–38, 251–52.

8. Ibid., 251–52; Wirt, *Sketches*, 125; R. Meade, *Patrick Henry*, 1:326.

9. GM to Martin Cockburn, 26 May 1774, *PGM*, 1:190–91; Randolph, *History of Virginia*, 178; Wirt, *Sketches*, 24, 421; Rutland, *George Mason and the War for Independence*, 28.

10. *DGW*, 24 March 1762, 1:295; 21 March 1763, 1:315; 30 March 1763, 1:317; 29 March 1764, 1:327–28; 30 May 1765, 1:337; 10 March 1775, 3:319.

11. Ibid., 27–28 November 1771, 3:71; 20 September 1773, 3:204; 1 December 1768, 2:114; 20–22 June 1769, 2:159–60.

12. GM to George Washington, 9 April 1768, Mason Papers, Gunston Hall; *DGW*, 10 May 1769, 2:150; 13 March 1770, 2:219; 18 April 1770, 2:229.

13. *DGW*, 27 August 1770, 2:264; 19 December 1770, 2:331–32; 15 February 1771, 3:8; 28 March 1771, 3:16.

14. Thomas Johnson to George Washington, 10 May 1772, *PGW-ColS*, 9:43–44; GM to George Washington, ca. 8 March 1775, *PGM*, 1:224–25; Copeland and MacMaster, *Five George Masons*, 118–22.

15. Henriques, "Uneven Friendship"; Cunliffe, *George Washington*, 127–29; George Washington to John Posey, 26 July 1769, *PGW-ColS*, 8:234–37; GM to George Washington, 17 October 1769, *PGM*, 1:113–15.

16. W. Meade, *Old Churches*, 2:227; Rowland, *Mason*, 1:112–14.

17. GM to George Washington, 18 February 1775, *PGM*, 1:223–24.

18. Flexner, *George Washington*, 1:313–14; Ellis, *His Excellency*, 63.

19. GM to Mrs. John Moncure, 12 March 1764, *PGM*, 1:59–60. See also GM to George Washington, 5 April 1769, ibid., 99–100; GM to George Washington, 17 October 1769, ibid., 113–14; GM to Charles and Landon Carter, 11 May 1770, ibid., 115–16; GM to George Washington, 17 February 1775, ibid., 220–22.

20. Mason Family Bible Entries, 4 April 1750–11 April 1780, ibid., 480–83; "Last Will and Testament," 20 March 1773, ibid., 147–60; Dunn, *Recollections of John Mason*, 65.

21. GM to George Brent, 2 October 1778, *PGM*, 1:433–39.

22. Branchi, "Memoirs of the Life and Voyages of Doctor Philip Mazzei, Part I," 169–70; Rakove, *Madison*, 13–14.

23. Edmund Pendleton to Joseph Chew, 15 June 1775, in Mays, *Pendleton Papers*, 1:110–13.

24. *PGM*, 1:8–9, 79–80.

25. Sosin, *Whitehall and the Wilderness*, 136–38; "Report of the Board of Trade and Plantations on the Western Problem," 7 March 1768, in Morison, *Sources and Documents*, 64; James, *Ohio Company*, 143–45.

26. GM to Robert Carter, 23 January 1768, *PGM*, 1:78–79; Robert Carter to GM, 10 February 1768, ibid., 80–83; "Memorandum on the Boundaries Proposed by the Ohio Company," ca. 20 February 1768, ibid., 85–89; GM to Robert Carter, 24 February 1768, ibid., 89–90.

27. GM to George Brent, 6 December 1770, ibid., 127–30; James, *Ohio Company*, 143–45.

28. James, *Ohio Company*, 146–50; Rowland, *Mason*, 1:155–58.

29. Sosin, *Whitehall and the Wilderness*, 189–90; Rowland, *Mason*, 1:155–58.

30. *PGM*, 1:125–26; GM to George Brent, 6 December 1770, ibid., 127–30; George Mercer to GM, 8 August 1771, ibid., 134–36; James Mercer to GM, 9 January 1772, ibid., 136–40.

31. GM to James Mercer, 13 January 1772, ibid., 140–43; James, *Ohio Company*, 265–66.

32. Ohio Company Advertisement, 5 August 1773, *PGM*, 1:162–63; James, *Ohio Company*, 156–58; Rowland, *Mason*, 1:119; Abernethy, *Western Lands and the American Revolution*, 127–28; Copeland and MacMaster, *Five George Masons*, 136–37; Morison, *Sources and Documents*, 79–100.

33. *PGM*, 1:161. See also ibid., at appendix B.

34. "Extracts from the Virginia Charters," ca. July 1773, ibid., 166. See also Stith, *The History of the First Discovery and Settlement of Virginia*.

35. "Extracts," *PGM*, 1:180–81.

36. Ibid., 182.

37. Ibid.; H. Miller, *George Mason: Constitutionalist*, 81.

38. "Extracts," *PGM*, 1:168.

39. Ibid., 173–75. Equally "Foreign" was Mason's commentary on the expansion of the vice-admiralty courts: "A plan so contrary to the first principles of Liberty & Justice, as would much better become the Divan at Constantinople, than the Cabinet of London." Ibid., 178.

40. "Petition for Warrants for Lands in Fincastle County," 17 June 1774, ibid., 193–97; Selby, *The Revolution in Virginia*, 16–17; Copeland and MacMaster, *Five George Masons*, 137–42; Boyd et al., *Papers of Thomas Jefferson*, 1:115–16.

41. As quoted in Alden, *American Revolution*, 105.

42. Arthur Lee to Richard Henry Lee, 18 March 1774, in Force, *American Archives*, 1:228–29; Edmund Pendleton to Joseph Chew, 20 June 1774, in Mays, *Pendleton Papers*, 1:92–96; Middlekauff, *The Glorious Cause*, 221–22, 230–31. The Intolerable Acts are reprinted in Jenson, *American Colonial Documents*, 779–85.

43. GM to Martin Cockburn, 26 May 1774, *PGM*, 1:190–91; "Petition for Warrants for Lands in Fincastle County," 17 June 1774, ibid., 193–97; Rowland, *Mason*, 1:170–71; Lord Dunmore to Earl of Dartmouth, 29 May 1774, in Force, *American Archives*, 1:352; Edmund Pendleton to Joseph Chew, 20 June 1774, in Mays, *Pendleton Papers*, 1:92–96. The 24 May 1774 resolution of the House of Burgesses is reprinted in Van Schreeven et al., *Revolutionary Virginia*, 1:93–95.

44. George Washington to Bryan Fairfax, 4 July 1774, *PGW-ColS*, 10:109–12; George Washington to John Augustine Washington, 11 July 1774, ibid., 111–13.

45. Grigsby, *The Virginia Convention of 1776*, 158; *DGW*, 3:260–61. Although Mason has almost universally been regarded as the author of the Fairfax Resolves, Sweig, "A New Found Washington Letter," 283–91, argues that they were primarily a committee effort. To be sure, other writers may have influenced the resolves; Richard Henry Lee had prepared his own draft before Dunmore dissolved the House of Burgesses, and undoubtedly Mason conferred with Lee when both men were in Williamsburg. Richard Henry Lee to Samuel Adams, 23 June 1774, in Force, *American Archives*, 4:445–46. But all the evidence points toward Mason as the principal, if not the sole, author of the Fairfax Resolves. The oldest known copy is in his handwriting, and he presented the resolves to the Fairfax freeholders. More significantly, drafting the resolves was the kind of task that often fell to Mason, and they echoed his voice, as when they declare the colonists were "Descendants not of the Conquered, but of the Conquerors," a line he had also used in his "Extracts from the Virginia Charters." *PGM*, 1:168, 201.

46. Fairfax County Resolves, 18 July 1774, *PGM*, 1:201–10. Did Mason mean to challenge Parliament's right to impose external taxes for purposes of regulating trade? One contemporary, Bryan Fairfax, believed Mason came late to questioning the legality, as opposed to the wisdom, of any Parliamentary taxation. Bryan Fairfax to George Washington, 5 August 1774, *PGW-ColS*, 10:143–50. Thomas Jefferson later claimed that, besides George Wythe, until Jefferson's *Summary View of the Rights of British America* was published in August 1774, no one believed Parliament had no authority in America. Edmund Randolph generally confirmed Jefferson's recollection, but it seems something of an overstatement. Richard Bland and Benjamin Franklin had entertained similar ideas. Malone, *Jefferson*, 1:180–90.

A denial of all Parliamentary authority was implicit in Mason's earlier writings, as when he said in his "Extracts from the Virginia Charters," that under the 1676 charter, "the subjects of Virginia are forever to remain under the immediate protection of the British Crown, & be subject *only to its Government here*." *PGM*, 1:179 (n. 14) (emphasis added). Yet Mason did not expressly reject taxes imposed to regulate trade, perhaps because he believed the prerevolutionary commercial relationship between England and America was mutually beneficial. See GM to George Washington, 5 April 1769, ibid., 99–100.

47. "Fairfax County Resolves," 18 July 1774, *PGM*, 1:201–10.

48. Robert Rutland believes Mason probably wrote a similar, if less well known, set of resolves for neighboring Prince William County. Perhaps he did. They show some of Mason's rhetorical fingerprints, but they also resemble the Westmoreland County Resolves, which were written by Richard Henry Lee. Mason and Lee may have collaborated in assisting some less eloquent patriots, but we cannot be certain. See "Prince William County Resolves," 6 June 1774, *PGM*, 1:191–93. See also "Westmoreland Resolves," 22 June 1774, in Force, *American Archives*, 1:437–38.

49. Sweig, "New-Found Washington Letter," 285; *PGW-ColS*, 10:127; Van Schreeven et al., *Revolutionary Virginia*, 1:109–11; *PGM*, 1:199–201.

50. Ironically, the most incisive critique of the nonimportation strategy may have

come from Mason's brother Thomson. In a series of letters to Rind's *Virginia Gazette* in the summer of 1774, Thomson Mason argued that nonimportation unfairly penalized innocent British manufacturers, merchants, and workers. But the younger Mason was no Tory; he advocated civil disobedience to parliamentary legislation on the theory that no acts passed since 1607 were binding in Virginia, an opinion not too far removed from the views of Bland, Jefferson, and his older brother. Van Schreeven et al., *Revolutionary Virginia*, 1:64–67, 169–203; Ragsdale, *A Planters' Republic*, 197–98.

51. Ragsdale, *A Planters' Republic*, 205–7; Force, *American Archives*, 1:686–90.

52. *DGW*, 30–31 August 1774, 3:271–72; Rowland, *Mason*, 1:172–75.

53. "Declaration and Resolves of the First Continental Congress," 14 October 1774, in Ford, *JCC*, 1:63–73; "The Association," 20 October 1774, ibid., 75–80; Middlekauff, *The Glorious Cause*, 147; Ragsdale, *A Planters' Republic*, 218–29.

54. "Fairfax County Militia Association," 21 September 1774, *PGM*, 1:210–12; Fairfax County Committee of Safety Proceedings, 17 January 1775, ibid., 212–13.

55. Lord Dunmore to Earl of Dartmouth, 24 December 1774, in Force, *American Archives*, 1:1061–63.

56. Mason agreed that an exception would be appropriate for Washington. GM to George Washington, 6 February 1775, *PGM*, 1:213–15; Fairfax County Militia Plan, 6 February 1775, ibid., 215–17; "Remarks on Annual Elections," April 1775, ibid., 229–32.

57. "Remarks on Annual Elections," ibid., 229–32.

58. GM to William Ramsay, 11 July 1775, ibid., 239–40; George Washington to Fairfax County Committee, 16 May 1775, ibid., 233–34. See also Force, *American Archives*, 2:165–72.

59. GM to William Lee, 1 June 1775, *PGM*, 1:236–39. The acts of Parliament to which Mason referred were probably the Restraining Acts, which put new restrictions on American trade and shipping.

60. "Remarks on Annual Elections," April 1775, ibid., 230–31; GM to George Brent, 6 December 1770, ibid., 129, 290; Maier, "John Wilkes and American Disillusionment with Britain," ibid., 373–95.

61. Selby, *Revolution in Virginia*, 14; Flexner, *George Washington*, 1:279–83; Peterson, *Thomas Jefferson and the New Nation*, 38–40; Sheridan, "The British Credit Crisis of 1772 and the American Colonies," 161–86; GM to Robert Carter, 23 January 1768, *PGM*, 1:78–79; GM to George Washington, 5 April 1769, ibid., 100; "Nonimportation Agreement," 23 April 1769, ibid., 107. See generally Breen, *Tobacco Culture*.

62. As quoted in Flexner, *George Washington*, 1:293. For an example of Washington's title imbroglios, see Sampson Darrell to George Washington, 8 October 1759, *PGW-ColS*, 6:367–68.

63. GM to George Washington, 17 October 1769, *PGM*, 1:113–15.

64. John Connally to George Washington, 1 February 1774, *PGW-ColS*, 9:464–66; Lord Dunmore to John Penn, 3 March 1774, in Force, *American Archives*,

1:252–55; John Penn to Lord Dunmore, 31 March 1774, ibid., 255–60; Eneas Mackay to John Penn, 4 April 1774, ibid., 269–71.

65. Billings et al., *Colonial Virginia*, 252–53; Wood, *Radicalism of the American Revolution*, 142–44. On the Separate Baptists, see Morton, *Colonial Virginia*, 2:821–22. Rhys Isaac seems to suggest that lower-status Baptists and Methodists were more anti-British than the Anglican gentry, which may be true, and that the gentry embraced resistance to maintain its leadership positions at home, which may be pushing the dissenters' influence a bit far. *The Transformation of Virginia*, 265–66. Woody Holton, *Forced Founders*, looks at other marginalized groups and makes a similar argument. John Gilman Kolp argues in *Gentleman and Freeholders*, 61–66, that Virginia elections were actually becoming less competitive in the 1760s and 1770s. Nevertheless, Virginians apparently believed an unhealthy partisanship was on the increase.

66. Breen, "Ideology and Nationalism," 29. See generally Rozbicki, *The Complete Colonial Gentleman*.

67. Force, *American Archives*, 2:1186; Van Schreeven et al., *Revolutionary Virginia*, 1:303–4.

68. Proceedings of the Third Convention, 19 July 1775, Van Schreeven et al., *Revolutionary Virginia*, 1:319, 324 (n. 6).

69. GM to Martin Cockburn, 5 August 1775, *PGM*, 1:245–46; Selby, *Revolution in Virginia*, 51–52.

70. GM to Martin Cockburn, 5 August 1775, *PGM*, 1:245–46; Rowland, *Mason*, 1:195–96.

71. GM to Martin Cockburn, 24 July 1775, *PGM*, 1:241–42.

72. Selby, *Revolution in Virginia*, 51–52; Rutland, *George Mason and the War for Independence*, 42.

73. "An Ordinance for Establishing a General Test Oath," 19 August 1775, *PGM*, 1:246–49; Proceedings of the Third Convention, 19 August 1775, in Van Schreeven et al., *Revolutionary Virginia*, 3:467–68; Rutland, *George Mason and the War for Independence*, 40–41.

74. GM to Martin Cockburn, 24 July 1775, *PGM*, 1:241–42; GM to Martin Cockburn, 22 August 1775, ibid., 249–52; Force, *American Archives*, 3:382.

75. GM to Martin Cockburn, 5 August 1775, *PGM*, 1:245–46; GM to Martin Cockburn, 22 August 1775, ibid., 249–52; GM to George Washington, 14 October 1775, ibid., 255–56.

76. GM to George Washington, 2 April 1776, ibid., 266–69; Force, *American Archives*, 3:87. On the fourth Virginia Convention and the Committee of Safety, see Van Schreeven et al., *Revolutionary Virginia*, 4:410 (n. 8); 5:26–27, 157–58, 164 (n. 15).

77. GM to Mr. Brent(?), 2 October 1778, *PGM*, 1:433–39; Grigsby, *Convention of 1776*, 154–55; Peters, *The Elder Pitt*, 172–83; Alden, *American Revolution*, 187.

78. GM to Maryland Council of Safety, 29 November 1775, *PGM*, 1:258–59.

79. Fairfax County Committee of Correspondence to John Hancock, 23 Novem-

ber 1775, ibid., 257–58; Resolution of Continental Congress, 10 November 1775, in Van Schreeven et al., *Revolutionary Virginia*, 4:361–62.

80. Fairfax County Committee of Correspondence to Charles Broadwater and George Mason, 9 December 1775, *PGM*, 1:259–62. See also Van Schreeven et al., *Revolutionary Virginia*, 5:88–90.

81. GM to George Washington, 2 April 1776, *PGM*, 1:266–69. See also GM and John Dalton to Maryland Council of Safety, 31 January 1776, ibid., 262–63; GM and John Dalton to Maryland Council of Safety, 15 March 1776, ibid., 264–65; Maryland Council of Safety to GM, 19 March 1776, ibid., 265–66. On the Potomac River defenses, see also materials collected in Van Schreeven et al., *Revolutionary Virginia*, 5:34–35; 6:130–31, 236–37, 514; 7:39, 41 (n. 5), 267–68, 294, 359.

Chapter Four

1. Force, *American Archives*, 6:1510–11; Chitwood, *Richard Henry Lee*, 97; Thomas Jefferson to Thomas Nelson, 16 May 1776, in Boyd et al., *Papers of Thomas Jefferson*, 1:292–93. Jefferson lacked the seniority to get excused temporarily, but a few months later he resigned his seat in order to serve in Virginia's new House of Delegates. Peterson, *Thomas Jefferson and the New Nation*, 100.

2. Edmund Pendleton to Richard Henry Lee, 7 May 1776, Mays, *Pendleton Papers*, 1:176–77.

3. Force, *American Archives*, 6:1512–15.

4. GM to Richard Henry Lee, 18 May 1776, *PGM*, 1:271–72; Certificate of Election, 15 April 1776, in Van Schreeven et al., *Revolutionary Virginia*, 6:391; 7:183–84 (n. 1); Isaac, *Transformation of Virginia*, 259; Holton, *Forced Founders*, 203; Rowland, *Mason*, 1:222.

5. "Resolutions of the Virginia Convention Calling upon Congress for a Declaration of Independence," 15 May 1776, in Mays, *Pendleton Papers*, 1:178–79; Selby, *Revolution in Virginia*, 97. See also Force, *American Archives*, 6:1524.

6. See Countryman, *American Revolution*, 109–13. See also Pierce, "The Independence Movement in Virginia, 1775–1776," 442–52.

7. Randolph, *History of Virginia*, 234; H. Miller, *Gentleman Revolutionary*, 130; Alden, *American Revolution*, 227–39; Selby, *Revolution in Virginia*, 66–94. For George III's proclamation of rebellion, see Jenson, *American Colonial Documents*, 850–51. For the Prohibitory Act, see ibid., 853.

8. GM to Richard Henry Lee, 18 May 1776, *PGM*, 1:271–72; GM to Mr. Brent(?), 2 October 1778, ibid., 433–39.

9. Randolph, *History of Virginia*, 255.

10. GM to Richard Henry Lee, 18 May 1776, *PGM*, 1:271–72; Force, *American Archives*, 6:1529–31; Rowland; *Mason*, 1:228–38; Randolph, *History of Virginia*, 252.

11. Edmund Pendleton to Thomas Jefferson, 24 May 1776, in Mays, *Pendleton Papers*, 1:180–81; Randolph, *History of Virginia*, 252; Reardon, *Edmund Randolph*, 32.

12. "First Draft of the Virginia Declaration of Rights," ca. 20–26 May 1776, *PGM*, 1:276–82; GM to Mr. Brent (?), 2 October 1778, ibid., 433–39.

13. See Boyd et al., *Papers of Thomas Jefferson*, 1:366–69; Hutchinson and Rachal, *Papers of James Madison*, 1:178; Brant, *James Madison*, 1:235–39, 257–59. See also Randolph, *History of Virginia*, 254.

14. "First Draft of the Virginia Declaration of Rights," ca. 20–26 May 1776, *PGM*, 1:276–82. For a discussion of the interplay of faith and secularism in American history, see Church, *The American Creed*.

15. "First Draft of the Virginia Declaration of Rights," *PGM*, 1:276–82. See also Brant, *Madison*, 1:428 (n. 5).

16. Proceedings of the Fifth Convention, 27 May 1776, in Van Schreeven et al., *Revolutionary Virginia*, 7:270–78.

17. Robert Rutland reads the sixth article of the committee draft to limit the suffrage to male property owners, but the literal language is not inconsistent with Mason's position in 1787 that landless parents, because of their concerns for the welfare of their children, had an interest in society sufficient to allow them to vote. See *PGM*, 1:285. The more liberal language is consistent with Mason's treatment of suffrage requirements in the draft constitution he wrote a few days later. See note 50 below.

18. Randolph, *History of Virginia*, 254; "Committee Draft of the Virginia Declaration of Rights," 27 May 1776, ibid., 282–86; GM to Mr. Brent,(?), 2 October 1778, ibid., 433–39; Rowland, *Mason*, 2:433–36. See also, Brant, *Madison*, 1:237–38.

19. Proceedings of the Fifth Convention, 27 May 1776, in Van Schreeven et al., *Revolutionary Virginia*, 7:270–76.

20. Thomas Ludwell Lee to Richard Henry Lee, 1 June 1776, Lee Family Papers, University of Virginia, Charlottesville; Henry Carrington Memorandum, 9 September 1851, Carrington Family Papers, Virginia Historical Society, Richmond; Randolph, *History of Virginia*, 253. See also Mays, *Edmund Pendleton*, 2:121–22.

21. Randolph, *History of Virginia*, 255. Mason may have misunderstood the common-law practice regarding ex post facto laws, wrongly thinking that a ban on such legislation would prohibit the enactment of retroactive laws in civil cases, when, in fact, only retroactive criminal statutes were defined in the law as ex post facto. See Levy, *Origins of the Bill of Rights*, 18.

22. Paine, "The Rights of Man" (1791), in Conway, *The Writings of Thomas Paine*, 2:325. See also Isaac, *Transformation of Virginia*, 274–80; Ketcham, *Madison*, 73; Banning, "James Madison, the Statute for Religious Freedom, and the Crisis of Republican Convictions," in Peterson and Vaughn, *The Virginia Statute for Religious Freedom*, 109–38.

23. Hutchinson and Rachal, *Papers of James Madison*, 2:174–75.

24. Ibid., 170–72. Randolph's account is garbled. He fails to distinguish among the different versions of the article on religious freedom and attributes its authorship to Henry. I have followed the reconstruction of Henry's role in Van Schreeven et al., *Revolutionary Virginia*, 7:456–58 (n. 33). See also Randolph, *History of Virginia*, 254; *PGM*, 1:290–91.

25. Proceedings of the Fifth Convention, 12 June 1776, in Van Schreeven et al., *Revolutionary Virginia*, 7:450. The evidence supporting Pendleton's sponsorship is questioned at ibid., 456–58 (n. 33), but see Hutchinson and Rachal, *Papers of James Madison*, 1:174–75; Brant, *Madison*, 1:247; Ketcham, *Madison*, 72–73.

26. Ketcham, *Madison*, 71–73.

27. Proceedings of the Fifth Convention, 10 June 1776, in Van Schreeven et al., *Revolutionary Virginia*, 7:417; Proceedings, 11 June 1776, ibid., 430; Proceedings, 12 June 1776, ibid., 449–50. See also Force, *American Archives*, 6:1557–61.

28. Schwartz, *The Bill of Rights*, 1:195–98.

29. Bailyn, *Ideological Origins of the American Revolution*, 182–84; Schwartz, *Bill of Rights*, 1:50–51.

30. Howard, "Rights in Passage," 3–15; *PGM*, 1:279–82; H. Miller, *George Mason: Constitutionalist*, 142–43. The idea citizens had a right to seek individual happiness was novel in 1776, but not original with Mason. The concept had appeared on occasion in the writings of John Adams, James Otis, and James Wilson. See Schlesinger, "The Lost Meaning of the Pursuit of Happiness," 325–27.

31. Schwartz, *Bill of Rights*, 1:179–80; Massachusetts Body of Liberties (1641), ibid., 69–84; Rhode Island and Providence Plantations Charter (1663), ibid., 95–107; Pennsylvania Frame of Government (1682), ibid., 130–44; Pennsylvania Charter of Privileges (1701), ibid., 169–75.

32. "Declaration and Resolves of the First Continental Congress," *JCC*, 1:63–74; Address to the Inhabitants of Quebec, ibid., 105–13.

33. See Howard, "From Mason to Modern Times," 95–112; Billings, "'That All Men Are Born Equally Free & Independent,'" 335–69; Levy, *Origins of the Bill of Rights*, 22–23.

34. Hening, *Statutes*, 9:170. See McDonald, *Novus Ordo Seclorum*, 46–49.

35. Billings, "'That All Men Are Born Equally Free,'" 349–50; Levy, *Origins of the Bill of Rights*, 63–64.

36. See Levy, *Origins of the Bill of Rights*, 105–22, 142, 167–68, 180–83. See also Wood, *The Creation of the American Republic*, 61, 608–10; and W. P. Adams, *The First American Constitutions*, 137–38.

37. GM to Richard Henry Lee, 4 March 1777, *PGM*, 1:333–34.

38. Rhode Island and Providence Plantation Charters, Schwartz, *Bill of Rights*, 1:97; New York Charter of Liberties and Privileges, ibid., 167; Selby, *Revolution in Virginia*, 121. New Hampshire and South Carolina adopted temporary constitutions that omitted religious tests and then reinstated them in their permanent constitutions. Kruman, *Between Authority and Liberty*, 45–49; Meadows, "The Virginia Constitution of 1776," 5–21.

39. See Pittman, "Jasper Yeates's Notes on the Pennsylvania Ratifying Convention, 1787," 304 (n. 12).

40. Pittman, Review of Richard L. Perry, ed., *Securing Our Liberties* (1951), 109–12. See also Howard, "From Mason to Modern Times," 101; Malone, *Jefferson*, 1:221; Chester, "George Mason," 128–46.

41. Schwartz, *Bill of Rights*, 1:231–32.

42. Wood, *Creation of the American Republic*, 376.

43. Kruman, *Between Authority and Liberty*, 7; Countryman, *American Revolution*, 125.

44. *PGM*, 1:295–99; John Adams to Richard Henry Lee, 15 November 1775, in Taylor et al., *The Papers of John Adams*, 3:307–8; Richard Henry Lee, "A Government Scheme," in Van Schreeven et al., *Revolutionary Virginia*, 6:367–68, 373–74 (nn. 1–2). See also Selby, "Richard Henry Lee, John Adams, and the Virginia Constitution," 387–400.

45. See Boyd et al., *Papers of Thomas Jefferson*, 1:333–34.

46. See generally Bailyn, *Ideological Origins of the American Revolution*, 272–73, 289–94; Colbourn, *Lamp of Experience*, 98–99.

47. John Adams, "Thoughts on Government," in Hyneman and Lutz, *American Political Writing*, 1:401–9; Peterson, *Thomas Jefferson and the New Nation*, 99–107.

48. Carter Braxton, "Address to the Convention of Virginia," in Van Schreeven et al., *Revolutionary Virginia*, 6:518–26, 531–33 (nn. 4–15); Richard Henry Lee to Edmund Pendleton, 12 May 1776, in Ballagh, *Lee Letters*, 1:190; Selby, *Revolution in Virginia*, 114–16.

49. Mason's Plan for the Virginia Constitution of 1776, *PGM*, 1:299–302; Boyd et al., *Papers of Thomas Jefferson*, 1:366–69.

50. Julian Boyd believes Mason intended to add the requirement of parenthood to the possession of a long-term lease as a basis for the right to vote, and thus restrict the suffrage. Boyd et al., *Papers of Thomas Jefferson*, 1:369 (n. 4). This seems to be a misreading of Mason's intent, and to be sure, Mason was not always a model of clarity. Robert Rutland's conflicting interpretation seems more persuasive. See *PGM*, 1:303.

Would Mason have supported female suffrage? Richard Henry Lee expressed sympathy for allowing property-owning widows to vote. Kruman, *Between Authority and Liberty*, 104–6. On issues of political and social reform, Lee was rarely to the left of Mason, so it seems likely that Mason would have approached the issue with an open mind, if it had ever been presented to him, but there is no evidence it was.

51. Lee, "A Government Scheme," in Van Schreeven et al., *Revolutionary Virginia*, 6:367–68; Adams, "Thoughts on Government," in Hyneman and Lutz, *American Political Writing*, 1:405–8; Greene, *Quest for Power*, 66–67.

52. "Thomas Jefferson to Thomas Nelson, 16 May 1776," in Boyd et al., *Papers of Thomas Jefferson*, 1:292–93.

53. Third Draft of Virginia Constitution, ibid., 356–65.

54. William Fleming to Thomas Jefferson, 15 June 1776, ibid., 386–87; William Fleming to Thomas Jefferson, 22 June 1776, ibid., 406; Edmund Pendleton to Thomas Jefferson, 22 July 1776, ibid., 187–88.

55. Edmund Randolph to George Baylor, 21 June 1776, quoted in Brant, *Madison*, 1:264.

56. Proceedings of the Fifth Convention, 24 June 1776, in Van Schreeven et al., *Revolutionary Virginia*, 7:594–98, 603–6 (nn. 18–40). Not only did the Cary com-

mittee fail to keep a record of its deliberations, but neither Mason's original draft nor the committee's final report has survived. Critical to recreating the evolution of the Virginia Constitution is William Fleming's letter to Jefferson of 22 June 1776, which contained an annotated copy of the printed constitution of 19–20 June, from which Mason's original can be reconstructed. Fortunately, a supplemental report from the committee to the convention, dated 24 June 1776, also survived. Julian Boyd collected and attempted to reconcile the surviving drafts in Boyd et al., *Papers of Thomas Jefferson*, 1:337–77. Boyd did the ground-breaking work; Van Schreeven et al., *Revolutionary Virginia*, sets out the transition from one draft to the next in minute detail but in an accessible fashion. Except for language that can be traced to Jefferson's draft, it is virtually impossible to know who originated a particular amendment.

57. George Wythe to Thomas Jefferson, 27 July 1776, in Boyd et al., *Papers of Thomas Jefferson*, 1:476–77.

58. Proceeding of the Fifth Convention, 24 June 1776, in Van Schreeven et al., *Revolutionary Virginia*, 7:598, 606 (n. 39); Third Draft of Virginia Constitution, in Boyd et al., *Papers of Thomas Jefferson*, 1:353–65, 385 (n. 19); *PGM*, 1:298.

59. Force, *American Archives*, 6:1589–98; Final Draft of Virginia Constitution, *PGM*, 1:304–9; Randolph, *History of Virginia*, 256. The ban on ministers illustrated the difficultly of reconciling a growing desire to separate church and state with a commitment to the free exercise of religion and raised the ire of at least one advanced liberal, the Philadelphia Universalist Benjamin Rush. Benjamin Rush to Patrick Henry, 16 July 1778, in P. Smith, *Letters of Delegates*, 4:474.

60. R. Meade, *Henry*, 2:122–23; Brant, *Madison*, 1:263–64; Wood, *Creation of the American Republic*, 149–50; Kruman, *Between Authority and Liberty*, 117, 124.

61. Proceedings of the Fifth Convention, 29 June 1776, in Van Schreeven et al., *Revolutionary Virginia*, 6:654–55.

62. Edmund Pendleton to Thomas Jefferson, 10 August 1776, in Mays, *Pendleton Papers*, 1:197–99; Maier, *The Old Revolutionaries*, 181; Selby, "Richard Henry Lee, John Adams, and the Virginia Constitution," 398.

63. Randolph, *History of Virginia*, 258; Peterson, *Thomas Jefferson and the New Nation*, 99–107; Brant, *Madison*, 1:251–56; 265–71; Jefferson, *Notes on the State of Virginia*, in Peterson, *The Portable* Jefferson, 162–76; Horrell, "George Mason and the Fairfax County Court," 427, 437–38. GM to Zachariah Johnston, 3 November 1790, *PGM*, 3:1208–11. Ironically perhaps, the Virginia framers showed little interest in democracy at the local level. The options considered for selecting members of the county court were limited to appointment by the governor or nomination by the court itself. None of the various drafts provided for the popular election of justices, and if the Jefferson and Mason drafts may be used as an index, the more liberal position in 1776 was to minimize local control and give the executive more discretion in making appointments.

The appointment formula adopted by the convention gave the Tidewater counties seventy-one delegates, as opposed to forty-six for the Piedmont, although the white populations of the two regions were comparable. Because the Piedmont was much larger geographically and gaining eligible voters at a faster rate, the malapportionment of the House of Delegates would only increase over time. See H. Miller, *George Mason: Constitutionalist*, 149.

64. Tucker, *Blackstone's Commentaries*, appendix, 1:113–19.

65. Randolph, *History of Virginia*, 251–52, 258; Vane, "A Healing Question" (1656), in Schwartz, *Bill of Rights*, 1:30–39; Kruman, *Between Authority and Liberty*, 20.

66. GM to Mr. Brent, 2 October 1778, *PGM*, 2:433–39.

67. Randolph, *History of Virginia*, 252–53; Tucker, *Blackstone's Commentaries*, appendix, 1:83–91; Thomas Jefferson to Edmund Pendleton, 26 August 1776, in Boyd et al., *Papers of Thomas Jefferson*, 1:503–6; W. P. Adams, *First American Constitutions*, 267–68; Peterson, *Thomas Jefferson and the New Nation*, 95; Kruman, *Between Authority and Liberty*, 55, 136. See also Selby, *Revolution in Virginia*, 115–17.

Chapter Five

1. GM to Richard Henry Lee, 21 July 1778, *PGM*, 1:429–31; GM to Richard Henry Lee, 4 March 1777, ibid., 333–35; Edmund Pendleton to William Woodford, 11 August 1778, in Mays, *Pendleton Papers*, 2:265–66; Alden, *The South in the Revolution*, 194–95; Middlekauff, *The Glorious Cause*, 432–33.

2. See generally Middlekauff, *The Glorious Cause*, 434–35, 493–95.

3. GM to Mr. —— Brent, 2 October 1778, *PGM*, 1:434.

4. As quoted in Selby, *Revolution in Virginia*, 157. See also Rutland, *Mason: Reluctant Statesman*, 67–73. On the "wartime malaise," see GM to George Mason Jr., 3 June 1781, *PGM*, 2:692–95; Isaac, *Transformation of Virginia*, 275–77; Wood, *Creation of the American Republic*, 416–18.

5. GM to Richard Henry Lee, 4 June 1779, *PGM*, 2:506–9; GM to Joseph Jones, 27 July 1780, ibid., 655–63.

6. Peterson, *Thomas Jefferson and the New Nation*, 109.

7. Mays, *Pendleton Papers*, 2:132. Abernethy, *Western Lands and the American Revolution*, 200, argues that the conservatives were the real expansionists, but see, Pierce, "The Independence Movement in Virginia." Bailey, "George Mason: Westerner," 409–17, places Mason squarely in the expansionist camp.

8. Thomas Jefferson, "The Autobiography of Thomas Jefferson," in Peterson, *Writings*, 36–37; Alden, *The South in the Revolution*, 311–12; Alden, *American Revolution*, 334–36.

9. Mason missed the May 1777 session while he was recovering from a smallpox vaccination. GM to George Wythe, 14 June 1777, *PGM*, 1:345–46. Smallpox ravaged America during the war. See Fenn, *Pox Americana*. Mason also missed the short session of May 1778. Habitually late for the start of the assembly, Mason was on the road to Williamsburg when the House adjourned. H. Miller, *Gentleman*

Revolutionary, 173. He also missed the October 1780 session, again apparently for health reasons. *PGM*, 2:663.

10. R. Meade, *Henry*, 2:127; Henry, *Henry*, 1:445–46; *PGM*, 1:325–27; 2:639–44.

11. *PGM*, 1:317, 319–22, 324–25.

12. Ibid., 1:521–22; Alden, *The South in the Revolution*, 344–45.

13. Leonard, *The General Assembly of Virginia*, 122–37.

14. Jefferson, "Autobiography," in Peterson, *Writings*, 37–38; *PGM*, 1:327–33; Boyd et al., *Papers of Thomas Jefferson*, 2:313–14; *Journal of the House of Delegates of Virginia, 1776*, 5 November 1776, 56.

15. Jefferson, *Notes on the State of Virginia*, in Peterson, *Writings*, 213; Boyd et al., *Papers of Thomas Jefferson*, 2:305.

16. *PGM*, 1:327–33; Jefferson, "Autobiography," in Peterson, *Writings*, 37–38.

17. Jefferson, "Autobiography," in Peterson, *Writings*, 44–45; R. E. Brown and Brown, *Virginia, 1705–1786*, 83–92; Keim, "Primogeniture and Entail in Colonial Virginia," 545–86; Alden, *The South in the Revolution*, 331. The abolition of primogeniture and entail are perhaps not the best illustrations of the limits of eighteenth-century reform. Bill No. 64 of the committee's legislative package set the penalties for homosexual acts: "If a man, by castration, if a woman, by cutting thro' the cartilage of her nose a hole of one half inch diameter at the least." Because the penalty at common law had been death, this was considered progress. See Boyd et al., *Papers of Thomas Jefferson*, 2:497.

18. Hening, *Statutes*, 10:129–30; Boyd et al., *Papers of Thomas Jefferson*, 2:476–78, 526–35; Jefferson, "Autobiography," in Peterson, *Writings*, 36. Citizenship was a sensitive topic, and subsequent legislatures continued to tamper with the law. An act passed in 1783 denied citizenship to former residents who had fought for Great Britain; it was intended to prevent them from bringing debt actions in Virginia's courts. Hening, *Statutes*, 11:322–24. In 1786 the General Assembly repealed the clauses on expatriation and the rights of citizens of other states. Ibid., 12:261–65.

19. *Journal of the House of Delegates of the Commonwealth of Virginia, 1777–80*, 20 October 1778, 20; 4 June 1779, 35; 5 June 1779, 36; 2 November 1779, 31; *PGM*, 2:594–95.

20. Peterson, *Thomas Jefferson and the New Nation*, 173; Main, "Government by the People: The American Revolution and the Democratization of the Legislatures," 391–407; Edmund Pendleton to William Woodford, 31 January 1778, in Mays, *Pendleton Papers*, 1:246–48.

21. *PGM*, 2:629–32; GM to Thomas Jefferson, 6 October 1780, ibid., 675–77; Hening, *Statutes*, 12:120–29. If Mason's proposal to deprive counties of representation was novel, his proposal to fine nonvoters was not. Georgia too fined nonvoting. Alden, *The South in the Revolution*, 314. Mason also chafed at the practice of some members of leaving while the House was in session. In a response that could not have endeared him to all his colleagues, Mason won adoption of a rule preventing delegates from drawing their salaries before the legislature adjourned. See GM to Richard Henry Lee, 19 June 1779, *PGM*, 2:522–25.

22. GM to George Wythe, 14 June 1777, *PGM*, 1:345–46; *Journal of the House of*

Delegates of the Commonwealth of Virginia, 1777–80, 22 May 1777, 24–25; Rowland, *Mason,* 1:282–84; Richard Henry Lee to George Wythe, 19 October 1777, P. Smith, *Letters of Delegates,* 7:146–47; Edmund Pendleton to William Woodford, 28 June 1778, Mays, *Pendleton Papers,* 1:214–15; McGaughy, *Richard Henry Lee of Virginia,* 130–32.

23. GM to Mr. —— Brent, 2 October 1778, *PGM,* 1:433–39.

24. GM to Richard Henry Lee, 19 June 1779, ibid., 2:522–25; GM to Richard Henry Lee, 4 June 1779, ibid., 506–9; Cyrus Griffin to Thomas Jefferson, 6 October 1778, in Boyd et al., *Papers of Thomas Jefferson,* 2:216–17. Mercer quoted in Brant, *Madison,* 1:360–63.

25. George Washington to GM, 27 March 1779, *PGM,* 2:491–94; Richard Henry Lee to Thomas Jefferson, 3 May 1779, in Ballagh, *Lee Letters,* 2:53–56; George Washington to Benjamin Harrison, 18 December 1778, in Fitzpatrick, *The Writings of George Washington,* 13:462–68.

26. GM to William Aylett, 8 June 1777, *PGM,* 1:343–45; GM to Thomas Jefferson, 3 April 1779, ibid., 2:494–97; GM to Richard Henry Lee, 4 June 1779, ibid., 506–9; GM to Richard Henry Lee, 19 June 1779, ibid, 522–25.

27. Sweig, "1649–1800," 108; GM to William Lee, 20 May 1775, *PGM,* 1:234–35. In 1789 Mason won a partial judgment, which Lee offered to pay. Mason rejected the settlement. *Mason v. Lee,* York County Court, 10 May 1789, *PGM,* 3:1155–56; William Lee to GM, 15 June 1790, ibid., 1202–3. Mason's other wartime business interests included partial ownership of a privateer, the *General Washington.* Copeland and MacMaster, *Five George Masons,* 199.

28. GM to Mr. —— Brent, 2 October 1778, *PGM,* 1:433–39; GM to James Mercer, 5 February 1780, ibid., 2:617–18.

29. As quoted in Copeland and MacMaster, *Five George Masons,* 208–9.

30. Ibid.

31. GM to Thomas Jefferson, 6 October 1780, *PGM,* 2:675–78; GM to Mr. Brent, 2 October 1780, ibid., 1:433–39; GM to James Mercer, 5 February 1780, ibid., 2:617–18; Dunn, *Recollections of John Mason,* 59.

32. JCC, 22 October 1778, 12:1043–49; GM to George Washington, 2 April 1776, *PGM,* 1:266–69. See also Middlekauff, *The Glorious Cause,* 512–19; Malone, *Jefferson,* 1:327; Flexner, *George Washington,* 2:340; Greene, *Quest for Power,* 108–9.

33. Greene, *Quest for Power,* 108–9, 120–25; Ferguson, *The Power of the Purse,* 21–22.

34. Randolph, *History of Virginia,* 261; Ferguson, *Power of the Purse,* 7–9, 26–33; Ketcham, *Madison,* 85–87; Brant, *Madison,* 1:357–58.

35. John Parke Custis to George Washington, 26 October 1777, *PGW-RWS,* 12:11–12; George Washington to John Parke Custis, 14 November 1777, ibid., 249–50; Selby, *Revolution in Virginia,* 152.

36. GW to Henry Laurens, 23 December 1777, *PGW-RWS,* 12:683–87; GW to Patrick Henry, 13 November 1777, ibid., 240–42; Flexner, *George Washington,* 2:200–201; Selby, *Revolution in Virginia,* 178, *PGM,* 1:352–54.

37. *PGM,* 1:357–62, 374–75; Hening, *Statutes,* 9:381, 385–87; Edmund Pendle-

ton to William Woodford, 29 November 1777, in Mays, *Pendleton Papers*, 1:238.

38. *PGM*, 1:357–62, 374–75; Hening, *Statutes*, 9:381, 385–87.

39. Richard Henry Lee to Thomas Jefferson, 29 April 1777, in Boyd et al., *Papers of Thomas Jefferson*, 2:13–14; Hening, *Statutes*, 9:275–80; Patrick Henry to Richard Henry Lee, 20 March 1777, in Henry, *Henry*, 2:513–14; Patrick Henry to Richard Henry Lee, 28 March 1777, ibid., 515; Edmund Pendleton to William Woodford, 15 May 1777, in Mays, *Pendleton Papers*, 1:208–10. Monroe quoted in Brant, *Madison*, 1:323.

40. Hening, *Statutes*, 9:337–49; *PGM*, 1:362–74; Edmund Pendleton to William Woodford, 29 November 1777, in Mays, *Pendleton Papers*, 1:238–40; Edmund Pendleton to William Woodford, 31 January 1778, ibid., 246–48; Selby, *Revolution in Virginia*, 135–37.

41. "From the Voters of Fairfax County," 20 August 1777, *PGM*, 1:346–49; Randolph, *History of Virginia*, 266–67; Hening, *Statutes*, 9:349–68; *Journal of the House of Delegates of the Commonwealth of Virginia, 1777–80*, 13 December 1777, 77–78; 6 January 1778, 102. See generally *PGM*, 1:375–97.

42. *PGM*, 1:373; Hening, *Statutes*, 9:454–56; Edmund Pendleton to William Woodford, 15 February 1778, in Mays, *Pendleton Papers*, 1:250–51.

43. *PGM*, 1:458–59, 462–64, 467–68; Hening, *Statutes*, 9:580–81, 474–77; Selby, *Revolution in Virginia*, 157–58.

44. Edmund Pendleton to George Washington, 22 December 1778, in Mays, *Pendleton Papers*, 1:276–77; Richard Henry Lee to Patrick Henry, 15 November 1778, in Ballagh, *Lee Letters*, 1:451–53; Boyd et al., *Papers of Thomas Jefferson*, 2:219; Hening, *Statutes*, 9:547–52.

45. GM to Richard Henry Lee, 4 June 1779, *PGM*, 2:506–9; GM to Richard Henry Lee, 19 June 1779, ibid., 522–25; Brant, *Madison*, 1:354–56; Selby, *Revolution in Virginia*, 209–10.

46. *PGM*, 2:598–612.

47. *JCC*, 14:561–62; Ferguson, *Power of the Purse*, 46–50.

48. *JCC*, 16:262–67; Ferguson, *Power of the Purse*, 51–56.

49. Selby, *Revolution in Virginia*, 248–51; Randolph, *History of Virginia*, 277–78; Chitwood, *Richard Henry Lee*, 143–44; R. Meade, *Henry*, 2:239; *PGM*, 2:633–37.

50. *PGM*, 2:645–52; Ferguson, *Power of the Purse*, 64–67.

51. Mason also grew increasingly sanguine about conscription and a standing army, writing Jefferson in 1780 that the "late Draught, for regular Service, was not only quietly, but chearfully executed in this, and the neighboring Countys." Little resistance would develop, he assured Jefferson, "where the leading men are true Whigs, & possessed of common Discretion." GM to Thomas Jefferson, 6 October 1780, *PGM*, 2:675–77.

52. John Adams to James Warren, 3 February 1777, in P. Smith, *Letters of Delegates*, 6:201–2; Caleb Wallace to James Caldwell, 8 April 1777, in Henry, *Henry*, 1:493–95. Ironically, at the same time Adams was praising Virginia for granting equal rights to religious dissenters, Wallace was complaining of continuing discrimination.

53. As quoted in Peterson, *Thomas Jefferson and the New Nation*, 185; George Washington to James Wilson, 31 March 1779, in Fitzpatrick, *Writings of Washington*, 14:311–14; George Washington to Joseph Reed, 12 December 1778, ibid., 13:382–85; William Fleming to Thomas Jefferson, 22 May 1779, in P. Smith, *Letters of Delegates*, 12:507–9.

54. Edmund Pendleton to William Woolford, 26 April 1779, in Mays, *Pendleton Papers*, 1:278–81; James M. Varnum to Horatio Gates, 15 February 1781, in P. Smith, *Letters of Delegates*, 16:716.

55. Richard Henry Lee to GM, 9 June 1779, *PGM*, 2:513–16. See also George Washington to John Augustine Washington, 26 November 1778, in Fitzpatrick, *Writings of Washington*, 13:334–37; Edmund Pendleton to George Washington, 27 April 1778, in Mays, *Pendleton Papers*, 1:255.

56. Selby, *Revolution in Virginia*, 122–23; Ferguson, *Power of the Purse*, 70–75; Abernethy, *Western Lands and the American Revolution*, 209–10. According to Abernethy, the "idea that Morris financed the Revolution out of his own pocket is purely mythological. The truth is that the Revolution financed Robert Morris." Ibid., 178.

57. As quoted in Abernethy, *Western Lands and the America Revolution*, 185.

58. Adair, "James Madison's Autobiography," 191–209, 204. See also Mann Page to John Page, 26 May 1777, in P. Smith, *Letters of Delegates*, 7:128–29; Meriwether Smith to Thomas Jefferson, 6 July 1779, ibid., 8:155–57; Hening, *Statutes*, 10:74–75; R. Meade, *Henry*, 2:208–9.

59. Edmund Pendleton to William Woodford, 1 November 1779, in Mays, *Pendleton Papers*, 1:302–4; Rutland, *Mason: Reluctant Statesman*, 68–69; Rutland, *George Mason and the War for Independence*, 57.

60. Buckley, *Church and State*, 12–15, 43.

61. Jefferson, "Autobiography," in Peterson, *Writings*, 34–35; Buckley, *Church and State*, 4, 11; Dreisback, "George Mason's Pursuit of Religious Liberty in Revolutionary Virginia," 18–19; "Memorial of the Presbytery of Hanover County," 24 October 1776, in Jenson, *American Colonial Documents*, 549–51; "Petition of Dissenters in Albemarle and Amherst Counties," ca. November 1776, in Boyd et al., *Papers of Thomas Jefferson*, 1:586–89; "Declaration of Virginia of Baptists," 25 December 1776, ibid., 660–61.

62. Jefferson, "Autobiography," in Peterson, *Writings*, 34–35; Boyd et al., *Papers of Thomas Jefferson*, 2:525–29; Buckley, *Church and State*, 21–30, 34–37; *Journal of the House of Delegates of the Commonwealth of Virginia, 1777–80*, 19 November 1776, 85.

63. *PGM*, 1:318–19; Selby, *Revolution in Virginia*, 145–47. See *Journal of the House of Delegates of the Commonwealth of Virginia, 1777–80*, 30 November 1776, 102–3, and entries through 9 December.

64. Buckley, *Church and State*, 45; *Journal of the House of Delegates of the Commonwealth of Virginia, 1777–80*, 15 November 1778, 64; 7 December 1778, 100–101.

65. Buckley, *Church and State*, 46–50.

66. Ibid., 56–61, appendix 1, 185–88.

67. Ibid., 21–30, 53–55; *PGM*, 1:318–19; Jefferson, "Autobiography," in Peterson, *Writings*, 34–35. For a Methodist petition favoring continuation of the establishment, see *Journal of the House of Delegates of the Commonwealth of Virginia, 1777–80*, 28 October 1778, 40.

68. *PGM*, 2:553–54, 590–92; *Journal of the House of Delegates of the Commonwealth of Virginia, 1777–80*, 11 December 1779, 85; 13 December 1779, 87.

69. See generally H. Miller, *George Mason: Constitutionalist*, 157–61.

70. Boyd et al., *Papers of Thomas Jefferson*, 2:555–58; Buckley, *Church and State*, 19–21, 69–70. The House of Delegates took seriously the ban in the 1776 Constitution on ministers holding public office. In November 1777 John Corbley from Monogalia County was refused a seat in the House because he was "a minister of the Gospel," although he said he was not paid for his preaching. *Journal of the House of Delegates of the Commonwealth of Virginia, 1777–80*, 1 November 1777, 9. At the same time, the House began its day with a prayer, employed a chaplain—Reverend James Madison, cousin of the future president—and even ordered Reverend Madison to prepare a Thanksgiving Day sermon. Ibid., 4 November 1777, 12.

71. GM to Richard Henry Lee, 12 April 1779, *PGM*, 2:498; ibid., 590–92. See also Selby, *Revolution in Virginia*, 147.

72. Randolph, *History of Virginia*, 272–73; Sosin, *Revolutionary Frontier*, 156–58; Selby, *Revolution in Virginia*, 141–44.

73. Randolph, *History of Virginia*, 259; Abernethy, *Western Lands and the American Revolution*, 164. Rutland has identified Mason as the likely author of the 24 June resolution. *PGM*, 1:313. Mason had complained earlier about the assembly's failure to address the question of Indian purchases. GM to George Washington, 9 March 1775, ibid., 224–26. To the contrary, see Van Schreeven et al., *Revolutionary Virginia*, 7:600–601 (n. 13).

74. GM to Robert Carter, 24 February 1768, *PGM*, 1:89–90; Jefferson, *Notes on the State of Virginia*, in Peterson, *The Portable Jefferson*, 183–84; "Opinion Relating to George Croghan's Title," 19 July 1777, in Mays, *Pendleton Papers*, 1:216–17; Randolph, *History of Virginia*, 259. A 1493 papal decree purported to divide the non-Christian world between Spain and Portugal.

75. See Rutland, *Mason*, 69–72; Abernethy, *Western Lands and the American Revolution*, 217–26; Malone, *Jefferson*, 1:257–59; Boyd et al., *Papers of Thomas Jefferson*, 2:137–38.

76. Hening, *Statutes*, 9:349–68.

77. *PGM*, 1:399–409; 414–22; Boyd et al., *Papers of Thomas Jefferson*, 2:133–38.

78. *PGM*, 1:424–25; Boyd et al., *Papers of Thomas Jefferson*, 2:64–65; *Journal of the House of Delegates of the Commonwealth of Virginia, 1777–80*, 24 January 1778, 134–36.

79. GM to Thomas Jefferson, 6 February 1778, *PGM*, 1:426–28, 444–51.

80. GM to Thomas Jefferson, 3 April 1779, ibid., 2:494–97.

81. GM to Richard Henry Lee, 4 June 1779, ibid., 506–7; GM to Richard Henry Lee, 19 June 1779, ibid., 522–25; Hening, *Statutes*, 10:35–65; Peterson, *Thomas Jefferson and the New Nation*, 120–22. See also *PGM*, 2:509–13, 518–19.

Mason had other real-estate battles to fight besides his campaign to vindicate the Ohio Company's land grants. A Maryland doctor, David Ross, challenged the company's title to several hundred acres it had bought outright around Wills Creek. The litigation continued until 1821, when Mason's heirs, who inherited what was left of the Ohio Company, sold out to Ross's estate. See Copeland and MacMasters, *Five George Masons*, 122–132.

Of greater importance to Mason were some 60,000 acres of headright claims he had purchased. Cary and Carter Braxton had attempted to amend the 1779 land office bill to abolish headrights. Mason thwarted their efforts, but he had to agree to pay county surveyors to resurvey his claims. GM to Richard Henry Lee, 19 June 1779, *PGM*, 2:522–25; Randolph, *History of Virginia*, 273. Mason received warrants from the land office in July 1779 confirming his headrights. Sloppy work by eighteenth-century surveyors, however, invited litigation, and undid Mason's dream of patenting 60,000 acres on the Licking River in Kentucky. In a lawsuit that lasted until 1804, a George Wilson successfully challenged Mason's title. Only a small tract on Panther Creek in Daviess County remained in the Mason family. See *PGM*, 1:451–52; 2:531–32, 829–30; Copeland and MacMaster, *Five George Masons*, 145–49.

82. GM to Richard Henry Lee, 12 April 1779, *PGM*, 1:497–500; Richard Henry Lee to Thomas Jefferson, 25 August 1777, in P. Smith, *Letters of Delegates*, 7:550–52; John Henry to Thomas Johnson, 10 March 1778, ibid., 9:258–59; Richard Henry Lee to Patrick Henry, 15 November 1778, in Ballagh, *Lee Letters*, 1:451–53. See also Alden, *American Revolution*, 344–47; Alden, *The South in the Revolution*, 220–23; Ketcham, *Madison*, 98–100; Brant, *Madison*, 2:89–92, 148–49.

83. GM to Richard Henry Lee, 12 April 1779, *PGM*, 2:497–500.

84. *JCC*, 15:1063–65, 1226–30; Samuel Huntington to the States, 30 October 1779, in P. Smith, *Letters of Delegates*, 14:134; Cyrus Griffin to House of Delegates, 9 November 1779, ibid., 166–67.

85. *PGM*, 2:549–50, 595–80; Selby, *Revolution in Virginia*, 242–44. Shortly before adopting the Remonstrance on 10 December 1779, Virginia had passed a law to discourage settlement northwest of the Ohio and on 24 January 1780 issued a proclamation requiring settlers in the area to return to Virginia proper. Hening, *Statutes*, 10:159–67; Boyd et al., *Papers of Thomas Jefferson*, 8:266–67. Intended as conciliatory gestures, they ironically paralleled the royal Proclamation of 1763 and had the same ostensible purpose: to avoid an Indian war.

86. William C. Houston to Robert Morris, 6 March 1780, in P. Smith, *Letters of Delegates*, 14:467–72; Joseph Jones to Thomas Jefferson, 30 June 1780, ibid., 15:393–96; John Walker to Thomas Jefferson, 11 July 1780, ibid., 433–34; Ketcham, *Madison*, 98–100.

87. GM to Joseph Jones, 27 July 1780, *PGM*, 2:655–63. In a letter to Clark that was also signed by Jefferson and Wythe, Mason had promised "some Further Reward in Lands" to the volunteers in Clark's campaign in the Ohio Valley. GM et al. to George Rogers Clark, 3 January 1778, ibid., 1:409–10.

88. *JCC*, 18:806–8, 915–16; Joseph Jones to George Washington, 6 September 1780, in P. Smith, *Letters of Delegates*, 16:29–31; James Madison to Joseph Jones,

19 September 1780, ibid., 94–96; James Madison to Joseph Jones, 21 November 1780, ibid., 190–92; Joseph Jones to James Madison, 2 December 1780, in Hutchinson and Rachal, *Papers of James Madison*, 2:218–20; *Journal of the House of Delegates of the Commonwealth of Virginia, 1777–80*, 2 January 1781, 80–81; Abernethy, *Western Lands and the American Revolution*, 242–47.

89. Abernethy, *Western Lands and the American Revolution*, 228; Randolph, *History of Virginia*, 272–73; H. Miller, *Gentleman Revolutionary*, 169–70; Sosin, *Revolutionary Frontier*, 154–55; Hinderaker, *Elusive Empires*, 204–7.

90. Bailey, *Ohio Company*, 291–93; James, *Ohio Company*, 163.

91. See Rutland, *Mason*, 69–72; Rowland, *Mason*, 1:328–29; Malone, *Jefferson*, 1:257–59.

92. GM to William Aylett, 19 April 1777, *PGM*, 1:338–40. For similar assessments, see Abernethy, *Western Lands and the American Revolution*, 217–26; and Rowland, *Mason*, 1:359.

93. GM to James Mercer, 5 February 1780, *PGM*, 2:617–18; George Washington to GM, 22 October 1780, ibid., 677–79.

94. Theodorick Bland to Richard Henry Lee, 5 March 1781, in P. Smith, *Letters of Delegates*, 17:13–15; GM to Virginia Delegates in Congress, 3 April 1781, *PGM*, 2:680–84; Henry Lee Sr. to Thomas Jefferson, 9 April 1781, in Boyd et al., *Papers of Thomas Jefferson*, 5:393–94.

95. GM to Pearson Chapman, 31 May 1781, *PGM*, 2:688–89; GM to George Mason Jr., 3 June 1781, ibid., 689–95. A May 1780 address from the general assembly to Congress suggests Mason's declining confidence in the militia. Dismissing the militia as "ineffectual," the address pleaded for a "speedy and powerful reinforcement of Continental troops." Although authorship of the address is uncertain, it has generally been attributed to Mason. See ibid., 623–25; Selby, *Revolution in Virginia*, 213.

Chapter Six

1. GM to Robert Carter, 27 October 1781, *PGM*, 2:700; Selby, *Revolution in Virginia*, 311–12.

2. GM to Arthur Lee, 25 March 1783, *PGM*, 2:765–68.

3. GM to Patrick Henry, 6 May 1783, ibid., 769–74.

4. GM to George Mason Jr., 8 January 1783, ibid., 759. For a sanguine view of the 1780s, see Jensen, *The New Nation*. See also McDonald, *Novus Ordo Seclorum*, 131–36, 143–44; and Alden, *The South in the Revolution*, 368–75. For a more critical view outlining the economic woes allegedly created by the lack of a competent national government, see Morris, *The Forging of the Union*, 130–49.

5. Rakove, *Original Meanings*, 26–31. See generally Marks, *Independence on Trial*, chap. 3.

6. Rakove, *Original Meanings*, 40–41; Wood, *Radicalism of the American Revolution*, 176; Wood, *Creation of the American Republic*, 476–77; Isaac, *Transformation of Virginia*, 319; Kulikoff, *Tobacco and Slaves*, 423–28.

7. Edmund Pendleton to Richard Henry Lee, 14 March 1785, in Mays, *Pendleton Papers*, 2:476–77.

8. As quoted in Ketcham, *Madison*, 160. See also Jensen, *The New Nation*, 52; Malone, *Jefferson*, 1:367; Buckley, *Church and State*, 71–72.

9. GM to Patrick Henry, 6 May 1783, *PGM*, 2:769–74; R. Meade, *Henry*, 2:253–54.

10. Jensen, *The New Nation*, 304–5, 311–12; R. H. Brown, *Redeeming the Republic*, 128–31.

11. GM to Edmund Randolph, 19 October 1782, *PGM*, 2:746–55; GM to George Mason Jr., 8 January 1783, ibid., 757–63; GM to William Cabell, 6 May 1783, ibid., 768–69; GM to Martin Cockburn, 18 April 1784, ibid., 799–800.

12. GM to George Mason Jr., 8 January 1783, ibid., 757–63; GM to Arthur Lee, 25 March 1783, ibid., 765–68; GM to George Washington, 5 April 1785, ibid., 823–24; GM to Martin Cockburn, 25 August 1786, ibid., 852–53.

13. The single most comprehensive statement of Mason's postwar views is probably his "Fairfax County Freeholders' Address and Instructions to Their General Assembly Delegates," 30 May 1783, ibid., 779–83. He opposed a state constitutional convention without "a Requisition from a Majority of the People." GM to William Cabell, 6 May 1783, ibid., 768–69.

14. "A Petition and Remonstrance from the Freeholders of Prince William County," 10 December 1781, ibid., 700–711.

15. H. Miller, *Gentlemen Revolutionary*, 212.

16. "A Petition and Remonstrance from the Freeholders of Prince William County," 10 December 1781, *PGM*, 2:700–711; Selby, *Revolution in Virginia*, 298–300; Evans, *Thomas Nelson of Yorktown*, 102–23.

17. "A Petition and Remonstrance from the Freeholders of Prince William County," 10 December 1781, *PGM*, 2:703–11.

18. Edmund Pendleton to James Madison, 31 December 1781, in Mays, *Pendleton Papers*, 2:382–84; *PGM*, 2:700–702; Selby, *Revolution in Virginia*, 315–17. For the act approving Nelson's conduct ex post facto, see Hening, *Statutes*, 10:478.

19. Hening, *Statutes*, 10:443, 468–69, 496; Richard Henry Lee to ——, 5 October 1781, in Ballagh, *Lee Letters*, 2:257. Arthur Lee had spent much of the Revolution in Paris as an American commissioner to France, but a bitter feud with his fellow commissioners, Franklin and Silas Deane, led to his dismissal. Lee returned to Virginia in 1780 and served in the House of Delegates from 1781 to 1784. Like Mason, he opposed ratification of the Constitution. See Potts, *Arthur Lee*.

20. GM to Samuel Beall, 9 May 1782, *PGM*, 2:712–14; Hening, *Statutes*, 10:456–57; Wood, *Radicalism of the American Revolution*, 248–52; Selby, *Revolution in Virginia*, 318–19; Ketcham, *Madison*, 175. See also R. H. Brown, *Redeeming the Republic*, 47–48.

21. GM to Arthur Lee, 25 March 1782, *PGM*, 2:765–68; GM to William Cabell, 6 May 1783, ibid., 768–69; GM to Arthur Campbell, 7 May 1783, ibid., 775–77; Hening, *Statutes*, 10:76, 136, 322. See also Jensen, *The New Nation*, 278–81.

22. "Fairfax County Freeholders' Address and Instructions to Their General As-

sembly Delegates," 30 May 1783, *PGM*, 2:779–83; "Fairfax County Petition Regarding Status of Prewar Debts Owed to British Creditors," 18 June 1783, ibid., 783–85; "Fairfax County Petition on Protesting Repeal of the Act to Prevent Extensive Credits," 18 June 1783, ibid., 785–87.

23. Jensen, *The New Nation*, 278–81; Richard Henry Lee to James Madison, 20 November 1784, in Ballagh, *Lee Letters*, 2:299–301; *PGM*, 2:787; Hening, *Statutes*, 12:528; *Ware v. Hylton*, 3 Dallas 199 (1795).

24. "Fairfax County Petition Protesting Certain Actions by Justices of the Peace," 8 June 1782, *PGM*, 2:733–37; "Deposition in Lawsuit over the *George Washington*," 29 September 1783, ibid., 789–90; "Protest from Fairfax County, Justices of the Peace," 22 March 1785, ibid., 822–12. See also ibid., 806–808; Horrell, "George Mason and the Fairfax County Court," 428–30.

25. Ketcham, *Madison*, 168–69; Brant, *Madison*, 2:315; Hutchinson and Rachal, *Papers of James Madison*, 8:64–66; Hening, *Statutes*, 11:402–4.

26. James Madison to Thomas Jefferson, 22 January 1786, in Hutchinson and Rachal, *Papers of James Madison*, 8:472–82; Philip Mazzei to Carissimo Amico, 15 June 1785, ibid., 294; GM to John Harvie, 29 August 1786, *PGM*, 2:853–55; GM to John Fitzgerald, 28 November 1786, ibid., 858–59.

27. David Stuart to George Washington, 8 November 1786, *PGW-ConfS*, 4:346–48; James Madison to Thomas Jefferson, 4 December 1786, in Hutchinson and Rachal, *Papers of James Madison*, 9:189–92.

28. "Protest by a Private Citizen against the Port Bill," November–December 1786, *PGM*, 2:859–64.

29. Jefferson, *Notes on the State of Virginia*, in Peterson, *The Portable Jefferson*, 217; Banning, *The Sacred Fire of Liberty*, 40–41; Ketcham, *Madison*, 168–69; *Journal of the House of Delegates of the Commonwealth of Virginia*, October 1786, 98, 101. For the various versions of the bill, see Hening, *Statutes*, 12:320–23, 434–38.

30. James Madison to Thomas Jefferson, 10 December 1783, *PGM*, 2:790–91.

31. Quoted in Rowland, *Mason*, 2:66–67.

32. *DGW*, 10 March 1785, 4:100; 11 March 1785, 4:101; 8 December 1785, 4:246; Flexner, *George Washington*, 3:27–28.

33. Lund Washington quoted in Henriques, "Uneven Friendship," 193. See also "Petition for a Protective Duty Levied upon Imported Tobacco-Snuff," 19 May 1783, *PGM*, 2:777–79.

34. John Harvie to Thomas Jefferson, 27 November 1781, in Boyd et al., *Papers of Thomas Jefferson*, 6:133–34; Joseph Jones to Thomas Jefferson, 29 December 1783, ibid., 428–30; James Currie to Thomas Jefferson, 9 July 1786, ibid., 107–11; *DGW*, 17 April 1786, 4:312.

35. James Madison to Thomas Jefferson, 12 May 1786, in Hutchinson and Rachal, *Papers of James Madison*, 9:48–54; James Madison to James Monroe, 13 May 1786, ibid., 54–57.

36. James Madison to James Monroe, 4 June 1786, ibid., 73–74; James Madison to Thomas Jefferson, 23 April 1787, ibid., 398–402. See also Edmund Randolph to Thomas Jefferson, 12 July 1786, in Boyd et al., *Papers of Thomas Jefferson*, 10:133–34.

37. Thomas Jefferson to James Madison, 11 December 1783, in Hutchinson and Rachal, *Papers of James Madison*, 7:405–48; James Madison to Thomas Jefferson, 16 March 1784, ibid., 8:6–15; James Madison to Thomas Jefferson, 15 May 1784, ibid., 34–35.

38. James Monroe to James Madison, 29 September 1786, ibid., 9:134–35; Henry Lee Jr. to George Washington, 11 October 1786, *PGW-ConfS*, 4:290–93; Rowland, *Mason*, 2:95.

39. GM to Thomas Jefferson, 27 September 1781, *PGM*, 2:697–99; *JCC*, 20:704–5; 21:1098; Sosin, *Revolutionary Frontier*, 158–60; Selby, *Revolution in Virginia*, 320–21.

40. Edmund Randolph to James Madison, 19 April 1782, in Hutchinson and Rachal, *Papers of James Madison*, 4:159–62; Rowland, *Mason*, 2:22.

41. GM to Samuel Purviance, 20 May 1782, *PGM*, 2:714–16; GM to Samuel Purviance, 17 July 1782, ibid., 738–41; Rowland, *Mason*, 2:22.

42. GM to Edmund Randolph, 19 October 1782, *PGM*, 2:746–55; James Madison to Thomas Jefferson, 15 July 1782, in Hutchinson and Rachal, *Papers of James Madison*, 4:32–36; Benjamin Harrison to Virginia Delegates, 27 September 1783, ibid., 7:360–61.

43. James Madison to Thomas Jefferson, 10 December 1783, *PGM*, 1:790–91; GM to Arthur Lee, 24 March 1784, ibid., 2:797–99, 1:9–10; *JCC*, 25:559–64; Selby, *Revolution in Virginia*, 320–21; Boyd et al., *Papers of Thomas Jefferson*, 6:571–75. Robert Rutland believed Mason "had all but abandoned the old Ohio Company claim" even before the Court of Appeals decision. *PGM*, 2:762–63.

44. Julian Boyd, for example, praised Virginia's magnanimity, writing "the Virginia Acts of Cession of 1781 and 1783 stand as a monument to the strength of national feeling in the post-Revolutionary period and to the solid accomplishments of the Confederation." Boyd et al., *Papers of Thomas Jefferson*, 6:574. See also GM to Joseph Jones, 27 July 1780, *PGM*, 2:655–63; H. Miller, *George Mason: Constitutionalist*, 165–66.

45. GM to George Mason Jr., 8 January 1783, *PGM*, 2:762–63; GM to Samuel Purviance, 17 July 1782, ibid., 738–41; Onuf, "Toward Federalism," 353–74.

46. Edmund Pendleton to Richard Henry Lee, 28 February 1785, in Mays, *Pendleton Papers*, 2:474–75; Wirt, *Sketches*, 260–63; Ketcham, *Madison*, 162–63; "A Bill Establishing a Provision for Teachers of the Christian Religion" (1784), in Buckley, *Church and State*, 188–89.

47. See Ketcham, *Madison*, 162–68; Levy, *The Establishment Clause*, 51–62; Curry, *The First Freedoms*, 134–48.

48. GM to Sarah Mason McCarty, 10 February 1785, *PGM*, 2:810; GM to George Washington, 2 October 1785, ibid., 830–31; George Washington to GM, 3 October 1785, ibid., 831–32; Richard Henry Lee to James Madison, 26 November 1784, in Ballagh, *Lee Letters*, 2:304–7; Alden, *The South in the Revolution*, 319–22; Buckley, *Church and State*, 135, 147–50; Brant, *Madison*, 2:350–52.

49. "Memorial and Remonstrance," in Hutchinson and Rachal, *Papers of James Madison*, 8:298–306.

50. Ibid.

51. John Page to Thomas Jefferson, 23 August 1785, in Boyd, *Papers of Thomas Jefferson*, 8:428–31. See also Buckley, *Church and State*, 147–15; Brant, *Madison*, 2:350–52; Ketcham, *Madison*, 162–68.

52. Buckley, *Church and State*, 137–38, 153–56.

53. Richard Henry Lee to Samuel Adams, 18 November 1784, in Ballagh, *Lee Letters*, 2:293–95; R. H. Brown, *Redeeming the Republic*, 19–20, 141–42; Marks, *Independence on Trial*, 56–59; Flexner, *George Washington*, 3:94–95.

54. Morris, *Forging the Union*, 41; Main, *The Antifederalists*, 92–94, 101–2.

55. Richard Henry Lee to Robert Wormley Carter, 3 June 1783, in Ballagh, *Lee Letters*, 2:281–82.

56. Edmund Pendleton to James Madison, 19 December 1786, in Mays, *Pendleton Papers*, 2:491–94; Main, *The Antifederalists*, 72, 111–13; Marks, *Independence on Trial*, 73–76, 86–88.

57. Alden, *The South in the Revolution*, 361–64, 377–78; R. Meade, *Henry*, 2:325–27; George Washington to Henry Lee Jr., 31 October 1786, *PGW-ConfS*, 4:318–20; Kukla, *A Wilderness So Immense*, 60–94.

58. "Fairfax County Freeholders' Address," 30 May 1783, *PGM*, 2:779–83.

59. James Madison to Thomas Jefferson, 10 December 1783, in Hutchinson and Rachal, *Papers of James Madison*, 7:401–6; Ketcham, *Madison*, 143; Brant, *Madison*, 2:306–10.

Madison did not explain how a national impost, in Mason's view, would undermine efforts to retaliate against Britain for the restrictions it had imposed on American shipping and exports. Mason may have still believed retaliation should be left to the states, and he may have seen a national impost as an entering wedge to federal supremacy over foreign commerce. Or he may have thought a Congress dependent on tariff revenues from British imports would likely be hostile to efforts to ban or otherwise restrict those imports.

60. "Resolutions Appointing Virginia Members of a Potomac River Commission," 28 June 1784, in Hutchinson and Rachal, *Papers of James Madison*, 8:89–90; Copeland and MacMaster, *Five George Masons*, 118–22; GM to George Washington, ca. 8 March 1775, *PGM*, 1:224–25.

61. Edmund Randolph to James Madison, 17 July 1785, in Hutchinson and Rachal, *Papers of James Madison*, 8:324; GM to James Madison, 9 August 1785, *PGM*, 2:826–28.

62. James Madison to Edmund Randolph, 26 July 1785, in Hutchinson and Rachal, *Papers of James Madison*, 8:327–29; *DGW*, 20 March 1785, 4:104–6; 22 March 1785, 4:106–7; 24 March 1785, 4:107–8; 25 March 1785, 4:108; 27 March 1785, 4:108; 28 March 1785, 4:109; James Madison to Thomas Jefferson, 27 April 1785, in Boyd et al., *Papers of Thomas Jefferson*, 8:110–16.

63. "The Compact between Maryland & Virginia Relating to the Jurisdiction and Navigation of the Potomac and Pokomoke Rivers," 28 March 1785, *PGM*, 2:816–22.

64. "Resolutions Authorizing an Interstate Compact on Navigation and Jurisdiction of the Potomac," 28 December 1784, in Hutchinson and Rachal, *Papers of*

James Madison, 8:206–7; "To the President of the Executive Council of the Commonwealth of Pennsylvania," 29 March 1785, *PGM*, 2:822–23.

65. GM and Alexander Henderson to the Speaker of the House of Delegates, 28 March 1785, *PGM*, 2:814–16.

66. Flexner, *George Washington*, 3:90; McDonald, *E Pluribus Unum*, 236–37. Brant also saw the two-state conference as an Anti-Federalist ploy; see Brant, *Madison*, 2:385. It was a curious affair. Article 6 of the Articles of Confederation required congressional approval for "any treaty, confederation, or alliance whatever" between two or more states. Mason's cover letter to the House of Delegates proposed that Virginia and Maryland seek leave of Congress to form a compact for naval defense, but it did not suggest that Congress needed to approve the Mount Vernon Compact itself. The agreement was apparently never submitted to the national legislature. McDonald has called "it . . . an overt flaunting of the Congress." *E Pluribus Unum*, 236. Madison had encouraged the Virginia legislature to convene the meeting, but when he prepared his "Vices of the Political System of the United States" in anticipation of the Constitutional Convention, he included the Mount Vernon Compact on a short list of improper "Encroachments by the States on the Federal Authority." For the "Vices," see Hunt, *The Writings of James Madison*, 2:361–69. George Mason may have concluded that Article 6 did not apply to interstate commercial treaties. What James Madison thought is a mystery. On Madison and the Mount Vernon Conference, see also Brant, *Madison*, 2:375–78.

While historians have treated the Mount Vernon Conference in the context of the move to reform or replace the Articles of Confederation, it must not be forgotten that at least some contemporary observers judged it on its own terms. Sometimes assembly delegate David Stuart condemned "the compact law of Col. Mason's" for doing nothing to advance the interests of the Potomac Navigation Company. David Stuart to George Washington, 25 December 1786, *PGW-ConfS*, 4:476–77.

67. James Madison to James Monroe, 22 January 1786, in Hutchinson and Rachal, *Papers of James Madison*, 8:482–84; GM to George Washington, 5 April 1785, *PGM*, 2:823–24; GM to George Washington, 2 October 1785, ibid., 830–31; GM to George Washington, 9 November 1785, ibid., 833–34; GM to James Madison, 7 December 1875, ibid., 835–38.

68. GM to James Madison, 9 August 1785, *PGM*, 2:826–28; GM to Benjamin Harrison, 8 December 1785, ibid., 838–39. Despite Mason's absence, the general assembly approved the Mount Vernon Compact without significant opposition.

69. James Monroe to James Madison, 3 September 1786, in Hutchinson and Rachal, *Papers of James Madison*, 9:112–14; Edmund Randolph to James Madison, 12 June 1786, ibid., 75–76. See also George Washington to David Stuart, 19 November 1786, *PGW-ConfS*, 4:387–88.

70. Edmund Randolph to GM, 6 December 1786, *PGM*, 2:864; James Madison to Thomas Jefferson, 23 April 1787, in Hutchinson and Rachal, *Papers of James Madison*, 9:398–402.

Mason seemed little concerned about Shays's Rebellion, an ill-fated uprising by cash-strapped farmers that was playing itself out in Massachusetts. The rebellion had frightened many among the better classes, but not Mason. He later defended the Massachusetts legislature, which had found itself deadlocked between pro-Shaysite and anti-Shaysite houses. He believed that in the midst of the rebellion, "it was right to be rigid. But after it was over, it would be wrong to exercise unnecessary severity." Memories of Shays's Rebellion may explain Mason's desire at Philadelphia to keep at least part of the state militia under state control, if that intermediate position required a particular rationale. *PGM*, 3:885, 961–62, 1098.

Chapter Seven

1. Farrand, *Records*, 3:558–63; McDonald, *We the People*, 32–33; Bowen, *Miracle at Philadelphia*, 19.

2. GM to George Mason Jr., 20 May 1787, *PGM*, 3:879–82. On Washington's silence at the Constitutional Convention, see Flexner, *George Washington*, 3:123. On Blair, see Bowen, *Miracle at Philadelphia*, 259; and Ferris, *Signers*, 145–46.

3. Farrand, *Records*, 2:559–61.

4. H. Miller, *George Mason: Constitutionalist*, 185; Richard Henry Lee to GM, 15 May 1787, *PGM*, 3:876–79; GM to Arthur Lee, 21 May 1787, ibid., 882–83.

5. GM to Edmund Randolph, 12 April 1787, *PGM*, 3:874–75; GM to Edmund Randolph, 23 April 1787, ibid., 875–76; GM to George Mason Jr., 20 May 1787, ibid., 879–82; H. Miller, *Gentleman Revolutionary*, 234.

6. Ketcham, *Madison*, 192–93; James Madison to Thomas Jefferson, 15 May 1787, in Farrand, *Records*, 3:20; George Reed to John Dickinson, 21 May 1787, ibid., 24–26.

According to Ketcham, Mason arrived in Philadelphia with Dr. McClurg on 17 May, but Madison's letter to Jefferson of 15 May reports that McClurg was already in Philadelphia and that Mason was expected "in a day or two." Mason wrote his son George that he had arrived on "Thursday evening," which would have been 17 May, so he could not have been traveling with McClurg.

7. GM to George Mason Jr., 20 May 1787, *PGM*, 3:879–82; Farrand, *Records*, 3:58–59.

8. GM to George Mason Jr., 20 May 1787, *PGM*, 3:879–92.

9. Richard Henry Lee to GM, 15 May 1787, ibid., 876–79.

10. GM to George Mason Jr., 20 May 1787, ibid., 3:879–92. Nothing should be made of George Washington's absence from the Virginia delegation. Washington went to Mass on 27 May. Freeman, *George Washington*, 4:94 (n. 94). As did Mason, Washington displayed, throughout his life, an irenic spirit in matters of faith. See generally Boller, *George Washington and Religion*.

11. Rossiter, *1787*, 104, 133–14; Farrand, *Records*, 1:45–52; Kramnick, "The 'Great National Discussion,'" 3–22. See generally W. Miller, *The Business of May Next*, 103–16.

12. GM to George Mason Jr., 27 May 1787, *PGM*, 3:884–85; GM to George Mason Jr., 1 June 1787, ibid., 890–94.

13. Farrand, *Records*, 3:94; H. Miller, *Gentleman Revolutionary*, 236; Van Doren, *The Great Rehearsal*, 131. On Washington's health, see Flexner, *George Washington*, 3:100, 108–12; and Bowen, *Miracle at Philadelphia*, 21.

14. GM to George Mason Jr., 1 June 1787, *PGM*, 3:890–94; Bowen, *Miracle at Philadelphia*, 87–89.

15. Ferris, *Signers*, 35, 143–44; Roche, "Founding Fathers," 799–816; Bowen, *Miracle at Philadelphia*, 37; McDonald, *E Pluribus Unum*, 263; C. Smith, *Wilson*, 221; Van Doren, *The Great Rehearsal*, 17.

16. McDonald, *E Pluribus Unum*, 288–89.

17. Brant, *Madison*, 3:49; McDonald, *Alexander Hamilton*, 106; Alexander Hamilton to George Washington, 3 July 1787, in Syrett, *The Papers of Alexander Hamilton*, 4:223–25.

18. Ferris, *Signers*, 183.

19. For a contemporary account, see Manasseh Cutler's journal entries in Farrand, *Records*, 3:58–59. For other impressions, see Brant, *Madison*, 3:84; C. Smith, *Wilson*, 219; and Bowen, *Miracle at Philadelphia*, 22–24.

20. Bowen, *Miracle at Philadelphia*, 22–24; GM to George Mason Jr., 1 June 1787, *PGM*, 3:890–94; Flexner, *George Washington*, 3:123. John Ferling has said of the convention's decision to deliberate in secret, "had the public known what was occurring behind closed doors, the popular clamor would have immediately stopped the proceedings." Ferling, *A Leap in the Dark*, 284.

21. Farrand, *Records*, 1:10.

22. Ibid., 18–24.

23. Ibid., 33–34.

24. Ibid., 34.

25. Ibid., 21, 35, 54. See also Rossiter, *1787*, 172–73; Rowland, *Mason*, 2:108–9.

26. Farrand, *Records*, 1:48–50. See also C. Smith, *Wilson*, 221–25; and Billias, *Gerry*, 160.

27. Farrand, *Records*, 1:132–34, 358–60; Kurland and Lerner, *The Founders' Constitution*, 2:43–50.

28. Farrand, *Records*, 1:133; Bowen, *Miracle at Philadelphia*, 74–75; Roche, "Founding Fathers," 140–41.

29. See C. Smith, *Wilson*, 229–30, 234–35.

30. Farrand, *Records*, 1:155–56, 407–8.

31. Ibid., 216, 378.

32. Ibid., 139–40; 2:74–78; *PGM*, 2:927–28.

33. Farrand, *Records*, 1:375.

34. Ibid., 428; *PGM*, 3:932–33.

Another future Anti-Federalist, Elbridge Gerry, also supported a property quali-fication for federal officeholders, which would seem to call into question the stereo-typical view of the Anti-Federalists as champions of grass-roots democracy opposed to the more aristocratic Federalists, as would Gerry's opposition to popular election of the House of Representatives. To further complicate matters, Gerry opposed a council of revision, a presumably undemocratic institution that Mason supported enthusiastically. On Gerry, see Ferris, *Signers*, 66; and Billias, *Gerry*, 181–82.

The delegates who opposed Mason's proposed requirements for federal office holding were not necessarily more egalitarian than he was. Madison hoped that "an enlargement of the sphere," that is, electing candidates from relatively large congressional districts, would attract better-qualified candidates than did state legislative races. The majority of the delegates wanted to raise the caliber of political leadership by opening up the process, not by restricting it. Rakove, *Madison*, 56; Rakove, "The Structure of Politics at the Accession of George Washington," 261–94.

35. Farrand, *Records*, 1:362.

36. Ibid., 380–81, 387–89; Kurland and Lerner, *Founders' Constitution*, 2:346–52. Madison's proposal was eventually approved by a one-vote margin late in the convention. Mason considered it "a partial remedy" (ibid., 347).

37. Farrand, *Records*, 1:176–79, 201–2.

38. Ibid., 234–37, 342–43.

39. Ibid., 322.

40. Ibid., 168, 336–40. On 17 July, the convention rejected a congressional veto on unconstitutional state laws, which it had approved on 31 May. Ibid., 2:21–22. Sentiment was moving toward what became the supremacy clause. See Hobson, "The Negative on State Laws," 215–35.

41. North Carolina Delegates to Governor Caswell, 14 June 1787, Farrand, *Records*, 2:46–47; Alexander Hamilton to George Washington, 3 July 1787, in Syrett, *Papers of Alexander Hamilton*, 4:223–25; George Washington to Alexander Hamilton, 10 July 1787, ibid., 225. For the view that the New Hampshire delegates, who were merchants, would have voted with the large-state bloc, see Collier and Collier, *Decision in Philadelphia*, 165.

42. GM to Beverly Randolph, 30 June 1787, *PGM*, 3:918–19. Mason's recommendation of Corbin is curious. Corbin had spent the Revolution studying law at London's Inner Temple and later became a Federalist. Mason and Corbin were not political allies, and Corbin's appointment would almost certainly have weakened Mason's position within the Virginia delegation.

43. Ibid., 313–22, 468, 510–11; Strayer, *The Delegate from New York*, 16; Roche, "Founding Fathers," 142–44; Ferris, *Signers*, 140–41.

44. Farrand, *Records*, 1:511–16; Brant, *Madison*, 3:90–91; Ferris, *Signers*, 53; Billias, *Gerry*, 176–77.

45. Rowland, *Mason*, 2:126–28; W. Miller, *Business of May Next*, 69; C. Smith, *Wilson*, 237–38.

46. Farrand, *Records*, 1:522–23; 3:189–90.

47. Ibid., 1:526–34; *PGM*, 3:919–20. Franklin apparently borrowed the idea for the Great Compromise from Roger Sherman of Connecticut, who suggested it on the floor of the convention, and hence it is also known as the Connecticut Compromise. See Brands, *The First American*, 680–82; Isaacson, *Benjamin Franklin*, 450–52.

48. McDonald and Mendle, "Historical Roots of the Originating Clause," 274–81; McDonald, *Novus Ordo Seclorum*, 25; W. Miller, *Business of May Next*, 99–101; Ferris, *Signers*, 56.

49. Brant, *Madison*, 3:121–22.

50. Farrand, *Records*, 1:544.

51. Ibid., 2:15; Ketcham, *Madison*, 212–15; Rossiter, *1787*, 190–93; Banning, "The Constitutional Convention," 112–31, 123–24.

52. Farrand, *Records*, 2:19–20; James Madison to Thomas Jefferson, 24 October 1787, ibid., 3:131; Ferris, *Signers*, 58.

53. Washington might not have accepted the presidency if it had consisted of a three-member executive committee, as Mason proposed. See Flexner, *George Washington*, 3:133–34; see also H. Miller, *Gentleman Revolutionary*, 245.

Forrest McDonald has suggested the delegates who developed reservations about the Constitution as it began to take shape—Mason, Martin, Gerry, and Randolph— may have intentionally agitated issues involving presidential power because the dissenters realized those issues divided the nationalists. McDonald, *E Pluribus Unum*, 303. However, there is no evidence that the views Mason expressed before the 27 July recess were insincere.

54. Farrand, *Records*, 1:88, 97; Bowen, *Miracle at Philadelphia*, 60.

55. Farrand, *Records*, 1:101–2, 110–14.

56. *PGM*, 2:895–98; Rossiter, *1787*, 245–47.

57. Farrand, *Records*, 1:88; 2:100–101.

58. Ibid., 1:68–69; 2:31, 118–19; Berkin, *A Brilliant Solution*, 126–29.

59. Farrand, *Records*, 1:68–69, 88; 2:33, 59, 118–20.

60. Ibid, 1:86; 2:41–42, 82–83.

61. Ibid., 1:101–2.

62. Ibid., 578–79, 582, 591–92.

63. Ibid., 581. Mason seemed open to counting slaves in some fashion and apparently did not object when the convention eventually adopted the "federal ratio" counting a slave as three-fifths of a free person for purposes of representation and taxation. The federal ratio had been proposed by the Articles of Confederation Congress in the early 1780s to apportion requisitions among the states. See W. Miller, *Business of May Next*, 121.

64. Farrand, *Records*, 2:47, 88–89, 127.

Chapter Eight

1. Farrand, *Records*, 2:97, 176. Mason's annotated copy of the Committee of Detail's report is reprinted in *PGM*, 3:934–48. See generally Rossiter, *1787*, 206–10.

2. Farrand, *Records*, 2:177–81; Rossiter, *1787*, 207.

3. Farrand, *Records*, 2:183–85.

4. Ibid., 185–86.

5. Ibid., 181–82; Rossiter, *1787*, 208.

6. Farrand, *Records*, 2:183, 187; Rossiter, *1787*, 209. See also Billias, *Gerry*, 173.

7. Farrand, *Records*, 2:183.

8. Ibid.

9. Ibid., 198–99.

10. Ibid., 251–52, 255–56, 260.

11. Ibid., 201–206.

12. Ibid., 216–19.

13. Ibid., 235–39.

14. Ibid., 270–72; *PGM*, 3:955.

15. Farrand, *Records*, 2:224–25.

16. Ibid., 230, 232–34.

17. Ibid., 273–80; Flexner, *George Washington*, 3:131.

18. Farrand, *Records*, 2:296–98.

19. Ibid., 283–89.

20. Ibid., 297–98.

21. Ibid., 305–8.

22. Ibid., 308–10.

23. Ibid., 340–44; Bowen, *Miracle at Philadelphia*, 214.

24. Farrand, *Records*, 2:314–15, 614.

25. Ibid., 326–27.

26. Ibid., 349. The definition of treason had immediate implications; it would affect the sanctions that might be imposed on Revolutionary War Loyalists.

27. Farrand, *Records*, 2:318–19.

28. Ibid., 326–33, 356; Billias, *Gerry*, 201.

29. Farrand, *Records*, 2:355–63.

30. Ibid., 364–65; McDonald, *E Pluribus Unum*, 180–81; Jordan, *White over Black*, 318.

31. Farrand, *Records*, 2:369–71; *PGM*, 3:965–66; Wilkins, *Jefferson's Pillow*, 62; W. Miller, *Business of May Next*, 124–27.

32. Farrand, *Records*, 2:371–73.

33. Ibid., 374–75. Mason is incorrectly identified at *PGM*, 2:967 as a member of the committee. Rutland and his coeditors confused the committee appointed on 18 August to consider issues related to state debts and the regulation of the militia with the committee appointed on 22 August to consider the slave trade and navigation acts.

34. Farrand, *Records*, 2:400; Memorandum of Thomas Jefferson, ca. 30 September 1792, *PGM*, 3:1275–76. See also GM to Thomas Jefferson, 26 May 1788, *PGM*, 3:1044–46; Jillson and Anderson, "Realignments in the Convention of 1787," 712–29.

35. Farrand, *Records*, 2:414–17.

36. Ibid., 3:253–54; Zahniser, *Charles Cotesworth Pinckney*, 87–97.

37. Farrand, *Records*, 2:370.

38. James Madison to George Washington, 18 October 1787, ibid., 3:129.

39. Rowland, *Mason*, 2:161–62. Rowland's denial of Mason's abolitionist tendencies commences a lyrical defense of "the old slave-holding aristocracy of the South." Mason is reborn as an abolitionist in Bowen, *Miracle at Philadelphia*, 95; and W. Miller, *Business of May Next*, 118.

40. Finkelman, *Slavery and the Founders*, 112, 161.

41. Farrand, *Records*, 2:412–14, 417; *PGM*, 3:967–68; Billias, *Gerry*, 190.

42. Farrand, *Records*, 2:417–18, 427, 437, 440–41.

43. Ibid., 449–51; 3:282.

44. Ibid., 2:445–52; Rossiter, *1787*, 217.

45. Farrand, *Records*, 2:453–54; William Blount et al. to Governor Caswell, 18 September 1787, ibid., 3:83–84; Brant, *Madison*, 3:123–26; Fehrenbacher, *The Slaveholding Republic*, 353 (n. 91).

46. Barry, *Mr. Rutledge of South Carolina*, 329–30. See also Ketcham, *Madison*, 223–25.

47. Farrand, *Records*, 2:375.

48. Ibid., 3:210–11; Zahniser, *Charles Cotesworth Pinckney*, 95.

49. McDonald, *E Pluribus Unum*, 291–302; Farrand, *Records*, 2:449; Pierce Butler to Weedon Butler, 5 May 1788, ibid., 3:301–4. A recent study has concluded that the "evidence only partly bears out" the theory that the slave trade was extended as part of a broader agreement in which New England received concessions on commercial regulations. Fehrenbacher, *Slaveholding Republic*, 34–36.

50. Ernst, *Rufus King*, 110–11; W. Miller, *Business of May Next*, 132–35; Boardman, *Roger Sherman*, 252–53.

51. James Madison to Robert Welsh, 27 November 1819, Farrand, *Records*, 3:436–38.

52. Memorandum of Thomas Jefferson, ca. 30 September 1792, *PGM*, 3:1276.

53. Farrand, *Records*, 2:478–79; Memorandum for Maryland Delegates, 31 August 1787, *PGM*, 3:974–75.

54. C. Smith, *Wilson*, 251; Farrand, *Records*, 2:477.

55. Farrand, *Records*, 2:497–502, 524–25; *PGM*, 3:975–78; Roche, "Founding Fathers," 144–45.

56. Farrand, *Records*, 2:511–15.

57. Ibid., 521–28.

58. Ibid., 522, 553–54; *PGM*, 3:980–81; Ketcham, *Madison*, 222–23; Kurland and Lerner, *Founders' Constitution*, 2:376–83.

59. Farrand, *Records*, 2:508, 553.

60. Ibid., 537–42; *PGM*, 3:978–79; Billias, *Gerry*, 163.

61. Farrand, *Records*, 2:560–64; H. Miller, *George Mason: Constitutionalist*, 210.

62. Farrand, *Records*, 2:581, 585–87.

63. Ibid., 587–88.

64. Ibid., 588.

65. Ibid., 565–80; James Madison to Thomas Jefferson, 24 October 1787, ibid., 3:135–36; Levy, *Origins of the Bill of Rights*, 30–31. See also Ferris, *Signers*, 80; Billias, *Gerry*, 197–98; Ketcham, *Madison*, 222.

66. As quoted in Bowen, *Miracle at Philadelphia*, 148.

67. Farrand, *Records*, 2:588–89, 607, 624; *PGM*, 3:982–83, 987–88.

68. Farrand, *Records*, 2:606–7, 617; *PGM*, 3:982. One of Gouverneur Morris's biographers considered the rakish New Yorker to have been *the* civil libertarian in

Philadelphia. Besides opposing bills of attainder, religious tests for holding office, and the suspension of habeas corpus in peacetime, Morris opposed Mason's sumptuary laws. Mintz, *Gouverneur Morris and the American Revolution*, 197–98. See also W. H. Adams, *Gouverneur Morris*, 145–68.

69. Farrand, *Records*, 2:612–19.

70. Ibid., 625–30.

71. Ibid., 631–32.

72. Ibid., 632–33.

73. Ibid., 641–49.

74. Account of Convention Expenses, 28 September 1787, *PGM*, 3:994–95.

75. W. Miller, *Business of May Next*, 141; Rossiter, *1787*, 252; Brant, *Madison*, 3:155–56; Ketcham, *Madison*, 229–30; Billias, *Gerry*, 204–5; Ernst, *Rufus King*, 116.

76. David Siemers has argued the delegates made "a brilliant move" in requiring nine states for ratification. A higher bar might not have been reached, and a lower requirement would have undermined the legitimacy of the new government. Siemers, *Ratifying the Republic*, 196.

77. On some of Mason's later objections, see GM to Thomas Jefferson, 26 May 1788, *PGM*, 3:1044–46.

78. James Madison to Thomas Jefferson, 24 October 1787, ibid., 135–36; Wallenstein, "Flawed Keepers of the Flame," 238–42.

The evolution of Mason's objections to the Constitution can be traced in the following documents, all in *PGM*, vol. 3: "Notes on the Committee of Detail Report," 934–48; "Notes on Proposed Changes to Committee of Style Report," ca. 13 September 1787, 983–85; "Objections on the Committee of Style Report," ca. 16 September 1787, 991–94; GM to Thomas Jefferson, 26 May 1788, 1044–46; Memorandum of Thomas Jefferson, 30 September 1792, 1275–76.

79. Bowen, *Miracle at Philadelphia*, 105. See also McDonald, *We the People*, 109–10. A sophisticated quantitative analysis of voting patterns shows that economic variables predicted Mason's vote on ten of the sixteen issues studied, which suggests economic factors influenced him less than they did most of the other delegates. See McGuire, *To Form a More Perfect Union*, 90–93.

80. For a succinct summary of the Framers' growing concern about "majoritarian excess," see Middlekauff, *The Glorious Cause*, 651–54. For the popular view of Mason as a champion of states' rights, see Rowland, *Mason*, 2:139–79. See also Bowen, *Miracle at Philadelphia*, 105, for the argument Mason believed "a strong central government lay counter to the republican ideas for which the Revolution had been fought." Irving Brant belabored the point but was close to the truth when he wrote "there was no dominating defensive force for State Rights in the Convention." Brant, *Madison*, 3:128. Luther Martin, who left the convention before the signing ceremony, may have been the one prominent Anti-Federalist with a coherent philosophy of states' rights. Cornell, *The Other Founders*, 61–62.

Chapter Nine

1. Daniel Carroll to James Madison, 28 October 1787, Hutchinson and Rachal, *Papers of James Madison*, 10:226–27; Robert Milligan to William Tilghman, 20 September 1787, *DHRC*, 10:13–14; GM to George Washington, 7 October 1787, *PGM*, 3:1001–4; James Madison to Thomas Jefferson, 24 October 1787, ibid., 1007.

2. Richard Henry Lee to GM, 1 October 1787, *PGM*, 3:996–1000; *JCC*, 33:540–44, 549; Middlekauff, *The Glorious Cause*, 660.

3. *PGM*, 3:994, 999; *DHRC*, 7:20.

4. Rossiter, *1787*, 275; George Washington to James Madison, 10 October 1787, *PGW-ConfS*, 5:566–68; Boyd, *The Politics of Opposition*, 47.

5. "Objections to this Constitution of Government," ca. 16 September 1787, *PGM*, 3:991–94; James Madison to George Washington, 18 October 1787, Farrand, *Records*, 3:129–31; Ketcham, *Madison*, 234.

6. GM to George Washington, 7 October 1787, *PGM*, 3:1001–4; *DHRC*, 13:346–48; James Madison to George Washington, 20 December 1787, *PGW-ConfS*, 5:499–501; Banning, "Virginia: Sectionalism and the General Good," 261–99; Rutland, *The Ordeal of the Constitution*, 32–33; Cornell, *The Other Founders*, 29–30; Denboer, "The House of Delegates," 122.

7. Rutland, *Ordeal of the Constitution*, 193–94; GM to Elbridge Gerry, 20 October 1787, *PGM*, 3:1005–7; ibid., 1002–3; Tobias Lear to John Langdon, 3 November 1787, *DHRC*, 8:196–98; *Virginia Journal*, 6 December 1787, ibid., 208–11.

8. *Virginia Journal*, 22 November 1787, *DHRC*, 8:174–75; James Madison to George Washington, 20 December 1787, Farrand, *Records*, 3:168; Cornell, *The Other Founders*, 74–78. A second Brutus essay appeared in the *Virginia Journal* on 6 December 1787. See *DHRC*, 8:212–16. Mason may have written a second Anti-Federalist tract that appeared in the *Virginia Independent Chronicle* on 17 October 1787, under the pen name Cato Uticensis, but the evidence for his authorship is weak. See *DHRC*, 8:70–76.

9. *PGM*, 3:993; Chitwood, *Richard Henry Lee*, 218–21; *Connecticut Courant*, 10 December 1787, *DHRC*, 8:229–31.

10. Tobias Lear to John Langdon, 19 October 1787, *DHRC*, 8:79–83; Tench Coxe to James Madison, 21 October 1787, ibid., 87–88; Rutland, *Ordeal of the Constitution*, 178; George Washington to James Madison, 10 October 1787, *PGW-ConfS*, 5:366–68; George Washington to David Stuart, 17 October 1787, ibid., 379–80.

11. *Pennsylvania Journal*, 17 October 1787, *DHRC*, 8:69–70; H. Miller, *Gentleman Revolutionary*, 272; H. Miller, *George Mason: Constitutionalist*, 218–19.

12. GM to Elbridge Gerry, 20 October 1787, *PGM*, 3:1005–7; *Philadelphia Independent Gazetteer*, 27 October 1787, *DHRC*, 8:125; Main, *The Antifederalists*, 249–56; Rutland, *Ordeal of the Constitution*, 184–85.

13. Cornell, *The Other Founders*, 11–12, 22–23; Boyd, *Politics of Opposition*, 121–22; Kenyon, *The Antifederalists*, xciii–xciv; Main, *Antifederalists*, 149–52;

Luther Martin, "Report to the Maryland Legislature," 29 November 1787, in Farrand, *Records*, 3:172–232.

14. Rutland, *Ordeal of the Constitution*, 76, 170; Briceland, "Virginia: The Cement of the Union," 209; Main, *Antifederalists*, 177; Siemers, *The Antifederalists*, 183–85; James Madison to Thomas Jefferson, 9 December 1787, in Hutchinson and Rachal, *Papers of James Madison*, 10:310–15; James Madison to George Washington, 20 December 1787, *PGW-ConfS*, 5:499–501.

15. Edmund Randolph, "Reasons for Not Signing the Constitution," 27 December 1787, *DHRC*, 8:260–75; Storing, *What the Anti-Federalists Were For*, 39.

16. Kenyon, *Antifederalists*, xxxix–xi; Cornell, *The Other Founders*, 72–73; Main, *Antifederalists*, 137–39; Allen and Lloyd, *The Essential Antifederalist*, 146–47, 234.

17. Storing, *What the Anti-Federalists Were For*, 21, 64–70; "Federal Farmer No. 2," 9 October 1787, in Kenyon, *Antifederalists*, 209.

18. Main, *Antifederalists*, 129.

19. Rutland, *Ordeal of the Constitution*, 5; Middlekauff, *The Glorious Cause*, 655–57; Storing, *What the Anti-Federalists Were For*, 9.

20. See, for example, Siemers, *Antifederalists*, 18.

21. Kenyon, *Antifederalists*, ixiii, lxvi–lxvii; George Washington to Henry Knox, 15 October 1787, *PGW-ConfS*, 5:375–76; George Washington to Bushrod Washington, 9 November 1787, ibid., 420–25; Boyd, *Politics of Opposition*, 41.

22. GM to George Washington, 7 October 1787, *PGM*, 3:1001–2; "Instructions from a Committee of Fairfax County Voters," 2 October 1787, ibid., 1000–1001; James Madison to William Short, 24 October 1787, in Hutchinson and Rachal, *Papers of James Madison*, 10:220–22; George Washington to James Madison, 5 November 1787, *DHRC*, 8:145–46.

23. *DHRC*, 8:113–14.

24. John Pierce to Henry Knox, 26 October 1787, *DHRC*, 8:123–24; Edmund Randolph to James Madison, ca. 29 October 1787, ibid., 132–35; John Pierce to Henry Knox, 12 November 1787, ibid., 155–56.

25. Edmund Randolph to James Madison, 23 October 1787, in Hutchinson and Rachal, *Papers of James Madison*, 10:229–31; George Washington to James Madison, 5 November 1787, *PGW-ConfS*, 5:409–10; *DHRC*, 8:110; Boyd, *Politics of Opposition*, 27–30.

26. *DHRC*, 8:114; *Journal of the House of Delegates of the Commonwealth of Virginia*, 25 October 1787, 15.

27. Archibald Stuart to James Madison, 2 December 1787, in Hutchinson and Rachal, *Papers of James Madison*, 10:290–93; George Washington to James Madison, 7 December 1787, *PGW-ConfS*, 5:577–81; *DHRC*, 8:183–93; *Journal of the House of Delegates of the Commonwealth of Virginia*, 30 November 1787, 77.

28. Rutland, *Ordeal of the Constitution*, 36–37; Boyd, *Politics of Opposition*, 27–30.

29. "Resolutions Condemning the Use of Paper Money," 3 November 1787, *PGM*, 3:1008–9; GM to George Washington, 6 November 1787, ibid., 1011–12; Archibald

Stuart to John Breckenridge, 6 November 1787, Mason Papers, Gunston Hall. See generally Main, "Sections and Politics in Virginia, 1781–1787," 96–112.

30. GM to George Washington, 27 November 1787, *PGM*, 3:1019–22; *Journal of the House of Delegates of the Commonwealth of Virginia*, 24 November 1787, 66.

31. GM to George Washington, 27 November 1787, *PGM*, 3:1019–22; *Journal of the House of Delegates of the Commonwealth of Virginia*, 17 November 1787, 51–52; ibid., 3 December 1787, 79–80.

32. *Journal of the House of Delegates of the Commonwealth of Virginia*, 12 November 1787, 41–42; Rutland, *Ordeal of the Constitution*, 175–76.

33. *Journal of the House of Delegates of the Commonwealth of Virginia*, 7 December 1787, 86; 18 December 1787, 106; 3 January 1788, 131. On Fitch's monopoly, see Hening, *Statutes*, 12:616–17.

34. *Journal of the House of Delegates of the Commonwealth of Virginia*, 28 November 1787, 73; 1 January 1788, 128–29. Slave owners would sometimes make fictitious transfers in an attempt to hide their slaves from their creditors. Mason's amendment made clear the ban on fraudulent transfers did not apply when possession of a slave had actually been conveyed to a new owner. The amendment appears at Hening, *Statutes*, 12:505–6.

35. *Journal of the House of Delegates of the Commonwealth of Virginia*, 13 November 1787, 44; George Washington to GM, 4 November 1787, *PGM*, 3:1009–10.

36. "To the Commissioners for Settling the Illinois Accounts," 31 December 1787, *PGM*, 3:1027–30; "Report of the Committee Investigating the Illinois Accounts," 7 January 1788, *PGM*, 3:1031–37.

37. "Fairfax County Petition Complaining about the Overseers of the Poor," 24 November 1787, ibid., 1013–16.

38. "Fairfax County Petition Protesting Road Laws," 24 November 1787, ibid., 1016–18.

39. *Journal of the House of Delegates of the Commonwealth of Virginia*, 28 December 1787, 122; Hening, *Statutes*, 12:573–80.

40. *Journal of the House of Delegates of the Commonwealth of Virginia*, 13 December 1787, 96; 18 December 1787, 106; Hening, *Statutes*, 12:522–27.

41. *Journal of the House of Delegates of the Commonwealth of Virginia*, 24 December 1787, 117; Hening, *Statutes*, 12:642–43. See also *PGM*, 3:1025–26.

42. Roeber, *Faithful Magistrates*, 174–79. See also Beeman, *The Old Dominion and the New Nation*, 32–33.

43. Archibald Stuart to James Madison, 2 November 1787, in Hutchinson and Rachal, *Papers of James Madison*, 10:234–35; Rutland, *Mason*, 94; GM to George Washington, 7 October 1787, *PGM*, 3:1001–2; GM to Elbridge Gerry, 20 October 1787, ibid., 1105–6. For a typical letter on John's behalf, see GM to Robert Carter, 30 April 1788, ibid., 1038.

44. Boyd, *Politics of Opposition*, 102–10.; Chitwood, *Richard Henry Lee*, 180–82; McGaughy, *Richard Henry Lee of Virginia*, 197–98. Henry has traditionally, and correctly, been seen as the public face of Virginia Anti-Federalism, with

Mason and Lee providing the intellectual leadership. See Rutland, *Ordeal of the Constitution*, 222–23. Lee's influence rested in large part on his assumed authorship of the anonymous "Letters from the Federal Farmer," but contemporary scholarship has questioned that assumption, see McGaughy, "The Authorship of the *Letters from the Federal Farmer*, Revisited" 153–70.

45. John Dawson to James Madison, 19 October 1787, *DHRC*, 8:78–79; John Hughes to Horatio Gates, 20 November 1787, ibid., 168–70; George Washington to James Madison, 5 February 1788, *PGW-ConfS*, 6:89–90.

46. George Washington to Thomas Jefferson, 1 January 1788, *PGW-ConfS*, 6:2–5; George Washington to James Madison, 5 February 1788, ibid., 89–90; Martin Oster to Comte de la Luzerne, 4 February 1788, *DHRC*, 8:343–44; James Madison to Thomas Jefferson, 19 February 1788, ibid., 384–85; Tobias Lear to Williams Prescott Jr., 4 March 1788, ibid., 455–56.

47. *Virginia Independent Chronicle*, 30 January 1788, *DHRC*, 8:331–40; *Winchester Virginia Gazette*, 25 January 1788, ibid., 325–29; *Petersburg Virginia Gazette*, 28 February 1788, ibid., 428–33; *Petersburg Virginia Gazette*, 13 March 1788, ibid., 492–503.

For Iredell's essays, published under the pseudonym "Marcus," see ibid., 4:548, 571, 596, 616, 630; 8:397.

48. Cyrus Griffin to Thomas Fitzsimmons, 18 February 1788, ibid., 8:382. Tobias Lear lumped Mason together with Henry in their "unabated violence" to the Constitution. Tobias Lear to John Langdon, 25 January 1788, ibid., 321–22.

49. *Philadelphia Independent Gazetteer*, 4 April 1788, ibid., 9:614; Tobias Lear to John Langdon, 3 April 1788, ibid., 698–99; Rutland, *Ordeal of the Constitution*, 196.

50. H. Miller, *George Mason: Constitutionalist*, 218–19.

51. Edward Carrington to William Short, 25 April 1788, *DHRC*, 9: 757–58; Richard Henry Lee to GM, 7 May 1788, *PGM*, 3:1041–44.

52. James Madison to Edmund Randolph, 10 January 1788, *DHRC*, 8:288–91; George Nicholas to James Madison, 5 April 1788, ibid., 9:702–5; James Madison to George Nicholas, 8 April 1788, ibid., 707–10; James Madison to Thomas Jefferson, 22 April 1788, ibid., 744–46.

53. GM to John Francis Mercer, 1 May 1788, *PGM*, 3:1039–41; GM to Thomas Jefferson, 26 May 1788, ibid., 1044–46; George Walker to Huie Reid & Co., 7 March 1788, Mason Papers, Gunston Hall.

54. James Duncanson to James Maury, 11 March 1788, *DHRC*, 8:478–80.

55. Ketcham, *Madison*, 266–69; *Providence Chronicle*, 24 April 1788, *DHRC*, 9:756–57; Risjord, *Jefferson's America*, 235; Thomas, "The Virginia Convention of 1788" 63–73.

56. Beeman, *Old Dominion*, 3–4.

57. George Washington to Marquis de Lafayette, 28 May 1788, *DHRC*, 9:766–69; Denboer, "The House of Delegates," 166–68; Johnstone, "Federalist, Doubtful and Antifederalist," 333–34. For newspaper accounts of the election results, see *DHRC*, 9:627–28.

58. GM to Thomas Jefferson, 26 May 1788, *PGM*, 3:1044–46; GM to John Francis Mercer, 1 May 1788, ibid., 1039–41.

59. Grigsby, *Federal Convention of 1788*, 1:25–26; *DHRC*, 9:910; Mays, *Pendleton Papers*, 2:228–20; H. Miller, *Gentleman Revolutionary*, 286–87.

60. Wirt, *Sketches*, 280; Grigsby, *Federal Convention*, 1:4, 69, 151, 188; *DHRC*, 9:905; James Duncanson to James Maury, June 1788, ibid., 10:1582–84; *PGM*, 3:1114; Kenyon, *Antifederalists*, xcv.

61. William Short to Thomas Lee Shippen, 31 May 1788, *DHRC*, 9:895–96; James Breckenridge to John Breckenridge, 13 June 1788, ibid., 10:1621; R. Meade, *Henry*, 2:360; Grigsby, *Federal Convention*, 1:70, 151; H. Miller, *Gentleman Revolutionary*, 287; Rutland, *Ordeal of the Constitution*, 181.

62. Grigsby, *Federal Convention*, 27–28.

63. *PGM*, 3:1048–50; James Madison to George Washington, 4 June 1788, *DHRC*, 10:1574; R. Meade, *Henry*, 2:344–45; Banning, "Virginia," 277–78. Jon Kukla believes Mason and Richard Henry Lee concocted the strategy of clause-by-clause debate as likely to produce support for amendments. Kukla, "Yes! No! And If . . . Federalists, Antifederalists, and Virginia's Federalists Who Are for Amendments," 43–78.

64. *DHRC*, 9:968, 1127–28, 1163; 10:1228.

65. Quoted in Mays, *Pendleton Papers*, 2:233. See also *DHRC*, 9:933.

66. *DHRC*, 9:947–48, 979, 987–88, 1019–20, 1023–24.

67. John Randolph of Roanoke quoted in Risjord, *Jefferson's America*, 233. See also H. Miller, *George Mason: Constitutionalist*, 222. Randolph's principal biographer argues that Randolph had few serious objections to the Constitution, and they were overcome by his fear of appearing to advocate disunion. Reardon, *Randolph*, 127–33.

68. See Banning, "Virginia," 279–80.

69. *PGM*, 3:1050–54, 1059–68, 1087.

70. *DHRC*, 9:1163–64. On the significance of the tax issue, see Madison's comment at ibid., 1142, and William Grayson's comments at ibid., 10:1184–86. Mason's predictions were essentially correct. One of the first acts of the new Congress was to adopt a liquor tax, which produced the republic's first tax revolt, the Whiskey Rebellion. See generally T. Slaughter, *The Whiskey Rebellion*.

71. *PGM*, 3:1073–81. Mason wanted to require approval of the state legislature before its militia could be marched beyond the adjacent state. Mason had objected to the militia clause in Philadelphia, but he raised new objections in Richmond. See Brant, *Madison*, 3:213. Opposition to a professional military was fundamental to republican thought; at the Richmond convention, William Grayson proposed limiting Congress's power to establish a navy. It was, he said, an unnecessary expense likely to provoke war with Europe. *DHRC*, 10:1314–16.

72. *DHRC*, 10:1259; Banning, "Virginia," 265.

73. *DHRC*, 10:1383, 1492–93.

74. Ibid., 1191–92; *PGM*, 3:1099–1101.

75. *DHRC*, 9:608–9. See also ibid., 1002–3; 10:1209, 1241.

76. *PGM*, 3:1101–13. See also Brant, *Madison*, 3:207–8, 220–21.

77. *DHRC*, 10:1425–28, 1430–38, 1454–55. See also H. Miller, *Gentleman Revolutionary*, 295.

78. *DHRC*, 10:1218–19; McDonald, *Novus Ordo Seclorum*, 259.

79. *PGM*, 3:1150, 1109, 1117–18.

80. Ibid., 1093; *DHRC*, 10:1372.

81. *PGM*, 3:1093; *DHRC*, 10:1373–74.

82. *PGM*, 3:1094–98.

83. Ibid., 1083–85, 1088–91.

84. Ibid., 1082–83, 1113.

85. Ibid., 1086, 1091–92.

86. Ibid., 1077–78.

87. Ibid., 1082–83.

88. *DHRC*, 10:1417.

89. *PGM*, 3:1052, 1059–60.

90. Ibid., 1060, 1077, 1097.

91. Richard Henry Lee to GM, 7 May 1788, ibid., 1041–44; "Resolutions for the Ratifying Convention," ca. 8 June 1788, ibid., 1054–57; Rutland, *Ordeal of the Constitution*, 224; H. Miller, *Gentleman Revolutionary*, 291.

92. GM to John Lamb, *PGM*, 3:1057–58.

93. "Proposed Amendment," ca. 11 June 1788, ibid., 1068–72.

94. Ibid., 1114; James Madison to George Washington, 23 June 1788, *DHRC*, 10:1668–69; William Short to Thomas Lee Shippen, 11 July 1788, ibid., 1700; William Nelson Jr. to William Short, ibid., 1700–17004.

95. "Proposed Amendments," 24 June 1788, *PGM*, 3:1115–18.

96. *DHRC*, 10:1537–42; H. Miller, *Gentleman Revolutionary*, 296–97.

97. Risjord, *Jefferson's America*, 235–36. Adair, *Fame and the Founding Fathers*, 194, to the contrary, concludes the debate did change a few votes. There is more evidence the delegates voted their economic interest, with debtors opposing ratification and holders of public securities supporting it. The economic interpretation is plausible but not irrefutable. According to a recent quantitative model developed to predict voting behavior, Mason was more likely, based on economic considerations, to support ratification than was James Madison. See McGuire, *A More Perfect Union*, 196–97, 204–6.

98. *PGM*, 3:1119–20; *DHRC*, 10:1512–15, 1551–58.

99. James Madison to George Washington, 27 June 1788, *DHRC*, 10:1688–89; James Madison to Thomas Jefferson, 24 July 1788, ibid., 1707–8. For newspaper accounts of the meeting, see ibid., 1560–61.

100. "Proposed Resolutions Reprimanding Governor Edmund Randolph," ca. 28 June 1788, *PGM*, 3:1120–22; Rutland, *Mason*, 95; Reardon, *Randolph*, 163–64.

101. "Notice to the Public," 8 July 1788, *PGM*, 3:1122–23.

102. See generally Banning, "Virginia," 287–89; Boyd, *Politics of Opposition*, 124–30; Rutland, *Ordeal of the Constitution*, 312–13.

Chapter Ten

1. Dunn, *Recollections of John Mason*, 73.

2. GM to Thomas Jefferson, 21 July 1788, *PGM*, 3:1125–26; GM to Beverly Randolph, 27 March 1790, ibid., 1192; GM to Robert Carter, 16 September 1791, ibid., 1239–40. See also GM to John Mason, 2 September 1788, ibid., 1128–30; GM to John Mason, 21 July 1788, ibid., 1126–27.

3. GM to John Mason, 31 July 1789, ibid., 1162–68; GM to John Mason, 23 January 1792, ibid., 1252–54.

4. GM to Thomas Jefferson, 21 July 1788, ibid., 1125–26.

5. GM to John Mason, 2 September 1788, ibid., 1128–30; GM to John Francis Mercer, 26 November 1788, ibid., 1132–34; Denboer, "The House of Delegates," 234–35.

6. GM to John Mason, 18 December 1788, *PGM*, 3:1135–40; Denboer, "The House of Delegates," 269; Boyd, *Politics of Opposition*, 153–58.

7. Rutland, *Ordeal of the Constitution*, 298; James Craik to George Washington, 24 August 1789, *PGW-PS*, 8:529–31; GM to John Mason, 18 December 1788, *PGM*, 3:1135–40; Horrell, "George Mason and the Fairfax County Court," 436–37; Sweig, "1649–1800," 134. According to David Siemers, the number of Anti-Federalist officeholders who refused to comply with the Oath Act was "remarkably small." Siemers, *Ratifying the Republic*, 37.

8. Beverly Randolph to GM, 25 March 1790, *PGM*, 3:1191–92; GM to Beverly Randolph, 27 March 1790, ibid., 1192; GM to Zachariah Johnston, 3 November 1790, ibid., 1208–11; Lund Washington to George Washington, 28 April 1790, *PGW-PS*, 5:353–56.

9. GM to John Mason, 31 July 1789, *PGM*, 3:1162–68; GM to Samuel Griffin, 8 September 1789, ibid., 1170–73. See also GM to Thomas Jefferson, 16 March 1790, ibid., 1188–91.

10. Thomas Jefferson to GM, 13 June 1790, ibid., 1201–2; GM to James Monroe, 30 January 1792, ibid., 1254–56. Useful on the acceptance of the Constitution in Virginia is Wren, "The Ideology of Court and Country in the Virginia Ratifying Convention of 1788," 389–408, which minimizes the philosophical differences between Virginia's Federalists and Anti-Federalists.

11. GM to Thomas Jefferson, 10 January 1791, *PGM*, 3:1216–19; GM to James Monroe, 9 February 1792, ibid., 1256–60; GM to John Mason, 10 September 1792, ibid., 1273–74; Bowling, "'A Tub to the Whale,'" 223–51.

12. GM to James Monroe, 30 January 1792, *PGM*, 3:1254–56; GM to James Monroe, 9 February 1792, ibid., 1256–60; Lund Washington to George Washington, 28 April 1790, *PGW-PS*, 5:353–56.

13. GM to Thomas Jefferson, 10 January 1791, *PGM*, 3:1216–19; Thomas Jefferson to GM, 4 February 1791, ibid., 1223–25; GM to John Mason, 12 July 1791, ibid., 1229–32; Thomas Jefferson to George Washington, 23 March 1792, *PGW-PS*, 10:408–14.

14. GM to John Mason, 13 March 1789, *PGM*, 3:1142–43.

15. Lund Washington to George Washington, 6 March 1789, *PGW-PS*, 1:369; George Washington to James Craik, 8 September 1789, ibid., 4:1–3; George Washington to Alexander Hamilton, 29 July 1792, ibid., 10:588–92. See also Copeland and MacMaster, *Five George Masons*, 232–33.

16. Horrell, "George Mason and the Fairfax County Court," 433–36; GM to Martin Cockburn, 1 December 1788, *PGM*, 3:1134; "Ruling on Levies," January 1789, ibid., 1140–41. Rowland, *Mason*, 2:309, provides a more heroic account in which Mason, by force of argument, persuaded the court to reverse itself, but even Rowland seems skeptical of her source—a young eyewitness who recalled the event almost forty years after the fact.

17. GM to Zachariah Johnston, 28 October 1789, *PGM*, 3:1179–81; "Petition Seeking Removal of the Fairfax County Courthouse from Alexandria," 3 November 1789, ibid., 1182–85; GM to Zachariah Johnson, 3 November 1790, ibid., 1208–11; "Petition Protesting Delays in Selecting a Courthouse Site," 11 November 1790, ibid., 1211–16.

18. "Protest against the Creation of a Fairfax-Loudoun District," ca. January 1791, ibid., 1219–23.

19. "Petition from Fairfax County Slaveholder," 20 October 1789, ibid., 1175–77; GM to Roger West, 9 November 1791, ibid., 1242–45; GM to Zachariah Johnston, 18 November 1791, ibid., 1245–46.

20. GM to John Mason, 2 September 1789, ibid., 1128–30.

21. GM to John Francis Mercer, 26 August 1791, ibid., 1235–37.

22. GM to Thomas Marshall, 16 October 1789, ibid., 1173–75; GM to John Mason, 23 January 1793, ibid., 1252–54; GM to John Mason, 3 July 1792, ibid., 1267–70; Richard Henry Lee to Charles Lee, 24 June 1789, in Ballagh, *Lee Letters*, 2:492–94.

23. GM to David Ross, 7 June 1791, *PGM*, 3:1229; Robert Carter to GM, 1 August 1791, ibid., 1232; GM to Robert Carter, 12 August 1791, ibid., 1232–33; Robert Carter to GM, 25 August 1791, ibid., 1235; GM to Robert Carter, 16 September 1791, ibid., 1239–40.

24. Rowland, *Mason*, 2:368.

25. GM to John Mason, 14 May 1789, *PGM*, 3:1148–54; Copeland and MacMaster, *Five George Masons*, 236–43.

26. GM to John Mason, 5 July 1792, *PGM*, 3:1267–70. See also GM to John Mason, 10 September 1792, ibid., 1273–74. George Mason IV died in 1796, outliving his father by only four years. Thomas Mason died in 1800 at the age of thirty.

27. GM to John Francis Mercer, 26 August 1791, ibid., 1235–37.

28. Quoted in H. Miller, *Gentleman Revolutionary*, 311–12. See also Copeland and MacMaster, *Five George Masons*, 245–61.

29. GM to John Mason, 12 June 1788, *PGM*, 3:1072–73.

30. GM to John Mason, 18 December 1788, ibid., 1135–40; GM to John Mason, 14 May 1789, ibid., 1148–55; GM to John Mason, 12 July 1791, ibid., 1229–32.

31. GM to James Monroe, 5 November 1788, ibid., 1131–32; Copeland and MacMaster, *Five George Masons*, 245–49.

32. GM to John Mason, 18 December 1788, *PGM*, 3:1135–40; GM to Thomas Jefferson, 16 March, 1792, ibid., 1188–91; GM to John Mason, 26 July 1790, ibid., 1203–6. For more on Mason's efforts on behalf of Joseph Fenwick, see GM to George Washington, 19 June 1789, ibid., 1157–61; GM to John Langdon, 3 June 1790, Mason Papers, Gunston Hall.

33. GM to Thomas Jefferson, 21 July 1788, *PGM*, 3:1124–25; GM to John Mason, ibid., 1128–30.

34. GM to John Mason, 31 July 1789, ibid., 1162–67.

35. GM to Samuel Griffin, 8 September 1789, ibid., 1170–73; GM to John Mason, 26 July 1790, ibid., 1203–6; GM to Thomas Jefferson, 10 January 1792, ibid., 1216–19.

36. GM to John Mason, 20 May 1790, ibid., 1198–1200; GM to John Mason, 5 July 1792, ibid., 1267–70; GM to John Mason, 10 September 1792, ibid., 1273–74.

37. Thomas Jefferson to George Washington, 17 September 1790, in Boyd, *Papers of Thomas Jefferson*, 17:466–67; Copeland and MacMaster, *Five George Masons*, 231–32; GM to Thomas Jefferson, 10 January 1791, *PGM*, 3:1216–19; GM to John Mason, 20 August 1792, ibid., 1271–73.

38. GM to James Monroe, 9 February 1792, *PGM*, 3:1256–60. The Cherokees hunted in Kentucky, and the British had recognized their rights in 1768 in the Treaty of Hard Labor. Some smaller upper Ohio Valley tribes also hunted in Kentucky. Holton, *Forced Founders*, 4–6. Mason, however, never seemed to take the Cherokees' claims seriously. GM to George Washington, 9 March 1775, *PGM* 1:224–25.

39. GM to John Mason, 13 June 1792, Mason Papers, Gunston Hall; GM to John Mason, 20 August 1792, *PGM*, 3:1271–73; GM to John Mason, 10 September 1792, ibid., 1273–74.

40. "Petition Regarding the Manufacture and Sale of Flour," September–October 1792, *PGM*, 3:1276–82.

41. "Notes of a Conversation with George Mason," 30 September 1792, in Boyd et al., *Papers of Thomas Jefferson*, 24:428–29; Thomas Jefferson to James Madison, 1 October 1792, ibid., 432.

42. James Monroe to Thomas Jefferson, 16 October 1792, ibid., 489–91; Thomas Jefferson to James Madison, 17 October 1792, ibid., 493–94; Copeland and MacMaster, *Five George Masons*, 233.

43. On Mason's influence, see generally Rossiter, *Seedtime of the Republic*, 327; Sweig, "1649–1800," 117; Chester, "George Mason: Influence beyond the United States," 128–46.

44. Wood, *Radicalism of the American Revolution*, 181–82.

45. Thomas Jefferson to George Washington, 23 May 1792, in Boyd et al., *Papers of Thomas Jefferson*, 23:535–41; Beeman, *Old Dominion*, xiii; Rutland, *Ordeal of the Constitution*, 310.

46. Siemers, *Ratifying the Republic*, 132, 161.

47. Ibid., 205–13; Murrin, "A Roof without Walls: The Dilemma of American National Identity," 346.

48. Denboer, "House of Delegates," 296–97; Ellis, "The Persistence of Anti-Federalism after 1789."

49. Wood, *The American Revolution*, 164–65. See also Wood, *Radicalism of the American Revolution*, 259; Ketcham, *The Anti-Federalist Papers and the Constitutional Convention Debates*, 20.

50. Cornell, *The Other Founders*, 299–307. See also McDonald, *Novus Ordo Seclorum*, 289–93. For a collection of essays on the persistence of Anti-Federalist attitudes, see Pacheco, *Antifederalism: The Legacy of George Mason*.

BIBLIOGRAPHY

Primary Sources

MANUSCRIPT COLLECTIONS

No single collection contains all of the Mason papers. The Library of Congress holds a significant amount of Mason materials, but its collection is far from comprehensive. Gunston Hall has custody of some of Mason's correspondence, as well as material pertaining to the Mason family and to the plantation itself. Fairfax County court records and the Alexandria newspapers, microfilm copies of which are generally available at the Library of Virginia, contain scattered references to Mason. I made use of these resources, but fortunately the vast majority of significant documents relating directly to Mason's life were collected by Robert Rutland and his coeditors and published in *The Papers of George Mason*. My account of Mason's career has relied almost entirely on his published papers and the other sources listed here.

PUBLISHED WORKS

Abbot, W. W., ed. *The Papers of George Washington: Confederation Series.* 6 vols. Charlottesville: University Press of Virginia, 1992–97.

Abbot, W. W., and Dorothy Twohig, eds. *The Papers of George Washington: The Colonial Series.* 10 vols. Charlottesville: University Press of Virginia, 1983–95.

Adair, Douglass, ed. "James Madison's Autobiography." *William and Mary Quarterly*, 3rd ser., 2 (April 1945): 191–209.

Allen, W. B., and Gordon Lloyd, eds. *The Essential Antifederalist.* 2nd ed. Lanham, Md.: Rowman & Littlefield, 2002.

Bailyn, Bernard, ed. *Pamphlets of the American Revolution, 1750–1776.* Cambridge: Harvard University Press, 1965.

Ballagh, James C., ed. *The Letters of Richard Henry Lee.* 2 vols. New York: Macmillan, 1911.

Boyd, Julian, et al., eds. *The Papers of Thomas Jefferson.* 31 vols. Princeton: Princeton University Press, 1950–2003.

Branchi, E. C., trans. "Memoirs of the Life and Voyages of Doctor Philip Mazzei, Part I." *William and Mary Quarterly*, 2nd ser., 9 (July 1929): 161–74.

———. "Memoirs of the Life and Voyages of Doctor Philip Mazzei, Part II." *William and Mary Quarterly*, 2nd ser., 9 (October 1929): 247–64.

Brock, R. A., ed. *The Official Records of Robert Dinwiddie.* 5 vols. Richmond: Virginia Historical Society, 1883–84.

Chase, Philander D., ed. *The Papers of George Washington: The Revolutionary War Series*. 14 vols. Charlottesville: University Press of Virginia, 1985–.

Conway, Moncure Daniel, ed. *The Writings of Thomas Paine*. 4 vols. New York: G. P. Putnam, 1896; reprint, New York: AMS Press, 1967.

Dunn, Terry K., ed. *The Recollections of John Mason: George Mason's Son Remembers His Father and Life at Gunston Hall*. Marshall, Va.: EPM Publications, 2004.

Farish, Hunter Dickinson, ed. *Journal and Letters of Philip Vickers Fithian, 1773–1774: A Plantation Tutor of the Old Dominion*. Williamsburg: Colonial Williamsburg, 1957.

Farrand, Max, ed. *The Records of the Federal Convention of 1787*. 4 vols. New Haven: Yale University Press, 1911–37.

Fitzpatrick, John C., ed. *The Writings of George Washington*. 39 vols. Washington, D.C.: U.S. Government Printing Office, 1931–44.

Force, Peter, ed. *American Archives*. 4th ser. 6 vols. Washington, D.C.: St. Clair and Force, 1837–46.

Ford, Washington C., ed. *Journals of the Continental Congress, 1776–1789*. 34 vols. Washington, D.C.: U.S. Government Printing Office, 1904–37.

Greene, Jack P., ed. *The Diary of Landon Carter of Sabine Hall, 1752–1775*. 2 vols. Charlottesville: University Press of Virginia, 1965.

Hening, William Walter, ed. *The Statutes at Large: Being a Collection of all the Laws of Virginia*. 13 vols. Richmond: Samuel Pleasants, 1819–123.

Historical Statistics of the United States: Colonial Times to 1970. Washington, D.C.: Government Printing Office, 1975.

Hunt, Gaillard, ed. *The Writings of James Madison*. 9 vols. New York: G. P. Putnam's Sons, 1900–1910.

Hutchinson, William T., and William M. E. Rachal, et al., eds. *The Papers of James Madison*. 17 vols. Chicago: University of Chicago Press; Charlottesville: University Press of Virginia, 1962–91.

Hyneman, Charles S., and Donald S. Lutz, eds. *American Political Writing during the Founding Era, 1760–1805*. 2 vols. Indianapolis: Liberty Fund, 1983.

Jackson, Donald, and Dorothy Twohig, eds. *The Diaries of George Washington*. 4 vols. Charlottesville: University Press of Virginia, 1976–78.

Jefferson, Thomas. *The Jefferson Bible: The Life and Morals of Jesus of Nazareth*. Boston: Beacon Press, 1989.

Jensen, Merrill, ed. *American Colonial Documents to 1776*. Vol. 9 of *English Historical Documents*. New York: Oxford University Press, 1969.

———, ed. *Tracts of the American Revolution, 1763–1776*. Indianapolis: Bobbs-Merrill, 1967.

Jensen, Merrill, et al., eds. *The Documentary History of the Ratification of the Constitution of the United States*. 20 vols. Madison: State Historical Society of Wisconsin, 1976–.

Jones, Hugh. *The Present State of Virginia*. Edited by Richard L. Morton. Chapel Hill: University of North Carolina Press, 1956.

Journal of the House of Delegates of the Commonwealth of Virginia. Richmond: Commonwealth of Virginia, 1776– .

Journal of the House of Delegates of the Commonwealth of Virginia, 1777–80. Richmond: Thomas W. White, 1827.

Journal of the House of Delegates of Virginia, 1776. Williamsburg: Alexander Purdie, undated.

Kennedy, John Pendleton, ed. *Journal of the House of Burgesses of Virginia, 1761–1765.* Richmond: Colonial Press, 1907.

———, ed. *Journals of the House of Burgesses of Virginia, 1766–1769.* Richmond: Colonial Press, 1906.

Ketcham, Ralph, ed. *The Anti-Federalist Papers and the Constitutional Convention Debates.* New York: Signet, 2003.

Kurland, Philip B., and Ralph Lerner, eds. *The Founders' Constitution.* 4 vols. Chicago: University of Chicago Press, 1987.

Labaree, Leonard W., ed. *The Papers of Benjamin Franklin.* 36 vols. New Haven: Yale University Press, 1959–2001.

Lipscomb, Andrew, ed. *The Writings of Thomas Jefferson.* 20 vols. Washington, D.C.: Thomas Jefferson Memorial Association, 1904–5.

Locke, John. *Two Treatises of Government.* Edited by Peter Laslett. Cambridge: Cambridge University Press, 1988.

Marchione, Margherita, ed. *Philip Mazzei: My Life and Wanderings.* Translated by S. Eugene Sealia. Morristown, N.J.: American Institute of Italian Studies, 1980.

Mays, David John, ed. *The Letters and Papers of Edmund Pendleton, 1734–1803.* 2 vols. Charlottesville: University Press of Virginia, 1967.

McIlwaine, H. R., ed. *The Journals of the House of Burgesses of Virginia, 1758–1761.* Richmond: Colonial Press, 1908.

Minutes of the Vestry: Truro Parish, Virginia, 1732–1785. Baltimore: Gateway Press, 1995.

Montagu, Edward Wortley. *Reflections on the Rise and Fall of the Ancient Republicks.* London: A. Millar, 1759.

Morison, Samuel E., ed. *Sources and Documents Illustrating the American Revolution, 1764–1788.* New York: Oxford University Press, 1929.

Mulkearn, Lois, comp. *George Mercer Papers Relating to the Ohio Company of Virginia.* Pittsburgh: University of Pittsburgh Press, 1954.

Peterson, Merrill D., ed. *The Portable Jefferson.* New York: Penguin Books, 1977.

———, ed. *The Writings of Thomas Jefferson.* New York: Library of America, 1984.

Randolph, Edmund. *History of Virginia.* Edited by Arthur Shaffer. Charlottesville: University Press of Virginia, 1970.

Reese, George, ed. *The Official Papers of Francis Fauquier, Lieutenant Governor of Virginia, 1758–1768.* 3 vols. Charlottesville: University Press of Virginia, 1980–82.

Rutland, Robert A., et al., eds. *The Papers of George Mason.* 3 vols. Chapel Hill: University of North Carolina Press, 1970.

Schwartz, Bernard, ed. *The Bill of Rights: A Documentary History*. New York: Chelsea House, 1971.

Sidney, Algernon. *Discourses on Government*. Edited by Thomas G. West. Indianapolis: Liberty Fund, 1996.

Smith, Paul H., ed. *Letters of Delegates to Congress, 1774–1789*. 26 vols. Washington, D.C.: Library of Congress, 1976.

Stith, William. *History of the First Discovery and Settlement of Virginia*. Williamsburg: W. Parks, 1747.

Strayer, Joseph R., ed. *The Delegate from New York: on the Proceedings of the Federal Convention of 1787, from the Notes of John Lansing, Jr.* Port Washington, N.Y.: Kennikut Press, 1967.

Syrett, Harold C., ed. *The Papers of Alexander Hamilton*. 27 vols. New York: Columbia University Press, 1961–87.

Taylor, Robert, ed. *The Papers of John Adams*. 12 vols. Cambridge: Harvard University Press, 1977– .

Trenchard, John, and Thomas Gordon. *Cato's Letters: Essays on Liberty, 1720–1723*. 2 vols. Edited by Ronald Hamoway. Indianapolis: Liberty Fund, 1995.

Tucker, St. George. *Blackstone's Commentaries with Notes of Reference to the Constitution and Laws of the Federal Government of the United States and of the Commonwealth of Virginia*. 5 vols. Philadelphia: William Young Birch & Abraham Small, 1803; reprint, New York: Augustus M. Keller, 1969.

Twohig, Dorothy, ed. *The Papers of George Washington: The Presidential Series*. 11 vols. Charlottesville: University Press of Virginia, 1987– .

Van Schreeven, William J., Robert L. Scriber, and Brent Tarter, comps. *Revolutionary Virginia: The Road to Independence*. 7 vols. Charlottesville: University Press of Virginia, 1973–83.

Wade, John, ed. *The Letters of Junius, Woodfall's Edition Revised and Enlarged by John Wade*. 2 vols. London: George Bell & Sons, 1904–5.

Secondary Sources

BOOKS

Abernethy, Thomas Perkins. *Western Lands and the American Revolution*. New York: Russell & Russell, 1937.

Adair, Douglass. *Fame and the Founding Fathers*. New York: W. W. Norton, 1974.

Adams, Willi Paul. *The First American Constitutions: Republican Ideology and the Making of State Constitutions in the Revolutionary Era*. Chapel Hill: University of North Carolina Press, 1980.

Adams, William Howard. *Gouverneur Morris: An Independent Life*. New Haven: Yale University Press, 2003.

Alden, John R. *A History of the American Revolution*. New York: Alfred A. Knopf, 1969.

————. *The South in the American Revolution, 1763–1789*. Baton Rouge: Louisiana State University Press, 1957.

Anderson, Fred. *Crucible of War: The Seven Years' War and the Fate of Empire in British North America, 1754–1766*. New York: Alfred A. Knopf, 2000.

Bailey, Kenneth P. *The Ohio Company of Virginia and the Westward Movement*. Glendale, Calif.: Arthur H. Clark, 1939.

Bailyn, Bernard. *The Ideological Origins of the American Revolution*. Cambridge: Harvard University Press, 1967.

Banning, Lance. *The Sacred Fire of Liberty: James Madison and the Founding of the Federal Republic*. Ithaca: Cornell University Press, 1995.

Barry, Richard. *Mr. Rutledge of South Carolina*. New York: Duell, Sloan, & Pearce, 1942.

Beeman, Richard R. *The Old Dominion and the New Nation, 1788–1801*. Lexington: University Press of Kentucky, 1972.

Beirne, Rosamond, and John Henry Scarff. *William Buckland, 1734–1774: Architect of Virginia and Maryland*. Baltimore: Maryland Historical Society, 1958.

Berkin, Carol. *A Brilliant Solution: Inventing the American Constitution*. Orlando. Fla.: Harcourt, 2002.

Berlin, Ira. *Many Thousands Gone: The First Two Centuries of Slavery in North America*. Cambridge: Harvard University Press, 1998.

Billias, George Athan. *Elbridge Gerry: Founding Father and Republican Statesman*. New York: McGraw Hill, 1976.

Billings, Warren M., John E. Selby, and Thad W. Tate. *Colonial Virginia: A History*. White Plains, N.Y.: KTO Press, 1986.

Boardman, Roger Sherman. *Roger Sherman: Signer and Statesman*. Philadelphia: University of Pennsylvania Press, 1938.

Boller, Paul F. *George Washington and Religion*. Dallas: Southern Methodist University Press, 1963.

Bowen, Catherine Drinker. *Miracle at Philadelphia: The Story of the Constitutional Convention, May to September 1787*. Boston: Little Brown, 1966.

Boyd, Steven R. *The Politics of Opposition: Antifederalists and the Acceptance of the Constitution*. Millwood, N.Y.: KTO Press, 1979.

Brands, H. W. *The First American: The Life and Times of Benjamin Franklin*. New York: Doubleday, 2000.

Brant, Irving. *James Madison*. 6 vols. Indianapolis: Bobbs-Merrill, 1941–61.

Breen, T. H. *Tobacco Culture: The Mentality of the Great Tidewater Planters on the Eve of Revolution*. Princeton: Princeton University Press, 1985.

Brinkley, Alan. *American History: A Survey*. 11th ed. Boston, Mass.: McGraw-Hill, 2003.

Brooke, John. *The Chatham Administration, 1766–1768*. London: Macmillan, 1956.

Brown, Robert E., and Catherine Brown. *Virginia, 1705–1786: Democracy or Aristocracy*. East Lansing: Michigan State University Press, 1964.

Brown, Roger H. *Redeeming the Republic: Federalists, Taxation, and the Origins of the Constitution*. Baltimore: Johns Hopkins University Press, 1993.

Buckley, Thomas E. *Church and State in Revolutionary Virginia, 1776–1787*. Charlottesville: University Press of Virginia, 1977.

Chitwood, Oliver. *Richard Henry Lee: Statesman of the Revolution*. Morgantown: West Virginia University Library, 1967.

Church, Forrest. *The American Creed: A Spiritual and Patriotic Primer*. New York: St. Martin's Press, 2002.

Colbourn, Trevor. *The Lamp of Experience: Whig History and the Intellectual Origins of the American Revolution*. New York: W. W. Norton, 1965.

Collier, Christopher, and James Lincoln Collier. *Decision in Philadelphia: The Constitutional Convention of 1787*. New York: Ballantine Books, 1986.

Copeland, Pamela C., and Richard K. MacMaster. *The Five George Masons: Patriots and Planters of Virginia and Maryland*. Lorton, Va.: Board of Regents of Gunston Hall, 1975.

Cornell, Saul. *The Other Founders: Anti-Federalism and the Dissenting Tradition in America, 1788–1828*. Chapel Hill: University of North Carolina Press, 1999.

Countryman, Edward. *The American Revolution*. New York: Hill & Wang, 1985.

Cunliffe, Marcus. *George Washington: Man and Monument*. Mount Vernon: Mount Vernon Ladies Association, 1998.

Curry, Thomas J. *The First Freedoms: Church and State in America to the Passage of the First Amendment*. New York: Oxford University Press, 1986.

Davis, David Brion. *The Problem of Slavery in the Age of Revolution, 1770–1823*. Ithaca, N.Y.: Cornell University Press, 1975.

Dinnerstein, Leonard, and Mary Dole Palsson, eds. *Jews in the South*. Baton Rouge. Louisiana State University Press, 1973.

Ebenstein, William, and Alan O. Ebenstein. *Great Political Thinkers: Plato to the Present*. 5th. ed. Fort Worth: Harcourt Brace, 1991.

Ellis, Joseph J. *His Excellency: George Washington*. New York: Alfred A. Knopf, 2004.

———. *Passionate Sage: The Character and Legacy of John Adams*. New York. W. W. Norton, 2001.

Ernst, Robert. *Rufus King: American Federalist*. Chapel Hill: University of North Carolina Press, 1968.

Evans, Emory G. *Thomas Nelson of Yorktown: Revolutionary Virginian*. Williamsburg: Williamsburg Foundation, 1975.

Fehrenbacher, Don E. *The Slaveholding Republic: An Account of the United States Government's Relations to Slavery*. Edited by Ward McAfee. New York: Oxford University Press, 2001.

Fenn, Elizabeth A. *Pox Americana: The Great Smallpox Epidemic of 1775–82*. New York: Hill & Wang, 2001.

Ferguson, E. James. *The Power of the Purse: A History of American Public Finance, 1776–1790*. Chapel Hill: University of North Carolina Press, 1961.

Ferling, John. *A Leap in the Dark: The Struggle to Create the American Republic*. New York: Oxford University Press, 2003.

Ferris, Robert G., ed. *Signers of the Constitution*. Washington, D.C.: Department of Interior, 1976.

Finkelman, Paul. *Slavery and the Founders: Race and Liberty in the Age of Jefferson*. Armonk, N.Y.: M. E. Sharpe, 1996.

Fischer, David Hackett, and James C. Kelly. *Bound Away: Virginia and the Westward Movement*. Charlottesville: University Press of Virginia, 2000.

Flexner, James Thomas. *George Washington*. 4 vols. Boston: Little Brown, 1965–72.

Freeman, Douglas Southall. *George Washington: A Biography*. 6 vols. New York: Charles Scribner's Sons, 1948–54.

Goldfield, David, et al. *The American Journey: A History of the United States*. 3rd ed. Upper Saddle River, N.J.: Pearson Prentice-Hall, 2004.

Greene, Jack P. *The Quest for Power: The Lower Houses of the Assembly in the Southern Royal Colonies, 1689–1776*. New York: W. W. Norton, 1972.

Griffith, Lucille Blanche. *The Virginia House of Burgesses, 1750–1774*. University: University of Alabama Press, 1970.

Grigsby, Hugh Blair. *The History of the Virginia Federal Convention of 1788*. 2 vols. Richmond: Virginia Historical Society, 1890–91.

———. *The Virginia Convention of 1776*. Richmond: J. W. Randolph, 1855; reprint, New York: De Capo Press, 1969.

Henri, Florette. *George Mason of Virginia*. New York: Macmillan, 1971.

Henry, William Wirt. *Patrick Henry: Life, Correspondence, and Speeches*. 3 vols. New York: Charles Scribner's Sons, 1891; reprint, New York: Burt Franklin, 1969.

Hinderaker, Eric. *Elusive Empires: Constructing Colonialism in the Ohio Valley, 1763–1800*. Cambridge: Cambridge University Press, 1997.

Holton, Woody. *Forced Founders: Indians, Debtors, Slaves, and the Making of the American Revolution in Virginia*. Chapel Hill: University of North Carolina Press, 1999.

Houston, Alan Craig. *Algernon Sidney and the Republican Heritage in England and America*. Princeton: Princeton University Press, 1991.

Isaac, Rhys. *The Transformation of Virginia, 1740–1790*. Chapel Hill: University of North Carolina Press, 1982.

Isaacson, Walter. *Benjamin Franklin: An American Life*. New York: Simon & Schuster, 2003.

James, Alfred P. *The Ohio Company: Its Inner History*. Pittsburgh: University of Pittsburgh Press, 1959.

Jennings, Francis. *The Creation of America: Through Revolution to Empire*. Cambridge: Cambridge University Press, 2000.

Jensen, Merrill. *The New Nation: A History of the United States during the Confederation, 1781–1789*. New York: Alfred A. Knopf, 1950.

Jordan, Winthrop D. *White over Black: American Attitudes toward the Negro, 1550–1812*. Chapel Hill: University of North Carolina Press, 1968.

Kenyon, Cecelia, ed. *The Antifederalists*. Indianapolis: Bobbs-Merrill, 1966.

Ketcham, Ralph. *James Madison: A Biography*. Charlottesville: University Press of Virginia, 1990.

Kolp, John Gilman. *Gentlemen and Freeholders: Electoral Politics and Political Community in Colonial Virginia*. Baltimore: Johns Hopkins University Press, 1998.

Koontz, Louis Knott. *Robert Dinwiddie*. Glendale, Calif.: Arthur H. Clark, 1941.

Kruman, Marc W. *Between Authority and Liberty: State Constitution Making in Revolutionary America*. Chapel Hill: University of North Carolina Press, 1997.

Kukla, Jon. *A Wilderness So Immense: The Louisiana Purchase and the Destiny of America*. New York: Alfred A. Knopf, 2003.

Kulikoff, Alan. *Tobacco and Slaves: The Development of Southern Cultures in the Chesapeake, 1680–1800*. Chapel Hill: University of North Carolina Press, 1986.

Lambert, Frank. *The Founding Fathers and the Place of Religion in America*. Princeton: Princeton University Press, 2003.

Lee, Richard H. *Memoir of the Life of Richard Henry Lee*. 2 vols. Philadelphia: H. C. Cary & I. Lea, 1825.

Leonard, Cynthia Miller, comp. *The General Assembly of Virginia, July 30, 1619–January 11, 1978: A Bicentennial Register of Members*. Richmond: Virginia State Library, 1978.

Levy, Leonard W. *The Establishment Clause: Religion and the First Amendment*. New York: Macmillan, 1986.

———. *Origins of the Bill of Rights*. New Haven: Yale University Press, 1999.

Maier, Pauline. *From Resistance to Revolution: Colonial Radicals and the Development of American Opposition to Britain, 1765–1776*. New York: Random House, 1972.

———. *The Old Revolutionaries: Political Lives in the Age of Samuel Adams*. New York: Alfred A. Knopf, 1980.

Main, Jackson Turner. *The Antifederalists: Critics of the Constitution, 1781–1788*. New York: W. W. Norton, 1961.

Malone, Dumas. *Jefferson and His Time*. 6 vols. Boston: Little Brown, 1948–74.

Mapp, Alf J., Jr. *The Faiths of Our Fathers: What America's Founders Really Believed*. Lanham, Md.: Rowman & Littlefield, 2003.

Marks, Frederick W., III. *Independence on Trial: Foreign Affairs and the Making of the Constitution*. Baton Rouge: Louisiana State University Press, 1973.

Mays, David John. *Edmund Pendleton, 1721–1803: A Biography*. 2 vols. Cambridge: Harvard University Press, 1952.

McCusker, John J., and Russell R. Menard. *The Economy of British America, 1607–1789*. Chapel Hill: University of North Carolina Press, 1985.

McDonald, Forrest. *Alexander Hamilton: A Biography*. New York: W. W. Norton, 1979.

———. *E Pluribus Unum: The Formation of the American Republic, 1776–1790*. 2nd ed. Indianapolis: Liberty Press, 1979.

———. *Novus Ordo Seclorum: The Intellectual Origins of the Constitution.* Lawrence: University Press of Kansas, 1985.

———. *We the People: The Economic Origins of the Constitution.* Chicago: University of Chicago Press, 1958.

McGaughy, J. Kent. *Richard Henry Lee of Virginia: A Portrait of an American Revolutionary.* Lanham, Md.: Rowman & Littlefield, 2004.

McGuire, Robert A. *To Form a More Perfect Union: A New Economic Interpretation of the United States Constitution.* New York: Oxford University Press, 2003.

Meade, Robert Douthat. *Patrick Henry.* 2 vols. Philadelphia: J. B. Lippincott, 1957.

Meade, William. *Old Churches, Ministers, and Families of Virginia.* 2 vols. Philadelphia: J. B. Lippincott, 1857.

Middlekauff, Robert. *The Glorious Cause: The American Revolution, 1763 – 1789.* New York: Oxford University Press, 1982.

Miller, Helen Hill. *George Mason: Constitutionalist.* Cambridge: Harvard University Press, 1938; reprint, Safety Harbor, Fla.: Simon Publications, 2001.

———. *George Mason: Gentleman Revolutionary.* Chapel Hill: University of North Carolina Press, 1975.

———. *George Mason of Gunston Hall.* Lorton, Va.: Board of Regents of Gunston Hall, 1958.

Miller, William Lee. *The Business of May Next: James Madison and the Founding.* Charlottesville: University Press of Virginia, 1992.

Mintz, Max M. *Gouverneur Morris and the American Revolution.* Norman: University of Oklahoma Press, 1970.

Morgan, Edmund S. *American Slavery, American Freedom: The Ordeal of Colonial Virginia.* New York: W. W. Norton, 1975.

Morgan, Edmund S., and Helen M. Morgan. *The Stamp Act Crisis: Prologue to Revolution.* Rev. ed. New York: Collier Books, 1963.

Morison, Samuel Eliot, Henry Steele Commager, and William E. Leuchtenburg. *The Growth of the American Republic.* 6th ed. 2 vols. New York: Oxford University Press, 1969.

Morris, Richard B. *The Forging of the Union, 1781 – 1789.* New York: Harper & Row, 1987.

Morton, Richard Lee. *Colonial Virginia.* 2 vols. Chapel Hill: University of North Carolina Press, 1960.

Moxham, Robert M. *The Colonial Plantations of George Mason.* Springfield, Va.: Colonial Press, 1974.

Nelson, John K. *A Blessed Company: Parishes, Parsons, and Parishioners in Anglican Virginia, 1690 – 1776.* Chapel Hill: University of North Carolina Press, 2001.

Pacheco, Josephine F., ed. *Antifederalism: The Legacy of George Mason.* Fairfax, Va.: George Mason University Press, 1992.

Pangle, Thomas L. *The Spirit of Modern Republicanism: The Moral Vision of the Founders and the Philosophy of John Locke.* Chicago: University of Chicago Press, 1988.

Peters, Marie. *The Elder Pitt*. London: Longman, 1998.

Peterson, Merrill D. *Thomas Jefferson and the New Nation*. New York: Oxford University Press, 1970.

Peterson, Merrill D., and Robert C. Vaughn, eds. *The Virginia Statute for Religious Freedom: Its Evolution and Consequences in American History*. Cambridge: Cambridge University Press, 1988.

Philyaw, L. Scott. *Virginia's Western Visions: Political and Cultural Expansion on an Early American Frontier*. Knoxville: University of Tennessee Press, 2004.

Pocock, J. G. A. *The Machiavellian Moment: Florentine Political Thought and the Atlantic Republican Tradition*. Princeton: Princeton University Press, 1975.

Porter, Roy, and G. S. Rousseau. *Gout: The Patrician Malady*. New Haven: Yale University Press, 1998.

Potts, Louis W. *Arthur Lee: A Virtuous Revolutionary*. Baton Rouge: Louisiana State University Press, 1981.

Ragsdale, Bruce A. *A Planters' Republic: The Search for Economic Independence in Revolutionary Virginia*. Madison, Wis.: Madison House, 1996.

Rakove, Jack. *Declaring Rights: A Brief History with Documents*. Boston: Bedford Books, 1998.

———. *James Madison and the Creation of the American Republic*. 2nd ed. New York: Longman, 2002.

———. *Original Meanings: Politics and Ideas in the Making of the Constitution*. New York: Alfred A. Knopf, 1997.

Randall, Willard Sterne. *George Washington: A Life*. New York: Henry Holt, 1997.

Reardon, John J. *Edmund Randolph: A Biography*. New York: Macmillan, 1974.

Reid, John Phillip. *Constitutional History of the American Revolution: The Authority of Law*. Madison: University of Wisconsin Press, 1993.

Reiss, Oscar. *Medicine in Colonial America*. Lanham, Md.: University Press of America, 2000.

Risjord, Norman K. *Jefferson's America*. 2nd ed. Lanham, Md.: Rowman & Littlefield, 2002.

Roark, James L., et al. *The American Promise: A History of the United States*. 2nd ed. Boston: Bedford/St. Martin's, 2002.

Robbins, Caroline. *The Eighteenth-Century Commonwealthman*. Cambridge: Harvard University Press, 1959.

Roeber, A. G. *Faithful Magistrates and Republican Lawyers: Creators of Virginia Legal Culture, 1680–1810*. Chapel Hill: University of North Carolina Press, 1981.

Rossiter, Clinton. *1787: The Grand Convention*. New York: W. W. Norton, 1966.

———. *Seedtime of the Republic: The Origin of the American Tradition of Political Liberty*. New York: Harcourt, Brace, 1953.

Rowland, Kate Mason. *The Life of George Mason, 1725–1792*. 2 vols. New York: G. P. Putnam's Sons, 1892.

Royster, Charles. *The Fabulous History of the Dismal Swamp Company: A Story of George Washington's Times*. New York: Vintage, 1999.

Rozbicki, Michal J. *The Complete Colonial Gentleman: Cultural Legitimacy in Plantation America*. Charlottesville: University Press of Virginia, 1998.

Rutland, Robert A. *George Mason and the War for Independence*. Williamsburg: Virginia Independence Bicentennial Commission, 1976.

———. *George Mason: Reluctant Statesman*. Baton Rouge: Louisiana State University Press, 1961.

———. *The Ordeal of the Constitution: The Antifederalists and the Ratification Struggle of 1787–1788*. Norman: University of Oklahoma Press, 1961.

Selby, John F. *The Revolution in Virginia, 1775–1783*. Williamsburg: Colonial Williamsburg Foundation, 1988.

Siemers, David J. *The Antifederalists: Men of Great Faith and Forbearance*. Lanham, Md.: Rowman & Littlefield, 2003.

———. *Ratifying the Republic: Antifederalists and Federalists in Constitutional Time*. Stanford: Stanford University Press, 2002.

Slaughter, Philip. *The History of Truro Parish in Virginia*. Philadelphia: G. W. Jacobs, 1908.

Slaughter, Thomas P. *The Whiskey Rebellion: Frontier Epilogue to the American Revolution*. New York: Oxford University Press, 1986.

Smith, Charles Page. *James Wilson: Founding Father, 1742–1798*. Chapel Hill: University of North Carolina Press, 1956.

Sobel, Mechal. *The World They Made Together: Black and White Values in Eighteenth Century Virginia*. Princeton: Princeton University Press, 1987.

Sosin, Jack M. *The Revolutionary Frontier, 1763–1783*. New York: Holt, Reinhart and Winston, 1967.

———. *Whitehall and the Wilderness: The Middle West in British Colonial Policy, 1760–1775*. Lincoln: University of Nebraska Press, 1961.

Storing, Herbert J. *What the Anti-Federalists Were For: The Political Thought of the Opponents of the Constitution*. Chicago: University of Chicago Press, 1981.

Stourzh, Gerald. *Benjamin Franklin and American Foreign Policy*. Chicago: University of Chicago Press, 1984.

Syndor, Charles S. *American Revolutionaries in the Making: Political Practices in Washington's Virginia*. New York: Free Press, 1965.

Tindall, George B., and David E. Shi. *America: A Narrative History*. 6th ed. New York: W. W. Norton, 2004.

Van Doran, Carl. *The Great Rehearsal: The Story of the Making and Ratifying of the Constitution of the United States*. New York: Viking Press, 1948.

Ward, Matthew C. *Breaking the Backcountry: The Seven Years' War in Virginia and Pennsylvania, 1754–1765*. Pittsburgh: University of Pittsburgh Press, 2003.

Wilkins, Roger. *Jefferson's Pillow: The Founding Fathers and the Dilemma of Black Patriotism*. Boston: Beacon Press, 2001.

Wirt, William. *Sketches for the Life and Character of Patrick Henry*. 2nd ed. Philadelphia: James Webster, 1818.

Wood, Gordon S. *The American Revolution: A History*. New York: Modern Library, 2002.

————. *The Creation of the American Republic, 1776–1789.* New York: W. W. Norton, 1969.

————. *The Radicalism of the American Revolution.* New York: Random House, 1991.

Zahniser, Marvin R. *Charles Cotesworth Pinckney: Founding Father.* Chapel Hill: University of North Carolina Press, 1967.

ARTICLES

Bailey, Kenneth P. "George Mason: Westerner." *William and Mary Quarterly,* 2nd ser., 23 (October 1943): 409–17.

Banning, Lance. "The Constitutional Convention." In *The Framing and Ratification of the Constitution,* edited by Leonard W. Levy and Dennis J. Mahoney, 112–31. New York: Macmillan, 1987.

————. "Virginia, Sectionalism and the General Good." In *Ratifying the Constitution,* edited by Michael Allen Gillespie and Michael Lienesch, 261–99. Lawrence: University Press of Kansas, 1989.

Beckerdite, Luke. "William Buckland and William Bernard Sears: The Designer and the Carver." *Journal of Early Southern Decorative Arts* 8 (November 1982): 7–40.

Billings, Warren M. "'That All Men Are Born Equally Free & Independent': Virginians and the Origins of the Bill of Rights." In *The Bill of Rights and the States: The Colonial and Revolutionary Origins of American Liberties,* edited by Patrick Conley and John P. Kaminski, 335–69. Madison, Wis.: Madison House, 1992.

Bond, Beverly W., Jr. "The Quit-Rent System in the American Colonies." *American Historical Review* 17 (April 1912): 496–516.

Bowling, Kenneth R. "'A Tub to the Whale': The Founding Fathers and the Adoption of the Federal Bill of Rights." *Journal of the Early Republic* 8 (Fall 1988): 223–51.

Breen, T. H. "Ideology and Nationalism on the Eve of the American Revolution: Revisions *Once More* in Need of Revising." *Journal of American History* 84 (June 1997): 13–39.

Briceland, Alan W. "Virginia: The Cement of the Union." In *The Constitution and the States: The Role of the Original Thirteen in the Framing and Adoption of the Federal Constitution,* edited by Patrick T. Conley and John P. Kaminski, 201–23. Madison, Wis.: Madison House, 1989.

Chester, Edward W. "George Mason: Influence beyond the United States." In *George Mason and the Legacy of Constitutional Liberty,* edited by Donald J. Senese, 128–46. Fairfax, Va.: Fairfax County History Commission, 1989.

DePauw, Linda Grant. "The Roots of American Federalism." In *Federalism: The Legacy of George Mason,* edited by Martin B. Cohen, 39–64. Fairfax, Va.: George Mason University Press, 1988.

Diggins, John Patrick. "Comrades and Citizens: New Mythologies in American Historiography." *American Historical Review* 90 (June 1985): 614–49.

Dreisback, Daniel L. "George Mason's Pursuit of Religious Liberty in Revolutionary Virginia." *Virginia Magazine of History and Biography* 108 (2000): 5–44.

Egnal, Marc. "The Origins of the Revolution in Virginia: A Reinterpretation." *William and Mary Quarterly*, 3rd ser., 37 (July 1980): 401–28.

Ellis, Richard. "The Persistence of Antifederalism after 1789." In *Beyond Confederation: Origins of the Constitution and American National Identity*, edited by Richard R. Beeman, Stephen Botein, and Edward C. Carter II, 295–314. Chapel Hill: University of North Carolina Press, 1987.

Evans, Emory G. "Planter Indebtedness and the Coming of the Revolution in Virginia." *William and Mary Quarterly*, 3rd ser., 19 (October 1962): 511–33.

Finkelman, Paul. "Slavery and the Constitutional Convention: Making a Covenant with Death." In *Beyond Confederation: Origins of the Constitution and American National Identity*, edited by Richard R. Beeman, Stephen Botein, and Edward C. Carter II, 188–225. Chapel Hill: University of North Carolina Press, 1987.

Freehling, William W. "The Founding Fathers and Slavery." *American Historical Review* 77 (February 1972): 81–93.

———. "The Founding Fathers, Conditional Antislavery, and the Nonradicalism of the American Revolution." In *The Reintegration of American History: Slavery and the Civil War*, edited by William W. Freehling, 12–33. New York: Oxford University Press, 1994.

Ganter, Herbert L. "The Machiavellianism of George Mason." *William and Mary Quarterly*, 2nd ser., 17 (April 1937): 239–64.

Henriques, Peter R. "An Uneven Friendship: The Relationship between George Washington and George Mason." *Virginia Magazine of History and Biography* 97 (April 1989): 185–204.

Hobson, Charles F. "The Negative on State Laws: James Madison and the Crisis of Republican Government." *William and Mary Quarterly*, 3rd ser., 36 (April 1979): 215–35.

Horrell, Joseph. "George Mason and the Fairfax County Court." *Virginia Magazine of History and Biography* 91(October 1983): 418–39.

Howard, A. E. Dick. "From Mason to Modern Times: 200 Years of American Rights." In *The Legacy of George Mason*, edited by Josephine F. Pacheco, 95–112. Fairfax, Va.: George Mason University Press, 1983.

———. "Rights in Passage: English Liberties in Early America." In *The Bill of Rights and the States: The Colonial and Revolutionary Origins of American Liberties*, edited by Patrick Conley and John P. Kaminski, 3–15. Madison, Wis.: Madison House, 1992.

Jillson, Calvin, and Thornton Anderson. "Realignments in the Convention of 1787: The Slave Trade Compromise." *Journal of Politics* 39 (August 1977): 712–29.

Johnstone, F. Claiborne. "Federalist, Doubtful, and Antifederalist: A Note on the Virginia Convention of 1788." *Virginia Magazine of History and Biography* 96 (July 1988): 333–44.

Katz, Stanley N. "Thomas Jefferson and the Right to Property in Revolutionary
    America." *Journal of Law and Economics* 19 (October 1976): 467–88.
Keim, C. Ray. "Primogeniture and Entail in Colonial Virginia." *William and Mary
    Quarterly*, 3rd ser., 25 (October 1968): 545–86.
Kramnick, Isaac. "The 'Great National Discussion': The Discourse of Politics
    in 1787." *William and Mary Quarterly*, 3rd ser., 45 (January 1988): 3–32.
Kukla, Jon. "Yes! No! And If . . . Federalists, Antifederalists, and Virginia Fed-
    eralists Who Are for Amendments." In *Antifederalism: The Legacy of George
    Mason*, edited by Josephine F. Pacheco, 43–78. Fairfax, Va.: George Mason
    University Press, 1992.
Lienesch, Michael. "In Defense of the Anti-Federalists." *History of Political
    Thought* 4 (Spring 1983): 65–87.
Lutz, Donald S. "Relative Importance of European Writers in Late Eighteenth
    Century American Political Thought." *American Political Science Review* 77
    (March 1984): 189–97.
Maier, Pauline. "John Wilkes and American Disillusionment with Britain." *Wil-
    liam and Mary Quarterly*, 3rd ser., 20 (July 1963): 373–95.
Main, Jackson Turner. "Government by the People: The American Revolution and
    the Democratization of the Legislatures." *William and Mary Quarterly*, 3rd ser.,
    23 (July 1966): 391–407.
———. "The One Hundred." *William and Mary Quarterly*, 3rd ser., 11 (July
    1954): 354–84.
———. "Sections and Politics in Virginia, 1781–1787." *William and Mary Quar-
    terly*, 3rd ser., 12 (January 1955): 96–112.
Marshall, P. J. "A Nation Defined by Empire, 1775–1776." In *Uniting the King-
    dom? The Making of British History*, edited by Alexander Grant and Keith L.
    Stinger, 208–21. London: Routledge, 1995.
McDonald, Forrest, and Michael Mendle. "The Historical Roots of the Originat-
    ing Clause of the United States Constitution: Article I, Section 7." *Modern Age*
    27 (Summer–Fall 1983): 274–81.
McGaughy, J. Kent. "The Authorship of the *Letters from the Federal Farmer*, Re-
    visited." *New York History* 70 (April 1989): 153–70.
Meadows, Milo. "The Virginia Constitution of 1776: Colonial Political Thought
    Leading to the Writing of the Virginia Constitution." *Filson Club Historical
    Quarterly* 43 (January 1969): 5–22.
Miller, Helen Hill. "John Mercer of Marlborough: A Portrait of an Irascible Gen-
    tleman." *Virginia Cavalcade* 27 (Autumn 1976): 74–85.
Murrin, John M. "Can Liberals Be Patriots? Natural Right, Virtue, and Moral
    Sense in the America of George Mason and Thomas Jefferson." In *Natural
    Rights and Natural Law: The Legacy of George Mason*, edited by Robert P.
    Davidow, 35–65. Fairfax, Va.: George Mason University Press, 1986.
———. "A Roof without Walls: The Dilemma of American National Identity." In
    *Beyond Confederation: Origins of the Constitution and the American National
    Identity*, edited by Richard R. Beeman, Stephen Botein, and Edward C. Carter
    II, 333–48. Chapel Hill: University of North Carolina Press, 1987.

Ohline, Howard A. "Republicanism and Slavery: Origins of the Three-Fifths Clause in the United States Constitution." *William and Mary Quarterly*, 3rd ser., 28 (October 1971): 563–84.

Onuf, Peter S. "Toward Federalism: Virginia, Congress, and the Western Lands." *William and Mary Quarterly*, 3rd ser., 34 (July 1977): 353–74.

Pierce, Michael D. "The Independence Movement in Virginia, 1775–1776." *Virginia Magazine of History and Biography* 80 (October 1972): 442–52.

Pittman, R. Carter. "Jasper Yeates's Notes on the Pennsylvania Ratifying Convention, 1787." *William and Mary Quarterly*, 3rd ser., 22 (April 1965): 301–18.

———. Review of Richard L. Perry, ed., *Securing Our Liberties* (1951). *Virginia Magazine of History and Biography* 86 (January 1960): 109–12.

Pocock, J. G. A. "Between Gog and Magog: The Republican Thesis and the *Ideologia Americana*." *Journal of the History of Ideas* 48 (April–June 1987): 325–46.

Rakove, Jack. "The Structure of Politics at the Accession of George Washington." In *Beyond Confederation: Origins of the Constitution and American National Identity*, edited by Richard R. Beeman, Stephen Botein, and Edward C. Carter II, 261–94. Chapel Hill: University of North Carolina Press, 1987.

Roche, John P. "The Founding Fathers: A Reform Caucus in Action." *American Political Science Review* 55 (December 1961): 799–816.

Rutland, Robert A. "George Mason and the Origins of the First Amendment." In *The First Amendment: The Legacy of George Mason*, edited by T. Daniel Shumate, 87–100. Fairfax, Va.: George Mason University Press, 1985.

Schauer, Frederick. "Free Speech and Its Philosophical Roots." In *The First Amendment: The Legacy of George Mason*, edited by T. Daniel Shumate, 132–55. Fairfax, Va.: George Mason University Press, 1985.

Schlesinger, Arthur H. "The Lost Meaning of the Pursuit of Happiness." *William and Mary Quarterly*, 3rd ser., 21 (July 1964): 325–27.

Schmidt, Frederika Teute, and Barbara Ripel Wilhelm. "Early Proslavery Petitions in Virginia." *William and Mary Quarterly*, 3rd ser., 30 (January 1973): 133–46.

Schwartz, Stephan A. "George Mason, Forgotten Founder: He Conceived the Bill of Rights." *Smithsonian* (May 2000): 143.

Selby, John. "Richard Henry Lee, John Adams, and the Virginia Constitution." *Virginia Magazine of History and Biography* 84 (October 1976): 387–400.

Senese, Donald L. "George Mason: Why the Forgotten Founding Father?" In *George Mason and the Legacy of Constitutional Liberty*, edited by Donald L. Senese, 147–52. Fairfax, Va.: Fairfax County History Commission, 1989.

Sheridan, Richard B. "The British Credit Crisis of 1772 and the American Colonies." *Journal of Economic History* 20 (June 1960): 161–86.

Steiner, Bruce E. "The Catholic Brents of Colonial Virginia: An Instance of Practical Toleration." *Virginia Magazine of History and Biography* 70 (October 1962): 387–409.

Sweig, Donald. "1649–1800." In *Fairfax County, Virginia: A History*, edited by Nan Netherton, 5–149. Fairfax, Va.: Fairfax County Board of Supervisors, 1978.

———. "A New Found Washington Letter of 1774 and the Fairfax Resolves." *William and Mary Quarterly*, 3rd ser., 40 (April 1983): 283–91.

———. "The Virginia Nonimportation Association Broadside of 1770 and Fairfax County: A Study in Local Participation." *Virginia Magazine of History and Biography* 87 (July 1979): 316–25.

Tarter, Brent. "Reflections on the Church of England in Colonial Virginia." *Virginia Magazine of History and Biography* 112 (2004): 338–71.

———. "Richard Bland." In *Dictionary of Virginia Biography*, edited by Sara B. Bearss et al., 2:10–13. Richmond: Library of Virginia, 2001.

Thomas, Robert E. "The Virginia Convention of 1788: A Criticism of Beard's *An Economic Interpretation of the Constitution*." *Journal of Southern History*" 19 (February–November, 1953): 63–73.

Wallenstein, Peter. "Flawed Keepers of the Flame: The Interpreters of George Mason." *Virginia Magazine of History and Biography* 102 (April 1994): 229–60.

Wren, J. Thomas. "The Ideology of Court and Country in the Virginia Ratifying Convention of 1788." *Virginia Magazine of History and Biography* 93 (October 1985): 389–408.

UNPUBLISHED WORKS

Brown, Bennie. "The Library of George Mason." Gunston Hall, Lorton, Va., December 1997.

Denboer, Gordon Ray. "The House of Delegates and the Evolution of Political Parties in Virginia, 1782–1992." Ph.D. dissertation, University of Wisconsin, 1972.

Dunn, Terry K. Gunston Hall Liberty Lecture, Lorton, Va., 18 February 2004.

INDEX